Linguistic Diversity and National Unity

Linguistic Diversity
and National Unity
Language Ecology in Thailand

William A. Smalley

The University of Chicago Press
Chicago and London

WILLIAM A. SMALLEY is professor emeritus of linguistics at Bethel College. A missonary linguist in Vietnam, Laos, and Thailand between 1950 and 1977, he is the coauthor of *Mother of Writing* (University of Chicago Press, 1990).

THE UNIVERSITY OF CHICAGO PRESS, CHICAGO 60637
THE UNIVERSITY OF CHICAGO PRESS, LTD., LONDON
© 1994 by The University of Chicago

All rights reserved. Published 1994
Printed in the United States of America
03 02 01 00 99 98 97 96 95 94   1 2 3 4 5
ISBN: 0-226-76288-2 (cloth)
        0-226-76289-0 (paper)

LIBRARY OF CONGRESS CATALOGING-IN-PUBLICATION DATA

Smalley, William Allen.
    Linguistic diversity and national unity:language ecology in
Thailand / William A. Smalley.
        p.   cm.
    Includes bibliographical references.
    Includes index.
    1. Thai language—Dialects—History. I. Title.
PL4159.S63 1994
495.9'17—dc20   93-48051
                                                            CIP

☉ The paper used in this publication meets the minimum requirements of the American National Standard for Information Sciences—Permanence of Paper for Printed Library Materials, ANSI Z39.48-1984.

In my ideal society of Siam, there should be unity without forced uniformity; there should be room for the non-conformist, the unique, the idealist, even the crank; members of the society should be able to discern truth, beauty and goodness and cherish them and discard superficial and false values; material and spiritual welfare should be available for all, not for the few; human dignity and freedom are each individual's sacred due, however humble he be.

— Puey Ungphakorn (1974)

Contents

Tables

Figures

Maps

Acknowledgments

The National Research Council of Thailand kindly granted me permission to undertake research in the country in 1985-1986. At that time I was supported by the Fulbright Foundation through the Thailand-United States Educational Foundation (Doris Wibunsin, Director), and was associated most helpfully both with the linguistics department of Chulalongkorn University (Peansiri E. Vongvipanond, Chair, and Theraphan L. Thongkum) and the Institute of Language and Culture for Rural Development at Mahidol University (Suriya Ratanakul, Chair). Bethel College (Dwight Jessup, Dean) granted me that year's sabbatical absence. In Thailand during the same period I also received extensive help from the library of the Tribal Research Institute, Chiang Mai, the Thailand Information Center in the library of Chulalongkorn University, Bangkok, and the Population Survey Division of the National Statistics Office, Bangkok (Sasithorn Jotikasthira). The names in parentheses above indicate those individuals who were most fully instrumental in extending the facilities of their institutions to me.

Earlier work on this book (1962-1978) was done under the auspices first of the American Bible Society and then of the United Bible Societies (Eugene A. Nida), greatly aided by my access in 1967-1969 to the Yale University libraries under a research fellowship in the anthropology department of that university (Harold C. Conklin, Chair).

My research assistant in 1985-1986 was Sureeporn Yaysa-nga. The following individuals provided typing and/or editorial help at various times: Jane A. Smalley, Leigh R. Kambhu, Carol J. Smalley, Umporn Suteeca, and Rita Carter. Lois Malcolm, Daniel Erickson, James Matcuk, Bruce Hagermeyster and Paul Berggren entered survey data or otherwise helped with the computer.

I have benefited by interviews, conversations or correspondence with many people. Where these led to incorporating specific information in the text the source is noted at the appropriate place. In addition, I have been helped by comments made by Amara Prasithrathsint, Amon Thavisak, Garland Bare, Benjamin Rittiwongsakul, Lois Callaway, C. W. Callaway, John Ellison, David Filbeck, David Griffiths, E. R. Hope, J. Edwin Hudspith, Beulah M. Johnston, Kalaya Tingsabadh, Paul W. Lewis, Richard Mann, David L. Morse, Jonathan Morse, Robert H. Morse, Stephen A. Morse, Mohamed A. Kadir, Samuel A. Mattix, James A. Morris, Pranee Kullavanijaya, Herbert C. Purnell, Rekha Thongsawad, Ruengdet Pankhuenkhat, Donald Schlatter, Sukhuma-Vadee Khamhirun, Surin Pitsuwan, Suwilai Premsrirat, Theraphan L. Thongkum, Harold Thiel, David Thomas, Dorothy Thomas, Vichin Panupong, Peter Wyss. My apologies to any whose names I neglected to record.

The following people read and criticized a late draft of the full book: Stanley J. Hanna, Paul W. Lewis, Edwin Zehner, and anonymous readers for the publisher. Other individuals have read earlier drafts of one or more chapters and provided helpful comments: T. David Anderson, Benjamin Rittiwongsakul, Frank Blair, James R. Chamberlain, David J. Clark, Christopher Court, C. J. Grijns, Howard A. Hatton, David W. Hogan, J. Edwin Hudspith, Samuel A. Mattix, Michael Moerman, James A. Morris, Norman A. Mundhenk, Kenneth L. Pike, Potchanat Samermit, Carol J. Smalley, Herbert C. Purnell, Philip C. Stine, David Strecker, David Thomas, Anne Wilding.

My profound appreciation to all individuals and institutions who have helped in various ways.

Introduction:
Thailand's Sociolinguistic Anomalies

A high school teacher in the provincial capital of Surin in northeast Thailand speaks the Northern Khmer language of the area to her neighbors and in many other informal situations around town. She learned it by living and working in the city for several years. On the other hand, she speaks Lao with her husband, a government official, because that is his mother tongue. She learned it (and met him) when she was in training as a teacher in the Lao-speaking area of the northeast. She teaches in Standard Thai, which she herself learned in school. She talks to her children in Lao or Northern Khmer or Standard Thai, as seems appropriate at the time. When she returns to her home village, an hour's ride by bus to the east of Surin, she speaks Kuy, her own native language, the language of her parents, the language in which she grew up.

Thailand is a country with eighty languages. This woman knows four of them well and also speaks some English. Yet Thailand gives outsiders and even many of its own people the impression of being almost monolingual. In surrounding countries diversity of that scope is divisive, the matrix of revolution, but in Thailand it is hardly noticed. What makes the difference?

Both the reality and some common misconceptions about the linguistic complexity of Thailand are exemplified in the following statement:

Varieties of Thai are spoken natively by about 91% of the population (Rustow 1968), thus Thai is an obvious choice as a sole official language. Thailand has never been under the dominion of a colonial power, another factor removing languages from competition. Speakers of languages other than Thai, mostly members of ethnic groups in specific regions (e.g. Malays in the south or Khmer in the north-east), or hill tribes, are normally educated in standard Thai; some Malays do attend Malay-medium schools. Members of urban minorities (especially the Chinese) also learn Thai; many of them speak it natively, in addition to a variety of Chinese (Gupta 1985: 12).

1

People who know Thailand generally agree with statements like these, and other authors have commented on the "homogeneity" of the country (Noss 1967:195; Kunstadter [ed.] 1967:393; Patya 1971: 175).[1] In important senses, however, the statement is misleading. The search for how the common perception of linguistic homogeneity in Thailand can be both true and false, how Thailand can be so linguistically diverse, yet so unified, is the central issue in this book.

Misconceptions and Puzzles

To highlight the false aspects of Gupta's statement, we can compare the language situation in India (Khubchandani 1983; Brass 1974). If Thailand were like India the Thai constitution would list Kammüang (the language of the northern provinces), Lao (the language of the northeast), and Paktay (the language of the southern peninsula), as well as Thai, as national languages. They would be the languages of separate states and the media of education. Ancient writing traditions would be vigorously maintained alongside those of Standard Thai. But none of this is true in Thailand.

If, instead, India were like Thailand, the quotation above would read "Varieties of Hindi are spoken natively by about 75% of the population. Thus Hindi is an obvious choice as a sole official language." But as a matter of fact, for Hindi to be made the sole official language of India would be bitterly opposed by millions of people.

The "varieties" as applied to India would include Bengali, Gujarati, and Marathi, no more distant in mutual intelligibility from Hindi than Kammüang, Lao and Paktay are from Standard Thai. These Indian languages, and some others more radically different from Hindi, are official languages in the Indian constitution, with their separate flourishing traditional writing systems. They are also languages of education and the widespread mass media in ways never imagined or desired by speakers of their counterparts in Thailand.

In India, furthermore, people have repeatedly rioted over language differences, whereas Standard Thai has not only achieved an unquestioned place in Thailand, but also gained that place relatively easily after the beginning of this century. This dominance continues although only a minority of people in Thailand, perhaps 20% (table B.1), is born to Standard Thai as its sole mother tongue. The many others who speak it have learned it in school to various levels of competence.

In Thailand native speakers often do not perceive major language differences to be politically important, or otherwise interpret them in some non-divisive way. The differences between the spoken Tai[2] languages are constantly minimized, and speakers of all such languages in the country are counted as speaking "Thai." In other countries trivial differences may be symbolically enlarged and sharpened in people's perceptions. In either case, the perception creates the social reality. But what creates the perception?

The statement is misleading on one level, although true on another, partly because "Thai" has more than one meaning. Sometimes "varieties of Thai" means differences on the scale of Spanish and Portuguese, at other times on the scale of Texas speech and Boston speech, and then again on the scale of educated and uneducated speech. Thus, some of the divergent varieties in "Thai" would elsewhere be classified without question as different languages.

The paragraph is misleading also because it begs numerous questions by lightly passing over the language diversity which does exist in Thailand. If it is true, in one sense, that "91% of the population" of Thailand natively speaks one or more "varieties of Thai," how did Thailand get that way when probably 20% of the people in the country have some Chinese ancestry, for example, as do 35% of the people in Bangkok? The presence of a Chinese-speaking population is divisive in some countries like Malaysia and Vietnam, but no Chinese language is of any political significance in Thailand. On the other hand, the English language, with virtually no native speakers, is critically important for the nation as a whole.

And how do the nearly eighty minority languages fit into the national picture? What are the patterns of multilingualism among their speakers? Whereas "varieties of Thai" have assumed a clearly dominant position over Chinese languages in modern times, and completely overwhelmed classical Mon, Khmer, and numerous smaller languages in older times, why have other languages nevertheless persisted? Ancestral forms of some languages still spoken in Thailand were present before the Tai languages arrived.

How did the fact that Thailand was not "under the domination of a colonial power" make a difference? Actually, before the modern colonial period the area was colonized by Tai-speaking people, among whom the people of central Thailand gained the ascendancy. But what in the language policy and practice of the Tai people created a different present-day situation from countries which were colonized by the West?

Why is it, furthermore, that "some Malays do attend Malay-medium schools" long after other native speakers of other languages were forbidden schools in their languages?

And yet, in spite of such anomalies, misconceptions and puzzling questions, clearly Standard Thai "is an obvious choice as a sole official language" in Thailand, although it is only part of what "Thai" means in the quotation.

Unity and Tension

For the most part, Thai people seem to feel secure in their unusual unity in the face of linguistic diversity, unity which the government works hard to promote through the educational system. But in spite of the general feeling of security, from time to time officials or newspaper writers become alarmed at some real or imagined threat from a minority group. King Rama VI in the first quarter of this century, and Prime Minister Phibunsongkhram in midcentury, both imagined danger from the Chinese population and used it to stir up factionalism. In the 1960s and 1970s communists were believed by many to pose a great threat, working to subvert restive minorities. Dissatisfaction on the part of the Pattani Malay-speaking population in the south is deep and of long duration.

Thai reactions to threats of these kinds, small and great, are not always measured and judicious. Xenophobic elements in Thai society are sometimes both vocal and powerful, most noticeable in some of the government officials and military people who run the country. Such people sometimes exploit ethnic differences for political, and especially military ends, even creating an enemy where danger is remote. Why officials differ from the generally laissez-faire attitude of the country toward language differences is one of the issues to be explored.

In Thailand, as elsewhere, more powerful people regularly exploit less powerful ones, whether they speak the same language or not, and injustice can be exacerbated by language and culture differences. Nevertheless Thai people also typically incorporate or accommodate differences in language and culture in more effective ways than many other countries, so that in spite of the consciousness in Thailand of a "minority problem," most people seem to accept the national unity which exists as the normal way of things. That incorporation, however, is not a particularly visible phenomenon to observers, Thai elite or foreigner. Like Gupta, above, others summarize the Western-influenced Thai elite attitude (Esman 1990:187-189) to the exclusion of the very different forces rooted in the past, and described here.

Government attempts at linguistic homogenization are a modern phenomenon everywhere. Only when universal school systems were instituted did requirements that each country have only one language even become imaginable in most countries. Language then often became a basis for political discrimination. Pressures result in loss of group identity and dignity or in intensified ethnic antagonism (Haugen 1987:4-5). Although efforts at such linguistic homogenization have been undertaken diligently by Thai bureaucrats in this century they have been successful in remarkably different ways from many other countries and from what the bureaucrats have intended.

For the most part, Thailand has been characterized by openness such as Margaret Mead described:

Throughout human history there has been a struggle between the proponents of closed and open systems, systems that could change their forms, accommodate to new ideas, retain the allegiance of new generations within them rather than goad them into rebellion or desertion, systems that welcomed the ideas, the questions, and the members of other systems, and those contrasting systems which hardened into exclusiveness and conservatism, so that wars of conquest, the rack, the ritual trial, the war on unbelievers in which one attained merit by killing them, became their destructive methods of self-perpetuation (Mead 1966:457).

This book describes some of those open characteristics which are at work in language relationships in Thailand. We will look, therefore, at the language diversity which exists in the country, and at the national unity which masks it, at how language functions on many levels and in many combinations of varieties. And we will seek to find the historic, structural, and functional reasons for the present relative unity in diversity.

On the other hand, answering the "why" and getting a balanced picture of complex interrelationships between languages and cultures over the whole country is difficult. Not only are the sources incomplete, but the range of relevant topics to be investigated is wide and complex. "A linguistic area is like a forest of mushrooms and fungi, interrelated and mutually dependent" (Mühlhäusler 1989:166). Obviously we will sample only a few elements of the forest in this book.

Language Ecology

In trying to answer the questions raised in this introduction we deal with issues called "language ecology," the study of the interactions between languages and their environments (Haugen 1971:19; Dil [ed.] 1972; Enninger and Haynes [eds.] 1984; Haarmann 1986). Here is how Haugen has laid out the field:

> For any given "language," then, we should want to have answers to the following ecological questions: (1) What is the *classification* in relation to other languages? . . . (2) Who are the *users*? . . . (3) What are the *domains* of use? This is a question of . . . discovering whether its use is unrestricted or limited in specific ways. (4) What *concurrent languages* are employed by its users? . . . (5) What *internal varieties* does the language show? . . . (6) What is the nature of its *written traditions*? . . . (7) To what degree has its written form been *standardized*, i.e. unified and codified? . . . (8) What kind of *institutional support* has it won, either in government, education, or private organizations, either to regulate its forms or propagate it? . . . (9) What are the *attitudes* of its users towards the language in terms of intimacy and status, leading to personal identification? . . . (10) Finally, we may wish to sum up its status in a *typology of ecological classification*, which will tell us something about where the language stands and where it is going in comparison with the other languages of the world (Haugen 1971:25).

Haugen's statement does not emphasize the historical processes by which existing ecological relationships are achieved, but such processes are a significant part of the picture in Thailand as well.

The organization of this book follows the hierarchical interrelationships between the varieties of language in the country. Hierarchy is part of Thai culture, part of the organization of Thai existence, and the particular hierarchy described here is created by patterns of multilingualism, by what languages people learn in addition to their mother tongue.

Part 1 deals with Standard Thai, the language of the Thai nation at home. Linguistic diversity in Thailand begins with important differences within Standard Thai, multiple varieties of it, and the complex patterns of its use. This section also touches briefly on English, the primary language of the nation in its dealings with much of the rest of the world.

Part 2, in turn, takes up each of the major regional languages of the country: Kammüang, Lao and Paktay, which were mentioned before; and Thaiklang, the regional language of the center of the country and the language on which Standard Thai is built. It describes some of the differences between these languages and Standard Thai, and the roles they play in relation to each other and to the nation.

Part 3 deals with marginal regional languages, smaller regional languages which overlap from neighboring countries around some of the borders of Thailand. The two most important ones—Northern

Khmer and Pattani Malay—differ sharply in the ways they fit into Thailand's diversity within unity.

Part 4 treats the other levels of the hierarchy: other Tai languages, the Chinese languages of the cities of Thailand, and other minority languages of different sizes, roles and importance. It sorts out some of the functional differences among them and discusses representative examples of the major types.

Part 5 then explores some issues which penetrate all of these levels of language role: whether or not languages other than Standard Thai should be written, and what function writing might have for them; the process of change and development of language as it has taken place in Thailand; the relationship between language and ethnicity. In the concluding chapter the language scene in Thailand is placed in a wider cultural and political context and some international comparisons are made.

This book is about the roles which languages play in the country, not about the linguistic form of different languages. Structural information (grammatical and phonological) is included from time to time only to throw light on language use.

Several major languages are missing from this book. Among them are specialized languages like Sanskrit, the classical language out of which high-level new vocabulary is formed in Thai; it gets only passing mention. Pali, the religious language of Thailand, is discussed even less. Modern languages of India spoken in Thailand, furthermore, are practically ignored. So is Vietnamese, spoken by a rather undigested minority in the northeast and in minority enclaves (often Catholic) in the central region. Little information has been published about speech groups among them and what I have read does not adequately describe language interactions. Little is said, also, about literature and literary language. All such omitted languages and varieties are nevertheless parts of the language ecology of the country.

Map 0.1. Provinces of Thailand. In almost every province the capital city of the province also bears the province name. Province names are keyed to the map by number and are listed below both alphabetically and numerically. In this book place names are spelled according to the conventions established in Royal Institute (1968).

Alphabetical order

6. Ang Thong
4. Ayuthaya
1. Bangkok
20. Buri Ram
13. Chachoengsao
9. Chai Nat
18. Chaiyaphum
16. Chanthaburi
36. Chiang Mai
37. Chiang Rai
14. Chon Buri
60. Chumphon
28. Kalasin
46. Kamphaeng Phet
52. Kanchanaburi
25. Khon Kaen
64. Krabi
40. Lampang
39. Lamphun
34. Loei
7. Lop Buri
35. Mae Hong Son
26. Maha Sarakham
29. Mukdahan
11. Nakhon Nayok
54. Nakhon Pathom
30. Nakhon Phanom
19. Nakhon Ratchasima
49. Nakhon Sawan
65. Nakhon Si Tham-
    marat
41. Nan
73. Narathiwat
33. Nong Khai
2. Nonthaburi
3. Pathum Thani
71. Pattani
63. Phangnga
67. Phatthalung
38. Phayao

51. Phetchabun
58. Phetchaburi
48. Phichit
47. Phitsanulok
1. Phra' Nakhon
42. Phrae
66. Phuket
12. Prachin Buri
59. Prachuap Khiri
    Khan
61. Ranong
55. Ratchaburi
15. Rayong
27. Roi Et
31. Sakon Nakhon
10. Samut Prakan
56. Samut Sakhon
57. Samut Songkhram
5. Saraburi
70. Satun
22. Si Sa Ket
8. Sing Buri
69. Songkhla
44. Sukhothai
53. Suphan Buri
62. Surat Thani
21. Surin
45. Tak
68. Trang
17. Trat
24. Ubon Ratcathani
32. Udon Thani
50. Uthai Thai
43. Uttaradit
72. Yala
23. Yasothon

Numerical order

1. Bangkok
   Phra' Nakhon
2. Nonthaburi
3. Pathum Thani
4. Ayuthaya
5. Saraburi
6. Ang Thong
7. Lop Buri
8. Sing Buri
9. Chai Nat
10. Samut Prakan
11. Nakhon Nayok
12. Prachin Buri
13. Chachoengsao
14. Chon Buri
15. Rayong
16. Chanthaburi
17. Trat
18. Chaiyaphum
19. Nakhon Ratchasima
20. Buri Ram
21. Surin
22. Si Sa Ket
23. Yasothon
24. Ubon Ratchathani
25. Khon Kaen
26. Maha Sarakham
27. Roi Et
28. Kalasin
29. Mukdahan
30. Nakhon Phanom
31. Sakon Nakhon
32. Udon Thani
33. Nong Khai
34. Loei
35. Mae Hong Son
36. Chiang Mai
37. Chiang Rai
38. Phayao
39. Lamphun

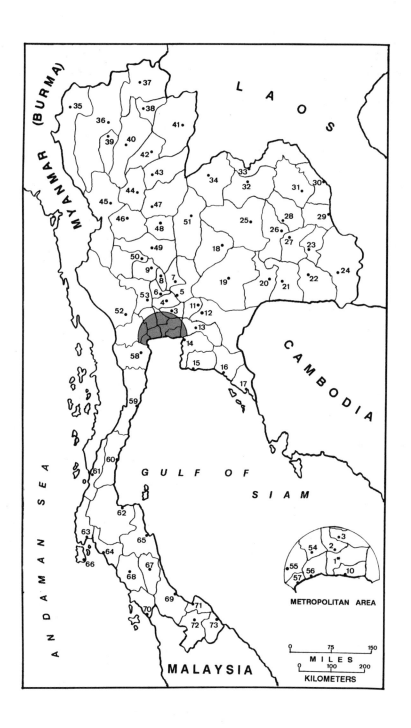

40. Lampang
41. Nan
42. Phrae
43. Uttaradit
44. Sukhothai
45. Tak
46. Kamphaeng Phet
47. Phitsanulok
48. Phichit
49. Nakhon Sawan
50. Uthai Thani
51. Phetchabun

52. Kanchanaburi
53. Suphan Buri
54. Nakhon Pathom
55. Ratchaburi
56. Samut Sakhon
57. Samut Songkhram
58. Phetchaburi
59. Prachuap Khiri
    Khan
60. Chumphon
61. Ranong
62. Surat Thani

63. Phangnga
64. Krabi
65. Nakhon Si Tham-
    marat
66. Phuket
67. Phatthalung
68. Trang
69. Songkhla
70. Satun
71. Pattani
72. Yala
73. Narathiwat

Part I

Languages of the Nation as a Whole
Introduction

Part 1 of this book is primarily about Standard Thai, the language which unifies Thailand, but its major theme is the diversity that lies within this unifying language. Standard Thai, carefully cultivated, prescribed and taught by government and elite, is a fascinatingly complex phenomenon.

One kind of diversity within Standard Thai is manifested at the soft borders of standardization, where not everyone talks the same even when they may agree on the "rules" for what is "correct" and "incorrect." Another is manifested when people use different varieties of the language in different social situations. Some varieties also reflect different social identities.

Standard Thai helps to unify the nation because it is the language of the nation as a whole, but only for internal purposes. English is the all-important external language of Thailand, universally taught in the schools. But in Thailand English is more diverse, also, than an outsider might expect. It includes forms of Thai-English which Thai people know and use as well as or instead of Standard English.

1

The Languages of Thailand
at Home and Abroad

That the language of Thailand is Thai is a truism even for Thai citizens, who know that many other languages are spoken within the borders of their country. When they hear about language conflict in India, where language riots frequently occur, knowledgeable Thai may give a passing thought to the Malay-speaking population in south Thailand, or to the Chinese population of the Thai towns and cities, but most are not seriously worried. They do not feel that the place of their Thai language is in any way threatened by the multiple languages spoken by citizens of the country.

To many Thai, as to some Westerners, the unquestioned place of one single language as the language of a country does not seem particularly worthy of comment. Because of their experience, Thai or Americans expect one country to have one language; Thai is the language of Thailand, and English is the language of the United States. Americans often feel that English is really the language even of large blocks of New York City or Miami where little else but Spanish is spoken, except to outsiders, or even of the thousands of square miles in the southwestern United States where little else but Navajo is spoken. They wonder how tiny Switzerland can possibly get along with three official languages. And many Canadians, faced with threats of secession by people in an important French-speaking area, wonder how it is possible for a nation to have two official languages.

To the citizens of many Asian countries, on the other hand, the fact that *the one* language of Thailand is Thai must seem very strange. For them large numbers of languages are axiomatic, and to have several official languages for a country is sometimes taken for granted. Their multiple languages are also often competing, symbols of division and sometimes of hatred.

Thai is therefore the unquestioned language of Thailand in a sense unusual for its surrounding area. It is the unrivalled language of education, the language of the major communications media, the language of prestige. Even the citizens of Thailand who do not speak

Thai do not question its role. "Those who are not born to it adapt to it or suffer the consequences" (Noss 1964:1).

Yet Thailand is linguistically complex. Probably more people in Thailand speak Lao as their mother tongue than are native speakers of Standard Thai. Languages spoken by over a million people and not even closely related to Thai are also to be found within Thai borders (table B.1).

When we chart the distribution of Thailand's many languages on a map and see the mosaic which results, and when we begin to sort out the roles which these many languages play in the country, we are forced to define the sense in which it is true that the language of Thailand is Thai. We are also forced to ask how these other languages fit into the scheme of things.

The Thai Which Is the Language of Thailand

The word *Thai* is often used loosely both in Thai and in English. As a start toward distinguishing between its different meanings we will use *Standard Thai* for the Thai which is the language of the country. Standard Thai is the official language, the legally appropriate language for all political and cultural purposes. Officially, internal government affairs and political activity are all conducted in Standard Thai. Formal high prestige cultural activity like public speaking or writing is normally carried out in Standard Thai, even by those who are not native speakers.

Standard Thai is not only the official language, but is also the national language, a symbol of identification for the Thai nation. Next to the King and along with the Buddhist religion, Standard Thai may be the strongest such symbol, even for those who speak it as a second language, or barely speak it at all.

There is no way of knowing exactly how many native speakers of Standard Thai are to be found in Thailand. Certainly most of the people of the upper classes would be included, even though some are native speakers of regional forms of Thai as well. We have estimated 10.4 million native speakers of Standard Thai who are not also native speakers of other languages (table B.1).

Standard Thai is therefore not a native language for most people in Thailand. For the majority, instead of being the language of the home and neighborhood, Standard Thai is learned in school. Sometimes such learning leads to a fully acceptable command of the spoken and written language. More often it leads to partial knowledge, usually adequate for most practical purposes, but sometimes hardly enough even for a rural person's limited need to use it.

As its official and national language, Standard Thai is also the written medium for Thailand. The origin of Thai writing is traditionally dated from A.D. 1283 because King Ramkhamhaeng's famous stone inscription of that date has been considered the earliest example of written Thai in existence. Likely writing was done on more perishable substances before that, but at any rate, Thai writing is over seven hundred years old.

The Standard Thai script, furthermore, is almost completely unique to the language.[1] It is as different from the most similar other script (that of Lao) as the Gothic script for German is from roman. Because the Thai nation, the Standard Thai language, and the Thai script are so nearly coextensive they have a mutually reinforcing effect on each other as symbols of national unity.

Publications proliferate in Standard Thai as they do in any major Asian language. Original writings and translated materials, classical and modern, poetry and technical prose, newspapers and pornographic magazines, Donald Duck and *Arts and Culture*, astrological advice and the diaries of King Chulalongkorn, fiction and history—all of these and much more are constantly flowing from Thai presses and flooding the bookstores.

Although the majority of the country does not speak Standard Thai except as it learns it in school, the unifying effect of the standard language is powerful. The more education spreads, develops, and deepens, the more universal a good knowledge of Standard Thai is becoming throughout the country. Other varieties of language are not necessarily disappearing, but the importance of Standard Thai, its widespread use and unifying force, is growing. So it is that Standard Thai is the language of Thailand. It is the language of the nation as opposed to parts of the nation. It symbolizes Thailand.

The Languages of Thailand Abroad

But even though the language of Thailand is Standard Thai, it is such only as the language of the nation at home. The language of Thailand abroad is English first of all, and then a few other languages to a much lesser extent. These latter include various Chinese languages, some European languages, some languages of India, plus a few other Asian languages like Malay, Lao, and Japanese.[2] All such languages except English are likely to be used internationally on a personal, cultural, or business level by individuals rather than on a national level.

Not only do Thai people communicate with foreigners in English, but foreigners like Japanese businesspeople often use English to communicate with other foreigners like their French or Indian counterparts in Thailand, as well. Because English is the international language of Thailand, the people of Thailand can participate in the most far-reaching communications network in the world (chap. 19). Thai people sometimes refer to English as the universal language.

Until the 1960s, most Thai people who could use English at all with foreigners were drawn from the small elite class. They include the people associated with the court and royal family, those with university education, the top of the political and business institutions, and some Western-oriented people. Now, however, many thousands of others have also learned to speak English of varying quality to get jobs with the ever-growing international community in the country and to carry on business with it. In a typical apartment complex in Bangkok, for example, the switchboard operators speak passable English to residents from countries like Iran, Indonesia, the Netherlands and Brazil as well as from English-speaking countries.

With respect to the place of English, however, Thailand is quite different from those of its neighbors which were once under English-speaking colonial rule. English is still important as a language of internal communication as well as one of external communication in India, Pakistan, Bangladesh, Myanmar (Burma),[3] Malaysia, Singapore, the Philippines, and Hong Kong. In some of these countries university education is conducted in English, or the option is available. In many cases English-medium educational tracks are also available at lower levels. Thailand has very few schools of higher learning in which English is the general medium of instruction, and allows no English-medium primary or secondary schools for Thai citizens. A functional knowledge of English is therefore much more pervasive in these other countries than in Thailand, even among people with modest education.

In neighboring countries, also, some individuals speak English as their language of the home, their mother tongue, or one of their mother tongues. Married couples from different parts of the country sometimes have no other language in common, and their children grow up in English-speaking homes (Platt and Weber 1980). That is rare among citizens of Thailand, restricted largely to homes in which one of the parents is originally from abroad.

As Thailand's language abroad, English is the most important language in which to obtain certain kinds of specialized information (Nida and Wonderly 1971). Although Thai universities are not English-medium institutions, students in the upper levels of many scholarly fields do much of their technical reading in English.

Occasionally lecturers from abroad teach university classes in English, and English language classes on some levels are sometimes conducted in English by Thai or foreign teachers. An occasional foreign lecturer will even require students to write or recite in English. Even in such cases, the level of English competence is generally low by comparison with students at the same stage in some other countries.

A great deal of specialized information filters to Thai people who do not know much English through people who are highly skilled in it, however. University professors educated in English abroad help students understand the English they are reading. Or they lecture and write books in Thai, transmitting to Thai people the information gained in English. So strong is the association some such people make between their academic subjects and English, that some of them are more comfortable discussing their technical subjects in English than in Thai. At meetings of a computer users' group in Bangkok the Thai people present talk more frequently about their computer experience in English than in Thai even to each other in private conversations.

English is a language of specialized information on lower levels as well. Numerous Thai read the English-language newspapers. Some people decipher the English directions on packages and appliances if there are none in Thai.

Other Functions of English in Thailand

English does have more functions in Thailand than international communication alone, however. One is to symbolize modernity, being a part of the larger world, being "with it." More English slogans seem to adorn shirts and other clothing than do Thai slogans, some of it fractured English like "To someone who like to Working for the lover." A bit of English often appears accenting a Thai message on posters or advertisements.

Foreign producers of some prestigious consumer products do not transliterate their brand names into Thai at all, but keep them in roman script, which is English so far as most Thai are concerned, even if the language of origin is not: Peugeot, Estée Lauder. Others transliterate them sometimes, but often both Thai and romanized forms are used: Toyota, Sony, Caltex. Mundane mass market products are more likely to be transliterated: Fab, Coke; but some come into Thailand as "modern," "Western" or stylish, and the use of English signs is prominent in relation to them: McDonald and A&W Root Beer fast-food restaurants. Some Thai storefront restaurants now have "Fast Food" prominently displayed in English on their signs, although the "fast food" served is Thai, like a bowl of noodles. The sign is not necessarily there to catch the eye of the foreigner, but because this Western concept with a Thai twist to it is "in" for middle-class Thai.

English is learned and maintained in Thailand primarily through formal education. It is not often learned socially, as people learn their mother tongues, or people in the Chinese community learn to speak Thai as children in Bangkok, or many upland people learn the regional language of the valleys below. A few do learn English on the job as household help or employees of foreigners, but most people learn what English they know in school from Thai teachers, who learned it from still other Thai, and have little contact with native speakers of English.

This cycle of learning English from Thai teachers creates a Thai English that Westerners have difficulty understanding. One time a man who had been through the Thai school system, including undergraduate university, came to interview me in Thai. When I asked him what his position was in the organization for which he was working, I did not know the Thai word with which he replied, so he said it in English. I understood that attempt at English, however, no better than I had understood the Thai. Finally he wrote it in English: public relations.

As a spoken language Thai English is rudimentary and incomplete, inadequate for extensive communication needs, but it nevertheless contributes to the function of gaining specialized information in Thailand, and provides prestige. Its primary function is to enable Thai to read or cite English, pronouncing it with Thai sounds (Brown 1976a).

English, of course, does not have to be pronounced in an American or British or Australian way to be a valid system of communication (Noss 1983; Kachru [ed.] 1982; Smith 1981). Indian English is sometimes hard for Americans to understand, but is neither rudimentary nor incomplete. It is a fully functioning variety used by thousands of speakers as a language of internal communication in India. Thai English is less developed and has a more limited role.

Thai English has some rather consistent features based on characteristics of the Thai language. Thai sounds are substituted for English ones according to rather regular patterns, but the degree of modification depends partly on the individual speaker's knowledge of more standard English forms. In its most extreme manifestation speakers of Thai English change most syllable-final English consonants to ones which occur in Thai, so that Standard English [s][4] often becomes [t] at the end of a syllable, for example. Standard English final consonant clusters are also reduced to a single consonant, so that Standard English *washed* [wašt] becomes [wát]. Stress is added to many English weak-stressed syllables, and English intonation is eliminated, so that the rhythm of the sentence is Thai.

The most pervasive modification is the addition of Thai tones to English words in systematic ways. Brown (1976a:72) cites a Thai TV commercial advertising a course teaching English to Thai. The announcer read off the names of six or seven English textbooks used, pronouncing the titles with English consonants and vowels, but with Thai rhythm and tones.

Even people who speak a Western form of English beautifully typically use elements of Thai English pronunciation at times. A leading Thai linguist with a Ph.D. from an American university, a specialist in English, has near-native control of American English. Nevertheless she typically cites sentence-long English language examples in Thai English embedded in her Thai lectures. To do so not only seems natural and appropriate in the Thai context, but may also be necessary to enable some people in the audience to understand the example.

Spoken by people like that, the grammar of the Thai English is likely to be standard. But for less-educated people, some of the grammatical forms which may show up in Thai English consist of Thai grammatical structure with English vocabulary (pronounced in Thai English fashion, of course). One maid said, *He wear shirt one body hat one leaf* 'He was wearing a coat and a hat'. *Body* and *leaf* are literal translations of the words used to classify the Thai nouns for 'coat' and 'hat' when specifying a number with them. People who have learned more English would not usually make substitutions as extreme as that.

Other characteristic grammatical forms in Thai English come not from Thai but from stripping off the complications of English as language learners regularly do (Adjamian 1976; Tarone 1980). So the person speaking Thai English says *Where do you go?* (parallel to *What do you see?* or *How do you feel?*) for 'Where are you going?'

not following any Thai construction, but reducing the complications of Standard English.

English Influence on Standard Thai

English influences the Thai language itself in many ways also. Some modern Thai type fonts, for example, are designed to give some of the letters an English appearance, a "mod" look.

More fundamentally, some people who translate English-language material into Thai assume that Thai is defective if it does not have a grammatical feature to match an English grammatical feature. So they try to "correct" it. Thai has several ways of expressing some of the ideas carried by the English passive, but only one of them, one which includes the word /thùuk/[5] in the sentence, has typically been called "passive" when Thai students learn to translate English. So many Thai have woodenly translated the English passive with that one Thai form, even though it did not really fit (Pongsri 1979).

In normal Thai contexts the Thai expression with /thùuk/ has a connotation of misfortune which does not apply to the English meaning. Thai people would typically use /thùuk/ in sentences like 'He was bitten by a dog'. But to translate the English *He was rewarded for his good deeds* with that particular Thai expression gives, or formerly gave, the effect of 'He had the misfortune of being rewarded for his good deeds'.

Amara Prasithrathsint (1983, 1985, 1988) has traced the use of different forms of the passive in Thai writings in the two-hundred-year "Bangkok Period" of Thai history. She noted the occurrence of passives of all kinds, and found that from 1802-1982 they increased from 0.15% to 6.66%. The use of /thùuk/ for the passive went from 0% to 26.3% of all passives used. Usage climbed to notable peaks at times, and then tapered off. She demonstrates that the peaks coincided with periods when English exerted its strongest influence.

The greatest effect of English on Thai may be as a source of modern loanwords. Borrowing vocabulary from other languages is nothing new for Thai, with other major sources in Chinese, Khmer, Sanskrit and Pali. But now English has become perhaps the leading source (Surai 1978, Gandour 1979, Karnchana 1979). Along with the information learned through English come English technical terms. And along with gadgets introduced from the West come English names for them. Thai people coined the word /thoorathàt/ 'television' out of classical roots meaning 'far away' and 'view'. But everyone says /thiiwii/ in informal usage, a borrowing of 'TV'. On the other hand, borrowing does not always win out over older patterns. A coinage of the same kind, /thoorasàp/ 'telephone' ('far away' plus 'word'), has not been superseded by any English borrowing.

Thai writers on technical materials will frequently write a Thai expression followed in parentheses by the English term they intend that expression to represent. Some readers do not know much English but get the general idea from the Thai, while others are helped by the English because the Thai usage may not be consistently recognized as a technical term.

English loanwords come into Thai on the other end of the scale as well. Some Thai slang is created from English loans, like /thék/ from *discotheque* or /mâat/ from *smart* (Payom 1985). In between the learned vocabulary and the slang lie several hundred English-derived ordinary words commonly used in everyday Thai, words like /píkník/ from *picnic* and /fiim/ from *film*.

English borrowings into Thai on any level are likely to undergo pronunciation changes like those of Thai English, and sometimes meaning changes as well. /chút/ from *suit* means 'a set of things that match, or go together', not just clothes. It includes teams, committees, glassware, books, etc. (Haas 1964:149-150). /fɛɛn/ means 'spouse' although derived from *fan* 'an admirer'. In pronunciation *valve* becomes /waaw/ as English [l] becomes Thai [w] after some vowels (Edwin Zehner personal communication). A vowel is inserted between the two initial consonants in *switch* to become /sawít/, and the final consonant cluster is reduced (Surai 1978). The vowels in both words are also adjusted to Thai.

Sometimes English affects the Thai spoken by one individual, or its effect may be temporary. Thai people sometimes return from abroad using Thai expressions modeled after English in ways that Thai friends who stayed at home do not immediately understand, or find strange (Wilaiwan 1979).

Learning the Languages of Thailand

The Thai school system[6] is organized as in table 1.1. Compulsory education was increased from four to six years in 1978, but by no means have all children ever received the minimal requirement because schools have not been available in the most remote areas, and the law cannot always be enforced. The present requirement of six years of primary education has been followed more completely in the cities than in the country and more in accessible areas than remote ones, although accessibility is constantly spreading. 47.6% of the population over twenty-five had no schooling at all in 1960, but that had dropped to 20.3% in 1980. Correspondingly, 0.6% had completed university in 1960, and 3.0% in 1980 (Wyatt 1984:291).

As already noted, the medium of instruction in all schools for Thai children is Standard Thai. Some children come to school speaking, or at least understanding, the language. These are primarily middle- and upper-class children in Bangkok or children raised by educated parents elsewhere. Other children initially have varying degrees of difficulty with the language of the schools. In most such cases children are not able initially to understand much of what the teacher says in class, but their own dialect is so close to Standard Thai that they quickly learn.

In a significant number of cases in some parts of the country, however, the children may speak a language entirely different from

Table 1.1. Organization of the Thai school system in 1986. Maximum years available at each level is shown in parentheses. Ages of entry are approximate.

Higher Education
    Alternatives. Age of entry: 20
        University (4)
        Teacher's college (2/4)
        Technical school (2/4)
        Military/police academy (5/4)
        Music/dramatic arts (2)
        Physical education (2)
Secondary Education
    Upper level alternatives. Age of entry: 17
        Academic (3)
        Teaching (2)
        Technical (2)
        Military (2)
        Music/dramatic arts (3)
        Physical education (2)
        Vocational (1/2)
    Lower level alternatives. Age of entry: 14
        Academic (3)
        Technical (3)
        Music/dramatic arts (3)
        Vocational (1/2)
Elementary Education (6). Age of entry: 7
Kindergarten/pre-primary (3). Age of entry: 3

any Tai language, and may take up to two years before they can adequately understand what is going on in class (chap. 16). All schools at lower levels must follow a uniform official curriculum which allows limited flexibility for private schools to make some adaptations. Thus some private schools offer more English, or offer it earlier, or offer a Chinese language for a limited number of hours, etc. In any case, one of the express purposes of education in Thailand is to teach all Thai children to use Standard Thai and another is to study some English (table 1.2).

However, many people in remote rural areas see little personal need for learning Standard Thai because their lives are circumscribed by their village and its immediate surroundings. Their regional language does well enough for that; reading and writing are not necessary parts of village life for most of them. Such areas are rapidly diminishing, however.

Many students have even less use for English and are not motivated to learn it. In poor rural areas English does not even have much snob appeal. Nor do such people have much need to read the directions on an imported item. The national need to use English for international communication likewise cannot compete with the family need to remove children from school to harvest rice, care for the younger children, or fulfill other responsibilities.

Standards of teaching English in the schools, especially in country areas, frequently remain low, as well. Teaching materials may not be available, or may be inadequate in poor schools. Although their own average education has improved markedly in recent years, some Thai teachers themselves have little command even of Thai English, since they have not had much more education than their pupils.

Table 1.2. Minimum weekly hours of language teaching in Thai schools, 1986. Some private schools teach 6-10 hours of a Chinese language as well. Where a range is given, the number of hours depends on other curricular choices. Private schools may teach more English than shown, and begin it earlier.

	Thai	English
Lower elementary	7	
Upper elementary	4	3-5
Lower secondary	4	4-6
Upper secondary	3-5	6-8

The opportunity and motivation to learn English vary in the towns and cities, also. Thai who can afford it, and who live in a city where it can be done, often send their children to private schools, some of them very prestigious, where the quality of education is considered to be higher than in most government schools. Many of these schools were originally founded by English-speaking missionaries and are still run by Thai Christian churches. Some of them employ native speakers of English among their teachers.[7] Even their Thai teachers of English often have greater English mastery than teachers in most other schools. Some students with aptitude gain considerable fluency in Standard English even under less ideal circumstances, however.

In the larger cities, furthermore, where tourists, business representatives and other foreigners congregate, some hundreds of people study English outside the school system, hoping to land better jobs working for foreign companies or for Thai companies dealing with foreigners. Numerous private institutions have English programs for adults, but Thai citizens may not attend English-medium primary and secondary international schools organized for expatriates in Thailand.

Thai who have a really good working knowledge of English often had part of their education abroad. Some studied in England, India, Australia or the United States when they were children or young people, sent there by wealthy parents or as beneficiaries of scholarships or of high school exchange programs. Others spent one or more years in foreign English-speaking universities. A few Thai have native or near-native mastery of English. People with such education are generally the ones who speak for Thailand to the outside world, or interpret for those who must speak only in Standard Thai.

But on the other hand, a Thai who is only educated abroad is handicapped for lack of opportunity to study Thai language and culture, and Thai is the indispensable internal language of the country. Thai skills in writing and speaking require years of schooling in Standard Thai. Thus, Sino-Thai families who formerly sent their sons to China to be educated found that those sons were at a disadvantage because of insufficient Thai when they returned to the family business in Thailand.

Summary

Thailand as a nation has two languages, Standard Thai and Standard English. The first is the internal language of the nation, the second its external language.

Standard Thai is a major national symbol, the official language, the language of government, education, media and high culture. For most Thai, however, it is not the language of their birth and home, nor of the region in which they live, but a language they learned in school, from the media, and through extensive use.

English, on the other hand, is the primary language which the nation uses in its external contacts. It is the language of international politics, advanced education outside the country, international media, culture and tourism. It is also a language which Thai people universally study in school.

But studying English has led also to a widespread Thai English, an interlanguage in which English is pronounced in a Thai manner and English grammar is modified both by Thai grammar and by reduction of the complexities of Standard English. Thai English is largely restricted to special functions like the citation of English words and sentences in Thai discourse and reading labels on imported packages. It is sometimes attempted with foreigners, who often have difficulty understanding it, but its primary use is internal to the country, not as a language of Thailand abroad.

Degrees of competency in Standard Thai range from zero to highly skillful among Thai citizens. Correspondingly, much smaller numbers manifest skills in English. But whether skillfully used or not, both languages are crucial to the country. Both are at the core of its linguistic diversity and national unity.

2

Standard Thai:
Variations about a Norm

As the internal language of the Thai nation, Standard Thai is a major source of unity in Thailand, but is itself a diverse phenomenon. Thai people generally agree that there are correct and incorrect ways of speaking and writing Thai, but well-educated ones will often unconsciously use some of the "incorrect" forms while they are talking about them as being incorrect. The issue of what "standard" means in relation to language is a complex one everywhere, and in Thailand it is one facet of the linguistic diversity of the country.[1]

The term *variety* has been used in the preceding pages as a general term for several kinds of systematic language differences. It is not used for haphazard slips of the tongue, or for individual peculiarities in language use, but for patterned variations in usage characteristic of groups of people, configurations such as those we will explore more fully in this chapter as they occur in Standard Thai. When varieties coincide with geographic distribution they are often called dialects. When they coincide with social status or behavior they are often called registers. When they are established as norms by the elite, the opinion makers, the bureaucracy or officialdom, they are referred to as standard and non-standard or substandard (or, more popularly, "correct" and "incorrect").

For our purposes, Standard Thai starts with that set of varieties which educated people in Thailand think they should speak or write, and which they take as norms when using the language carefully. But all such speakers vary from these norms in myriad ways, and most variations which are not stigmatized still pass unnoticed as Standard Thai. Thus anyone who speaks or writes without markedly non-standard usage is generally interpreted as speaking Standard Thai.

The existence of such a standard language implies a process of codification, of overt and covert decision making concerning what is to be acceptable (Weinreich 1968:314-315), what will go into a dictionary or a grammar book, what will be taught in school, what will be condemned.[2] The need for such codification is felt by the elite, or by officials of a government, or a school system, in part because some of the diversity which exists in the language is too great for such institutions to tolerate. If a standard is truly to be achieved, however, these norms must also be accepted by a significant part of the population (Stewart 1968:534).

The rigidity with which a standard is maintained varies for different parts of the language. Table 2.1 shows a continuum of standardization along which some language features can vary more than others. Table 2.2 also shows roughly how that variability is greater within the spoken standard than within the written standard, and suggests degrees of variability within each of these as well.

The most tangible, least variable aspects of Standard Thai are the writing system and spelling. Unlike European languages, the writing system itself, including the basic shapes of the letters, is uniquely Thai. On the other hand, one Thai type font varies from another in the shapes of its letters, as does one typewriter model from another, and one person's handwriting from another's. Advertisers and logo designers create eye-catching variations also. But people read all such variants as Thai, still manifestations of the one Thai writing system. Shapes of the individual letters vary within limits of recognizability, but no other system will be accepted as Standard Thai writing.

Table 2.1. Examples of elements in the continuum of variation between some vigorously promoted language forms and other vigorously repudiated ones.

	Most vigorously promoted
Standard	Ideal written
	Actual written by relevant elites
	Ideal spoken
	Actual spoken by relevant elites
Neutral	Non-stigmatized colloquial
	Non-stigmatized regionalisms
Non-standard	Mistakes, slips of the tongue
	Interlanguage
	Stigmatized regionalisms
	Stigmatized colloquial
	Non-vulgar
	Vulgar
	Most vigorously proscribed

Table 2.2. Degrees of variability in different components of Standard Thai.

More limited variability	
Writing system	
Spelling	
Reading pronunciation	
Written grammar	Spoken pronunciation
Written vocabulary	Spoken grammar
Written usage	Spoken vocabulary
	Spoken usage

Greater variability

As in most languages with an established writing tradition, not much variation is allowed in Thai spelling, either. Normally a given word is to be spelled in one particular way considered correct, even if that spelling is inconsistent with other spellings. For example, the correct way of writing /thân/ (respectful term of address to a man), which is spoken with a vowel of short duration, is ท่าน. According to the regular spelling rules, however, this spelling would normally represent a vowel of long duration, as though it were */thâan/[3] similar to ทาน /thaan/ 'eat'. Or the correct way, really the only way, of writing /hɔ̂ŋ/ 'room', spoken with a vowel of short duration, is ห้อง, although such a spelling would commonly represent a vowel of long duration.

To be sure, the spelling of a few Thai words has varied over time. Occasionally the spelling of one word has changed with shifting pronunciations, while the spelling of other words has not. In a form of Tai which preceded modern Thai, for example, ยาง (a kind of tree) and อยฺาง 'rubber' were both pronounced and spelled differently, but in time they came to be spoken alike, and the spelling of 'rubber' shifted also to ยฺาง, like 'tree' (Brown 1965:146-147, 159-160). Nevertheless, in spite of a few such cases, little variation in spelling is tolerated in Standard Thai.

Beyond the writing system and spelling, an understanding of just what constitutes Standard Thai becomes more vague. The difficulty linguists have had in defining Standard Thai and its relationship to other forms of Thai has been expressed as follows:

Standard Thai has been called a national language, a regional dialect, a language for use in schools, an equivalent of Central Thai, an equivalent of Bangkok Thai, an equivalent of educated Central or Bangkok Thai, a language not equivalent to, but closely resembling Central (and Bangkok) Thai, a prestige dialect of educated speakers regardless of origin, and a model of what Central Thai is supposed to be (Beebe 1974:74).

Precisely because many misconceptions concerning Standard are held by Thai people themselves as well as by foreign researchers, we need to clarify its nature and diversity. In many respects the generalizations in this chapter and the next do not differ much from those which could be made concerning other standard languages, but they are often overlooked and misunderstood in Thailand, and need to be emphasized here.

Variation in Bangkok Thai Pronunciation

Beebe (1974, 1975, 1979) examined recorded interviews with Thai people of different professional classes for ways in which their pronunciations conformed or did not conform to Standard Thai norms. The words selected for observation are spelled in Thai with certain initial consonant clusters, or sequences of consonants consisting of the Thai script equivalents of {pr phr pl phl tr kr khr kl khl kw khw}.[4] In ideal Standard Thai these clusters are supposed to be fully pronounced, with no consonants dropped or changed from what the writing indicates.

Figure 2.1 shows the percentage of occurrences in which words spelled with {r} or {l} or {w} in consonant clusters were actually pronounced that way in Beebe's sample. Clusters with {w} were generally pronounced as written, especially in the more educated occupational classes, but {l} and {r} were pronounced much less frequently by all classes. The use of a pronunciation other than [kw] for {kw} was an indicator of lower-class occupation on a graded scale, but the use of some other pronunciation than [př] for {pr} was more nearly universal, not related to any professional class. Frequency of [pl] for {pl} lay between. In the upper professional classes the people interviewed must be presumed to be largely speakers of Standard Thai, but most of them regularly do not pronounce some of these clusters in the way the norms of ideal spoken Standard Thai would specify.

These findings are presented in more detail in figures 2.2 and 2.3. In figure 2.2 [kw] is the standard pronunciation, while [f] is common to non-standard colloquial speech in Bangkok and the surrounding area. Standard Thai speakers say that pronunciations other than the

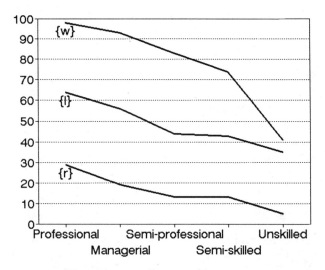

Fig. 2.1. Average percentage of full cluster retention in words spelled with clusters involving {w}, {l} and {r} as the second member, according to occupational class (after Beebe 1974:157-158; Beebe 1975:57).

[kw] in figure 2.2 seem provincial, uneducated, and many would feel uncomfortable using them.

In figure 2.3 [př] is the ideal standard pronunciation, while [p] represents cluster reduction, and [pl] results from lack of contrast between [l] and [ř], as discussed below. Most of the other pronunciations are scattered attempts to produce some kind of [r], either retroflexed [ɹ] (as in many dialects of English) or trilled [r̄]. In this case, [př], the ideal standard form, often feels and sounds unnatural and awkward to good speakers of Standard Thai. Tai languages have long been undergoing cluster reduction that has been especially strong with {r} clusters, so that many Tai languages have no clusters of this kind left, and Standard Thai is headed in that direction.

The distinction drawn between the "ideal" and the "actual" standard in table 2.1 is the difference between what is promoted, advocated by purists, and taught in the schools as "correct," on the one hand, and what upper-class and educated people actually do use in the various kinds of formal and semi-formal situations reflected in figures 2.1-2.3, on the other. The actual spoken standard is what such people sense as normal, what they are comfortable using, what seems appropriate to the kind of situation in which the language is used.

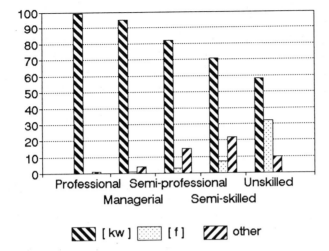

Fig. 2.2. Pronunciations of Standard Thai {kw} by speakers of different occupational classes (after Beebe 1975).

In the next chapter we will see something of how the particular situation in which Standard Thai is spoken affects what varieties are used. Since Beebe's data come from interviews, and since people can be expected to be careful about their language in such situations even though language was not the focus of their attention in the interview, it is likely that even more instances of pronunciations which do not match ideal standards are actually spoken by the same subjects in less guarded situations. I have heard a Thai accountant switch pronunciation of the same word instantaneously from [kw] spoken to me, to [f] spoken to our taxi driver.

Origins of Standard Thai

The standardization of Thai presumably began in the kingdom of Ayuthaya, centered north of Bangkok. It was there that classical Central Thai culture was developed in the fifteenth to the eighteenth centuries. The city and the rich rice-growing plain, which was the economic base of the kingdom, were populated by people who spoke a number of different languages, and some mutually intelligible Tai dialects. The writing system, which had been developed earlier, was also used in the court at Ayuthaya, and writing conventions reflected that usage.

Ayuthaya was destroyed by the Burmese in 1767, but within a few years a new capital was established at Bangkok under the first king in the present Chakri dynasty. As much as possible of Ayuthayan culture was reestablished there in spite of the enormous loss of wealth, cultural treasure, religious objects, archives and libraries of the earlier capital. The new royal family, the surviving power elite, intellectuals and religious leaders continued as the upper class in this new location, bringing their spoken language with them, as well as their writing traditions. However, the common people of the Bangkok area spoke a different dialect.

Smaller differences between the speech of the elite and of ordinary people had doubtless already been present at Ayuthaya, caused by many factors. Certainly one was the use of vocabulary borrowed from Khmer and Sanskrit (Gedney 1947) by the upper classes. Also, different ages and classes of people everywhere accept changes in sound, grammar, and vocabulary at differing rates and/or from different sources, creating different patterns of speech in a diverse population.

But the differences between the spoken Bangkok dialect and the one brought by the Ayuthayan elite doubtless increased the gap separating upper-class language from that of the ordinary people. In time the city also grew larger, drawing people of different languages and dialects from more outlying regions, and from abroad in the case of

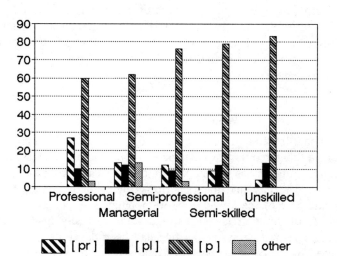

Fig. 2.3. Pronunciations of Standard Thai {pr} by speakers of different occupational classes (after Beebe 1975).

Chinese, South Asians and Europeans. Contacts with English affected what was considered to be standard (Amara 1988; Diller 1988). Education and occupation created more social differentiation. Today the metropolitan area has a staggering spectrum of different linguistic patterns and influences at work.

In this mosaic, the Royal Institute in Thailand has for many years been charged with the development, purification and standardization of ideal Standard Thai, as they see it. Its influence is extended through publications such as its dictionary and encyclopedia. It represents one strand of purist perspective in Thailand which sees standard forms as intrinsically right, not just as social or cultural reality (Diller 1988).

But more powerful than such arbitrary prescriptivism in shaping people's sense of actual Standard Thai is the speech and writing of relevant elites, beginning with the King and court. The aristocracy, the wealthy, the writers, the intellectuals, the journalists, the TV, movie and radio performers all contribute to the formation of actual Standard Thai.

Maintenance and Change in Standardization

Among Beebe's subjects, older people tended to approximate the ideal standard norms more closely than younger people, which gives evidence of the direction of change. Some of the dynamics of typical language change can be seen in figure 2.4, where change due to education moves down from the upper classes, but some other kinds of change move up from the lower classes. In either case the change may seem inappropriate to some groups of people, who refuse to adopt it, creating points of resistance where it slows down, or beyond which it does not penetrate. Those points differ for different traits, different groups, different individuals, and at different times.

As changes take place in the speech of the young, for example, and spread through part of the population, a segment of the older population may resist it. If it continues to spread even though it slows down, the point of resistance gradually rises higher on the scale, and more nearly universal usage may increasingly lower the resistance in more people. Or older people may die off and be replaced by people who have earlier made the change.

Likewise, lower-class people may resist forms introduced through education or other higher-class activity because they sound snobbish

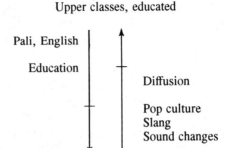

Fig. 2.4. Some forces of language change.
The horizontal lines symbolize variable points
of resistance.

or bookish to them. Now that the loss of spoken /r/ is virtually universal in most of Thailand, attempts by educators to promote it get tacit resistance from most of the population. The existing patterns of speech do not readily give way to attempts to reestablish the distinction in people's pronunciation. Many feel stuffy speaking that way.

Non-standard and Neutral Usage

Table 2.1, with its gradation between what is most intensely promoted as standard and what is most intensely proscribed as non-standard, includes a category of mistakes, or slips of the tongue. Thai people, like everyone else, catch themselves saying things they do not intend, and although the mistakes themselves may not be standard they do not detract from hearing the variety the person is using as standard, other things being equal. In fact, most such lapses are not even noticed, and when noticed are automatically forgiven.

Interlanguage, furthermore, is the language of people who do not speak Thai well because their mother tongue is not Thai, but a Chinese language, or Pattani Malay, or Lisu, or something else (Tarone 1980). Pronunciation and grammar are affected by interference from the mother language, and the speakers are unable to handle the complexities of Thai, so that they do communicate to some degree, sometimes fluently and extensively, but not with accuracy or naturalness. But although interlanguage is not standard, it is usually tolerated, marking the people who use it as lying outside the real Thai orbit.

Stigmatized forms are not so easily forgiven, however. Standard language norms are sometimes easier to identify by what they are against than by what they promote. In American English, for example, forms like "he ain't" and "he don't" are widely stigmatized.

Thus, to use our Standard Thai {pr} example again, [př] pronunciation is promoted as standard, but most people, even educated ones, would feel silly using it in anything but very formal situations, and many would even feel silly using it there. [p] for {pr}, therefore, is not stigmatized by most people using the spoken standard. But [f] and some other variants are stigmatized as pronunciation for {kw}, considered rustic and uneducated, so people speaking Standard Thai under most circumstances not only avoid these pronunciations but also have negative feelings about them.

Language usage may be stigmatized because it is borrowed from a different geographic dialect, the "regionalisms" of table 2.1. But not all regionalisms are stigmatized, some sounding exotic, or quaint, and so tolerated. More typically a usage is stigmatized when it is identified with lower classes, the uneducated, minority groups, or other people looked down upon. Thus, /nə́/ or /də́/ used where Standard Thai would have /ná/ (a final particle with various functions) sounds rural, lower class, and therefore non-standard.

Vulgar usage is stigmatized for use in some situations, although it may be appropriate in others. In itself it is not standard, but some of it may be sprinkled in otherwise standard speech. Thai has many words for 'eat' on different levels of elegance. /dɛ̀ɛk/ and /yát/ are vulgar, non-standard in themselves, but nevertheless used for effect within some types of standard discourse (chap. 3).

Most actual language usage lies between what is actively promoted as a symbol of correctness and what is stigmatized. This neutral area

Table 2.3. Standard and non-standard elements occurring separately or in various degrees of mixture.

	Promoted	Neutral	Stigmatized
Pure	Standard Thai	Standard Thai	Non-standard
Mixed	Standard Thai + special effect or mistake	Standard / Non-standard	Non-standard + promoted forms

in the continuum of table 2.1 is common both to speakers of Standard Thai and to others from Bangkok. If it occurs in discourse without stigmatized elements, it is standard. If it occurs with markedly stigmatized elements, the whole discourse seems non-standard (table 2.3).

Standard Thai around the Nation

But although no clear-cut, objective, strictly definable Standard Thai can be identified, any more than can any such rigidly definable Standard American English, Standard Thai is nevertheless very real in Thai culture, education, self-understanding, and values. It is a cultural concept with variable manifestations, some loose and relatively unformulated and others about which strong opinions exist.

Children born and raised in an upper-class home where Standard Thai is spoken regularly learn it at home and build on that foundation through education and use. For them education serves to develop their skills for higher and more formal levels of speaking and writing.

Children born in the central plains, but in families where Standard Thai is not normally used, or used only in special circumstances, have to learn a partially different tone system, change their pronunciation of many words from their native speech, and substitute some entirely different words when they speak Standard Thai. But still, learning to speak it primarily involves making modifications in what they already know, and building on that. This is because Standard Thai is based on Thaiklang, the regional language of central Thailand (chap. 7). Such people therefore select varieties along a continuum between the colloquial variety of Thaiklang they know and ideal Standard Thai. The selection differs with the person, age, occupation, education, situation, person spoken to, people listening, and much more.

People born in other regions of the country, in families where Standard Thai is not normally used, have more difficulty. For them Standard Thai is a different language from their own, and learning to use it correctly takes longer. In rural areas, once out of school many such people retain only scraps of spoken Standard Thai, although they may still understand quite a bit. Others mix what they retain with local usage. A few go on to learn Standard Thai well.

The Thai school system has spread Standard Thai throughout the country in what its officials consider to be a pure form, maintaining remarkable uniformity as spoken by sufficiently educated people with different mother tongues. Reinforcing and supplementing education is the ubiquitous Standard Thai of the radio, widespread television, and print media in all but the most remote rural areas.

But on the other hand, just as Standard Thai is not an unvarying entity as used by educated speakers in Bangkok, neither is it completely uniform as it occurs across the country. Slightly divergent geographic dialects are to be found, as in any other major language. Most of these have been introduced into Standard Thai from regionalisms, but in one respect at least, some outlying ones are closer to ideal Standard Thai than is the actual Standard Thai of Bangkok.

Ideally, for example, spoken Standard Thai requires people to pronounce written {r} and {l} as [ř] and [l] respectively.[5] We are speaking now of single consonants, not of these sounds in the clusters discussed above. {rót} 'to water, sprinkle' is supposed to be pronounced differently from {lót} 'to lower, reduce', or {rɔɔŋ} 'place beneath' from {lɔɔŋ} 'try out, try on'. Children are drilled in school on making this distinction, and an occasional article deplores the fact that many people do not in fact regularly do so.

Among educated Bangkok speakers of Standard Thai some will sometimes make this distinction in pronunciation when they are being extra careful. Perhaps a few regularly make it. But most speakers of Standard Thai throughout the country pronounce words with these spellings sometimes one way, sometimes the other, most commonly giving an [l] pronunciation to both. Many Thai are like speakers of Chinese, Japanese or Korean, in that they sometimes cannot even hear the difference between [r] and [l]. In a set of experiments highly educated Thai speakers distinguished them only 80% of the time (Abramson 1962:6-9).

So difficult is the distinction for less educated speakers that they may even reverse pronunciations when they are trying hard to be proper. An agent who was showing us a house to rent told us that the street on which it was located was [sɔɔy răŋ sǔan], and actually wrote down for us in roman letters: Soi Rang Suan. The name of the street, as written in Thai, and as pronounced when people are not trying to be extra careful, is [sɔɔy lǎŋ sǔan]. The main thing this person seems to have learned from the classes where she was drilled on pronouncing a difference between {l} and {r}, was that [l] is wrong; you must say [ř].

In an even more startling example, a Thai woman told a story to family and friends, pronouncing each {l} and {r} naturally for her speech as [l]. She then turned and repeated the whole story to an American who was present, pronouncing each {l} and {r} as [ř], an

exaggerated variant used by some people trying to pronounce {r} in a
deliberate way (Beebe 1974:131).

So {l} and {r} are a problem for most speakers of Standard Thai,
who believe they should pronounce a distinction, but whose internal
grammatical rules, as distinct from what they are told in school, do
not provide one. There are areas of the country, however, where a
clear distinction does exist with most speakers. In the Northern
Khmer-speaking areas of Surin, Buri Ram and Si Sa Ket provinces of
northeast Thailand, for example, speakers of Standard Thai whose
mother tongue is Northern Khmer distinguish between /r/ and /l/ in
their Standard Thai because they have such a distinction in their variety of Khmer (Smalley 1976c:47; Noss 1966).

In much of the southern peninsula, from Chumphon Province
south, with the exception of the border provinces of Songkhla, Yala
and Satun, furthermore, the local Thai languages and dialects have a
distinct /r/ (Noss 1964:2; Brown 1965:117, 119-123, 126-128, 130-
131, 133-135; Premchit 1983), and Noss implies that this carries over
into their Standard Thai as well. U Thong District in Suphan Buri
Province likewise has a distinct /r/ in its local dialect (Brown 1965:
85), as do some districts in Nakorn Ratchasima Province (Chalida
1977). In these and other cases like them, many people use /r/ regularly in their Standard Thai.

However, such people do not all necessarily carry the distinction
over into Standard Thai even though they already have it from their
mother tongue. In Surat Thani, one of the southern provinces which
does have the distinction, young people are often reluctant to use it in
their Standard Thai because they do not hear it in the speech of people
from Bangkok (Theraphan L. Thongkum personal communication).

Some people, furthermore, have a regional accent when speaking
Standard Thai. Many northerners whose mother tongue is Kammüang, for example, pronounce the sound represented by ค {kh} of
ideal Standard Thai (similar to the sound represented by {c} in
English *cat*) as [x] (similar to the sound represented by {ch} in
German *ach*) or as [kx]. Thus, Standard Thai /khon/ 'person' is often
heard as [xon] or [kxon] when some northerners are speaking.
Likewise, some people from parts of northeast Thailand will say [s]
or [ts] for {ch} in words like Standard Thai ฉัน /chān/ 'I', which they
pronounce [săn] or [tsăn].

Furthermore, the vocabulary of Standard Thai varies slightly as
used in different sections of Thailand, frequently creating non-
stigmatized regionalisms. The Kammüang word /dɔɔy/ 'mountain',

for example, is in common use in otherwise Standard Thai discourse in the north. In Chiang Mai people will often say, in Standard Thai: /pay thîaw bon dɔɔy/ 'go for a trip up the mountain' and /yùu bon dɔɔy/ 'live in the mountains'. This then carries over in a limited way into Bangkok Standard Thai when people are talking about an experience in the north or the northern hill tribes.

I noticed in the 1960s, both in the north of Thailand and in the northeast, that I was addressed with Standard Thai /naay/ (used as a title 'Sir' or 'Mr.') more than I was in Bangkok, where I was more frequently addressed with /'acaan/ 'Professor', if not /khun/ 'you'. The meaning of /naay/ is probably not different in Bangkok from what it is in the other areas, but its frequency seemed to be. Doubtless many differences in the frequency and usage of Standard Thai terms occur in this way, partly due to carryover from local varieties of speech and partly to the different roles which Standard Thai and local varieties of speech play.

Summary

So Standard Thai is not a monolithic, invariable, static language, any more than any other living language is. It serves to establish some order among varieties, reflecting centers of power. We have characterized ideal Standard Thai as what people are taught, what the language brokers insist they should speak and write. This ideal standard is much less complex, however, than what speakers of Standard Thai actually do speak and write, even those who follow the ideals most closely. Their repertoire of speech and writing contains far more variation than the ideal presupposes.

People would sound stilted if they spoke only according to the norms of ideal Standard Thai. Instead, they adapt their speech and writing to myriad situations, and so long as they do not sound too much as though they are using some regional dialect or language, or do not sound like uneducated people in some way, or do not use otherwise stigmatized words or pronunciations, these variations raise no questions in the minds of Standard Thai-speaking hearers or readers.

What is to be accepted as standard is problematic in Thai as in any other standardized language. Standard Thai is the result of developments through different historical processes, carried by the various elites, propagated and enforced by the school system. Although the rules for ideal Standard Thai often seem categorical, much variation in usage is actually accepted even by purists, while other variation is stigmatized even by the people who use it. The cline between standard and substandard speech is therefore uneven and ill defined at the borders. People in different parts of the country, furthermore, sometimes have partially different problems with learning and using standard forms. Standard Thai is always changing in some respects, too, although highly stable in others.

But although Standard Thai is in some ways an artificial construct, it is nevertheless highly functional, widely used, highly desired and greatly admired by Thai on almost all levels of national life. It is essential to national unity in spite of its internal diversity. And although someone's use of Standard Thai depends in most cases on that person's level of education, it is nevertheless the language of the whole nation, not just of educated people. Thai people throughout the nation agree that "Thai," meaning Standard Thai, is the language of Thailand, whether they can use it or not.

3

Social Dimensions of Standard Thai

Standard Thai varies in a number of multidimensional ways beyond the different approximations of ideal standard which were discussed in the last chapter. As they talk, speakers combine interdependent varieties taken from each of several dimensions of the language, depending on social factors in the speech situation.[1]

The types of varieties discussed in this chapter are not unique to Standard Thai, except in a few features and many details. The pervasive presence of multiple dimensions of varieties in Standard Thai needs nevertheless to be emphasized as a part of Thailand's diversity within national unity. The diversity inherent in the Standard Thai language is so much taken for granted that its significance goes largely unnoticed.

The Dimension of Social Distance

If we listen to a Thai government official giving a speech at the opening of a new public building, and then conversing with a cluster of people who gather around him at the reception afterwards, we are struck with how his use of Standard Thai changes. The decided "speaking to a crowd" projection of the speech is gone, of course, but the differences extend much beyond that.

For one thing, the speaker's pronunciation is partially different. All major syllables in Standard Thai have tones—characteristic pitch or pitch movement—which are as essential to the word in which they occur as are the consonants and vowels. However, tones on some words are different in a formal speech from the way they are in conversation. For example, some people say [kʰǎw] 'third person, respectful' or [lɨ̌] 'question word' with a rising tone in a speech-making situation, but in normal Standard Thai conversation they say [kʰāw] or [lɨ̄] instead, with a high tone which is different from any of the five tones usually counted as the tones of Standard Thai.

41

With many speakers, furthermore, first- and second-person pronouns differ sharply in speech and social conversation. In the official's speech /khâaphacâw/ is used for the first person and /thân/ for the second person, whereas in the social conversation at the reception the pronouns are /phǒm/ and /khun/.

In speeches the word meaning 'eat' is generally /rápprathaan/, whereas in a conversation at a reception it is often /thaan/. 'Give' in a speech may be /mɔ̀ɔp/ or /mɔ̂ɔp hây/, but in a conversation it may well be /hây/. Speech makers generally use status particles such as /khráp/ or /khâ/ much less than people engaged in conversation (table 3.2). Grammatical differences include more frequent repetition of the subject of the sentence in a speech than in a conversation, where the listener is expected to know by context what the subject is.

In a conversation some speakers use the particle /nã/ as much as every two or three sentences, signalling that they want the hearer to respond. Most do not use it at all during a formal speech, although some (especially women) may use it in a less formal one, such as a classroom lecture.

Thus, anyone listening to tape recordings of the official talking in both of these events would have no trouble identifying which was the speech and which the conversation.

When the reception is over, the speaker drives home with a good friend, a former schoolmate, a colleague with much the same social position. He now speaks another variety of Standard Thai. First person now probably becomes /kuu/, and second person /mɨŋ/. These pronouns express camaraderie and relaxed freedom (Cooke 1968:11, 16) when used in this situation, but would be most disrespectful under other circumstances or to people other than close friends. They would not normally be used in the presence of women or superiors.[2]

'Eat' is no longer /thaan/ or /rápprathaan/ but /kin/. Slang may be used more extensively. The status particles are gone from the ends of sentences, although they still occur as responses, with the meanings of 'yes, uh-huh, go ahead, I'm listening'. Sentences are shorter, less carefully formulated than in the conversation. More is left unexpressed because the men know each other so well that they do not need to be explicit about everything. Less attention is paid to care and preciseness in pronunciation. Whole syllables are regularly left off words.

But this is not necessarily "sloppy" speech. If the friends talked with each other in the car as they were talking with people at the reception they would feel as though a social barrier stood between them. Talk at the reception sounds friendly, polite, but distant. Instead, the conversation in the car sounds personal, warm, and close.

These three major ways of speaking used in one afternoon by the same person are three varieties along the Standard Thai dimension of social distance. They are sometimes called public, as in speech making, consultative, as in the conversation at the reception, and personal, as in the conversation in the car.[3]

Of these social distance varieties, the consultative (characteristic of social interaction with acquaintances or strangers) is the basic one in the sense that the others can be derived from it. The public variety is formed from the consultative by elaborations in grammar, pronunciation, vocabulary, and discourse organization. These usually require considerable education to handle effectively. The personal variety, on the other hand, is formed from the consultative by such processes as deletions, ellipses, and contractions, as well as differences of vocabulary, and greater use of slang.

Social distance varieties correlate to some degree with the physical distance between speakers and hearers (Hall 1966, 1968). In Standard Thai the public variety is normally used in speaking to a group, at least some members of which are normally several or more feet away. The larger the group and the greater the physical distance, the more marked the indicators of public variety often become. The personal variety is normally used with no more than two or three individuals—perhaps around a table, walking along together, or chatting in a little cluster. Because the consultative variety is the basic one it can be used in a greater number of situations, although the participants who use it in a small cluster of people are not likely to be in as close physical proximity as with the personal distance variety.

Varieties in the dimension of social distance, or any other sets of varieties in Standard Thai, should never be thought of as rigid categories, however. They are gradations along a continuum with archetypical manifestations but porous boundaries. Speakers also vary in their selections along the continuum in one direction or another. Some talks to fairly large groups in informal settings show reduced public distance, for example, tending more toward consultative distance. But such deviation cannot go too far, or the language sounds inappropriate, and if extreme enough, offensive.

The Dimension of Social Relationship

If we continue to follow the Thai official the next day we can find him at his office in one of the large government buildings in Bangkok. His responsibilities give him contact with different types of people, including the cabinet minister in charge of the ministry in which he works, his own superiors, his equals, his immediate subordinates, clerks, messengers and chauffeurs. When he talks with any of these people he uses primarily the consultative variety of Standard Thai, although he may also shift occasionally into the personal variety when a colleague of long-standing drops in for a moment. He does not talk the same to all of these levels of people, however, but modifies the consultative variety according to the different social relationships.

For one thing, the official selects from several different first- and second-person pronouns, depending on the person to whom he is talking. Table 3.1 shows just a few of the possibilities.[4] The pronouns used with the cabinet minister show great deference. Pronouns for immediate superiors, equals, and almost-equals imply slight deference. They politely elevate almost-equals and equals to the level of slight superiors. English-derived pronouns, on the other hand, indicate equality and camaraderie. Other pronouns explicitly place the addressees lower than the speakers, but if appropriately used are not necessarily disrespectful, as they may seem to Westerners. An inappropriate term may be disrespectful, however, if it is lower than is required, or may indicate mock deference if it is higher than required. On the other hand, this social relationship dimension does not imply that every particular type of combination of speaker and hearer re-

Table 3.1. Some pronoun combinations which express the dimension of social relationship in Standard Thai. They are shown from the perspective of the illustrative official in the text.

Social rank of addressee	First person	Second person
The Minister	krăphŏm	thân
Immediate superiors, equals	phŏm	khun
Western-oriented equals	'ay (Eng. *I*)	yuu (Eng. *you*)
Clerks and lower-rank subordinates in general	chăn	khun
Young female clerk with whom official has considerable contact	chăn	thəə
Lower-class Chinese who runs the small restaurant where the official eats his lunch	'úa	líi

quires a corresponding particular pronoun. In fact, speakers sometimes switch pronouns in the same discourse, with the same hearer,
for a variety of reasons (Angkap 1972:29, 103-120), such as to suggest that the relationship is shifting in actuality or in·mood.[5]

Standard Thai status particles[6] are other frequently recurring sig-
nals of social relationship. They occur in sentence-final or phrase-final
position, or speakers respond with them as independent utterances to
indicate assent or attentiveness in conversation (table 3.2). They are
not used in all discourse, their presence depending on social distance
and other factors, such as whether or not the speaker feels like being
polite. If they are used, however, the particle chosen reflects the
social relationship.[7]

The following quotation presents some useful rules of thumb for
foreigners learning to use status particles in Standard Thai. An alternative set of usages from another source (Wichuda S. Zehner personal
communication) has been added in brackets within the quotation as
well. The minor differences between the two sets may be due to
differences in the social classes of the sources, individual differences,

Table 3.2. Status particles in Standard Thai, showing norms which apply to
consultative social distance (after Noss 1964:215-217). Pronunciation of
these particles varies widely. For example, one of them ranges from /khrãp/
through /khãp/, and /hãp/ to /hã/. ?=question, O=other.

Addressee		Man speaking	Woman speaking
To highly superior, sacred, or noble person	?	khrãphŏm	câwkhã or khã
	O	khrãphŏm	câwkhâ or khâ
To equal or superior	?	khrãp	khã
	O	khráp	khâ
To intimate, younger or inferior	?	cã, khrãp or nothing	cã, khã or nothing
	O	câ, khráp or nothing	câ, khâ or nothing
To intimate or equal; otherwise rude and vulgar	?	wã	wã
	O	wâ	wâ
Impolite	?	yã	yã

or changes in practice over the twenty-five years since the paragraph was written.

With your own servants, no particle; but with servants at the boss's house, /câ/ [no particle]. With your friends at the office or at school, no particle; but with their parents, /khráp/ or /khâ/. With a taxi driver or salesman, no particle [/khráp/ or /khâ/ if the person is considerably older]; but with his children, /câ/ [depends on one's own relationship to the person addressed]. A romance usually proceeds from /khráp/ to /câ/ to no particle (/câ/ corresponding to "sweet talk") (Brown 1967:1).

Usage does change with time. In 1985-1986 some young men had taken to using /khrāphǒm/ in some relationships where a previous generation would have used only /khráp/. It remains to be seen whether this was a passing fad or part of a long-term shift.

The status particles themselves express social relationship, but some of them can also be modified by substituting a rising tone for their normal tone to indicate social distance as well. Thus, a woman may say /cǎa/ to a friend, which intensifies the intimacy of the basic form /câ/, or /khǎa/, which intensifies the deference of the basic form /khâ/ (Jones, Mendiones, and Reynolds 1976:45).

Pronouns and status particles correlate with relative rank between people talking, or between speakers and the people about whom they are talking. Titles, on the other hand, express a more fixed rank. Someone may be addressed or spoken of with the title of /'acaan/ 'professor' by a servant, a student, a fellow professor, or the Prime Minister, especially at public or consultative distance. The servant or student, however, would stick to the title or some other equally deferential term at personal distance when the peer or superior might shift to a more relative term.

The indicators of social relationship have other meanings also. They are frequently used in Thai to imply a range of moods from camaraderie to flattery or insult. Any unexpected or unusual use of status particle, pronoun, or other social relationship indicator is likely to be charged with emotion. If the social relationship indicators in the discourse do not match the perceived relationships between the people involved they carry emotional overtones, as does any change in them during the discourse.

Interplay of Social Distance and Social Relationship

More interplay between social distance and social relationship dimensions is manifested in the many complex terms of address to be found in Standard Thai. These are made up of a combination of pronoun, kin term, rank, title/occupation, name and expressive phrase (Amara and Kalaya 1985). The elements must occur in that order, and any combination is theoretically possible, from any single item in the set to the whole string. However, a combination of three of the elements or fewer is most typical. These terms of address may also be concluded by a status particle.

In such complex terms of address the individual terms indicate social relationship. But in combination they differ also in social distance. A title indicates more social distance than a name or a kin term, for example. Thus, the successive terms of address in the following two sets of examples reflect increasing social distance along with the social relationship inherent in the basic term.

pâa 'aunt'	mɔ̌ɔ 'doctor'
khunpâa 'you-aunt'	luŋmɔ̌ɔ 'uncle-doctor'
	khunmɔ̌ɔ 'you-doctor'

In table 3.3 use of the name alone as a term of address shows relative non-deference (social relationship) and/or intimacy (social distance). Thus a superior will use the inferior's name, but not vice versa. Names are freely used between friends of equal status. Use of the pronoun alone, however, shows relative deference and/or remoteness, and so is often used in addressing a superior. It sounds cool and distant between friends. The social implication of pronoun plus name is intermediate between name alone and pronoun alone. For a lower-status person addressing a higher-status person, the name added to the pronoun reduces deference and/or remoteness. For a higher-status person speaking to a lower-status person, the pronoun added to the name reduces non-deference and/or intimacy.

Table 3.3. Interrelationship between social relationship and social distance in three types of Thai terms of address (after Amara and Kalaya 1985).

Social relationship	Term of address	Social distance
non-deference	name	intimacy
	pronoun + name	
deference	pronoun	remoteness

Other factors with social distance implications also affect selection
of terms of address. Among members of the academic community in
Lopburi Province, teachers in rural areas used terms which manifested closer social distance when talking to each other than did those in
urban areas. Colleagues of the opposite sex at high schools spoke to
each other with greater social distance than did those at grade schools.
Still greater social distance was manifested between such colleagues in
the college (Charuwan 1982).

Terms of address found in 157 Thai novels and short stories written over the last two hundred years show that some patterns have
changed and others have not. More lower-status people are pictured
as regularly using pronoun-plus-name in addressing higher-status
people, for example. Some wives also started addressing their husbands by name alone after the democratic revolution of the 1930s.
Such practice is still less common for wives than pronoun-plus-name,
but no other lower-status people use names alone in addressing
higher-status people. With some couples the marriage relationship
itself has doubtless become more nearly egalitarian, with corresponding changes in terms of address (Amara and Kalaya 1985).

The Dimension of Social Value

Thai words for 'eat' illustrate categories from elegant to vulgar along
the dimension of social value. This dimension expresses the relative
weight and dignity given to different vocabulary items in Standard
Thai (table 3.4). The more distant the social dimension, the higher the
social relationship of the person spoken to, the more formal the situation, and/or the more written the style (as opposed to spoken), the
higher the dimension of social value which is appropriate.

Table 3.4. Thai words for 'eat' showing some of the possibilities in the
social value dimension. On the relation of vulgar terms to Standard Thai,
see chapter 2. The difference between "sacred" and "ordinary" will be discussed in chapter 4.

Social value	Ordinary	Sacred (priests)	Sacred (kings)
Elegant	bɔɔriphôok, rápprathaan, thaan	krathamphattakit	sawŏəy
Simple	kin	chǎn	rápprathan
Slang	cía, fâat, lɔ̀ɔ		
Vulgar	yát, dɛ̀ɛk		

A Thai popular song which swept the country years ago illustrates how a person of meager education and humble standing can have problems with the elegant value of Standard Thai. As the song goes, Village Headman Lee /phûuyày lii/ received an order from higher-ups in the government requiring him to see that more pigs were raised in his village. The order came in the elegant variety, in which the word for pig is /sukɔɔn/, whereas in the simple variety it is /mǔu/.

So Headman Lee dutifully told the villagers that the government wanted them to raise more /sukɔɔn/. A villager asked what /sukɔɔn/ were, and Headman Lee replied, "/mǎanɔɔy mǎanɔɔy thammadaa/ 'little dogs, ordinary little dogs'!" He confused the elegant word for pig with the elegant word for dog, which is /sunák/. The song was a dig at the country bumpkin, pompous officials who try to communicate in elegant language with uneducated villagers, and the complexity of Standard Thai, all in one.

The simple variety in the dimension of social value is the variety for everyday situations. Most of its vocabulary is descended from the ancient Tai parent language called Proto-Tai (chap. 11). Elegant terms, used in more specialized circumstances, tend to be built on roots taken from the three classical sources of borrowed words in Standard Thai: Khmer, Pali and Sanskrit. Sanskrit was the ancient learned language of northern India, and Pali was a related language through which much of Thailand's Buddhist culture was imported. Khmer was the language spoken by the empire from which the Thai took over domination of the area, and from whom they took much of the court culture and vocabulary.

But words were not simply borrowed from these languages to become fixed items in Standard Thai. Rather, Standard Thai constantly adds to and enriches its vocabulary by forming compounds out of many of these elements, combining them with each other and with "native" Thai roots (Gedney 1947:ii).

Thailand has borrowed and is borrowing from other languages as well, today notably from Chinese languages and from English. Such new Standard Thai words feel different, however, not normally carrying elegant social value. Some are used extensively with simple social value, others as slang, sounding innovative. One often senses a set of mental quotation marks around many Standard Thai words borrowed from English for imported technical concepts. Some of them are not felt to be genuinely Thai in the sense that Sanskrit borrowings are.

Some typical examples of terms with simple and elegant value are to be seen in table 3.5. Not all elegant terms are known to all speak-

Table 3.5. Examples of simple and elegant social value.

Meaning	Simple	Elegant
child (kin term)	lûuk	bùt
father	phɔ̂ɔ	bidaa
mother	mɛ̂ɛ	maandaa
wife	mia	phanlayaa
husband	phǔa	sǎami
restaurant	láanahǎan	pháttaakaan
doctor	mɔ̌ɔ	phɛ̂ɛt
dog	mǎa	sunák
pig	mǔu	sukɔɔn

ers of Standard Thai, for education and experience is required to learn many of them. The ability to understand the elegant variety is almost always greater than the ability to speak or write it, but may not be widespread among rural people of little education.

The elegant variety of the social value dimension is almost always used at public distance, and shows deference when used at consultative distance. It virtually disappears at personal distance, where it is inappropriate because of the formality and deference associated with it.

Slang, on the other hand, is strongest at personal distance. Vulgar language is usually reserved for special effect, or is the result of argument or anger if it occurs at greater than personal distance. In the latter case it is crude and disrespectful. It frequently shows camaraderie between close friends of the same sex and age at personal distance.

But although such correlations are strong between social distance and social relationship, on the one hand, and social value on the other, they are still partially independent variables. A man talking to an equal at consultative distance may say either /lûuk/ or /bùt/ for 'child', the first being simple and the second elegant in the social value dimension.

Self-categorizing Varieties

In the social distance, social relationship and social value dimensions, speakers slip freely from one variety to another as they change speech situations. The varieties therefore do not markedly categorize, classify, identify or characterize the speaker. Self-categorizing varieties, on the other hand, are not so easily changed. They reflect the areas from which speakers come, like the north or northeast, or some types of groups to which they belong, like Sino-Thai or the educated class. Table 3.6 includes this type of difference between dimensions which characterize and those which do not. It also lists a few other dimensions of Standard Thai which have not been discussed so far.

In the last chapter we saw varieties of Thai used according to occupational and educational levels of the speakers. These were examples of self-categorizing varieties along the dimension of social status, although we did not call them that at the time. In their approximations of real (as opposed to ideal) Standard Thai, speakers sounded educated or uneducated, or sounded like professionals or unskilled laborers. The use of [f] instead of [kw] for {kw} particularly stamped the speaker as less educated, not likely to be of the professional class.

One more example of this social status scaling of pronunciation involves four variants of /s/ in Thai. For simplicity we will divide them into two groups, pronunciations that sound much like English /s/ and others that sound much like English /Θ/ (as in /Θiŋ/ *thing*). Figure 3.1 shows percentages of their occurrence in the speech of people of different social classes.

Here we apparently also have an example of language in the process of changing, as also discussed in the last chapter. Beebe (1976:17-25) showed limited evidence that the [Θ] pronunciation might be spreading upward from lower-class people. By 1991 it was becoming common among university students (Janpanit Surasin personal communication).

Table 3.6. Examples of types of varieties within Standard Thai. Those in parentheses, and others, are not discussed in this book.

Varieties	Not self-categorizing	Self-categorizing
Unidimensional	Social distance Social relationship Social value (Jargon) (Topic)	Social status
Multidimensional	Range Medium	Dialect Standardization- related Education-related Sex-related Time-related

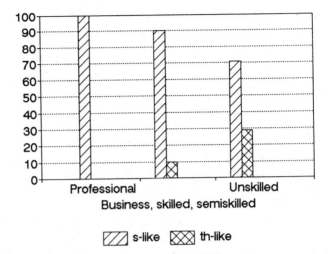

Fig. 3.1. Frequency of occurrence of variants of /s/ in the social status dimension of Standard Thai (after Beebe 1976: 17-18).

Summary

Standard Thai has numerous dimensional varieties appropriate to different kinds of social situations and relationships. Those dimensions described in this chapter are all simultaneously in effect in almost all Standard Thai discourse.

Speakers select among varieties along the social distance dimension according to such factors as the formality or intimacy of a situation, the degree of public or private character it has, and the closeness of the relationship between the speakers. A speaker will quickly change from one of these varieties to another in response to ever-changing social situations. The varieties are marked, among other things, by the degree of grammatical elaboration, simplification or contraction.

Speakers select among varieties along the social relationship dimension according to the kind of status and roles they have with respect to each other. The same speaker will tend to use much the same social relationship variety each time he or she talks with the same hearer, although that choice may be modified by other factors in the social situation as well. Social relationship varieties are strewn with words which imply deference or superiority in various degrees, or relative equality.

Speakers select among varieties ranging from elegant to vulgar along the social value dimension, according to how fancy they feel the discourse should be, and how much deference they want to show. Social value dimensions are marked primarily by vocabulary choices.

Speakers use varieties associated with their class and rank along the social status dimension. Unlike the previous varieties, which vary with situation, social status varieties depend most of all on factors like the speaker's family, education and position, although the speaker may modify them somewhat in different social situations. Social status varieties therefore categorize the speakers themselves in ways which previously described varieties do not. Pronunciation differences are often important markers of social status varieties.

4

Multidimensional Varieties:
Ranges and Media

A barber in the northern city of Chiang Mai told me about being summoned to the King's summer palace on Suthep Mountain overlooking the town. He was talking with me in Standard Thai, but emphasized how nervous he had been, not only at the thought of cutting His Majesty's hair, but also at having to address the King, or respond when spoken to, because he did not know how to talk to a king. King Bhumibol, however, had told him not to be concerned and to speak to him just as he would to anyone else. To the barber, this was an indication of the King's great kindness, because in Standard Thai to talk to the King just as you would talk to anyone else is to talk to the King disrespectfully.

The last chapter dealt primarily with some unidimensional varieties of Standard Thai, but table 3.6 listed multidimensional varieties as well. The language used for talking about royalty is part of one such set or range of dimensions which we call the sacred range of Standard Thai (Hatton 1978:35-40). And the Standard Thai which has been discussed so far, correspondingly, is the ordinary range. Both ranges are multidimensional in that each incorporates a repertoire of dimensions, as already shown for the ordinary range.

The Sacred Range of Standard Thai

Thai people who have problems using the sacred range are not limited to Chiang Mai barbers. A collection of folktales for Thai children includes this comment in the introduction:

Being intended for children, the style of this book is simple. Therefore, the court terms have likewise been simplified as in all children's stories and should not be taken as correct usage for kings (Maniratana 1966).

Well-educated northerners in Thailand have said that when they talk about the King they much prefer to talk in Kammüang (Northern

Thai), which does not have the same elaboration of special language for royalty that Standard Thai has. Some well-educated Thai are even rumored to speak English in audience with the King so as not to speak disrespectfully in Standard Thai or be guilty of flagrant malapropisms. Prince Chula mentioned that

members of the Chakri Family [the present ruling dynasty] have often written to one another in English to avoid the elaborate language required for the different ranks amongst relatives (Chula 1960:271).

The variety appropriate to royalty is called /raachaasàp/ 'royal words, high language' in Standard Thai. It consists of a special set of vocabulary plus prefixes which elevate ordinary words when special ones are not available. Table 4.1 illustrates the radical difference between terms for royalty and the ordinary vocabulary of Standard Thai.

In these examples the first group illustrates verbs which are completely different from the corresponding ordinary range. In the next group, on the other hand, the root of the verb in the two varieties is the same but a prefix /soŋ-/ elevates the word to royal status. Many of the nouns in royal vocabulary correspondingly begin with a prefix /phrā-/, as in the next group. In the final three examples the nouns in the two columns are entirely different.

The sacred variety of Standard Thai appropriate for royalty extends in part, however, to a very important class of commoners as well—to monks in the Buddhist religious hierarchy. Important differences in

Table 4.1. Examples of ordinary and royal vocabulary.

English	Standard Thai	Royal vocabulary
speak	phûut	tràt
give	hây	prathaan
tell	bɔ̀ɔk	thuun
build, create	sâaŋ	soŋsâaŋ
have	mii	soŋmii
name (simple)	chɨ̂ɨ	
name (elegant)	naam	phrānaam
seat	thîinâŋ	phrāthîinâŋ
eye	taa	phrānêet
foot	tháaw	phrābàat
heart, spirit	cay	phrāthay

detail between vocabulary used about royalty and that used about monks create two subvarieties, but both are subsumed in the same overall range. The range also extends to discussion of sacred beings, supernatural or otherwise, and sacred objects like statues of the Buddha and amulets.

We have already seen that most nouns in the sacred range are prefaced with the element /phrā-/. When used as an independent noun, /phrá'/ refers to a monk, a Buddha statue, a sacred object, a deity, or royalty. In compounds it has the effect of elevating the word with which it is compounded by adding the meaning of 'sacred, powerful, charged with sacred power'. /phrá'/ is *mana*, or sacred power which is not due to the presence of any spirit but which is inherent in the very sacred thing itself.

A major reason why royalty, monks, and sacred objects are included in the same range of Standard Thai is that in Thai Buddhism sacredness is the basis for royalty as much as it is for religion (Kirsch 1967:5; Kukrit 1955). This royal sacredness is not the former European idea of the divine right of kings, a sacredness conferred by God, but is intrinsic (Wright 1968:2). The King is king because he is sacred. The very fact that he is king shows his accumulation of merit from previous incarnations (Hanks 1962; Wilson 1962:52, 74; Keyes 1966:352). He is a "special order located somewhere between the natural and the supernatural" (Wilson 1962:89-90). Although the King pays deference to monks, and so in theory is not the most sacred person in Thailand, the combination of his sacredness with his position in society does, in fact, place him at the peak of the pyramid.

The sacredness of royalty developed in Tai-speaking states, particularly Ayuthaya, during the fourteenth century. The concept was already strong in the Khmer capital, and Khmer culture was already exerting influence on Tai courts when Ayuthaya conquered the Khmer center of Angkor Thom. The conquering forces brought back learned men who taught the Ayuthayan court the system of sacred kingship with all of its protocol and associated language, adapting it from Khmer to Thai (Kukrit 1955:82; O'Connor 1978:74-75).

A reverse trend, the "humanizing" of the throne, began under King Chulalongkorn, who reigned from 1868 to 1910 (Hall 1961: 584; Wilson 1962:99-100). Later the coup of 1932, which sought to substitute constitutional government for the absolute monarchy, brought major changes in the role of the king. Now, increasing secularization in the cities, increasing contact with other worldviews, and many other forces lessen the sacredness of the king and other sacred beings and objects. Despite linguistic and other symbols carried over from the past, the secular bureaucracy—including the military—may now in fact rank as high as the hierarchy of monks in the social structure of Thailand (Chai 1985:34, 47). But Thai feelings about royalty and religion run deep, and although the sacred language is built on social conditions of the past, it is by no means only a relic.

Because sacredness rather than simple royalty is fundamental to the varieties of Standard Thai under discussion, the range is here called the sacred range in spite of the Thai term, which means "royal language." Some of its vocabulary refers only to royalty and some only to the monkhood or sacred objects, but sacredness pervades the whole range and royalty does not.

Use of the Sacred Range

Although speakers of Standard Thai with modest education sometimes find discourse in the sacred range unintelligible to them, the two ranges are not different languages. The unintelligibility is in some ways analogous to non-mathematicians trying to understand a technical lecture in mathematics or nuclear physics, or someone unfamiliar with a sport listening to two enthusiasts talking. The language is the mother tongue, but the listener cannot understand much of the vocabulary and usage.

However, the range is also different even when the concepts and content are completely familiar to the speaker of ordinary Standard Thai. Less educated speakers, for example, would have no trouble understanding the ordinary Standard Thai for the following passage.

He went to see his father. His younger brother went with him, carrying some betel. His father stroked the back of his head and said admiringly that he was very good looking, and had another younger brother by another wife take him to look at some pictures (translated from Phunsrikasem 1957:2-3).

As originally written in the sacred range, however, understanding would be more limited among less well educated people. The magnitude of the difference between the ordinary and sacred ranges may be seen in a comparison of the passage as expressed in both of them (table 4.2).

The difference between the ordinary and sacred ranges of Standard Thai generally consists only of parallel sets of vocabulary (Gedney 1961). The only grammatical difference lies in the prefixed elements

Table 4.2. Comparison of the same passage in sacred and ordinary ranges.

Sacred: phrābàat sŏmdèt phrācâwyùuhŭa sadèt phrārâachadamnəən maa
Ordinary: khāw   maa
English: he   came

S: fâw   sŏmdèt phrābaromachonkanàat. phrā'anuchaa   chəənphrāsĭi
O: hăa   khunphɔ̀ɔ .   nɔ̀ɔŋchaay   thĭimàak
E: to see   (his) father.   younger brother   carrying betel

S: taam sadèt khâwpay fâw dûay. phrābaromachonkanàat soŋlûup phrāsĭan
O: taam   pay   dûay. khunphɔ̀ɔ   lûup   sĭisà'
E: went along   also. (his) father   stroked head

S: phrābàat sŏmdèt phrācâwyùuhŭa talɔ̀ɔt phrāprìtsadaaŋ. lɛ́ɛw damràt
O: khāw   talɔ̀ɔt   lăŋ.   lɛ́ɛw klàaw
E: his   whole   back.   then declared

S: sănsə̆ən wâa mii phrāsirirûup ŋaam,   lɛ́' prɔ̀ot hây phrācâwlûukthəə
O: chom   wâa mii rûuprâaŋ   ŋaam,   lɛ́'   hây nɔ̀ɔŋchaay
E: praised   that have appearance beautiful, and   had younger brother

S: phrā'oŋ nìŋ phaa sadèt pay thɔ̀ɔtphrānêet rûupphâapkhĭan.
O: khon   nìŋ phaa   pay duu   rûupphâap.
E: one (of his)   take   go   look at   pictures.

and special compounding forms. The different vocabularies of the ordinary and sacred ranges, furthermore, are generally equivalent in meaning except for the respective kinship terminologies. Selected examples of differences between kinship terms are shown in table 4.3, where some terms in the ordinary range correspond to two different terms in the sacred, and vice versa. More than that, some meanings split so decidedly that a word like /phrāmaatùtchăa/ 'mother's sister' in the sacred range not only divides into two different words in the ordinary range, but these two ordinary range words also have additional meanings not included in /phrāmaatùtchăa/. This is because the ordinary range makes the distinction between older and younger sibling primary, while the sacred range makes the distinction between the sex of the siblings primary.

However, the total number of words peculiar to the royal variety of the sacred range is relatively small, including ninety-two terms for parts of the body, some kinship terms, sixty-six terms for animals and objects and seventy-three terms for actions of various kinds (Gedney 1961:109-110). On the other hand, all nouns and verbs used in reference to royalty are additionally marked for the sacred range through the use of compounding or grammatical prefixes if no special term exists.

Table 4.3. Differences in the meanings of selected kinship terms in ordinary and sacred ranges (after Rachamanop 1965:8-12).

Relationship	English	Ordinary range	Sacred range
father's father	grandfather	pùu	phrã'ayyakaa
mother's father	grandfather	taa	phrã'ayyakaa
father's mother	grandmother	yâa	phrã'ayyíkaa
mother's mother	grandmother	yaay	phrã'ayyíkaa
father's older brother	uncle	luŋ	phrãpìtùlaa
mother's older brother	uncle	luŋ	phrãmaatùlaa
mother's younger brother	uncle	náa	phrãmaatùlaa
mother's younger sister	aunt	náa	phrãmaatùtchǎa
mother's older sister	aunt	pâa	phrãmaatùtchǎa
father's older sister	aunt	pâa	phrãpiitùtchǎa
father's younger sister	aunt	'aa	phrãpiitùtchǎa
father's younger brother	uncle	'aa	phrã'aa
child's child	grandchild	lǎan	phrãrâachanàtdaa
sister's child	niece/nephew	lǎan	phrãphaakhìnay

The sacred range is supposed to be used automatically in reference to royalty but except for terms of address is not used when talking to royalty about non-royalty. Thus, the ordinary range word for any part of the body may be used in addressing the King, so long as it is used of the body of a commoner (Gedney 1961:110). Furthermore, people in the royal family do not use the sacred range when speaking of themselves, but do use it when they refer to other royalty (Kukrit 1955:85).

Speaking or writing the sacred range properly is a strong social marker for people who live or aspire to live in upper circles, and to use the prefix /soŋ-/ or /phrã-/ in the wrong places is a trap for neophytes. These prefixes must be used only with ordinary range roots to elevate them to sacred range, so if the root is already in the sacred range adding the prefix is gauche. Thus, to say /soŋtràt/ (table 4.1), furthermore, would be decidedly substandard (Kukrit 1955:85).

Use of some parts of the sacred range is declining and becoming less precise. Not only the secularizing and democratizing tendencies noted earlier, but even increased education, which theoretically makes the sacred range more widely known, also tends to weaken its use. Education is no longer restricted to upper-class people and to royalty who hear the sacred range regularly as a dynamic communication system. The ever-growing middle-class educated group is more likely to learn it superficially and speak it more inconsistently.

Dimensions in the Sacred Range

The sacred range incorporates various social dimensions, but also sometimes includes higher levels than those that occur in the highest levels of the ordinary range (table 3.1). In table 4.4, for example, the word /sadèt/ of the sacred range is part of expressions meaning both 'go' and 'come', but it has no ordinary language counterpart. It indicates royal movement or change of state, and is used in some other sacred language forms such as /sadèt sawǎnkhót/ 'to die, go to heaven'. /sadèt/ would not be used of an ordinary monk, nor is it used of lower nobility, but is reserved for the king, his family, and the supreme patriarch, the highest person in the Buddhist hierarchy of Thailand.In table 4.4 the first entry is a relatively simple-level royal variety word, although it would be elegant from an ordinary-range standpoint. The last is much more elegant, honorific, and formal. The skillful user of the royal variety can suit the right degree of social value elaboration to any situation. Less skillful people, even if familiar with the terms, may reveal their inability to use the royal variety correctly by either too much or not enough elegance for the situation.

The royal variety, especially in its higher social relationship and social value dimensions, gives ordinary Thai people the most trouble in the sacred range. Lower varieties shade into the usage of the elegant variety of the ordinary range. The language used of ordinary monks is also simpler and more widely known, so most people who speak Standard Thai well do not have as much trouble with it.

In Thailand's social structure the descendants of a king lose a bit of their royal sacredness with each passing generation, until the fifth generation descendants are commoners. The level of the sacred language used in reference to them decreases correspondingly.

Table 4.4. Social value differences in the sacred range, the longer the term the more elegant.

English	Ordinary range	Sacred range
go, come	pay, maa	sadèt
go, come	pay, maa	sadèt pay, sadèt maa
go, come	pay, maa	sadèt phrǎrâachadamnəən

Multidimensional Media

This book deals generally with spoken varieties of Standard Thai rather than written ones, but we note here briefly that many varieties are available within the written medium as well. Written Standard Thai is multidimensional, a set of varieties including both sacred and ordinary ranges, with all of their dimensions.

Standard Thai written language, however, is not identical with spoken language in any of these varieties, although it comes closer to some of them than to others. The writing system, for example, represents most of the structurally significant sound distinctions of Standard Thai, but not all. It has no way of showing the difference of vowel length on some vowels like /ə/ and /əə/, as between /ŋən/ 'money, silver', and /dəən/ 'walk', for example.

Furthermore, a reader cannot always tell the correct pronunciation of a word simply by its spelling. Sometimes the spelling is ambiguous, as when เสมอ could theoretically be read either as /samɔ̌ə/ or /sěemɔɔ/, whereas it actually represents a word pronounced in the first way, meaning 'same, even'. Another inconsistency results from an occasional bad "fit" between writing and speech: ประวัติ would theoretically represent /prawát/, but actually corresponds to /prawàt/ 'story'.[1]

Like all other languages, Standard Thai has words which sound alike although they differ in meaning. As in English, many such homophones are distinguished by spelling. This is convenient for the educated person who knows how to spell well, but is difficult for less educated people who cannot simply spell consistently what they pronounce.

A Thai folktale about Chiang Miang, a legendary trickster, includes an incident involving two such words: บาท /bàat/ 'a unit of weight' and บาตร /bàat/ 'bowl in which a monk receives offerings of food'. The king offered Chiang Miang four or five /bàat/ of silver, which in Standard Thai clearly means บาท 'unit of weight', a relatively modest sum. Chiang Miang, however, lined up five บาตร 'monk's bowl' to be filled with silver worth about four thousand บาท 'unit of weight' (Maniratana 1966).

The Standard Thai writing system also differs from speech in the order of its symbols. Thai writing is primarily alphabetic, which means that characters usually represent phonemes (structured sound units). However, the order in which the characters are written left-to-right does not necessarily correspond to the sequence in which the phonemes are spoken. Some vowels which follow a consonant in speech are written after the symbol for the consonant, but others are written before it, above it, below it, before and after it, before and above it, or before, above and after it (chap. 16).

Another difference between the spoken and written medium is that the Standard Thai written language does not show all of the complexity of contractions, elisions, and reductions which are characteristic of speech and help to give it many different dimensions.

In general, the written medium also has even less dialect variation than the spoken medium. As we have seen, however, whereas most features of written Standard Thai are based on Standard Thai as spoken in Bangkok, written Standard Thai makes a difference in writing between {l r} ล ร, a distinction which most Bangkok speakers do not make in speech.

By and large, the most important differences between written and spoken Standard Thai lie in vocabulary, grammar, and style. To talk as you write sounds bookish. Some such differences—as seen by Thai language teachers—are listed in a book on how Standard Thai should be written (Faculty of Arts 1980:53-58). Sometimes the teachers simply ask for elegant terms to be used in writing, rather than simple ones:

Spoken: /kraday/ 'stairway' (simple social value)
Written: /banday/ (elegant social value)

In some cases the elegant written form is supposed to be longer and more flowery than the spoken:

S: /wanphálíhàt/ 'Thursday'
W: /wanphálíhàtsabɔɔdii/

Fewer contractions are supposed to be used in writing:

S: /mâydâypaythîawnǎy/ 'didn't go off for a good time'
W: /mâydâypaythîawthîinǎy/

Some grammatical particles and affective words characteristic of speech are not part of written language, at least from this ideal standard point of view:

S: /mâychâykhoncay'ɔɔnrɔ̀knǎ/ 'not at all a weak person'
W: /mâychâykhoncay'ɔ̀ɔn/

Beyond such details, written language at public distance uses the public distance features more fully and more systematically than does spoken language. At consultative distance it incorporates more public distance features than would be incorporated in speech. Written language also tends to be more elegant, to show more deference, and often to be more archaic. What is suitable in writing may be too elegant or too distant if spoken, and what is spoken may be too simple or imply too close a social distance if written. All of this varies, too, in different written genres.

Other Multidimensional Varieties

Ranges and media are not self-categorizing types of multidimensional varieties (table 3.6), but Standard Thai does have some such self-categorizing multidimensional sets of varieties.

Sex-related Varieties

The speech of men and women is distinguished in Standard Thai more obviously than in English. For example, some frequently used particles of social status differ with the sex of the speaker (table 3.2), as do many of the most commonly used pronouns, especially in the consultative variety of the social distance dimension and in some of the higher ranks of the social relationship dimension (table 4.5). Kinship terms used by speakers referring to themselves and as terms of address sometimes also involve the sex dimension.

At least one special intonation is used by women, although not generally by men. It consists of a high rising pitch on the first syllable when a stative verb ("adjective") is doubled, to give it an intensified meaning (table 4.6).

Table 4.5. Some examples of sex difference in the use of Standard Thai pronouns. The upper three are in the ordinary range, the lower three in the sacred range (after Cooke 1968:23-27; see also 38-39, 49, 56-57, 66).

Situation	Man speaking	Woman speaking
to equal or superior, deferential	phǒm	dichǎn
to high-ranking superior	kraphǒm	dichǎn
to higher-ranking superior	klâawkraphǒm	dichǎn
to lesser royalty	kramɔ̀m	mɔ̀mchǎn
to lesser royalty, more deferential		kramɔ̀mchǎn
to higher royalty	klâawkramɔ̀m	klâawkramɔ̀mchǎn

Table 4.6. An intonation said to be characteristic primarily of women's speech. In the first syllable the tone is changed to indicate the intensification ('very . . .'). It is shown here as high tone, but actually is pronounced above a normal high tone (Haas 1964:130).

English	Not intensified	Intensified
pretty	sǔay	sǔaysǔay
long	yaaw	yáawyaaw
good	dii	díidii
heavy	nàk	náknàk

Time-related Varieties

Every language is constantly changing. Some words, pronunciations, and grammatical forms are slowly going out of use and others are coming in. The language of our grandparents may sometimes have a slightly old-fashioned sound to it, and teenage speech a modern one. We sometimes notice differences also when we read books written one hundred or more years ago. Sometimes people who read much classical literature preserve a few archaisms in some of the dimensions of their own speech and writing. On the other hand, some other speakers and writers like to use recent borrowings or coinages with a modern flavor.

When we look at the time dimension comprehensively, the great bulk of Standard Thai lies in the middle—contemporary language not notably archaic or modern. At one end of the scale archaic language ranges from slightly old-fashioned to obsolete. At the other end modern language ranges from slightly avant-garde to new coinages made every day. When speakers consistently use either end of the scale their speech is self-categorizing.

People sometimes do change time-related varieties for special effect, however. The effective Thai storyteller may use touches of archaism when the story is set in the past.

An older translation of the Bible into Standard Thai sometimes tends toward archaisms, not only because it was made years ago but also because translators wanted to keep the old flavor of this very ancient book. A more recent revision is more contemporary, but at one stage in its formation critics said that it was "too modern" in some details, some of the language sounding as if it belonged too much to the age of electronics and space.

Still a third translation struggled with the problem of translating the pronouns for "I" and "you" when Jesus was talking with his disciples. Social relationship and social distance were both involved. Christian belief places Jesus in a high position, and counts him as sacred, yet the stories describe his role as an itinerant teacher with disciples who were close to him. In older translations, when Jesus speaks he uses /raw/ 'we, royal I' and /thân/ 'you'. The /raw/ was suitable for modern Christian concepts of Jesus' sacredness and role, but the /thân/ spoken to disciples who were close personal friends did not fit at all. It was too deferential at personal distance, and although suitable for public distance, was too remote for the more intimate situations described in the stories.

To use what many teachers in Bangkok today would use with adult students, however, was felt to be anachronistically modern: /phǒm/ 'I' and /khun/ 'you'. Compromises along the time dimension as well as in social distance and social relationship had to be made.

The pair /raw/ 'royal I' and /câw/ 'you (spoken to an inferior)' were finally selected as the most fully in keeping with the Christian reader's understanding of Jesus' role in the gospels where the relationship was that of master and disciple. However, the social distance reflected in that pair is really much too great to be true to the actual historical situation and the social relationship is much too authoritarian, a king/subject relationship. It also has an archaic tone.

Many of the differences in the dimension of time are simply due to shifts in the uses of vocabulary, words going out of use and others taking their place. The older words are still to be found in older books, but modern writers or speakers do not use them (table 4.7). Innovations are words which have not been used widely enough to lose the feeling of being new.

Table 4.7. Examples of archaic and contemporary forms.

English	Archaic Form	Contemporary form
1st, 2nd person pronoun, royalty to female commoner	lɔn	thəə
2nd person pronoun, elegant, to superior	tâaytháaw	thân
1st person pronoun	tuukhâa	chǎn
stunted, stubby	cêɛ	tîa
shine, be bright	cêɛŋ	sawàaŋ
why?	yay	thammay

On the other hand, a good deal of the dimension of time in Standard Thai comes also from the changing sociolinguistic situation. Some extreme differences of social relationship are now seen to be derogatory, and are going out of style with the increasing democratization of society. So with the growing numbers of middle-class educated professional people, forms like /khâa/ 'I, me' and /câw/ 'you', spoken by a superior to an inferior, have an old-fashioned sound to them, as if they belong in a history book or in an old tale.

The dimension of social relationship is not out of date by any means, but some of the terms which place the hearer in a lower or unfavorable position are affected by modern ideas. The increasingly widespread use of /phǒm/ 'I' and /khun/ 'you' is modern in flavor. In similar fashion, the word for 'domestic servant' found in most dictionaries and widely used in the 1960s was /khoncháay/ 'person to use'. In the 1980s the commonly heard term is the more dignified /khonŋaan/ 'person who works'.

Summary

The dimensions of Standard Thai come in multidimensional sets. In this chapter we described two of them, the sacred range (in contrast to the ordinary range of chapters 2 and 3) and the written medium (in contrast to the spoken medium). We also touched on some multidimensional self-categorizing varieties such as those spoken by men and women, and by people of different ages.

The sacred range consists of a selection of varieties used to and about sacred individuals and objects, most notably royalty, priests, statues of the Buddha, and the paraphernalia of Buddhist ritual. It is characterized most notably by special vocabulary and by prefixual elements which raise ordinary vocabulary to a sacred level. It is generally more highly elaborated and elegant than the ordinary range as well.

The written medium is manifested in a unique script which matches Standard Thai speech well but not perfectly. Writing also tends to be more elegant than speech and incorporates more public distance features than would conversation with the same receptor.

Part II

Major Regional Languages
Introduction

By the end of Part 1 we saw that although Standard Thai is all one language it is made up of many varieties, and that probably nobody controls all of them. These varieties have their respective functions, however, and are intermingled according to those required in any discourse. Together they create the diverse richness of the language.

But for most people in Thailand Standard Thai is a learned language, not the language of their home and neighborhood. The native languages of most Thai people are the four regional languages, each spoken in a different part of the country (map II.1). Those languages are featured in the following chapters.

Each regional language of Thailand is the internal language of a primary section of the country. Each is used as a language of wider communication by speakers of minority languages within the region. Each dominates those minority languages in the sense that minority language speakers tend to learn the regional language, but not vice versa. Each regional language is dominated by Standard Thai.

With minor exceptions, none of these regional languages are themselves used significantly as languages of wider communication outside their region, because within the country that is the role of Standard Thai. They are, however, sometimes spoken in extra-regional pockets or enclaves of displaced peoples (chap. 11). Lao spoken in communities near the Myanmar border, for example, does not function as a regional language even though it contributes to the total complexity of the communication networks in that part of the country.

Estimates of the number of speakers for whom each of the four regional languages is their native language, together with their percentages of the total population of the country, are as follows:

Thaiklang (Central Thai)[1]	14,400,000	26.99%
Lao (Northeastern Thai)	12,200,000	22.87%
Kammüang (Northern Thai)	4,800,000	8.99%
Paktay (Southern Thai)	4,300,000	8.06%

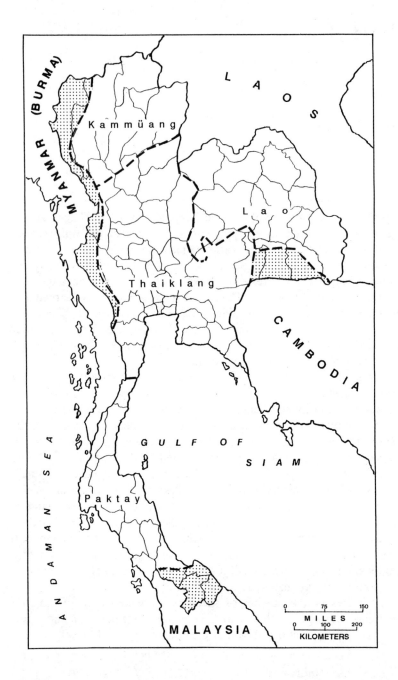

Map II.1. Areas of the four regional languages of Thailand. The shaded areas are dominated by marginal regional languages (chaps. 8-10).

World/international languages

English, etc.
External languages of the country

National language

Standard Thai
Internal language of the country, external language of the regions

Regional languages

Thaiklang	Lao	Paktay	Kammüang
(Central Thai)	(Northeastern Thai)	(Southern Thai)	(Northern Thai)

Internal languages of respective regions,
external languages for lower-level linguistic groups within the regions

Marginal regional languages

Phlow	Northern Khmer	Pattani Malay	Sgaw	Tai Yai

Internal languages of the marginal regions, external languages
for lower-level linguistic groups within the marginal regions

Other categories of languages

Enclave	Town and city	Displaced Tai	Marginal

Internal languages only

Fig. II.1. Hierarchy of relationships among most of the categories of languages which make up the linguistic diversity in Thailand. The hierarchy is based on language learning patterns and aspirations, as adults tend to learn languages higher than their own but not ones on their level or lower. It also implies other role relationships which will be developed in due course.

Of course, the actual number of speakers for each of these languages is considerably larger than shown because the languages are also extensively used by non-native speakers.

These regional languages are at the heart of the critical issue of linguistic diversity and national unity in Thailand. The language riots of India take place because of antagonisms at the regional level, and it is among speakers of regional languages that resentment of the national language of the Philippines is found. The chapters in this section describe the contrasting Thai situation. Chapters 18 and 19 will provide more interpretation.

Within Thailand, the regional languages have much in common among themselves and in their functional relations to Standard Thai, but also manifest significant differences. We approach each of them somewhat differently in their respective chapters, highlighting some of those differences as well as portraying some of the characteristics which they have in common. The discussion of Kammüang, for example, emphasizes its linguistic differences from Standard Thai so as to demonstrate that it is really a different language in spite of similarities and in spite of the contrary viewpoint of many Thai people. The discussion of Lao emphasizes how language symbolizes regional identity in tension with national unity. The discussion of Paktay emphasizes the striking sociolinguistic levels within Paktay itself. The discussion of Thaiklang emphasizes the special conditions resulting from its being the regional language out of which Standard Thai was formed.

The functional relationship of these regional languages to Standard Thai and English helps us to begin to see the structure of Thailand's linguistic diversity within national unity, a hierarchy of language use created by people's learning patterns (fig. II.1). Most speakers of regional languages learn to use at least some Standard Thai, many of them learning it well. Adult native speakers of Standard Thai, on the other hand, do not normally learn any regional language. Many native speakers of either Standard Thai or regional languages, however, learn English if they can.

5

Kammüang (Northern Thai)

When the government official of chapter 3 takes his family to Chiang Mai in northern Thailand, the children are amused or puzzled by some unfamiliar pronunciations and expressions which they hear at different places along the eight-hundred kilometer bus route. Then in Chiang Mai itself people speak to them in Standard Thai, sometimes with an accent, but when they overhear people talking with each other they often do not understand what is said. Sometimes they understand a phrase or two but then get lost again. Their father explains to them that they are listening to /phaasǎa nǐa/ 'northern language'.

Internal and External Languages of the Northern Region

Earlier we described Standard Thai as the internal language of Thailand, the language of the nation, and English as its primary external language. The travelling official and his family are now finding that in northern Thailand Standard Thai is the external language of the region, the language used with outsiders, and a regional language is used instead for internal communication. Like Thai people elsewhere, northerners insist that Standard Thai is the language of the country, and those with any education insist that it is *their* language, but when they are thinking of their region of the country they say that their language is Kammüang /kammian/ 'language of the city/political center/state'.[1]

The strength of this distinction between Kammüang (Northern Thai)[2] as the internal language of the major part of northern Thailand, and Standard Thai as its external language, can be seen when the government official and his wife are invited out to a restaurant by old friends, northerners whom they knew in Bangkok during their university days. They are some of Chiang Mai's leading citizens, perhaps a doctor, a lawyer, and a government official or two.

These northerners converse directly with their guests in good Standard Thai. Normally, however, when one of them turns to speak to another northerner the language switches to Kammüang. They slip back and forth between the languages without the slightest hesitancy or confusion.

Kammüang, however, is not the internal language of the northern region under all circumstances. The dinner party adjourns to a formal meeting, a benefit program for a private school, where one of the northerners who was at dinner is the featured speaker. During the program everything of a formal nature is conducted in Standard Thai, with only an occasional humorous interjection in Kammüang. The meeting is strictly a regional affair, strictly for internal communication, but Standard Thai is used instead of Kammüang for the public variety of the social distance dimension.

Dialects of Kammüang

Map II.1 shows an L-shaped line through northern Thailand, north and east of which Kammüang is the native tongue of the vast majority of people, and south and west of which it is not. South of the line Thaiklang (Central Thai) is another regional language (chap. 7). Marginal regional languages are spoken west of the line (chap. 8).

This Kammüang language area is considerably smaller than the Thai government's northern administrative area, the boundary of which lies to the south. Not clear from the map is also the fact that the border of Kammüang is not as sharp as it looks, but more like a transition zone (Kalaya 1985a:85-87) where features of pronunciation or vocabulary characteristic of both Kammüang and Thaiklang are intermingled in varying proportions.

Isolated pockets of Kammüang-speaking people are located elsewhere in Thailand as well; some of them settled as prisoners of war brought from the north over a hundred years ago. More recently, Northern Thai people have also moved into the western border regions of the north. In areas such as these Kammüang is not the immediate regional language, but a displaced language (chap. 11), a little drop of oil in a basin of water, generally maintaining some of its own characteristics and its own identity, although surrounded by people speaking other languages.[3]

The Kammüang area itself manifests considerable diversity, with different major dialects grouped in the provinces of Chiang Mai,

Table 5.1. Examples of vocabulary differences between Chiang
Mai and Phrae.

English	Chiang Mai	Phrae	Standard Thai
guava	bàkūay	màkɛ̌ɛw	falàŋ
older sister	pîi	yĩay	phîisǎaw
maize	khãwsàlii	khãwpôot	khâawphôot
loin cloth	phãatʼɔɔŋ	phãahǔa	phâakhǎawmáa
jump	dòot	cǒn	kradòot

Chiang Rai-Phayao, Lampang, Nan-Phrae, and Tak, and outside the
main Kammüang area in the Mae Sariang District of Mae Hong Son
Province. Table 5.1 shows a few examples of vocabulary difference
between two of the dialects, with Standard Thai included for comparison. Geographic dialects do not come in tidy bundles, of course, and
within each of these major dialects considerable additional variety is
to be found.

Kammüang and Standard Thai

But in spite of their diversity, the dialects of Kammüang share features which are consistently different from the other major Tai languages in Thailand. Linguistically, Kammüang is significantly and
sometimes systematically different from Standard Thai in sound system, grammar, and vocabulary. We demonstrate this by presenting
more strictly linguistic information about it than is typical of most
chapters in this book.

Tones

For one thing, although tone pronunciations vary all over north
Thailand, the Kammüang dialects share a characteristic tone system
which is significantly different from Standard Thai and from the language of every other region (chap. 11; Brown 1965:79-82, 86; Jones
1966). Standard Thai, for example, has a falling tone which is written
in various ways, partially illustrated in table 5.2. This correspondence
between the one tone in Standard Thai and the two in Kammüang is
characteristic of scores of words.

Also, because two Kammüang tones correspond to a single falling
tone in Standard Thai, Kammüang has six distinct tones, as opposed

Table 5.2. Standard Thai spellings for the falling tone /ˆ/, with contrasting tones in Kammüang. Not all of the illustrative syllables shown here are actual words.

Standard Thai spelling	Standard Thai pronunciation	Kammüang pronunciation
ป้า	pâa	pāa
ผ้า	phâa	phāa
ฟ้า	phâa	pâa
พาด	phâat	pâat

to five full tones in Standard Thai.[4] The Kammüang tones contrast with each other as in the following examples (Mundhenk 1966:viii):

káa	'do business'	sɔ́ɔn	'stack up'
kâa	'value'	sɔ̂ɔn	'hide'
kāa	'dare'	sɔ̄ɔn (sɛ́')	(kind of fishing)
kaa	(question particle)	sɔɔn	'repair (roof)'
kǎa	'crow'	sɔ̌ɔn	'teach'
kàa	(positive particle)	sɔ̀ɔn	'delve into'

Another systematic difference between Kammüang and Standard Thai is shown in table 5.3, where the initial consonants /p t c k ' b d/ all work alike in their relation to tone in Standard Thai, but split into two groups which work differently from each other in Kammüang. The first group in the Kammüang column has rising tones. In the second group the pronunciation varies from one dialect to another, but in any one dialect all three have the same tone. Again, this phenomenon is characteristic of many words (chap. 11).

Consonants and Vowels

For the most part, when a word is shared by Standard Thai and Kammüang, the consonants are the same in both. Table 5.4 shows some important systematic differences, however. The last example illustrates the fact that many words written with {r} in Standard Thai are pronounced [h] in Kammüang. This is the {r} which is ideally pronounced [ř] in Standard Thai but is actually more often pronounced [l]. Two of the examples also illustrate that some words pronounced with /y/ in Standard Thai have /y/ in Kammüang also, while others have /ñ/, which does not occur at all in Standard Thai.

Table 5.3. Tone correspondences between Standard
Thai and Kammüang when the syllable-initial
consonant is /p t c k ' b d/ and no tone diacritic is
written in the Standard Thai orthography.

Standard Thai spelling	Standard Thai pronunciation	Kammüang pronunciation
ปา	paa	pǎa
ตา	taa	tǎa
จา	caa	cǎa
กา	kaa	kǎa
อา	'aa	'aa
บา	baa	baa
ดา	daa	daa

The first eight examples illustrate a type of correspondence
between Standard Thai and Kammüang initial consonants, also shown
in the consonants of table 5.2, where a single consonant sound in
Standard Thai corresponds to two consonant sounds in Kammüang.
There า is the symbol for the vowel /aa/, ป the spelling for /p/, and ต
for final /t/. /ph/ has two spellings, ผ and พ, which correspond to
two different consonants in Kammüang. In each case the Standard
Thai consonants are aspirated (spoken with a puff of air represented

Table 5.4. Correspondence of some initial consonants in Standard Thai and Kammüang (after
Mundhenk 1966:ix).

English	Standard Thai	Kammüang
cloth	phâa	phãa
thousand	phan	pan
ask	thǎam	thǎam
road	thaaŋ	taaŋ
tear	chìik	sìik, chìik
name	chîi	cîi
leg	khǎa	khǎa
word	kham	kam
be at	yùu	yùu
long	yaaw	ñaaw
boat	lia	hia

Table 5.5. Clusters with /l/ and /r/ in ideal Standard Thai but with no corresponding cluster in Kammüang.

English	Ideal Standard Thai	Kammüang
pepper sauce	namphrík	náamphík
family	khrôopkhrua	khôopkhua
fish	plaa	pǎa
dare	klâa	kǎa

by /h/ in our transcription), whereas the Kammüang consonants divide into aspirated and unaspirated ones, with an additional complication in the fifth example. However, in each pair of examples the words are spelled in Standard Thai with different initial consonant symbols, reflecting an earlier difference in pronunciation there also.

In Standard Thai consonant clusters involve /l/ or /w/ as the second member, as we have seen—the /l/ spelled {l} or {r} (chap. 2). Kammüang, however, has no clusters with /l/ or /r/ (table 5.5). Kammüang does, however, have more clusters with /w/ as the second member than does Standard Thai (Benchawan 1963; Mundhenk 1966:x; Mundhenk 1967; Mundhenk 1968):

/swaam/	'to feel, rub'
/jwàat/	'to fall off'
/cwàap/	'to bite, nibble (of fish)'
/ŋwáay/	'to turn around'

Many such clusters are gradually disappearing, and on some words speakers fluctuate between pronunciations with and without /w/. The clusters remain common, however, especially after /s/ and /ŋ/.

Grammar

The foregoing paragraphs are enough to illustrate that in spite of differences within Kammüang, important common phonological characteristics distinguish Kammüang from Standard Thai. Although the grammars are largely the same, furthermore, they are not fully so, and even small grammatical differences sometimes create more of a barrier to comprehension than do sound differences.

Compound words, for example, may be formed from the same elements in the two languages, but the order may be reversed, as in the top group of examples in table 5.6. When the Kammüang order does

Table 5.6. Differences from Standard Thai in the formation of some compound words in Kammüang. In these examples /náam nám- nãm-/ means 'water' (after Purnell 1965).

English	Standard Thai	Kammüang
river	mɛ̂ɛnáam	námɛ̂ɛ
metal dipper	kɔ̂knáam	námkɔ̀k
tap water	nãmkɔ̀k	
well	bɔ̀ɔnáam	námbɔ̀ɔ
well water	nãmbɔ̀ɔ	
water pot	mɔ̂ɔnáam	námmɔ̂ɔ
pitcher	khonthoo	námtõn
coconut-shell dipper	krabuay	námbuay
woven water bucket	khrú'	námthũuŋ
metal pail	thăŋ	námkhú'
drain	thɔ̀ɔ	námlin

does occur in Standard Thai it sometimes carries an entirely different meaning. Kammüang, furthermore, sometimes has words based on this compounding sequence, where Standard Thai does not have a compound at all.

Particles meaning 'very, much, many, a lot, intensely, extremely' provide another illustration. In some cases the usage is similar, as in the first group in table 5.7, in others different, as in the second group.

Vocabulary

While much Kammüang vocabulary is easily recognizable as corresponding to Standard Thai, many words show little or no resemblance

Table 5.7. Intensifiers in Kammüang and Standard Thai (after Purnell 1965).

English	Standard Thai	Kammüang
too hot	lɔ́ɔnkəənpay	hɔ̀ɔnlámpay
too many	mâakkəənpay	nãklámpay
scrumptious	'arɔ̀ylə̂kəən	lamtɛ́ɛlamwâa
worn out	nɬaymâakciŋciŋ	'ittɛ́ɛ'itwâa
very heavy	nàklə̂kəən	nàktɛ́ɛnàkwâa

Table 5.8. Examples of words where Kammüang and Standard Thai are different. In some cases the words occur in both languages, but with different meanings (after Purnell, Hope, and Yuang 1966 and Met 1965).

English	Standard Thai	Kammüang
market	talàat	kàat
twenty	yîisìp	saaw
delicious	'arɔ̀y	lam
mosquito net	múŋ	sut
classifiers	fɔɔŋ	kèn
for eggs,	phǒn	kèn
fruits, etc.	lûuk	kèn
priest	phrá'	tú'
novice priest	neen	phá'
be defeated	phɛ́ɛ	káan
win	chaná'	pɛ́ɛ
be allergic to	phɛ́ɛ	pɛ́ɛ

whatsoever, and a few are confusingly "opposite" in meaning (table 5.8). Vocabulary, however, is one part of the language where changes toward Standard Thai take place most noticeably. Some Standard Thai words are slowly taking the place of Kammüang words, more rapidly in urban areas than in rural (Gunyarat 1979).

Social Dimension Varieties

Kammüang has a dimension of social relationship, but it is not as elaborately developed as the one in Standard Thai. Status particles, among other things, are more limited. /kháp/ (man speaking) and /cāw/ (woman speaking) are mild status particles corresponding to Standard Thai /khráp/ and /khâ/, respectively. /bà/ is used with friends, usually males.

The Kammüang pronoun system, likewise, is less complicated than the Standard Thai system, but distinguishes at least three levels of social relationship (table 5.9). Of these pronouns, /phǒm/ 'first person, man speaking,' is a borrowing from Standard Thai, and Standard Thai /thân/ 'second person singular' is frequently heard instead of the older Kammüang /tâan/ (Kingshill 1960:220).

Table 5.9. Pronouns of Chiang Rai and Chiang Mai Kammüang, with Chiang Mai pronunciation (Purnell, Hope, and Yuang 1966:12). As in Standard Thai, titles and names are also used in pronominal ways.

English	To superiors	To equals	To intimates, inferiors, etc.
I (man speaking)	phŏm	haw	kuu (inferiors) pə̂n (women) haa (male age-mate) khã (wife)
I (woman speaking)	cãw khãcaw	haw khã	pə̂n (husband, female agemate)
you (singular)	tâan	tâan	miŋ (goes with kuu) tŭa (goes with pə̂n) khiŋ (goes with haa) sŭu
he, she	tâan	pə̂n khăw	pə̂n khăw man
it	man	man	man
we	haw mùuhaw	haw mùuhaw	mùutŭa
you (plural)	tântaŋlăay	tântaŋlăay sŭukhăw	mùusŭu
they	pə̂n khăw mùupə̂n	pə̂n khăw mùupə̂n	pə̂n khăw mùupə̂n

Something of the force of social relationship correlated with social distance in the Kammüang pronoun /sŭu/ 'you' may be seen in a northern Thailand researcher's rapport with Mla'bri' informants (chap. 16). The term is normally used with a close friend, but can be insulting when used with someone at a greater social distance, so the Mla'bri' individuals were upset when the researcher addressed them with it. On another occasion however, the researcher (an older person than they) called himself /pɔ̀ɔ/ 'father', and addressed them with /lûuk/ 'child', which was acceptable (Kraisri 1963:179).

We have seen, however, that educated northerners tend to substitute Standard Thai for Kammüang when speaking a public variety under formal or semi-formal circumstances. The higher up on the scale of social distance, the more likely they are to use Standard Thai. The lower on the scale, the more likely they are to use Kammüang, with fluent, automatic, and unhesitating switching between the two, according to the requirements of the situation.[5] Such use of two languages to express different social dimensions is known as diglossia or situational bilingualism.[6]

The feeling that Standard Thai should be used at public distance is strong, but at times may also be a manifestation of cultural insecurity. Whereas sometimes officials from central Thailand who do not really speak Kammüang will try to show solidarity with northerners by throwing in some Kammüang words when making speeches to village people in the north, northern officials may tend to use pure Standard Thai even though villagers do not understand. On one occasion an anthropologist's northern assistant remarked with weary disapproval that northerners who become officials never use Kammüang in public because they want to show their status and how proper they are (Michael Moerman personal communication).

Buddhist sermons in the rural north provide at least one important exception to this generalization about the public use of Standard Thai. They are more likely to be delivered in Kammüang than are other public addresses. In one village, for example, extemporaneous sermons by northerners were always given in Kammüang, which the people understood and loved to hear. When visiting monks from outside the north came to preach and did not speak Kammüang, their sermons were less effective (Kingshill 1960:118).

Although sermons stored in the temple of that rural village were largely in Kammüang, some written in Standard Thai were also available, but were shorter than the Kammüang ones. Monks and novices found them harder to read aloud, and they were not delivered upon local demand, but only upon orders from higher up (Kingshill 1960:117). Doubtless the increasing knowledge of Standard Thai in recent years reduces the disparity in such situations, but Kammüang remains strong.

Teachers in all schools in Thailand are supposed to teach only in Standard Thai, but those teachers able to do so speak in Kammüang in the classroom when necessary, and when no outsider is thought to be able to overhear. Otherwise the younger children would not understand, and little would be accomplished in the early grades (Kingshill 1960:69, 219). That unofficial and illegal practice is part of what has made the Thai educational system work in the north. In the city of Chiang Mai the threshold of Kammüang is lower than in rural areas, of course, so Standard Thai is understood, expected, and accepted at a younger age and more often.

Psychological Identity

The speakers of Kammüang have a distinct ethnic name for themselves, /khonmiang/ 'people of the country', as well as for their language, /kammiang/ 'language of the country'. Some neighboring people call them Yuan, a term which some of the ancestors of the Kammüang-speaking people earlier used of themselves (Kraisri 1965b). An elegant Thai term for them, gaining in usage, is Lanna Thai, the name of an ancient northern kingdom.

In addition to their separate name, their situational bilingualism contributes to the psychological distinctiveness of Kammüang. To be sure, some educated speakers of Kammüang feel that Standard Thai is in some way "better," a feeling related often to writing it. But these same people generally manifest no rejection of, or embarrassment because of colloquial use of Kammüang, such as sometimes occurs with situational bilingualism elsewhere (Ferguson 1964:431).

Kammüang traditional writing and literature also contribute to the psychological identity of the language and people, limited as their use now is. At one time the language of various kingdoms of northern Thailand, Kammüang has an alphabet derived from Mon, which has a different appearance from Standard Thai. Writing was typically scratched on a palm leaf with a metal stylus, after which a black substance was rubbed over the surface to make the scratches visible. The palm-leaf pages were loosely bound into volumes with string. Today this process is still occasionally used, but some sermons are written in ordinary school notebooks instead (Kingshill 1960:114).

After the Bangkok kingdom took over northern Thailand, reading and writing in Kammüang were eventually eliminated from the schools, except for temple schools. The last instruction in Kammüang given in Prince Royal's College, one of the prominent private schools in Chiang Mai, was in the 1920s. The traditional Kammüang writing system is no longer normally used in government affairs, business, or regular correspondence, but it is still used some in the Buddhist temples.

In addition to that continuing religious use, a revival of ancient Kammüang writing is also taking place in some academic circles in northern Thailand. The study of old documents on palm leaf is a major part of this work, as is the production of bilingual and trilingual dictionaries in Kammüang, Standard Thai, and English (Ronald Renard 1990 personal communication). On the other hand, the Social Research Institute at Chiang Mai University has a program of transliterating traditional Kammüang texts into Standard Thai script,[7] which could reduce the need for the Kammüang script, although not for the language.

On the more popular level, learning to read and write the Kammüang script has traditionally been a male prerogative, and some temple boys are still required to learn it for the priesthood in at least some Kammüang-speaking villages (Kingshill 1960:101, 119; Rhum 1987:10). As it is used primarily for religious purposes the skill is believed to generate magical and religious power. Copying texts and donating them to the temple also brings merit (Rhum 1987:5-7). The Standard Thai script which students learn in school is also used by some individuals to write in Kammüang, producing letters, columns in newspapers, folktales, and descriptions of Kammüang culture. Some young people write their courtship letters in the Kammüang language but Standard Thai script because writing anything that personal in the Standard Thai language itself seems too distant a social dimension (Moerman 1966:157). Books in the Kammüang language but Standard Thai script are published from time to time.

When people do write the Kammüang language in Standard Thai script the spelling is generally inconsistent because Standard Thai and Kammüang sound systems are so different. Standardizing the spelling of some of these differences to provide a highly functional Standard Thai script for the Kammüang language would be possible (chap. 16), but has not been done. The spelling problems created by the language differences contribute to a sense of Kammüang identity.

Although not many northerners write Kammüang, speech in the regional language is alive and vigorous among nearly five million native speakers plus others who need it as a second language. Because of population growth many more people speak Kammüang today than when Standard Thai became the official language of northern Thailand.

As Standard Thai has become better known in northern Thailand it is not replacing Kammüang, but many more people have become situationally bilingual. Kammüang is changing, to be sure, becoming more dependent, "lower" in some of the dimensions of language, and more like Standard Thai, but its place among Thailand's diverse languages is not remotely threatened.

In spite of a strong sense of Kammüang and Northern Thai identity, however, northerners also share the feeling that Kammüang is "Thai." It is not Standard Thai or Thaiklang; it has a distinct identity from them, but is nevertheless a manifestation of a larger Thai language. From the Kammüang point of view, Standard Thai and Kammüang are different kinds of Thai, along with many other languages in the country as well.

Intelligibility

When two varieties of speech are as much alike as Kammüang and Standard Thai, various criteria need to be used in deciding whether to classify them as the same language or as different languages. One of the most important of these is intelligibility, the degree to which the use of one variety is intelligible to speakers of the other who have had no previous experience with it (chap. 17). Such intelligibility may be bilateral (mutual intelligibility) or unilateral.

Intelligibility criteria, however, are not always easy to apply in a rational way (Gleason 1961:441; Hockett 1958:321-329). We have already run into some of the problems. Within Standard Thai itself, for example, not all native speakers can understand everything in the sacred range. Neither would they understand many lectures in science classes in the university. Yet Standard Thai is all one language, as we will define "one language."

Between the Tai languages, furthermore, people often experience partial understanding. The government official visiting Chiang Mai finds that when the elderly lady who runs the restaurant speaks to him in Kammüang about his order he can understand her for the most part, but when his Kammüang companions are talking to each other he understands much less, and when he is out in a country village understanding is even more difficult.

In some cases people are trying to help him understand by simplifying what they say to him in Kammüang, stating it in an easier way rather than the most natural way or the way that first comes to mind. When they see that he is not understanding they try another wording. Furthermore, when they talk to him they talk in the consultative variety of Kammüang, without the contractions and slang of the personal variety.

Villagers can understand more of the official's Standard Thai than he can understand of their Kammüang. What they learned in school is not all completely lost since it has been reinforced down through the years by radio and television and by hearing people speak Standard Thai.

It is important, therefore, to make a technical distinction between *intelligibility* and *comprehension*. Intelligibility is an intrinsic degree of similarity between language varieties, while comprehension is skill learned through contact with the other language. Intelligibility depends on how different the dialects or languages are, comprehension on how speakers have adjusted to the difference (Blair 1990:2). Intelligibility between Kammüang and Standard Thai is not complete, but speakers of the one gain comprehension easily if they have and use the opportunity to do so. On the whole, Standard Thai is more comprehensible to Kammüang speakers than the reverse because they have greater exposure to it.

We will reserve the term intelligibility, furthermore, to describe a relationship between varieties such that native speakers of one have full and unhesitating understanding of the other, with only the normal misunderstandings which native speakers of the other also make in their own languages, plus a few occasional ones for differences of pronunciation, vocabulary, or idiom. Such understanding is true of all normally intelligent speakers using the consultative level with non-technical varieties of the ordinary range on all subject matter familiar to them. Ideally intelligibility should be measured against speakers who have never had contact with any other closely related language or dialect, but that is impossible in Thailand, and rarely possible anywhere. Nevertheless, by the inexact observations we can make under these criteria, clearly Standard Thai and Kammüang are not mutually intelligible, and are therefore to be considered different languages.

But, as we have also seen, this is not the whole story, and it would not be right to imply that Standard Thai and Kammüang are as different as Standard Thai and English. Some languages which are not mutually intelligible are readily learnable. That is, they easily become comprehensible if the opportunity and interest are there (Noss 1964: 2).

Our criterion of "readily learnable" involves a variable period of adjustment.

[In Africa] inhabitants of village A describe the dialect of adjacent village B as a "two-day" dialect, and that of the somewhat more remote village C as a "one-week" dialect, and so on. What is meant is that in the first case two days of working towards the goal are enough to establish a basis for easy intercommunication about practical matters, whereas in the second case the adjustment requires a week (Hockett 1958:326-327).

Two languages which are not mutually intelligible are readily learnable only if they have much in common. In the case of Standard Thai and Kammüang this is their "Thainess." The communication distance between them can be measured by the time it takes for the speaker of one to learn the other to the point of full comprehension. For most people of central Thailand learning Kammüang to this degree would take several weeks if they had had no previous contact.

In actual fact, the learnability of Standard Thai for a native speaker of Kammüang is very much greater than that of Kammüang for a native speaker of Standard Thai. People outside the north do not have much opportunity for concentrated exposure to Kammüang. Furthermore, adults are usually more highly motivated to learn a language which is considered to be higher than one which is lower. Thus, people from the central plains are not generally motivated to learn Kammüang, but many speakers of Kammüang are highly motivated to learn Standard Thai as the language of education and the major media, a vehicle of communication outside of the region, the prestige form, the language of social mobility and the language of the nation.

Even with all of these qualifications, however, this typology of language/dialect difference may be too categorical for some northerners in Thailand. Standard Thai and Kammüang are two languages with a high degree of learnability for most people, but for northerners with sufficient education, brought up as native speakers of both languages, they may have effectively become a single language with different ranges selected according to co-speakers or as different dimensions selected according to the formality of the situation. The borderline between bilingualism and the development of integrated varieties in the same language is very narrow here.

Summary

Kammüang is the internal language of the northern region of Thailand, and Standard Thai is its external language. Kammüang has several major subregional dialects, of which the most important is spoken in Chiang Mai and its environs.

All dialects of Kammüang differ from Standard Thai in a number of common distinctive ways, especially in the tone system and part of the system of initial consonants. Extensive vocabulary differences and some grammatical ones are to be found as well.

Kammüang has a number of social dimensions, but not as many as Standard Thai, and some of them not as elaborate. One important feature of the diglossia which these two languages represent is that Standard Thai itself is used as the upper level of some Kammüang dimensions like public distance.

Kammüang was formerly written in its own script, which is still preserved for some religious and cultural purposes, but most northerners who want to write anything now do so in Standard Thai.

Kammüang and Standard Thai are not mutually intelligible although most northerners have learned at least enough Standard Thai to follow simple discourse in that language. Few people from outside the north can follow any extended discourse clearly in Kammüang although they will get the drift of some of it. The languages are readily learnable, however. Speakers from other parts of the country could adjust to understanding and speaking Kammüang simply by interacting with it over a period of time, but speakers of Standard Thai rarely do this. Speakers of Kammüang do quickly learn Standard Thai or Thaiklang if they spend extended periods of time in central Thailand, however. This non-reciprocal learning pattern is a manifestation of the language hierarchy (fig. II.1).

In spite of significant structural differences between Standard Thai and Kammüang, and the lack of mutual intelligibility, speakers of Kammüang identify with the nation as well as with the northern region, and consider Standard Thai to be the language of the nation even if they do not speak it well.

6

Lao (Northeastern Thai)

The part of Thailand which bulges out to the east, sharing a common border with Laos and Cambodia, is generally called /phâak'isăan/ 'Isan, the northeast region', obviously from the perspective of Bangkok to the southwest. It is generally poorer than most other parts of the country because of more limited resources, less rainfall, land which is less ideally suited to rice cultivation than some other parts, and relative economic neglect. Inadequate rainfall for seasons on end means a precarious existence for the majority of the population, which depends on growing rice both for food and for cash (Kanala 1977:195).

For the most part people in the northeast are apolitical, accepting their fate with passivity, most comfortable conforming to their assigned place in the social hierarchy, and exhibiting a high tolerance for capricious superiors who treat them with force and discrimination (Kanala 1977:256). But at times economic conditions and the feeling of being ignored by the government have given rise to political restiveness in some segments of the northeastern population. Some people have therefore responded to messages promising them a better world, so that in the 1960s and 1970s, for example, a small insurgency persisted in remote areas of the region, encouraged and aided by Vietnam and China, through Laos. The northeast is the one region of Thailand where the threat of disunity has sometimes begun to surface in a major language group.

Under that threat the government, goaded and backed by the United States, undertook major economic development projects, many of them of little permanent value because they ignored local priorities and participation. But other changes, particularly improvements in the infrastructure, did provide the ground on which adjustments in life could be built. So electrification and the building of roads, for example, have been widespread, and some irrigation has also been useful in raising the standard of living for some of the people in the northeast.[1]

After the end of the Vietnam War, China and Thailand established friendly relations, and China no longer supported Thai insurgents. Vietnam continued to do so, with Soviet help for a while, but without even what little success it had before. In the meantime, the economic situation in the northeast improved for some people and a series of governments within Thailand has been less harsh than either the regime of the Vietnam War years or the especially repressive government of the mid-1970s. The threat of insurgency has correspondingly diminished, at least for now.

Like many countries, Thailand has a small, extremely wealthy upper class, a rapidly growing but relatively small middle class, and a large percentage of extremely poor people. Even during occasional periods of elective government it has been ruled in effect by military power and by an all-pervasive and relatively inflexible bureaucracy. In the view of country villagers all of this is legitimized, but also tempered, by the sacred monarchy.

People in power are oriented toward Bangkok as the economic, cultural and political center of the country. Concentric spheres of interest radiate from there, the more peripheral the area the less important to centralized bureaucrats, unless elements out on the fringe pose some kind of threat. Traditionally, civil servants were punished by being sent to the more remote provinces, which also received less money, less thought, less education, and less development. Banditry and lawlessness also occurred there more commonly than in central areas, and were less diligently checked. In recent years, however, the central spheres of interest are getting larger, the remote margins of the country smaller.

In the meantime, also, some aspects of the economy of the northeast have been booming, fueled in part by wages earned by thousands of northeasterners working abroad for Middle Eastern oil concerns, or as laborers in such countries as Japan, Taiwan, Singapore and Brunei (Samuel A. Mattix personal communication). Large two-story cement houses built by returned oil workers sometimes rise above small villages of otherwise more traditional wooden and bamboo homes.

But the poverty of huge sectors of Thailand's population is nevertheless more conspicuous in parts of the rural northeast than anywhere else in the country except the slums of Bangkok. And a high percentage of the dwellers in those slums came there from the northeast.

Lao

The northeast contributes greatly to the linguistic diversity of Thailand. It has more different Tai languages and dialects than any other region. Some of these are displaced languages and dialects (chap. 11), while others are dialects of the regional language. Non-Tai languages are spoken there as well, including Northern Khmer and Kuy (chap. 10), which have some of the largest populations among minority languages in the country.

The people of the northeast call their regional language /phaasaa phiin mian/ (tones vary according to dialect) 'local language' or more commonly /laaw/ (tone varies) 'Lao'. They may refer to themselves as Thai or Lao, depending on the context. In Standard Thai people frequently also refer to Lao as /phaasǎa'isǎan/ 'northeastern language', which northeasterners also use in a Thai-ized Lao.

Lao, of course, is also the name of the people and language in the neighboring country of Laos,[2] although 80% or so of all ethnic Lao live in Thailand. The major Lao dialect divisions run right across the border, so that the Loei Province dialect in Thailand is more similar to the Luang Prabang dialect in Laos than it is to the Khon Kaen dialect in Thailand. Lao in Laos, however, has a writing system which looks somewhat different from Standard Thai writing, and since people in Thailand tend to identify the regional languages with Thai, the different appearance of Lao writing in Laos makes some of them think that spoken Lao in Thailand and in Laos are less alike than they really are.

Lao Dialects

The major Lao dialect divisions, classified primarily by differences in the tone systems, are called the Luang Prabang or northern group, Vientiane or central group, and southern group (Brown 1965; Hartmann 1976, 1980). Luang Prabang and Vientiane are, of course, towns in Laos. In addition to the tongue of the Luang Prabang group, which extends down into Loei Province, the Vientiane group overlaps the border east and south of that. But the largest number of Lao dialects in Thailand belong to the southern group, which extends into southern Laos.

Within these Lao dialect groupings in the northeast itself, various provinces, many districts, even villages have their small differences of dialect, so that people can often tell where another person comes from

Table 6.1. Comparison of tones in two Lao dialects and Standard Thai (data from Prapart 1980; Wantanee and Dee 1978).

English	Standard Thai	Loei (Na Pho)	Khon Kaen
monkey	liŋ (mid)	liŋ (high rising)	liiŋ (high falling)
red	dɛɛŋ (mid)	dɛɛŋ (high rising)	dɛɛŋ (low falling)
rice	khâaw (falling)	khaw (high rising then falling)	khaw (low falling)
father	phɔ̂ɔ (falling)	phɔɔ (mid falling)	phɔɔ (mid level)
chicken	kày (low)	kay (mid falling)	kay (high level)
turtle	tàw (low)	taw (mid falling)	taw (high level)
tongue	lín (high)	liin (mid rising)	lin (mid falling)
sky	fáa (high)	faa (mid rising)	faa (mid rising)
garden	sŭan (rising)	suan (high falling)	suan (low rising)
sweet	wăan (rising)	waan (high falling)	waan (low rising)

by that person's pronunciation. Mutual intelligibility, however, extends right across the northeast among Lao dialects.

Examples of the tone differences within Lao, and their differences from Standard Thai, may be seen in table 6.1, along with an occasional difference of vowel length, or duration, symbolized by single and double letters in the examples. The Loei dialect shown there is from the Luang Prabang group, and the Khon Kaen dialect is from the southern group. The examples represent scores of other words with the same tones corresponding between the dialects in the same way. Some characteristic consonant differences between Lao and Standard Thai may be seen in table 6.2. These, too, are quite regular except as Lao dialects currently borrow pronunciations of some words from Standard Thai, skewing the system. Included also are a few examples of words which are completely different between Khon Kaen Lao and Standard Thai.

Normalized Lao

Along with all of the individual local dialects, somewhat more generalized forms of Lao are used in public media and by people who travel about in northeast Thailand. They are based on the spoken Lao of educated people in various cities and larger towns like Khon Kaen. They are also the ones generally used when Lao is written for publication in Thai script (Keyes 1967:3). In these varieties localisms are reduced, and the influence of Standard Thai is strong.

These varieties are not "standardized" (Keyes 1966:304, 350), as no government has established their position, no school system promotes them, and no dictionaries or grammar books are recognized as normative. Nevertheless a social process analogous to standardization is at work, as these varieties partially transcend the multitude of local dialects.

Such normalized varieties arise for numerous pragmatic and psychological reasons. Radio and television announcers cannot broadcast in all of the varieties which make up the Lao of the northeast. If they did use those dialects natural to their hometowns they would bring to the radio some of the linguistic diversity of the countryside, but different social values, many inappropriate to radio, are ascribed to different ways of speaking. Some sound rural, quaint, backward, others urban, modern, progressive. Media people are much more likely to opt for the urban than for the rural, even if their background is rural. The process is self-reinforcing, for when mildly prestigious forms are extensively used by influential speakers these forms become still more prestigious.

As a result, a graded range of normalized varieties extends from the dialects of the major centers of the northeast at one end of the continuum, to something close to Standard Thai at the other end, the latter often spoken with northeastern colloquialisms and a Lao accent

Table 6.2. Examples of differences between Lao (Khon Kaen dialect) and Standard Thai in initial consonants, as well as in entirely different words (Wantanee and Dee 1978).

English	Standard Thai	Khon Kaen Lao
spoon	chɔ́ɔn	sɔɔn (mid falling)
elephant	cháaŋ	saaŋ (mid falling)
to wipe	chét	seet (mid level)
grandmother	yâa	ñaa (mid level)
mosquito	yuŋ	ñuŋ (high falling)
long	yaaw	ñaaw (high falling)
rainbow	lúŋ	huŋ (mid falling)
boat	lɨa	hɨa (high falling)
house	lɨan	hɨan (high falling)
friend	phɨ̂an	siaw (mid level)
nose	camùuk	daŋ (low falling)
I	chǎn	khɔɔy (low falling)

(Gedney 1967:791; A. Thomas Kirsch personal communication). Most northeasterners, however, speak primarily their local dialects, although they hear and understand many others, local and normalized. People coming to the northeast from central Thailand, on the other hand, usually find themselves understood up to a point, but are unable to understand much of what they hear in town, and less of what they hear in rural villages (Gedney 1967:791).

Writing Lao

There are four different writing systems for Lao in northeast Thailand. One is the traditional writing system of Buddhist texts, called /tuatham/ (tones vary) 'doctrine letters (symbols), Dharmic writing'. It is similar to the traditional writing system used for Kammüang in the north.

Increasingly rare, this temple script is generally learned in monasteries so that monks can read the sacred books and consult the astrological tables. Even a generation or two ago, few people wrote in it and most of those who "wrote" simply copied texts which were loaned back and forth freely between monasteries. Now even that copying function has been taken over largely by the printing press using Standard Thai script (Tambiah 1968:93-99, 105).

An ancient Khmer script also used in the northeast is now primarily restricted to amulets, tattoos, charms, and the charts of fortune tellers (Paitoon 1984:164).

The official system of writing in Laos is also to be found in Thailand, but is now restricted to minor use for poetic and romantic literature (Tambiah 1970:118-120). Sometimes documents contain mixtures of the temple and Lao scripts. Derived from the Sukhothai system from which the Thai system was taken, Lao writing is considerably simpler than modern Standard Thai writing although now strongly influenced by it. The form used in some older Lao manuscripts in Thailand, however, is sometimes an archaic earlier stage (James R. Chamberlain personal communication).

Finally, the Standard Thai system itself is increasingly used to write Lao, a more recent development spurred by the school system and by decreasing knowledge of the other systems. It is taking over for religious and secular purposes ranging from informal letter writing to publications on northeastern traditional culture. One company, Sritham Publishers in Ubon, regularly publishes Lao books in Thai script; its publications include the history and ancient customs of the northeast, proverbs, traditional stories, and other northeastern lore. It has also published a major Lao-Thai-English dictionary with extensive citations from Lao literature (Preecha 1989). This dictionary of more than a thousand pages, distributed widely with assistance from the Toyota Foundation, may strengthen the growing legitimacy of writing Lao in Thai script.[3]

Lao and Standard Thai

Lao is used for communication with contiguous areas of Laos, in peaceful times extensively so, as people crisscross the Mekong River between the two countries. But such use does not make it one of the external languages of the Thai nation. The cross-border communication is regional, not national, not official, and not in competition with the place of Standard Thai or English.

Instead, Standard Thai impinges directly on many people in the region. The military draft draws young men into urban and national centers where they mix with men from other parts of the country (Keyes 1966:311). Many northeasterners migrate to central and south Thailand, especially to Bangkok. Some of them go seasonally, to work there during the slack part of the agricultural cycle at home, while others spend several years away, the majority eventually returning to the northeast (Lightfoot, Fuller, and Peerasit 1983; Fuller et al. 1983). And although northeasterners tend to cluster together when in Bangkok, speaking Lao and eating northeastern food (Textor 1961), they come home with a much stronger use of Standard Thai, or at least Thaiklang, the regional language of the center. The education they had in Standard Thai before they went also fortified them for that trip into the other language area (Keyes 1966:179).

Lao is closer to being mutually intelligible with Standard Thai than is Kammüang.[4] A speaker of Standard Thai would need less time to learn good Lao when immersed in a Lao environment, than to learn Kammüang under analogous circumstances. However, it took Thai researchers from Bangkok a month to get used to the Lao of Udon enough to be sure of reasonable understanding. And even then, problems kept cropping up (Tambiah 1968:89).

One reason for greater intelligibility is that Lao speakers have borrowed more vocabulary from Standard Thai than have Kammüang speakers, due to their greater movement into and out of the central region. Another is the greater intrinsic difference in the northern sound system. Between Lao and Standard Thai, also, considerably more of the common original vocabulary is pronounced the same, if we ignore tones.

Many people in the towns of the northeast are fully competent in everyday Standard Thai, spoken and written, particularly in the consultative dimension, whereas in outlying villages many women and some men have lost most of what ability they gained in school. They have become illiterate again, retaining only a meager memory which helps them understand some spoken Standard Thai, but not speak it. And throughout the northeast people are to be found at every gradation between.

By present trends, functional bilingualism between Lao and Standard Thai could in time become universal for northeasterners. Lao, furthermore, will be increasingly altered by the influence of Standard Thai, influence which will make such bilingualism easier to attain.

Most government officials from outside the northeast, on the other hand, do not understand much Lao, and make no effort to learn it, considering it rustic and inferior. They content themselves with a few standard jokes about it, and may even refuse to acknowledge what they do understand. Because they have contact primarily with more educated Lao and because the lowly would not think of asserting themselves, they have no idea of how little they are really understood, a situation particularly critical for community development workers. Fortunately other officials come from the region itself, and so can communicate with the villagers, relate to them, and better understand their situation.

If officials of goodwill from outside the region tried to understand Lao and to gain facility in using it, the effort would pay off enormously in rapport and communication. But such learning is contrary to powerful assumptions built into the language hierarchy, so that many people are embarrassed to speak a language below their own. To speak Lao would carry some of the feelings which an educated American would have in using working-class English with its "ain't" and "he don't," a dialect which is not nearly as different from Standard English as Lao is from Standard Thai. Speakers of higher-level languages sometimes feel that they are protecting themselves from social pollution by not learning lower ones.

Values of a Thai Education

As in other parts of the country, the spread of government education has increased both multilingualism and what people can understand of

Standard Thai when they are not themselves able to speak it. Students in the northeast do not achieve fully developed use of the national language in four to six years of school any more than do those in the north or south, but they are prepared for gaining such fluency whenever the opportunity arises to use enough Standard Thai (Keyes 1966: 179).

Teachers, with their superior education and Thai-ized values, are also major windows which villagers have to the outside world.[5] The Thai educational system is the most powerful force for spreading Thai national values in general, and Standard Thai language in particular. Its first objective is to cement people to the nation, preparing them to accept, cope with and participate in a Thai-dominated world. The objective is met primarily through teaching spoken and written Standard Thai, so that all texts in the first grades except arithmetic texts are primarily or secondarily Thai-language readers.

In northeastern schools teachers spend much more time on Standard Thai than is required by the country-wide curriculum designed in Bangkok (Keyes 1966:164-166). But in order to teach children who do not know Standard Thai, Lao-speaking teachers break the rules and use Lao, like their peers use other regional languages elsewhere in the country. The teachers share with the curriculum planners in Bangkok the goal of instilling Standard Thai, but they know that the children in early grades cannot learn much content if they teach in Standard Thai exclusively. Informally, Standard Thai gets phased in until it is used exclusively on upper levels. Thus, the fact that most teachers come from the region partially saves the educational system from its own rigidity. By bending the system teachers are better carriers of the national culture and language to the children.

But in spite of widespread public schools, like much of the rest of rural Thailand children in northeastern country villages cannot get enough schooling in their own community to ensure their knowledge of Standard Thai. Anything beyond four to six grades must be taken in town, where they must board in the home of a relative, friend, or stranger. At ten to twelve years of age the children who do go away are often treated as servants in the foster home and shown little affection, so many do not stay. Most parents are not able even to arrange this much, and many children do not continue their education.

In earlier times, in all Buddhist villages education was centered in the village temple. If boys who studied there went on for more education it was to temples in the towns, eventually some to temples in

Bangkok. Traditional village education was very closely tied to life in the village (Hanks 1958), and was immediately applicable. It was an important merit-making activity for a boy and his family, and so had intrinsic religious value whether other values were perceived or not.

The village monks, furthermore, taught morality as seen from a village perspective, and how to deal with the uncertainties of life through rituals for propitiating supra-human forces. In other words, boys learned how to live in the natural and supernatural world of the village. To be sure, the literacy gained was not needed by everyone in the community, but some literate people were needed to be able to read for the community.

Modern education, however, brings no religious benefit and little apparent value for traditional rice-farming village life. Although Buddhism is taught, it is an abstract and remote Buddhism, not much concerned with the spirits all around which affect everyday life. The perspective is national, not village. This literacy and education, furthermore, are in a strange language which nobody ever uses in the village.

Modern education is for life outside the village, for people in the towns and cities, for semi-secularized people, in spite of its overt Buddhist content. It is education in the language of the nation, the values of the nation, the religion of the nation, the culture of the nation. Even the northeast region in which the students live gets only passing mention.

Modern education prepares people to work in government offices, to be business owners or employees, or to be teachers. If people want to get out of the village they may be motivated to have a modern education, but most northeasterners would simply prefer an adequate life where they are.

However, as national life impinges more on rural life villagers in the northeast as well as in other parts of the country can no longer escape its consequences. They need some education to check how much the rice mill operator is trying to cheat them as he weighs their harvest of rice on his scales and pays them their tiny total cash income for the year. Somebody needs to understand what government directives mean as the village becomes less and less isolated. But people who do reasonably well in school often move on into the town, into employment or the incessant search for often non-existing jobs. Meanwhile, in the more out-of-the-way villages some of their classmates lapse back into illiteracy, with minimal use of Standard Thai.

Lao Identity

Although in most respects Lao is typical of the regional languages of Thailand, native speakers have greater ambivalence toward it than northerners do toward Kammüang. The stigma of being rustic and backward is attached to Lao much more than to Kammüang by the respective native speakers as well as by people from the outside. The people of the northeast do not have a simple-level term for themselves with the same positive connotations that northerners have, either. Nearest to it is the elegant Thai term *Isan*, which some northeasterners also use, especially to designate region-wide traits.

But in spite of its rustic image, the region has a great deal to hold it together and to stimulate group identity. One factor already mentioned is the political response to severe economic conditions and a consciousness of regional need. Along with increased knowledge of Standard Thai, the northeasterner brings back from his working trip to Bangkok a stronger sense of his differences from the people of central Thailand. While away from home he missed most keenly those things he had in common with others from the northeast (Keyes 1966:324).

Radio and television, contributing as they do to the hearing of Standard Thai, nevertheless also contribute to northeastern identity through their secondary use of normalized Lao, and especially through a popular and productive traditional musical form, the /lam laaw/ (tones vary). This is a powerful cultural tradition which extends throughout the region, transcending individual local dialects. Current events, social commentary, traditional narratives, folktales, history, satire, love poetry, burlesque are sung by performers at fairs and on the public media (Keyes 1966:304, 294-295).

The form of the song is rather loosely constructed rhyming verse. Some songs are transcribed in written texts, in any of the three principal scripts, and many are also transmitted in oral form. The singer has wide room to exercise creativity, to improvise, and to engage in repartee (Tambiah 1968:115-117). But even here, this thoroughly northeastern form of oral music/literature also has its nationalizing effect as performers increasingly sing stories from the central and northern regions.

In spite of the fact that Buddhism is a nation-wide religion, northeastern Buddhism is another unifying factor for the northeast. An important body of Buddhist sermons in the northeast is built around characteristic northeastern stories, formerly written in the temple script, but now increasingly in Thai script. Villagers sometimes choose the sermons which are to be read by the monk; they greatly appreciate this northeastern type with which they can identify, and which, in turn, reinforces their regionality (Tambiah 1968:102). There are even Lao temples in Bangkok (Wyatt 1966).

Other Lao literature in Thai script, scanty as it is, is used in some areas, especially in the temples. It tends to record and emphasize northeastern history, culture and traditions, as well as religion.

So many forces like these are working toward greater cohesiveness in Lao identity, many more than have been noted here. And it seems that in recent years embarrassment over Lao identity is sometimes changing to pride, at least among intellectuals. Programs in Lao studies are now offered in universities of the northeast, and the Isan Cultural Institute has been established in Mahasarakham. One northeastern university professor, when asked at a conference why being singled out as a northeasterner is embarrassing, made the startling statement, "I do not know about the rest of you, but as for me, I am Lao." As the Lao identity is losing its stigma, Lao restaurants in Bangkok are also becoming more popular than ever before. Lao-style music dominates the pop-music field, and Lao comedians are popular in nightclubs (James R. Chamberlain personal communication).

Television talk shows and commercials, as well as educated Thai people in groups made up of individuals from different parts of the country now frequently inject regional language to spice up Standard Thai conversation, to be funny, and to show appreciation for different regions. In such a setting someone who knows a regional language in addition to Standard Thai has an advantage. The Lao are benefiting from this general loosening of the popular view that Standard Thai alone is of value (Samuel A. Mattix personal communication).

But along with such increasing regionalism Lao-speaking people in Thailand have a strong sense of being Thai citizens, of belonging to the Thai nation, of being under the Thai king. They recognize fully that Standard Thai is the language of that nation and its people, no matter how little they may speak it. They feel this way not only because of education and the political authority over them, but for pragmatic and ideological reasons as well.

The contrast may be seen in the different attitudes of northeasterners toward Laos and Thailand. People in Laos speak the same language as the northeasterners do, and many northeasterners are geographically nearer Laos than they are central Thailand, but Laos does not exercise the pull on people in Thailand's northeast that Bangkok does. The northeast may be the poorest region of Thailand, but neighboring Laos is no alternative. What improvement may come to the northeast will come through Bangkok.

In peaceful times people in the border areas trade extensively across the river which separates them from Laos. Many have friends and relatives on the other side. But even the guerrilla insurgents who have operated at different times in the remote areas of the northeast, and who were trained and supplied through Laos, have not been oriented toward Laos. They are looking for a different social order in Thailand.

Ideologically the pull is toward Bangkok as well. The King and the Supreme Patriarch of Thai Buddhism are in Bangkok. The sacredness, the mana-like spiritual energy which these beings have can be tapped at the local level by the use of the symbols of kingship and of Buddhism. The pictures and images of the King and the ever-present evidence of Buddhism focus this power for the villagers. The sound of the King's voice on the radio has far more significance to the villager than the intrinsic meaning of his words. Villagers will listen to the King or watch him on television not because they understand him but because they respect him and gain merit through this ritual.

Bangkok, the location of the King, is the sacred center of the universe. The nation, with its flag and national song, is the domain of that sacred center (Keyes 1966:302, 354-355). It is in Bangkok that the most sacred and powerful religious objects are located, and there the primary rites for insuring the fertility of the land and a good harvest take place, conducted by members of the royal family. Bangkok is the hub around which Thailand rotates, and the northeast is one of its spokes. Standard Thai, in turn, is the language of religious, economic and political power in Bangkok, the power that makes the country run. Even a resurgent pride in Lao does not threaten that.

Summary

Next to the center, the northeast is the largest region of Thailand, and has the most Tai languages and dialects. It is also the poorest and the most subject to discontent.

Lao is the regional language of the northeast. It consists of numerous dialects in three major groups. The dialects in some of the major towns have become somewhat normalized to the point where many villagers in neighboring areas speak them as well as their village dialects.

There are four different ways of writing Lao, but none is in widespread use as most people who want to write do so in Standard Thai instead.

Lao is not mutually intelligible with Standard Thai, but the latter is widely known, especially in the towns. Although education in Standard Thai is widespread, it does not fully meet the needs of many villagers, to whom the earlier pattern of educating boys in the monasteries was more suited.

People in central Thailand have traditionally looked down on the northeast and its Lao language, causing some northeasterners to be somewhat ashamed to be known as Lao. That condition is changing, however, and confidence in Lao identity seems to be getting stronger.

Even the feeling of being poor, neglected and marginalized has not caused more than small eruptions of protest and dissent from northeasterners in the past. The people of the northeast see their destiny as inextricably linked with Thailand for cultural, religious and pragmatic reasons.

7

Paktay (Southern Thai)
and Thaiklang (Central Thai)

The two remaining major regional languages of Thailand have important similarities to Kammüang and Lao in their relationships to Standard Thai, as well as important differences. In the south some normalized varieties of Paktay (Southern Thai) are more similar to
Standard Thai than those described for the northeast, but many local
dialects are even more different from Standard Thai than are the corresponding Lao dialects. In central Thailand, on the other hand,
Standard Thai is itself a variety of Thaiklang (Central Thai), mutually
intelligible with other Thaiklang dialects, although it functions on a
different level in the language hierarchy.

Paktay, the Southern Regional Language

Paktay /pàktâay/ is spoken in the southern panhandle, south of the
provincial center of Prachuap. Some of the Paktay-speaking population is descended from, or partly descended from Malay-speaking
people and perhaps others who preceded Tai-speaking people in the
area. Still other ancestors include Tai-speaking settlers who stayed in
the area after participating in military expeditions from the twelfth
century on or who migrated into the area (Wyatt 1984:33).

For example, in one community in the Sai Buri District of Pattani
Province people say they are descended from Thaiklang elephant
troops who deserted a Thai government military campaign after they
lost their elephants several generations ago. Their dialect is at present
not very remote from Paktay, but includes in its everyday speech
words which are otherwise found only in the sacred range of Standard
Thai (Anne Wilding personal communication).

Such villagers were not the primary force, however, in extending
the influence of earlier central Thailand kingdoms down the peninsula. Rather, a southern elite plus officials and military garrisons from
Tai-speaking states to the north extended their control as far south as

Nakhon Si Thammarat by the twelfth century, where they ruled Malay-speaking people (chap. 10).

By the seventeenth and eighteenth centuries, a local southern urban elite spoke Thaiklang as well as the Paktay which had developed as the language of the region. Some of their sons were sent to the capital as royal pages, some to return as leaders oriented toward Bangkok. Some of their daughters entered the harem in the king's inner palace, cementing relationships between their families and the court (Diller 1976:11).

In those earlier times, on the other hand, the Paktay-speaking villagers and lower-class urban people had little contact with Thaiklang. Villagers from other regions who moved in occasionally, and groups of prisoners from the northeast and the north, were usually assimilated to speaking Paktay in due course (Diller 1976:11-12).

A class-based diglossia or situational bilingualism thus emerged early among the elite in the south, and has continued for centuries. In modern times with mobility of populations, education, and easy communication, it has pervaded the population more extensively, and has gained complexity to the point where all natively Tai-speaking people in the south participate to varying degrees in an intricate set of situational dialect/language selections. Their situation foreshadows what the use of multiple forms of Tai will become in the north and the northeast.

Like Kammüang and Lao, Paktay has many local dialects, most of them similar to each other.[1] Southerners often refer to individual local dialects of Paktay as "the local language of X" (naming the place). The term Paktay, however, may refer to anything from such a local dialect to southern forms of speech very close to Thaiklang.

Standard Thai occupies its regular place in the region as the language of the government and education, with the usual qualifications that Paktay will be used between southern government officials in informal situations, and by southern schoolteachers helping their pupils who do not know Standard Thai. Standard Thai is the public distance variety for the region, the language of public meetings and the primary language of the media, although Paktay is also used on the radio. Standard Thai is the language which anyone with the education to do so uses with outsiders from other parts of Thailand. It is also the language of royal or high-born characters in the shadow plays, which people watch by the hour. Peasants and demons in those plays use Paktay (Court 1975).

Varieties of Paktay

Between Standard Thai and the local dialects lies a series of inter-mediary varieties, but as was noted for Kammüang, nobody has any doubt which language is being used. In the examples which follow, two extreme forms of Paktay are illustrated, both from Songkhla, the "Educated" recorded from professionals and the "Rural" from vil-lagers (Diller 1976, 1979).

In the examples of table 7.1 the primary difference between Stan-dard Thai and the Paktay varieties is in tone. As in Kammüang and Lao, furthermore, a given tone in Standard Thai is not always matched by a single tone in Paktay. In fact, the Standard Thai low tone corresponds to three tones in Paktay: high, high falling, and low rising. Even so, tones in Standard Thai do correspond systematically to ones in Paktay, and among Paktay dialects, just as they do in Kam-müang and Lao (chap. 11).

This means that people using the Educated Paktay variety recog-nize the corresponding tones in Standard Thai when they hear them. Likewise, native speakers of Standard Thai going to the south for the first time begin picking up the ability to hear the corresponding tones in Educated Paktay. They normally understand (but cannot speak) this variety because it does not differ a great deal from Standard Thai except for tones. Rural Paktay, however, takes longer to understand.

Table 7.2 shows some correspondences of initial consonants be-tween the same three varieties. In some words the consonants are the

Table 7.1. Examples of correspondences between Standard Thai, Educated Paktay and Rural Paktay in which consonant and vowel phonemes are the same, but tones differ between Paktay and Standard Thai (after Diller 1979: 61). Tone contours are described in parentheses.

English	Standard Thai	Educated Paktay	Rural Paktay
leg	khǎa (rising)	khaa (high)	khaa (high)
a rhizome	khàa (low)	khaa (high)	khaa (high)
to kill	khâa (falling)	khaa (high falling)	khaa (high falling)
value	khâa (falling)	khaa (low)	khaa (low)
thatch grass	khaa (mid)	khaa (mid falling)	khaa (mid falling)
to do trading	kháa (high)	khaa (high falling)	khaa (low falling)
to lack	khàat (low)	khaat (high falling)	khaat (high falling)
to polish	khàt (low)	khat (high)	khat (high)
to bite	kàt (low)	kat (low rising)	kat (low rising)

Table 7.2. Examples of consonant correspondences between Standard Thai, Educated Paktay and Rural Paktay (after Diller 1979:62).

English	Standard Thai	Educated Paktay	Rural Paktay
right side	khwǎa (rising)	khwaa (high)	khwaa (high)
lid	fǎa (rising)	faa (high)	khwaa (high)
lonely	ŋǎw (rising)	ŋaw (high)	haw (high)
hair louse	hǎw (rising)	haw (high)	haw (high)
grass	yâa (falling)	yaa (high falling)	ñaa (high falling)
father's mother	yâa (falling)	yaa (low)	yaa (low)
to ache	mîay (falling)	mîay (low)	mlîay (low)

same in all three, as they were in table 7.1, but in others they differ, with Educated Paktay grouped this time with Standard Thai, not with Rural Paktay.

Pairs of words pronounced alike in any one variety, furthermore, are not necessarily pronounced alike in the others. The words for 'right side' and 'lid' both sound the same in Rural Paktay, but have different initial consonants in Standard Thai and Educated Paktay. The same is true of the words for 'lonely' and 'hair louse'. However, the words for 'grass' and 'father's mother' are both pronounced with the same consonants and vowels in Standard Thai and in Educated Paktay, but with different ones in Rural Paktay. The pairs of words which are pronounced alike in Standard Thai are nevertheless not spelled the same in that language. The spelling difference reflects an older difference in Standard Thai pronunciation.

Table 7.3. Examples of vowel correspondences between Standard Thai, Educated Paktay and Rural Paktay (after Diller 1979:62).

English	Standard Thai	Educated Paktay	Rural Paktay
group	mùu (low)	muu (high)	moo (high)
pig	mǔu (rising)	muu (high)	muu (high)
to fight	sûu (falling)	suu (high falling)	soo (high falling)
chain	sôo (falling)	soo (high falling)	soo (high falling)
fever	khây (falling)	khaay (high falling)	khaay (high falling)
stockade	khâay (falling)	khaay (low)	khaay (low)
egg	khày (low)	khay (high)	khay (high)

Table 7.4. Examples of words in which tones differ between Standard Thai, Educated and Rural Paktay (after Diller 1979: 62-63).

English	Standard Thai	Educated Paktay	Rural Paktay
island	kɔ̀' (low)	kɔ' (low rising)	kɔɔ' (mid)
Year of Rabbit	thɔ̀' (low)	thɔ' (high)	thɔɔ' (high falling)
to patch	pà' (low)	pa' (low rising)	paa' (mid)
more	kwàa (low)	kwaa (low rising)	waa (high)

The vowels of Educated Paktay are most often like those of Standard Thai (table 7.3). The word for 'fever', however, is an example where the Educated Paktay vowel is the same as the one in Rural Paktay.

The words for 'group' and 'pig' are pronounced alike in Educated Paktay, whereas in Standard Thai they are distinguished by tone, but not vowel, and in Rural Paktay they are distinguished by vowel, but not tone. Table 7.4 also provides examples of another, less frequent pattern in which the tones of all three varieties are different.

Although Tai languages are often referred to as "monosyllabic," hundreds of words in Standard Thai have more than one syllable, especially words borrowed from languages like Sanskrit, Pali and Khmer. Rural Paktay words which correspond to them often have only one syllable, however, and if more than one they are often still

Table 7.5. Examples of shorter words in Rural Paktay as against Standard Thai, Educated Paktay and Rural Paktay (after Diller 1979:63-64). Tones are described only for syllables which correspond to the Rural Paktay.

English	Standard Thai	Educated Paktay	Rural Paktay
handbag	klapǎw (rising)	krapaaw (mid)	paaw (mid)
market	talàat (low)	talaat (high falling)	laat (high falling)
door	platuu (mid)	pratuu (low rising)	tuu (low rising)
comfortable	sabaay (mid)	sabaay (low rising)	baay (low rising)
to growl	khamlaam (mid)	khamlaam (mid falling)	mlaam (mid falling)
to carve (meat)	chamlɛ̂' (low)	chamlɛ' (high)	mlɛɛ' (high)
clock	naalikaa (mid, mid)	naalikaa (mid falling, low rising)	naakaa (mid falling, low rising)

Table 7.6. Examples in which Rural Paktay has entirely different words from Educated Paktay and Standard Thai (after Diller 1979:72). Paktay tones are not necessary to the point of the table.

English	Standard Thai	Educated Paktay	Rural Paktay
why?	thammay	thammay	saay
how?	yaŋŋay	yaŋŋay	phrɨɨ
much	mâak	maak	luy
to throw	paa	paa	liw
to chase	lây	laay	yik
fish net	'uan	'uan	kat

shorter than the corresponding Standard Thai word. Educated Paktay, however, has the longer words (table 7.5).

Whereas in our earlier examples the corresponding words in the three varieties were clearly related to each other, some Rural Paktay words are completely different from Educated Paktay and Standard Thai. A few of them may be seen in table 7.6.

Tables 7.1-6 are a bit misleading, however, in that pronunciation of some consonants and vowels differs more than the transcription would seem to indicate. In the Rural variety, for example, /s/ is pronounced [ṭṣ], something like /ts/ in the English word *hits*, but with the tongue curved up a bit. There are, likewise, a number of different pronunciations for {tr} in Rural Paktay. But most important, in syllable-final position /aw/ and /ay/ are pronounced with a different vowel, [ʌw] and [ʌy] respectively. These are common sounds, and this pronunciation is one of the most noticeable markers of Rural Paktay (Diller 1979:67).

Adding to the complexity of the relationship between these three varieties are numerous differences among the meanings of words, as in table 7.7. Different words which are pronounced alike in one variety may not be in the other, just as *merry, marry* and *Mary* are pronounced alike in some dialects of English but differently in others.

As indicated earlier, the two varieties of Paktay we are using as examples are not as discrete as the columns in the tables could imply, but are the ends on a continuum of usage (Diller 1976, 1979). Some older villagers speak a fairly "pure" Rural Paktay. Educated people reading Standard Thai texts aloud in Paktay may use a "pure" Educated Paktay. But conversations slide along a scale between the two, tending more toward the Educated variety with educated people, more toward the Rural variety with rural people. The mixture is also based partly on communication circumstances.

However, mixing Paktay features into Standard Thai is strongly disapproved. If Standard Thai tones are used, no Paktay features of pronunciation or meaning of any kind should also be used, but when the Paktay tone system is used, a whole set of gradations of mixture between Standard Thai and Paktay is acceptable (Diller 1979:78). People differ in their abilities to handle the two languages and the scale of variation within Paktay. Southern professionals and administrators tend to have a good command of Standard Thai and Educated Paktay, but only a moderate ability to speak and understand Rural Paktay. Rural southerners with little education have good Rural Paktay and a moderate understanding of Educated Paktay and Standard Thai, but only a weak ability to speak Educated Paktay and no ability to speak Standard Thai. One of the effects of this disparity of abilities is that people with lower control of Standard Thai avoid it for fear of making embarrassing mistakes, about which jokes abound (Diller 1976:209-210).

Different varieties have different emotional affects as well. On the positive side, Standard Thai has overtones of power and economic opportunity, of being modern, and correct, of sounding deferential and reserved. Rural Paktay has overtones of preserving local values, of being direct and trustworthy, and of sounding warm and personal. On the negative side, however, Standard Thai has overtones of being a threat to local values, legalistic, aloof and alienating, and Paktay of backwardness, of being incorrect and outdated, coarse and unrestrained (Diller 1979:83).

Table 7.7. Examples of non-equivalence in meaning between Standard Thai and Educated Paktay on one hand and Rural Paktay on the other (after Diller 1979:74-75). Paktay tones are not necessary to the point of the table.

English	Standard Thai	Educated Paktay	Rural Paktay
more, any more	'ìik	'iik	ləəy
again	'ìik	'iik	laaw
cool	yen	yen	yen
cold	năaw	naaw	yen
honey	nămphîŋ	namphiŋ	namphiŋ
sugar	nămtaan	namtaan	namphiŋ
sugar syrup	nămtaan	namtaan	namtaan
green	khĭaw	khiaw	khiaw
dark blue	nămŋən	namŋən	khiaw
light blue	fáa	faa	khiaw

As in Kammüang, the range from Standard Thai through local varieties provides social dimensions. Standard Thai is used for greater social distance, and has more elegant social value. Its social relationships are more deferential. Paktay reflects closer social distance, simpler social value, and less deferential social relationship, with more use of kinship terminology. As elsewhere in the country, however, these norms may not always be followed. A public speaker who senses hostility may win the crowd over through the use of Paktay, thus switching to a closer social distance (Diller 1979:86).

Malay Influence on Paktay

Some of the local, rural southern dialects of Paktay have been influenced by varieties of Malay (chap. 10), both because of proximity and because many native speakers of some forms of Paktay are descendants of native speakers of Malay. Ancestors would therefore have been bilingual at some time, even if present people are not.

Satun, one of the Thai provinces on the border of Malaysia, has a large population in which many people are switching or have switched to the primary use of Paktay even though they are recently descended from Pattani Malay-speaking people. Consequently, large numbers of Malay loanwords have been borrowed into Paktay as spoken in Satun. Sometimes both a Tai-related and a Malay-related word is in use for the same meaning. Using the Malay vocabulary in a case like that helps symbolize partial Malay identity, even when speaking Paktay. The words are altered to fit Paktay phonological patterns, including addition of tone, which Malay does not have. But Paktay is also modified in the process, creating Malay-Rural Paktay, another variety by which people can symbolize their relationships (Court 1975).

The Psychological Validity of Paktay

The Educated and Rural varieties of Paktay are all called Paktay by native speakers, different from what they call Standard Thai or Thaiklang, even though Educated Paktay is very similar to Standard Thai. From the standpoint of the south, all forms of Paktay are insider languages, and Standard Thai or Thaiklang are in several respects outsider languages. Tones are salient throughout Thailand for distinguishing between "us" and "them," and in Paktay tone is certainly the great divider from Standard Thai. The "separateness" of Standard Thai is also fostered by its standardization, which sets it outside of the sliding scale of variation within Paktay.

By intelligibility criteria alone, Educated Paktay and Standard Thai may be the same language, and Rural Paktay a different one. Sociolinguistically, however, the two extremes of Paktay belong together, and Standard Thai is separate at least on that level. On still a higher level, as with Tai varieties in the rest of the country, all three are "Thai."

Thaiklang (Central Thai)

Thaiklang is different from the other regional languages in that Standard Thai is linguistically part of it, both historically and by the measure of intelligibility. Functionally, however, the relationship between Standard Thai and Thaiklang is like that between Standard Thai and the other regional languages.

Because intelligibility between Standard Thai and other Thaiklang dialects is not a major problem, the two types of varieties are easily confused. Both Thai people and foreigners, for example, often say that Standard Thai is the speech of Bangkok, although in Bangkok as elsewhere many people regularly speak with stigmatized patterns of grammar and pronunciation. Part of the confusion also comes from the Thai expression /phaasǎaklaaŋ/ 'central language', which is used both for Standard Thai and for the language of the central region. /klaaŋ/ means both 'central' and 'common' in the sense of "common to the whole country."

In earlier stages the forerunner of Standard Thai was the most prestigious dialect of the central region, spoken in the court. It then became the basis for the standardized form in the central region, where Bangkok's power was strongest. Only in this century has a concerted effort been made to extend it to the other regions as they came more fully under Bangkok's control. Only in the 1930s did Standard Thai education become widespread throughout the country, and only in the 1960s did it begin to penetrate extensively into the less accessible hinterland.

Thaiklang is the internal language of the central region, so Standard Thai, as one of the Thaiklang dialects, is used more for internal purposes in that region than in others. A higher percentage of the people native to the central area, especially Bangkok, regularly use Standard Thai for communication internal to the region. A much larger percentage of the population is also monolingual in Standard Thai than in other regions.

Even so, for most people in the center, Standard Thai is learned primarily through education, as in the rest of the country. However, school children who do not speak it when they first go to school do not have the same difficulty understanding their teachers as their counterparts have in other regions.

As in the other regions, people in the center can often tell where others come from by their pronunciation. Thaiklang also has vocabulary differences from dialect to dialect, such as terms for folk medicine and for bodily functions (Richard Carlson personal communication). Speakers of Standard Thai often react to such terms as "vulgar," "uneducated," "rural," or "provincial." Social gradations are also present in Thaiklang, some dialects more rural than others, some having more prestige, especially those most like Standard Thai.

But no clear boundary can be drawn between Standard Thai and the regional language except on a few stigmatized details. Instead, a mostly seamless continuum extends between ideal Standard Thai and any local dialect (chap. 2). Situational bidialectism in the center, furthermore, is analogous to the situational bilingualism elsewhere. People select between varieties, including those of Standard Thai, to indicate greater or lesser social distance and other relationships with their co-speakers.

At present the pronunciation of Standard Thai does not coincide with the pronunciation of any one local Thaiklang dialect either. It has been characterized as having the "vowels common to all dialects of the Central region, the consonants of Suphan Buri, and the tones of Bangkok" (Brown 1967:xii). So in this way also it is a Thaiklang dialect with a difference.

Standard Thai, furthermore, is the most aberrant of all the Tai languages, let alone of the Thaiklang dialects. The heavy borrowings from Indic languages, Khmer, and now English, have changed it a great deal. Standard Thai has also been modernized more than any other Tai language in the country, so that people can communicate more easily about things foreign to traditional Thai culture, about ideas and goods that come into the country from elsewhere. Standardization, on the other hand, has also helped to preserve vestiges of older forms of Thai, like the distinction in pronunciation discussed earlier between what is written with {l} and {r} (chap. 2).

More linguistic study has gone into the three other regional languages than into non-standard Thaiklang. And most research on Standard Thai has been on idealized Standard Thai, little on extensive recording of what people actually say in their everyday use of the language. Ongoing work, however, should eventually give a clearer picture of the overall central region, and situate Standard Thai within it with greater clarity (e.g., Kalaya 1980, 1985a, 1985b).

Expansion of Thaiklang

Thaiklang is the only regional language of Thailand which borders on all of the others. The transitional nature of the border areas between the different regional languages can be seen most clearly in the area between Paktay and Thaiklang because it lies in the narrow southern peninsula where the gradations are easy to plot. Thaiklang vocabulary diminishes and Paktay vocabulary increases from north to south through the transitional zone, as shown in figure 7.1. Much the same transitional pattern is to be found in the tone differences in this border area as well (Kesmanee 1983).

One other border dialect of Thaiklang needs special mention here because it throws light on one process of language assimilation and language retention in the country. Map II.1 shows Thaiklang bulging up into the northeastern geographic region of Thailand in Nakhon Ratchasima (Khorat) Province and neighboring provinces. The variety of speech in that area, known as Khorat Thai /thaykhoorâat/, is mutu-

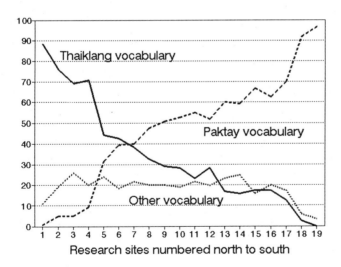

Fig. 7.1. Transition between Thaiklang and Paktay vocabulary, with research sites numbered 1-19 from north to south.

ally intelligible with Thaiklang, in spite of having an atypical tone system for a Thaiklang dialect.

This dialect of Thaiklang may have arisen by a process of language change in which a Lao dialect or Nyo, a displaced Tai language, was gradually modified in the direction of Thaiklang (Brown 1965:113). The major features of the sound system of the earlier language may have been kept, or slightly modified, while Thaiklang vocabulary was borrowed over a period of time. The pronunciation of the Thaiklang words was changed to conform to the local pronunciation, producing a new dialect mutually intelligible with Thaiklang, but not with Lao or any other language in the northeast.

This could well be one process by which Thaiklang has spread or is spreading along its borders. The wholesale borrowing of Thaiklang vocabulary with local pronunciation is of course common among all languages of Thailand, but this Khorat Thai pattern is a step farther along in linguistic assimilation.

If this supposition is correct, Korat Thai was produced by a process similar to that which produced Educated Paktay, where Paktay tones are kept, but the words are otherwise generally Standard Thai. The difference between the two is that Khorat Thai is not identified with Lao, as Educated Paktay is with Paktay. The intelligibility of the two with Standard Thai may be the same, but the identity of one is Thaiklang, the other not. The first case brings intelligibility with Thaiklang into one of the dialects of the regional language, the other expands Thaiklang.

The area in which Khorat Thai is spoken is growing. It is steadily, if slowly, moving eastward across Buri Ram Province, absorbing primarily Northern Khmer as it goes. The border shown in maps II.1 and 9.1 should be interpreted as consisting of pockets and tongues of Lao, Northern Khmer and Khorat Thai interpenetrating each other. Varying percentages of Thaiklang and Northern Khmer vocabulary, as against Lao, are used in the border zones (Vichin 1985). A similar situation may also exist on the northern edge of the Thaiklang region in Laplae District, Uttaradit Province, this time with Kammüang phonology and Thaiklang vocabulary (Norman A. Mundhenk personal communication).

As a result of such Thaiklang spread, and except for the diversity of languages to be found in the cities, the central region has fewer different language groups than the north or northeast.

Summary

Paktay in the southern panhandle of Thailand differs from Kammüang and Lao in having a much more fully normalized variety of Educated Paktay along with its more typical multiple varieties of Rural Paktay. Educated Paktay generally has the vocabulary of Standard Thai, but the tones of Paktay. It is mutually intelligible with Standard Thai but is classified as Paktay by native speakers and outsiders alike, for whom tone is the most salient categorizing feature. Rural Paktay is not mutually intelligible with Standard Thai and many rural people cannot understand Educated Paktay either.

Thaiklang is the regional language out of which Standard Thai is formed. It differs from the other regional languages, therefore, in being mutually intelligible with Standard Thai. It has numerous dialects distinguished largely by tone, with some differences of other sounds and vocabulary as well. The Thaiklang region is slowly spreading into each of the other regions through processes of language change along its borders.

Part III

Marginal Regional Languages
Introduction

The four major regional languages described in earlier chapters do not completely fill the political boundaries of Thailand (map II.1). The leftover areas are occupied by people speaking marginal regional languages, dominant within their regions because they are used by speakers of other languages for wider communication within those areas. Thus they have some similarities to the major regional languages, but on a smaller scale (map III.1). Estimates of their respective populations are

Northern Khmer	1,100,000
Pattani Malay	1,000,000
Sgaw	252,000
Tai Yai	40,000
Phlow	40,000

Marginal regional languages are different from the major regional languages in other ways as well. They are not as conspicuous to the rest of the country, and their character as regional languages has not been frequently noticed or well understood. They tend to be lumped with the "minority languages," which statistically they are, but they differ in important ways from other categories of languages to be described later. They are sometimes thought of as "trade languages," but they differ from strictly trade languages like Lahu or Yunnanese Mandarin Chinese precisely because they have a regional base.[1]

With one exception, marginal regional languages are not Tai languages either. Tai Yai (Shan), the exception, is as different from the other Tai languages, roughly, as the major regional languages are from each other. The remaining marginal regional languages, however, are not descended from Proto-Tai at all. To be sure, they share many grammatical characteristics common to the whole area, some vocabulary, and elements of a similar semantic structure, but the communication distance between them and the Tai languages is large.

115

Map. III.1. Locations of marginal regional languages.

The marginal regional languages, furthermore, are not in the mainstream of Thai life. The people who speak some of them are geographically isolated, often even more limited educationally than typical speakers of regional languages. The differences among languages lower than the regional languages are also widely ignored by the general Thai population, who tend to lump the Sgaw and the Phlow, for example, with the Hmong and other groups as 'hill tribes' /chaaw khǎw/ even though they are significantly different. Even the valley-dwelling, Tai-speaking Tai Yai are sometimes called a "hill tribe."

Finally, marginal regional languages are another step down in the hierarchy of communication networks in the country (fig. II.1). For speakers of the major regional languages Standard Thai is the language of wider communication within Thailand beyond the region. Speakers of marginal regional languages potentially have two languages of wider communication: the nearest major regional language, which gives them communication channels into the major region near which they are situated, and Standard Thai. They, in turn, dominate languages below them in the hierarchy in their region.

Geography helps to isolate some marginal regional languages. Most people who speak the major regional languages as their mother tongues live primarily in easily accessible valleys and on the plains, although the number of exceptions in the mountains is growing as population pressures increase. But two marginal regional languages, Sgaw and Phlow, are spoken primarily in the mountains running along the Myanmar border for half the length of the country, including the river valleys and flatlands within those mountain ranges as well.

Although the people who speak Tai Yai and Pattani Malay, are not mountain peoples, intervening mountains and jungles nevertheless formerly helped to shield many of them from intensive contact with Kammüang- and Paktay-speaking people respectively, and therefore helped to preserve Tai Yai and Pattani Malay as marginal regional languages.

The exception to geographical isolation among those languages is Northern Khmer in northeastern Thailand. The primary area in which it is spoken is neither mountainous nor shielded from the rest of Thailand by mountains. On the contrary, it is somewhat separated from related dialects in Cambodia by a mountain range, jungle, and sparsely settled territory.

Marginal regional languages are classified as "marginal" because they extend into Thailand as fringes of larger groups on the other side

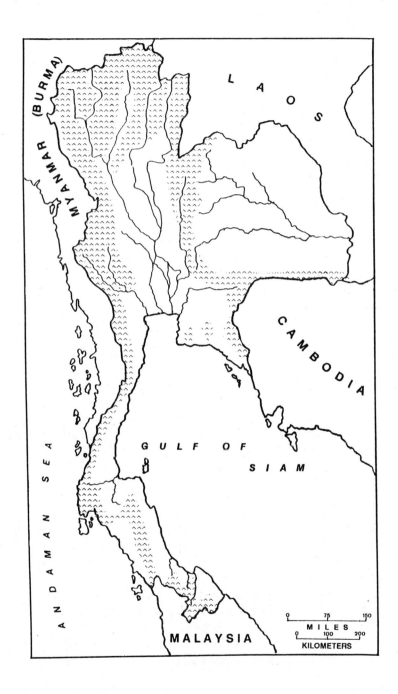

Map. III.2. Mountains and rivers of Thailand.

of the border where they are located. In two cases they are linguistically closely related to the dominant groups in neighboring nations, Northern Khmer to Khmer (Cambodian) and Pattani Malay to Malay in Malaysia. In the other cases they are related to people who are dominant in neighboring border areas of Myanmar although not in that country as a whole. This marginal character is functionally very different from the overlap of Lao between Thailand and Laos, where the overwhelming majority of the speakers are in Thailand, not Laos.

Such marginality is significant to the issue of linguistic diversity and national unity, especially in the case of Pattani Malay (chap. 10). Some Thai also imagine it to be significant in the case of Sgaw (chap. 8). Each marginal regional language tests or illuminates Thailand's unity within diversity in a different way.

8

Tai Yai (Shan), Sgaw (Karen), Phlow (Karen), plus Non-regional Phlong (Karen)

Tai Yai (Shan)

Directly north of Thailand lie the Shan States of Myanmar, where Tai Yai (Shan) speakers are the most numerous, politically most important, and culturally most dominant people. Tai Yai communities and individuals overlap also into adjacent parts of northern Thailand, and in the extreme northwest corner of the country they are again the most numerous and culturally dominant group. Speakers of some other languages in that area therefore use Tai Yai as a language of wider communication, which makes Tai Yai a marginal regional language (map III.1).

The communication distance between Tai Yai and Kammüang or between Tai Yai and Standard Thai is much like the distance between the major regional languages and Standard Thai. Some differences are due to vocabulary borrowed from different sources, Tai Yai having had centuries of contact with Burmese and other languages in Myanmar. Others include Tai Yai tone patterns and other sounds which do not fully match those of Kammüang and Thaiklang.

Tai Yai-speaking people have a long writing tradition with a script based on Burmese. Many ambiguities and other difficulties plagued that traditional system, however, especially as tones were not represented. Beginning in 1955 an orthographic reform was introduced in Myanmar, and many books have been converted into the new system in the Shan States. Some men and boys learn one or another of the scripts as novices in the temple. Other boys and girls learn them as students in school.

In Thailand the Tai Yai writing system is used primarily to record traditional healing activities and other traditional lore. In some villages practitioners use it to prepare and prescribe herbal medicines, diagnose illness, and determine auspicious and inauspicious days (Durrenberger 1983:120).

Tai Yai is still vigorous as an individual language, but its role as a regional language may be weakening. Kammüang, the neighboring major regional language, is penetrating ever more deeply into the Tai Yai area along with new roads and other means of communication. Use of Standard Thai is also increasing, spread by the schools and media. In the hills of the Tai Yai region and extending considerably to the south of it, Sgaw (Sgaw Karen) is another competing regional language.

Aside from its marginality, size and remoteness from the rest of the country, there is little to distinguish Tai Yai from the major regional languages. This additional Tai language does not present significant new issues to linguistic diversity and national unity.

Karen Marginal Regional Languages

Other than English, with its specialized roles, all of the languages discussed in this book so far have been Tai languages. Among them, Standard Thai is diligently promoted by the central government and the educational system. English is sustained in part by a major civilization of world scope and by powerful economic and political bases elsewhere. Now we begin to think about the roles of the many other languages which are not Tai and in most cases are not undergirded by such powerful external forces.

We begin at the northern half of Thailand's western boundary, shared with the Kayah and Karen states in Myanmar, where the majority of the people speak Karen languages. Several of these overlap also into Thailand as marginal languages there. Some of them, like Keyeh and Pa-O (Taungthu) are not regional languages, however, because they do not dominate other languages across any region (part 4). They are spoken by small groups in western Mae Hong Son Province, with Pa-O also to be found in western Kanchanaburi Province.

But Sgaw, with the largest population of any Karen language in Thailand, is a marginal regional language in part of the area where it is spoken. In addition, a language called Pwo Karen in Myanmar is related to at least two different languages in Thailand. One of these, Phlow (Pwo Karen), is a marginal regional language through at least some of the area where it is spoken, while the other, Phlong (Pwo Karen), is a marginal language, almost an enclave language (part 4).

The Karen are called /karìaŋ/ in Thaiklang/Standard Thai, and /yaaŋ/ in Kammüang. Writers often use the generic term "Karen" or its Thai equivalent no matter which of the Karen languages is spoken by the group they are discussing. Linguistically this is something on the order of lumping French, Spanish, Portuguese, and Italian people together as "Romance," as in "the Romance live in Western Europe." The reader cannot always be sure whether an author is using "Karen" generally for the range of people speaking various Karen languages, or whether she is substituting it for the name of one particular linguistic or ethnic group such as the Sgaw.

Unlike "Romance," however, "Karen" does reflect a genuine ethnolinguistic grouping, not just a linguistic one. Many Karen think of themselves as being Karen as against non-Karen on one level of their identity. The meaning of this identity varies among the particular kinds of Karen and according to circumstances. One reason why Karen attempts at gaining independence in Myanmar have been fragmented is that local identities are strongest. People tend to act as members of small local groups or followers of a local leader, not as Karen against Burmese (Kunstadter [ed.] 1967:76-77, after Lehman 1967).

Contact between Karen-speaking and Kammüang-speaking peoples began in the late eighteenth century in northern Thailand, when Northern Thai kingdoms had relations with Karen principalities in Kayah State. Some Karen people also came to work in the teak lumber business in Thailand while others were forcibly rounded up from Myanmar to live in undersettled areas of the country. Sgaw and Phlong Karen also began moving into the mountains of the western border region under the domain of the northern kingdoms, especially the kingdom of Chiang Mai (Keyes 1979b:36-44).

Farther south, Karen peoples began to come into contact with the people of central Thailand at about the same time. By 1872 Karen descendants of war captives were living far from the Myanmar border on the eastern side of central Thailand, in the mountains between the central plains and the northeastern plateau. The people of central Thailand were also fighting the Burmese during that period, which brought their armies into contact with Karen in the mountains that divided the two countries. Later, because of disturbances within Myanmar, more Sgaw, Phlow, and Phlong settled in the border regions of Thailand (Keyes 1979b:44-45).

Over this long period of contact, these three Karen groups in Thailand have developed a stable relationship with their dominant Tai-speaking neighbors, as well as with the other peoples of the area. Many Thai officials and members of the public farther away, however, are sometimes disturbed by their presence. They apply a "hill tribes" label to Karen, with mistaken implications. In the popular Thai stereotype "hill tribes" raise opium and destroy the forests, but neither opium production nor destruction of the forest through agricultural methods is historically characteristic of the Karen peoples. Of those living in the mountains, many do clear patches of the forest to plant their crops, but theirs has traditionally been the stable, non-destructive, ecologically regenerative "short cultivation, long fallow" system (chap. 13; Keyes 1979a:14-16).

Then again, Karen peoples have been in revolt against the Burmese ever since World War II. Military activity near the border increases and decreases, with Thai newspapers regularly carrying stories of the fighting. Some Thai are therefore afraid that the Karen in Thailand will also revolt, although there has never been any hint of any such inclination.[1]

Some Thai interpret the insurrection in Myanmar as Christian Karen fighting Buddhist Burmese, and fear a repeat in Thailand. They overlook the fact that Christians are a small minority among the Karen peoples—10% in Myanmar, less in Thailand (Hovemyr 1989: 26)—and that Buddhist Karen are also fighting the Burmese, as are Buddhist Shan (Tai Yai), a people among whom there are virtually no Christians.

The Thai perception that the Karen are Christians may be due to the fact that although Karen Christians remain a small minority, they do tend to be more conspicuous to Thai people than many Buddhist or animist Karen. They tend to be the best-educated Karen, are the most literate, and have the most conspicuous institutions such as churches; and many live in more accessible villages, towns and cities, where they interact with the Northern Thai population and Thai officials (Hovemyr 1989:9-10).

But circumstances and relationships have been entirely different for the Karen in Myanmar and Thailand. In spite of many problems with the Thai bureaucracy and strained relationships due to overpopulation in the areas in which they live, Karen peoples who still have contacts across the border consider themselves much better off in Thailand than they would be in Myanmar, complaining that they were looked down upon and mistreated by the Burmese (Benjamin Rittiwongsakul personal communication; Kunstadter 1979:148).

Sgaw

The Sgaw (Sgaw Karen, Skaw Karen) constitute the largest Karen group in Thailand, probably numbering 250,000. Sgaw regional language status is due primarily to speakers of Lavüa' (Lua', Lawa) languages, who often use Sgaw as a language of wider communication (chap. 15). Some Hmong people in the hills also use it (Benjamin Rittiwongsakul personal communication).

Sgaw's role may be seen vividly in the Mae Sariang District of Mae Hong Son Province, where different communities speak Sgaw, a Lavüa' language, a Chinese language or languages, Tai Yai, and Kammüang, respectively. The town of Mae Sariang is about half Sgaw, making Sgaw the largest language group in town. Sino-Thai and Indian/Pakistani merchants speak it to the townspeople who know it and to people coming in from the hills. Even clerks in the banks need Sgaw to deal with some of their customers (Benjamin Rittiwongsakul personal communication).

Twenty years ago bilingualism with Kammüang or Thai was spotty among Sgaw speakers (Kunstadter 1964:15, 16). Now Kammüang and Standard Thai are known much more widely. Many Sgaw have found that life is much easier when some people in the family can speak, read and write Standard Thai, and can communicate with officials. Among them, Sgaw adults who have worked for logging companies, or as day laborers, or who hire out the labor of their elephants, sometimes speak Standard Thai or Kammüang or both. People in one Sgaw village near Mae Sariang speak good Standard Thai. Many parents there and elsewhere send their children to school because they want them to become teachers and other kinds of government workers with regular salaries.

Many Sgaw people in Myanmar under the British had considerable education in English, Burmese or Sgaw. In Thailand, some Sgaw were among the first of the borderland minority peoples in the north to want a Thai education, and are educationally the most advanced at the present time (Rekha Thongsawadi personal communication), largely due at the beginning to Christian mission hostels and other church programs in support of Thai education (Keyes 1979a:21). A Thai education is prized in the Sgaw church, and whereas the church uses the Sgaw language, and has the Bible and other religious materials in Sgaw, Thai literacy and Thai education open other horizons to those who seek it, spurred by values encouraged in the church.

One effort to bring Thai education to children in the hills around Mae Sariang, for example, was a children's hostel started by the American Baptist Mission in the mid-1950s. It was run by a remarkable Sgaw refugee couple from Myanmar, the late Benjamin and Lah Say Rittiwongsakul.[2] Some of their former wards are headmasters, teachers, agricultural extension workers, clerks, and businesspeople. The majority are carrying out these tasks back in the hills, where they are better able to tolerate the minimal modern conveniences than are their Tai-speaking colleagues from the valleys (Benjamin Rittiwongsakul personal communication).

In the earlier days, children knew no Kammüang or Standard Thai whatsoever when they first came to the hostel, but more recently the majority had been to school in Standard Thai in the hills for several years before continuing in Mae Sariang. In Mae Sariang they learn to play in Kammüang, and quickly reach a point where it is one of the languages they use regularly in town. Standard Thai, however, comes harder. Children with no previous knowledge of it require about two years in school, whether in town or earlier in the village, before they can understand. Children who went to school in their village before coming to Mae Sariang usually have to drop back a grade because their Standard Thai is not good enough to handle schoolwork at the grade level they had reached in the village (Benjamin Rittiwongsakul personal communication).

Sgaw itself has been written for over 150 years. In fact, two rival systems are used in Thailand, and a minority is literate in each. The primary system was developed in 1832 by Jonathan Wade, a missionary in Myanmar. Based on the Burmese script, it represents efficiently the Sgaw speech of the Moulmein area (Jones 1961:v; Smalley 1976a:4-5). It works well in Thailand also, despite differences of dialect. The second system is a roman one developed by Joseph Séguinotte in 1954 (Smalley 1976a:5).

These systems are used primarily by Christian Sgaw, Protestants and Catholics respectively. Christian missionaries and Sgaw church leaders have produced the bulk of the literature in both systems as well.

Phlow (and Phlong)

Phlow (Pwo Karen) is a marginal regional language near the Myanmar border in Kanchanaburi Province (Stern 1965), and perhaps in other parts of the border area. Another dialect (or another very closely related language) is to be found in Phetchaburi and Ratchaburi provinces (Anderson 1987) but is probably not regional in function there. In addition, Phlong /phlôn/ or /phlôn syù/,[3] also generally called Pwo Karen by others, is spoken in scattered areas of the north, where it is not regional because speakers of other languages do not normally learn it as adults. Together Phlow and Phlong constitute a close language cluster in Thailand, part of the Karen category, itself a larger, more inclusive language cluster.

The Pwo were not exclusively and perhaps not even primarily a mountain-dwelling people in Myanmar. In the early part of the century, at least, many lived near the seacoast or in river valleys (Marshall 1922:1; Stern 1979:64), in symbiotic relationship with the Mon peoples, who had a more complex culture (Keyes 1979b:30). And although the Phlow do inhabit the western mountains in central Thailand, they often cultivate wet-rice fields in the valleys of those mountains, as well as dry rice on the mountain slopes (chap. 13).

The Phlow in Thailand, like their relatives in Myanmar, had extensive contacts with the Mon (chap. 13), and many follow the Mon form of Buddhism. By 1826 the Phlow were engaged with the Mon in finding and trading forest products and in producing cotton and cotton cloth, taking their trade goods by raft to Bangkok (Stern 1979:66).

Otherwise, they were isolated by distance, jungle and rugged territory from the Thai in central Thailand. In the mid-1830s, however, Phlow district officers were put in charge of the area by the Thai government, were awarded Thai titles, and were made responsible to the governor of Kanchanaburi Province. The last such Phlow official in a system of Thai indirect rule retired in 1924 (Stern 1979:66-67).

Although the Phlow are no longer as isolated as they were in the nineteenth century and the first half of the twentieth century in Thailand, they remain a truly marginal people, between two worlds. Stern describes how the Phlow in Thailand argue about which of two words for 'cup' or 'table' is the "real" Phlow word, one actually having been borrowed from Mon or Burmese, and the other from Thai. And such a term as 'customs duties' is in part a Burmese borrowing and in part Thai (Stern 1979:67).

The population of the small district center of Sangkhla Buri epitomizes the linguistic complexity of the western border regions of the country. It has speakers of Phlow (one-quarter of the population), Pa-O (another Karen language), Mon (chap. 13), Lao, Thaiklang and Standard Thai (Stern 1965; Stern 1979:69, 73-78). In this population the Standard Thai-speaking group is an administrative and professional elite with roots elsewhere, although a few people are permanent residents. The Lao came from Laos about seventy-five years ago.

In this town, where Phlow is not even the majority language, it "enjoys a particular linguistic dominance," so that even some Lao sometimes speak it at home, and some Thai officials who have been there long enough have picked up a smattering of it (Stern 1965:12; Stern 1979:78). Phlow-speaking people constitute a much larger percentage of the people living on the mountain slopes away from the rivers. It would seem that if Phlow has this regional language position in Sangkhla Buri itself, it likely does for considerable distances to the north and south as well.

The Phlow have long accepted Thai schools, and in the past the chief deterrent to elementary education was the distance from school (Stern 1965). Parents would strain their resources to send children to school if they could. In 1965 Phlow children made up 50% of the school population of Sangkhla Buri, although they were only 27% of the actual number of school-age children in town (Stern 1979:76). Opportunities for education are greater now.

The Phlow have other types of contact with the Thai as well. Thai officialdom, lumber operations, mines, and dam construction have all had their influence. Under these circumstances, and with the increase of Standard Thai and Lao languages, it is difficult to know whether or not the Phlow language will keep its regional function, or for how long.

Pwo Karen is written in three different writing systems in Myanmar, each over a hundred years old. All of them are found in the Sangkhla Buri area as well, although none of them is widely used there. The first system was the mission script developed by Francis Mason. It was adapted from the Burmese-based system developed for Sgaw by Jonathan Wade, and underwent various revisions.

A second script is believed to have been developed by Phu Ta Mai, a Pwo Karen Buddhist monk, who was stimulated by his monastic contacts with Mon clergy. This monastic script is used primarily for secular purposes, although largely by monks (Stern 1968a:2).

The third Phlow writing system is associated with a messianic Buddhist sect among the Phlow called the Leke (Marin 1943; Stern 1968b). This script seems so unusual and appears so complicated that it is called "chicken-scratch writing" by those who do not know it (Stern 1968a:2).

On the other hand, the closely related Phlong in southern Mae Hong Son, Chiang Mai, and Lamphun provinces, where their language is not a marginal regional language, find the language of books written in the mission script in Myanmar all but unintelligible. They do not use any of the three scripts described above, but a few people use a Thai-based writing system revised from Cooke, Hudspith, and Morris (1976).

Phlong-speaking people in the north have long lived side by side with Kammüang-speaking people in the wide river valleys, and now roads extend through to many of their mountain villages as well. Acculturation to northern Thai ways and the use of Kammüang are considerably greater in the valleys than in the mountains, but are everywhere rapidly increasing. In Lamphun, Lampang, and Phrae provinces, valley villages are often nominally Buddhist, in contrast to the non-Buddhist traditional spirit religions of the Karen in general (Truxton 1958:67).

Many Phlong children in formerly remote areas now go to school, as the government is paying more attention to the needs of minority peoples. Multilingualism has increased and is reinforced by the radio, on which people prefer Kammüang programs over Standard Thai because the generally elegant variety of Standard Thai used is too difficult.

Roots in Myanmar, marginal role, different language family, people of a different culture—from the perspective of the typical Thai these three Karen languages stand out as the most extreme instances of diversity among languages discussed so far. It might be well, therefore, to note Stern's concluding remarks (1965:13):

This is not to say that the Karen in village and town do not consider themselves Thai citizens. They pay their taxes and register their irrigated lands; they were well represented among the volunteer detachment recently trained; and their houses commonly display pictures of Their Majesties. While they may sympathize with the Free Karen in their struggle against Burma, there are few, indeed, that would see their future in a Karen State. What they want instead is more of the advantages which Thailand can offer them.

The Karen Village of Huay Tom

One Karen village is not at all typical, but nevertheless illustrates some of the dynamics of maintenance and change in language use by different groups in Thailand. It is the village of Huay Tom in southern Lamphun Province, south of Chiang Mai.

Since 1935, a Sgaw-speaking northern Thai Buddhist monk by the name of Ba Chai Wong Sa Phatthana, or Ba Wong, has regularly visited Karen villages, both Sgaw and Phlong, in the provinces of Chiang Mai, Lamphun, Tak and Mae Hong Son. He preaches and teaches Buddhism and Thai values, and has developed a considerable following. Huay Tom is Ba Wong's center, where he has his temple and where a community of over three thousand people has been formed. In 1982 85% of the school children were Sgaw, 14% Phlong, and 1% Northern Thai. Sgaw predominates in Huay Tom in spite of the fact that this village is on a plateau inhabited mostly by Northern Thai, and that the Karen population in the province is primarily Phlong. There are teachers, doctors, and other Thai and Northern Thai professionals in the village in addition to Ba Wong.

In Huay Tom the Phlong language is used only by Phlong people, who speak Sgaw to other Karen.[4] Thus the regional language role of Sgaw in the northwestern part of Thailand extends into this rather atypical village outside the Sgaw region. How people rated their ability to use Sgaw, alone or in combination with Kammüang and Standard Thai, is shown in fig. 8.1. More males were able to use languages other than Sgaw than were females, the majority of whom could not speak any Tai language.

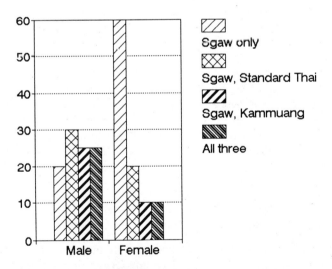

Fig. 8.1. Monolingualism and multilingualism among male and female Sgaw native speakers in Huay Tom (after Yawalak 1984).

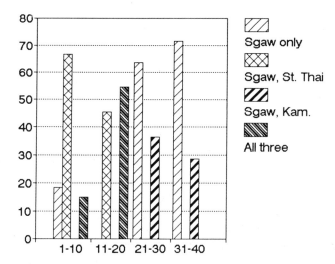

Fig. 8.2. Monolingualism and multilingualism among Sgaw native speakers in Huay Tom, by age category (after Yawalak 1984:34).

Figure 8.2 shows that multilingualism in Huay Tom is related to the age of the speaker. No one between the ages of eleven and twenty is monolingual, for example; the majority in that age group speak all three languages. The minority speaks only Sgaw and Standard Thai. On the other hand, education alone accounts for knowledge of Standard Thai in Huay Tom. Nobody over twenty-one speaks Standard Thai at all, due to an earlier lack of educational opportunity.

When asked what language they would speak to a government official who knew Sgaw, the people interviewed in Huay Tom answered as in figure 8.3. Some such officials with Sgaw background do live in the area, and considerably fewer people would speak Standard Thai exclusively to them than were able to do so. Even those with four to six years of education would prefer to speak Sgaw or Sgaw along with Standard Thai. Only 10% of students over ten years old used Sgaw as well as Standard Thai with teachers, however, but 38.8% of students ten or under used both.

Also of significance to the issue of individual identity in a culturally mixed situation was people's preference to be classified as Sgaw or Thai (fig. 8.4). Few people over twenty wanted to be classified as Thai only, but almost half under that age did.

Thai publications are generally of more interest than Sgaw publications to people in the village of Huay Tom, although someone does

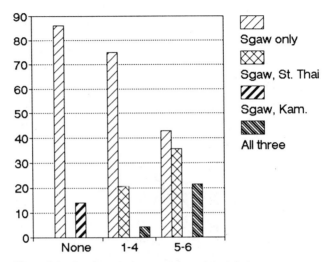

Fig. 8.3. Preferred languages when speaking with a government official who can speak Sgaw, by education, in percentages (after Yawalak 1984:49).

₃ach Sgaw writing to children. Written materials available in Sgaw re limited. The government Sgaw language radio broadcasts are not f much interest in this community either, partly because the dialect is

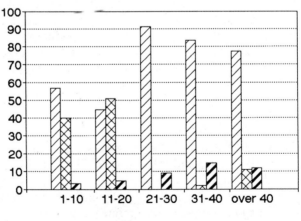

Fig. 8.4. Preferred ethnic labels among Sgaw native speakers in Huay Tom, by age category (after Yawalak 1984:85).

different. Younger people turn on Thai radio programs, however, especially for their music.

Thus Huay Tom provides a case study of a Karen village which has been in intensive contact with Kammüang and Standard Thai for a short time. It is not typical for several reasons, particularly because of a charismatic Northern Thai leader who molds the character of the village and who has drawn around him a group of self-selected people who want what he has to offer. Nevertheless, Sgaw's regional language function is maintained, although we do not know whether or not marginal ties to the other side of the border are still active. Kammüang plays its role as the regional language, and so does Standard Thai as the language of contacts outside the region, and with teachers or doctors or government officials when the regional languages will not suffice. The village is becoming trilingual, but it is too early to tell what stable linguistic interrelationship will ultimately result.

Official Status of the Karen-speaking Peoples in Thailand

In spite of the fact that ancestors of some of the Karen-speaking peoples came to Thailand two hundred years ago or more, some Sgaw, Phlow and Phlong have ambiguous status in the country. Their situation is complicated by new arrivals from Myanmar each year, so that government officials do not always know how to distinguish old residents from new immigrants.

The valley-dwelling or town-dwelling people among the Karen have the least difficulty in some ways. Many own land or have employment, have been registered as citizens, and carry identity cards. But because people speaking the same languages in the mountains are "hill tribes" by government category, they are sometimes assumed to be recent immigrants, even illegal aliens, and therefore cannot be registered as citizens (Keyes 1979a:17).

Some people whose births were duly registered and so should be counted as Thai citizens still have trouble. Names of people from hill villages were often incorrectly recorded in district office records, and any irregularity can hold up registration of their land or their appointment as civil servants (Kunstadter 1979:148-149). When such unregistered mountain Karen do laboriously prepare the more level areas of land along the streams for irrigated rice they sometimes lose those fields to Northern Thai people from the valley, who defraud them by simply registering the Karen-cleared land in their own names.

On the other hand, some Thai officials have been genuinely concerned for Karen-speaking peoples and have helped them. Central Thai and Northern Thai teachers have taken Karen children from the mountains into their homes so they could attend school at higher levels than are available in their villages (Rekha Thongsawadi personal communication). Tai language-speaking medical and agricultural workers and teachers in the mountains have sometimes befriended the local villagers. Many officials, furthermore, have deliberately not enforced a law prohibiting cultivation of land in the hills because they know the mountain peoples have no alternative to such agriculture (chaps. 13, 14).

But above all it is the King who is the conscience of Thailand when it comes to the poor, the backward, the remote peoples of the country. He is genuinely the king of the Sgaw and the Phlow and the Phlong as well as of the Lao and the speakers of Kammüang and Thaiklang. His money, his example, his personal attention have made a huge difference, to the point even of creating resentment among some Thai, who feel that he is doing too much for non-Tai poor.

In some ways the problems of the Karen peoples and other minorities in Thailand are little different from those of poor peoples considered "Thai" in a narrower sense, however. The whole peasant agricultural sector of the country is suffering. Everybody has to deal with corrupt officials. All low-status people are subject to contempt and exploitation. Injustices are common in Bangkok and the surrounding plains as well as in the mountains of Mae Hong Son Province. But the marginality of the Karen and their lack of "Thainess" does multiply the hardships.

There is no racism, as such, involved. The barriers are communication, inability to cope with the Thai world, lack of knowledge of the Thai way of doing things, lack of resources, lack of power, and wrong perceptions on the part of people in more powerful positions. Some of these problems can be corrected by language use and education. Even the lack of resources may be somewhat less significant when education and communication make other alternatives possible.

But although marginality is sometimes an uncomfortable position, few Karen are giving up their Karen language as they take on others. Sgaw are Sgaw and speak Sgaw under some circumstances. They are Karen in other circumstances, although they do not have a corresponding Karen-wide language.

In some cases they are almost Northern Thai, and many speak Kammüang under appropriate circumstances.

More and more they are Thai, and many speak Standard Thai when that is required.[5]

And, ironically, a few older Sgaw people who came as refugees from Myanmar, who had their high-school education during the British colonial years, and are now living in remote towns like Mae Sariang, speak better English, by international communication standards, than most university-educated Thai. But although their English and Burmese are good, and their Thai is only passable, they are neither British nor Burmese. They are Sgaw; they are Karen; and now they are Thai, whether they have citizenship papers to show it or not.

Summary

The smaller three (out of the five) marginal regional languages in Thailand are Tai Yai, Sgaw and Phlow. The first of these is a Tai language, the latter two Karen, an unrelated language family. These three languages overlap from Myanmar, but in no case does this marginality create a base for disunity within Thailand.

In spite of serious weaknesses, even injustices in Thai treatment of such minority peoples, their speakers do not entertain serious resentment of the Thai government and people. They are not like speakers of the same or closely related languages in Myanmar, whose resentment toward the government of that country has been the basis for long-standing revolution. These languages fit their niches in the language hierarchy of Thailand with little friction in spite of extensive poverty among their speakers and neglect by the authorities.

9

Northern Khmer
plus Non-marginal Kuy

Across the country from Tai Yai, Sgaw, and Phlow lies the region in which Northern Khmer is spoken, another marginal regional language, but one with many more speakers than the three previous ones combined. The Northern Khmer region itself stretches along the Cambodian border, spanning much of the southern tier of the northeastern provinces (map III.1). No mountains shield it, and a railroad line has crossed it since early in the century, from which a network of roads now penetrates extensively into the countryside.

Nor does the Northern Khmer-speaking region have within it as many minor languages with small populations as do the Tai Yai and the Karen marginal regions. Instead, the closely related Kuy, with 275,000 speakers, is a sizable language, as minority languages in Thailand go. Standard Thai and Chinese languages (chap. 12) have their usual places (Suwilai 1986). The government has also opened up some tracts of land for farmers from other regions to resettle, along with local people, contributing to the language mix. Lao borders on and is intermingled with Northern Khmer on the north, and the Khorat Thai dialect of Thaiklang lies to the west. The regional role of Northern Khmer is thus maintained among sizable, important language populations.

The provinces of Buri Ram, Surin, and Si Sa Ket, in which Northern Khmer is primarily located, do experience major language encroachment, however. Bilingualism is increasing and assimilation is occurring, such as must have also taken place over much of the plains and valleys of Thailand as Tai languages worked their way through the country across the centuries.[1]

Northern Khmer

The Northern Khmer language /khəmɛɛr/ (/khaměen/ in Thai) is a mosaic of mutually intelligible dialects, with local differences all across the area. We do not know how far intelligibility extends into northern Cambodia. The border area in both countries is relatively sparsely populated and a mountain range with rather steep cliffs separates them at some points. Cross-border contacts certainly exhibit nothing of the intensity and significance that they have for the Pattani Malay population in southern Thailand (chap. 10).

Northern Khmer is apparently a different language from Standard Khmer (Cambodian). Khmer informants in the northeast uniformly reported difficulty in understanding Phnom Penh radio, with its vocabulary and sound differences.[2] So Northern Khmer seems to be in a decodable relationship to Standard Khmer rather than an intelligible one (chap. 17). But whether or not that is true, its speakers clearly identify with Thailand rather than with Cambodia. In their own words, the Northern Khmer-speaking people are "Thai who speak Khmer" (David Thomas personal communication).

Northern Khmer is not a Tai language, but belongs to the Mon-Khmer language family, another of the major widespread families of mainland Southeast Asia (chap. 17). It is also the first non-tonal language to be discussed in this book, aside from English.

Khmer-speaking peoples and Khmer civilization extended into much of what is now Thailand in the ninth and tenth centuries, before Tai-speaking peoples gained dominance. They have therefore probably lived where they are now for over a thousand years, although the populations may have been sparse (Jenner 1974, Paitoon 1984:50-51). Significant new Khmer migration came into the area in the eighteenth century as well.

Northern Khmer as a Regional Language

Maps 9.1-9.3 show most of the 1964 distribution of the populations under discussion. A distinction is made in them between solid core language areas and intermingled areas. In the latter, villages speaking different languages exist side by side, or communities of people in the same village/town are native speakers of different languages. Not shown are isolated individuals or families which are native speakers of other languages, often living in and near the towns. Nor do the maps show multilingualism, which is widespread.

Map 9.1 shows that Northern Khmer is spoken in almost all of Surin, more than half of Buri Ram, and half of Si Sa Ket provinces, and that it overlaps into Ubon Ratchathani and Roi Et, which were not surveyed. The solid core area is cut in two from north to south at

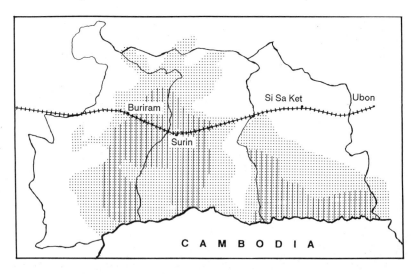

Map 9.1. Distribution of Northern Khmer in the survey area of northeast Thailand. Double shading shows the solid core areas where there is little intermingling of communities speaking other languages.

the Surin-Si Sa Ket border by the Kuy language, to be discussed later in this chapter. The other broken patch inside the solid core Northern Khmer area results from rapid new settlement, with communities of Thaiklang, Lao and Kuy intermingled with the comparatively sparse Khmer population already in southwestern Surin and southeastern Buri Ram.

Map 9.2 shows how the Lao and Thaiklang regional languages give way to Northern Khmer in this part of the northeast. Of course Lao is widely known in the Northern Khmer region, but is neither the internal language of communities nor the primary regional language through much of the region. As the nearby major regional language, Lao dominates Northern Khmer for communication outside the Northern Khmer area, however (fig. II.1). Undoubtedly the extent of territory with Lao communities is growing as well. Southwest Surin and south central Si Sa Ket, for example, were two areas where Lao communities were known to be increasing in 1964, due to government resettlement policies.

Of the three provinces, however, only in southwestern Buri Ram is any Thaiklang dialect solidly entrenched as a domestic language. This is the edge of the slowly expanding Khorat Thai dialect (chap. 7). Many individual native speakers of Thaiklang dialects, especially

Standard Thai, also live as minorities in other communities of the Northern Khmer region, most commonly in the provincial centers and along the railroad line. Schoolteachers and government officials who speak Standard Thai, often as a second language, are scattered as individuals through the whole area as well.

Northern Khmer is a regional language because in these provinces many native speakers of other languages, especially Kuy and the Chinese languages, need it for wider communication. It is not a regional language over all the area in which it is spoken, however. Around the edges lies a band where Lao or Thaiklang (Khorat Thai) is the regional language, and Northern Khmer is simply a marginal language (part 4). Likewise it is doubtless not a regional language for the populations which speak it in neighboring Ubon Ratchathani and Nakhon Ratchasima provinces. However, the territory where Northern Khmer does function as a regional language is larger than its solid core area alone.

In light of the distributions on maps 9.1 and 9.2, analyzed in relation to the underreported 1980 census, the 1989 Northern Khmer population would seem to be roughly 1.1 million. Although the Northern Khmer are a minority people in Thailand at large and in the northeast-

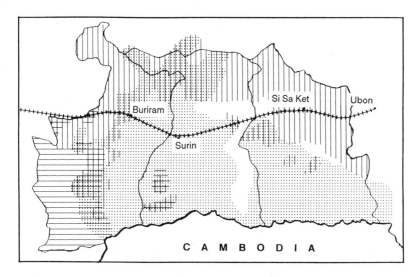

Map 9.2. Areas of Lao and Thaiklang interface with Northern Khmer in the survey area. Distribution of Lao communities is shown by vertical shading, that of Thaiklang by horizontal shading, and Northern Khmer by dots. Overlap in shading shows areas where communities speaking the respective languages are intermingled.

ern region, they are the large majority in much of these three provinces. They probably constitute the largest non-Tai, non-Chinese language population in Thailand.[3]

Given the size and importance of Northern Khmer in its own area, the population which speaks this language is remarkably invisible to the nation at large. Northern Khmer people fit so perfectly into the language hierarchy that they are not generally noticed even though theirs is not a Tai language. Their immediate Tai-speaking neighbors know about them, of course, but the Northern Khmer exhibit no linguistic competition, no Khmer nationalism, no secessionism. They live on the margin of the country and cause no problems, so they are largely ignored as being a separate people.

At least fifteen thousand other Khmer-speaking people (probably many more than that) live in Thailand besides those in these provinces and the immediately adjacent ones (1980 census). They presumably speak forms of Khmer different from Northern Khmer. Gainey and Theraphan (1977) report Khmer populations along the Cambodian border in southeastern Thailand and in scattered places elsewhere in the country,[4] but no form of Khmer is likely to be a regional language outside of these three provinces of the northeast.

Writing Systems

In older times Northern Khmer-speaking Buddhist monks in the northeast learned as many as four scripts for three languages, one for Khmer, two for Lao, and one for Thai. The sacred Khmer script, called Khom, also learned at the time by Thai in central Thailand, was used by the Northern Khmer for religious texts, magic formulas and protective tattoos. The Lao script was used for official Lao documents, and the sacred temple script was used for Lao religious texts. The Standard Thai script was learned largely in the towns and larger district centers (Paitoon 1984:164, 166-168). In 1964 we found little evidence of anyone reading Khmer at all, and written Standard Thai had become widespread.

A Thai-based writing system was devised for Northern Khmer in 1964 (Smalley 1976c), with occasional subsequent modifications, the most recent in 1987 (Thomas 1987; Suwilai et al. 1987; Suwilai and Sophana 1990). At a few points the system seems troublesome to the reader of Thai because the languages are different, but it remains workable, and some publications have been produced in it. These include a Northern Khmer wordbook (Institute 1986), conversation lessons for learning Northern Khmer (Kheuan, Suwilai, and Thomas 1984), a dictionary (Teel 1988), a health manual (Suwilai et al. 1988), some folktales (Kheuan 1987), and a variety of Christian religious materials. A dictionary by Dhanan and Chartchai (1978) uses a similar system.

Multilingualism among Northern Khmer Speakers

Figure 9.2 shows the increase in multilingualism among Northern Khmer-speaking people over the generations preceding our 1964 survey, as respondents reported their own languages and those of various relatives. We found more people to be quadrilingual than monolingual, speaking and/or understanding Kuy, Lao, and Standard Thai as well as Northern Khmer (fig. 9.1). The largest group was bilingual in Northern Khmer and Standard Thai, the second largest group trilingual in Northern Khmer, Standard Thai and Lao.

In these provinces, as elsewhere, competence in Standard Thai depends primarily on education, with travel outside the region often contributing significantly as well. Standard Thai occupies its special place as the language of the nation and is used by many people in the area when educated language is appropriate, especially at public dis-

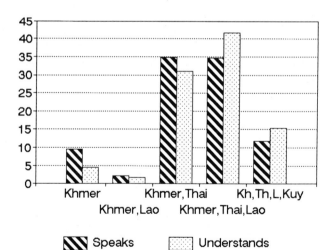

Fig. 9.1. Multilingual speaking abilities in Northern Khmer communities (after Smalley 1988b:399). Additional combinations of languages (Khmer-Lao-Kuy, Khmer-Thai-Kuy, and Other) each had less than 3.5%.

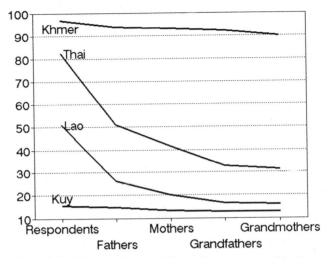

Fig. 9.2. Change in multilingualism among Northern Khmer over generations. The 2,409 respondents were asked what languages they spoke and what languages various relatives spoke (after Smalley 1988b:404).

tance (chap. 3). It also provides a way of communicating with people from outside the northeast.

How much Lao Northern Khmer-speaking people know, on the other hand, is based primarily on proximity to Lao-speaking areas orto some towns, or the railway, or the major roads. People in areas of considerable interpenetration sometimes need Lao as the language next up in the hierarchy, the immediate language of wider communication. Lao may be losing out to Standard Thai, on the other hand, among speakers of Northern Khmer more distant from the areas of Lao interpenetration, as education, TV, and radio provide greater exposure to the national language. In fact, a few Lao-speaking peoples in more solidly Northern Khmer areas actually learn Northern Khmer (David Thomas personal communication).

So pervasive and important is multilingualism that even jokes told by Northern Khmer-speaking people sometimes center around it, and reflect the language hierarchy:

It is expected that the Chinese merchants will know both Khmer and Thai, and it is expected that Khmers can speak Thai, so jokes about deficiencies in this direction are funny. But it is not expected that Thais will know Khmer, or that either Thais or Khmers will know Chinese, so jokes about them are

not noteworthy or funny. The language acceptability scale is Chinese →
Khmer → Thai. Kui [Kuy] is seldom mentioned, but would probably be
ranked with Chinese (i.e. below Khmer). Lao . . . is more often mentioned
and would seem to rank close to or perhaps just slightly higher than Khmer
(Thomas and Thomas 1982:94).

Education in Standard Thai

Even more multilingualism doubtless exists in the Northern Khmer
area at present than was found at the time of our survey, and is becoming increasingly characteristic of older people as well as younger
ones. In 1964 elementary schools with four grades had been established in almost every corner of this three-province area. As elsewhere in Thailand, however, education beyond four or six grades is
not available in village schools. Village children have the opportunity
for additional schooling only if they live near larger centers or can
move in with families living there.

The school is the most fundamental, grass-roots experience in
which the national language and national culture and values impinge
on the average Northern Khmer child. As elsewhere, the language of
instruction is Standard Thai, with no official difference in curriculum
from that used in other language areas. Unofficially, of course, teaching is inevitably affected when few of the pupils know the language of
instruction.

For the Thaiklang-speaking child on the central plains, schooling
means linguistic enrichment in the direction of the national language,
standardization, and the addition of a written medium and more
dimensions to the spoken language the child already knows. For the
Northern Khmer-speaking pupil, schooling means learning a new language which she or he does not yet speak at all. The Northern
Khmer-speaking teacher yields to this difference and makes explana-
tions in Northern Khmer to the children who do not understand.
Those teachers who are not Northern Khmer have to spend more time
getting pupils to understand, flounder longer, improvise more, until
such time as the children have learned enough Standard Thai to be
able to participate.

As one example of the difficulty, school children's ability to hear
the tones of the Thai language was sampled from third and fourth
graders whose native languages were Northern Khmer and Kuy, plus
Pattani Malay in southern Thailand, and compared with children from
Bangkok and vicinity whose native language was Standard Thai or

some other dialect of Thaiklang. The non-Thai-speaking children were almost exactly one year or grade poorer than Thai-speaking children in their ability to hear tones. That is, fourth graders were not statistically different from Thai-speaking children in third grade (Isara 1962).

Bilingual language jokes told by the Northern Khmer highlight the same problem by lampooning both the imperfect learning of tones exhibited by some people and the superiority felt by those who do master them (Thomas and Thomas 1982:91):

A Khmer came back from the big city boasting about how well he could now speak Thai. His admiring neighbors wanted to learn more Thai, so asked him,

"We have heard that the Thai use a word /maa/ ['come', mid tone]. Can you tell us what it means?"

"Yes, that's easy. It means /ckɛɛ/ ['dog']."

"Then how about /mǎa/ ['dog', rising tone]."

"That means /ckɛ̌ɛ/ ['dog']."

"And /máa/ ['horse', high tone]?"

"Oh, that's /ckɛ́ɛ/ ['dog']."

The average child eventually learns to speak Standard Thai rather fluently on a simple level, and to "read and write" in the sense of being able to handle the basic mechanics of the Thai writing system. Some, of course, go beyond that. Figure 9.3 shows the effect of the spreading school system over the decades preceding the 1964 survey. Schools are even more accessible now.

The literacy rates of the younger people shown in figure 9.1 look impressive, but they actually reflect school attendance better than they do functional literacy. Even more than in the Lao areas already discussed, to learn mechanical literacy skills does not necessarily lead to the continuing ability to read. An investigation of literacy in the northeast (Coordination Center 1965:11) found that people in a Northern Khmer-speaking area of Si Sa Ket Province had the lowest degree of comprehension of Thai written materials of any village surveyed. 78% could not comprehend the lowest level reading materials. After that, the next poorest reading comprehension was in Surin Province, in which half of the villages surveyed were Northern Khmer. The additional years of schooling available since then do make a difference, but even today the Northern Khmer region remains the area where students score the lowest on national tests in all of the country (Dorothy Thomas personal communication).

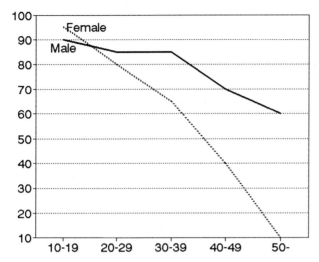

Fig. 9.3. Ability to read Thai, by age and sex, from self-reports in the 1964 survey, shown in percentages.

The Bureaucratic Hierarchy

Northern Khmer villages and village clusters (/tambon/ in Thai) generally have Northern Khmer headmen. All teachers and all officials higher than village cluster headmen are appointed from above, so that Thaiklang, Lao, Northern Khmer, and sometimes Kuy officials are usually mixed in the district centers. In 1964 the Northern Khmer were well represented at all levels, however, including the deputy governor of Surin Province. In 1986 the mayor of Surin, the district chief and the provincial governor were all Northern Khmer (David Thomas personal communication).

Thus, officials with whom villagers deal typically know Northern Khmer, and are not a primary stimulus to, or reinforcement for, multilingualism. On the district level the non-Khmer officials in government offices do contribute more to bilingualism, but many Northern Khmer officials work there also. The higher the level, and the more formal the situation, the more the feeling that Standard Thai is the appropriate language to use. But even so, Northern Khmer is the typical language a person will use in most government offices in Surin.

Travel

The railroad and the spreading network of roads which cross the region link it with such Tai-language provincial capitals as Si Sa Ket, Ubon Ratchathani and Nakhon Ratchasima, and with Bangkok. The Northern Khmer region is churning, and through their mobility thousands of people come into contact with speakers of other languages. Many people leave each year to work elsewhere, most of them coming back within five months. People also travel for pleasure, especially to places where relatives live.

Some people travel only to a nearby center like Surin, others farther along the railroad or bus line to other destinations in the southern part of the northeast. Still others go completely outside the area to Bangkok, Chon Buri (southeast of Bangkok), and Rayong (farther south than that). Although Northern Khmer-speaking people tend to cluster together when they leave the area, such trips stimulate multilingualism in ways already described for Lao.

Population Centers

Northern Khmer can be heard everywhere on the streets of the provincial capital of Surin as local people talk to each other in it most of the time. But even though Surin is a Northern Khmer city, numerous officials, teachers, and business people who are not speakers of Northern Khmer live there as well. The mixed population is an important stimulus to multilingualism, along with education, and most people in town can respond to outsiders normally in Standard Thai. Strangers are sometimes misled by this ready use of Standard Thai and do not realize the pervasiveness of the Northern Khmer language. The 1980 census was so far off that it recorded only 570 speakers who used Northern Khmer as the language of the home in the municipal area.

The function of the provincial centers in stimulating multilingualism, especially use of Standard Thai, is echoed in a more limited way in some district centers. In the solid core areas most individuals in district centers can speak Northern Khmer, but the few who do not sometimes force Northern Khmer speakers to use Standard Thai or Lao. In non-core areas usually one language is statistically predominant, but some people cannot use it or use it with difficulty, which again stimulates the Northern Khmer to use a higher language.

As is the custom with the Lao in much of the rest of the northeast, many Northern Khmer men live in their wives' villages after marriage. In most cases of intermarriage between native speakers of different languages, the husbands therefore tend to adopt the wife's language. Usually a person who marries into the village already speaks the language of the village and people forget that he or she was not originally from that language community.

Ease of Learning Another Language

For a speaker of Kuy to learn Northern Khmer, or vice versa, does not require a long period of contact. The languages are closely related, share much vocabulary, and have many predictable pronunciation correspondences (chap. 17). The sound systems are similar, although Kuy is complicated by "voice register," which Northern Khmer does not have (Johnston 1976, Theraphan 1985b).

For a speaker of Northern Khmer to learn a Lao dialect or Standard Thai is more difficult, however. Tai languages are not related to Northern Khmer, as Kuy is, or as Thaiklang and Lao are to each other. More divergence is to be found in grammar, and the basic vocabulary—as opposed to borrowed vocabulary—is quite different. Because the Tai languages are tone languages and Northern Khmer is not, when Northern Khmer-speaking people learn a Tai language they have to learn a type of sound system to which they are not accustomed.

On the other hand, some parts of the task are not so difficult. Tai-language vowel and consonant systems, for one thing, are generally simpler than those of Northern Khmer, so that aspect of pronunciation gives learners relatively little trouble.

Speakers of Khmer and Tai languages each recognize some vocabulary when they hear the other (chap. 17) because of mutual borrowing between them for centuries, or because of common borrowing from other languages like Sanskrit. Therefore, anyone who knows Standard Thai recognizes a significant proportion of the Northern Khmer vocabulary, even when reading texts about simple village activities (Smalley 1976c:76-83; Kheuan, Suwilai, and Thomas 1984). Such words common to both languages are often pronounced differently in each, but many of the differences are predictable because certain sounds in one language correspond quite regularly to certain other sounds in the other language. A large portion of the vocabulary is therefore fairly easy to learn.

National Identification

Northern Khmer-speaking people share the usual dissatisfaction with officialdom to be found elsewhere in provincial Thailand. Anti-government agitation has even occurred at times, fed by discontent in this economically depressed area. But unlike some Pattani Malay who have wanted to secede from Thailand (chap. 10) nobody thinks being part of Cambodia or having an independent Northern Khmer state would be an improvement.

On the contrary, Thailand has much more attraction for the Northern Khmer than do neighboring countries. Symptoms of national identification include a sense of belonging, the direction in which people habitually look for benefit and development, the direction of aspirations when young people want to rise above their village level, the language cultivated if people seek an education, and the communication ties people seek.

Northern Khmer is thus a marginal regional language, spoken by a large population, which fits into the language hierarchy of Thailand almost as neatly as though it were a Tai language. The area where it is spoken is an archetype of linguistic diversity and national unity, with its stratified situational multilingualism involving two major language families. In spite of the size of the Northern Khmer population and the pervasiveness of the use of the language, the lack of competitiveness between it and Tai languages and cultures is so complete that the diversity of the area virtually goes unnoticed except by local residents or outside specialists. And even such people often do not seem to sense how large and remarkable the phenomenon is.

Kuy, a Marginal Language

Kuy /kuuy/ (Suay) is not a marginal regional language, but marginal, because although it overlaps from neighboring countries, non-Kuy people do not normally learn it as adults. It therefore really belongs in a later chapter, but like Phlong in the last chapter it is included here because the region in which it is found cannot be discussed adequately without reference to it.

Map 9.3 shows the solid core areas for Kuy and areas of intermingled Northern Khmer and Kuy communities in 1964. Only a narrow strip of solid core Kuy remains, located in Surin Province, primarily at the Si Sa Ket border. The areas of interpenetration with Northern Khmer are especially revealing of historical processes, as they largely surround the main Northern Khmer solid core areas. Add

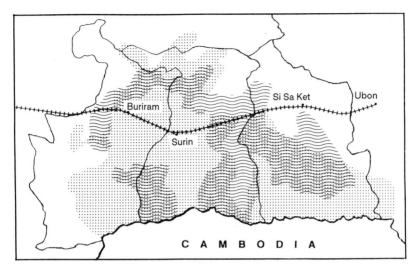

Map 9.3. Distribution of Kuy in relation to Northern Khmer. Kuy is shown by wavy shading. Overlap in shading shows areas where communities speaking the respective languages are intermingled.

to this the traditions which portray Surin and other Northern Khmer centers as former Kuy towns (Prasert 1978:iii-iv; Paitoon 1984:52), and the maps show the expansion of Northern Khmer at the expense of Kuy.

As the Northern Khmer population increased and grew in importance, Kuy speakers gradually switched to Northern Khmer over most of this territory. Seidenfaden (1952:178-179) made the comment that "the Khmer, unlike their Kuy cousins, do not give up their proper language." However, he noticed primarily the Kuy loss to Lao, although Kuy loss to Khmer itself may have been greater.

Ancestors of the Kuy may have been the aboriginal inhabitants of the area centuries before the Lao, long before the Khmer empire, as much as three thousand years ago (Paitoon 1984:46). Immigration from Laos increased the population in the seventeenth century. In the first part of this century Kuy stretched from Surin to the border of Laos (Seidenfaden 1952:181).

But although the Kuy-speaking area has shrunk with respect to both Khmer and Lao, the Kuy have not diminished in population. Seidenfaden (1952:159) estimated 100,000 in 1917. Johnston (1976: 259) estimated 150,000 in 1954. The present estimate is 275,000. Kuy people often have large families, as do other rural populations of

Thailand, so natural increase continues. Seidenfaden's (1952:156) prediction that "in another generation or two at the most there may be no Kui-speaking people left in the whole of Northeast Siam" was not just premature, it was wrong. Kuy is not at all an endangered language. It is today spoken by the largest number of people of any marginal—but not regional—language in Thailand (chaps. 13, 14). The Kuy population, however, is probably not increasing as fast as the rest of the population in the country because some communities are gradually becoming speakers of Northern Khmer and Lao.

The marginal language status of Kuy is due to a population overlap primarily from Cambodia (Schrock et al. 1970:1-2). Smaller populations also live in Laos, from where the most recent migration of Kuy supposedly came to Thailand in the seventeenth and eighteenth centuries, settling primarily in Surin Province (Prasert 1978:ii). But Kuy marginality is psychologically tenuous in Thailand. Kuy people have little memory of other Kuy in Laos, and no memory of those in Cambodia (Van der Haak personal communication).

Among the many dialects of Kuy (Prasert 1978:xix-xxiii), speakers of the two principal ones call themselves /kuuy/ and /kuay/, respectively (Van der Haak and Wykos 1987).[5] In Surin Province Kuuy is spoken in the area of Samrong Thap on the railroad line in the solid-core Kuy area near the Si Sa Ket border, and in patches elsewhere. Kuay is spoken to the south of that in Sangkha and Sikhoraphum districts and in patches to the northwest (Van der Haak and Wykos 1987, Beulah M. Johnston personal communication). It is not clear how far these dialects may be spoken beyond that.

A Thai-based writing system based on the Kuuy dialect has been designed (Johnston 1976), and a New Testament, some primers, and a small selection of Christian reading materials have been published in it. Kuuy people who can already read Thai learn to read the Kuy system very quickly, and some previously non-literate people have learned it also. A dictionary (Prasert 1978) records Kuy in a different Thai-based transcription.

Many Kuy use Northern Khmer, the next language up in the hierarchy, for wider communication, but that is not universal throughout this area. Around Samrong Thap, in the solid core area, they generally know Lao before they know Northern Khmer, if they know the latter at all.

On the other hand, although Kuy is a marginal language, low in the hierarchy, and not generally learned by people speaking languages above it, exceptions do occur. Merchants (usually Sino-Thai) do use it in Samrong Thap. A Kuy teacher married a man who is half Central Thai, half Chinese, but they speak Kuy in the home. A Central Thai woman married a Kuy man and in the space of two to three years claimed to have forgotten her Thai. She seemed to have become Kuy in speech and culture (Beulah M. Johnston personal communication). Individual needs, personalities and such circumstances as location influence culture change (chap. 18), and complicate the larger picture.

Trends and Possible Developments

Given the widespread and increasing multilingualism in the Northern Khmer region, some people ask, "How long will it be before the Northern Khmer (or the Kuy) disappear?" Put that way, the question is misleading. Rather, the issue is how long will it be before young people say, "Before my grandfather died he used to talk Khmer (or Kuy) with his old friends, but nobody knows it any more"? And in what language will they say it?

In answer to that question, Keyes (1967:8) made the following prediction:

In a linguistic sense if no other, the Lao have shown greater flexibility to absorb the Khmer with whom they have come into contact than have the Khmer the Lao. In consequence, the number of Khmer-speaking people remaining in the Northeast has slowly diminished to the present-day (1960) size of not more than half a million out of a total population of nine million. Even the remaining Khmer are bilingual and I would predict that their distinctiveness will also disappear in time.

It is true that over the last four hundred years Lao dialects have slowly replaced some languages and dialects closely related to Northern Khmer, and Northern Khmer itself in some areas. In fact, the whole expanse of the northeast probably contained people speaking Mon-Khmer languages before the Tai languages spread so widely. Thus the area in which Mon-Khmer languages is spoken has shrunk, although some other Mon-Khmer languages still remain in the northeast besides the ones we are discussing.

But shrinking territory does not necessarily mean shrinking population. Twice as many people speak Northern Khmer as their mother tongue in 1989 as did at the time of our 1964 survey. Nor is it unusual for minority languages to grow. Although many Native American (Indian) languages have died out, some others are spoken by many times more people than ever spoke them before the arrival of Europeans in the New World.

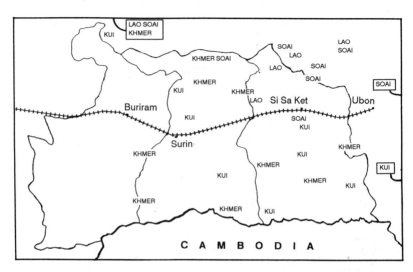

Map 9.4. Seidenfaden's map of Northern Khmer and Kuy in Surin and Si Sa Ket provinces, 1910 (Seidenfaden 1952). His spellings have been preserved.

A second qualification required of Keyes's statement is that the shrinkage of territory occupied by a language is easily exaggerated. Map 9.4 shows data from a 1910 map, made by Eric Seidenfaden, superimposed on the basic map of the three provinces used in this chapter. Seidenfaden's labels and spellings have been kept for eth-nolinguistic designations. Kui, Soai and Khmer Soai are subgroups of Kuy in his terminology. "Lao Soai" and "Khmer Soai" refer to acculturated Kuy groups which no longer used their ancestral Kuy language, or did not use it much.

How the area in which Kuy is spoken has shrunk with the expansion of Lao in this century may be seen by comparing this map with map 9.1. The Kuy area has shrunk significantly both to the north and to the east. Kuy is not a regional language, so it has less to bolster its existence, although it is still strong. Northern Khmer, a regional language, has been much more resistant to shrinking. The extent of Kuy shrinkage may be somewhat distorted in this comparison, however, because the 1964 survey did not reach into Ubon Province, where Seidenfaden indicated Kuy groups. Gainey and Theraphan (1977) also show communities there.

Seidenfaden's map does not include populations in Buri Ram, and Kuy, not Khmer, was the focus of his article, but eighty years later we find no evident shrinkage of the parts of the Northern Khmer-speaking area which he shows, except for one pocket to the north, off the map.

The multilingualism of the area, another of Keyes's points, has already been described, but does not in itself mean the disappearance of distinctiveness. Some populations in the world have been 100% multilingual for centuries. Multilingualism and ethnic consciousness are sometimes virtually the only distinctive features they have left.

The Northern Khmer-speaking population in Thailand is large, vigorous, and growing. The Kuy-speaking population is also relatively large and growing, but more slowly. Their distinctiveness could disappear within two hundred years, or even one hundred years, but that is doubtful, especially for Northern Khmer. For the foreseeable future the populations using these languages will probably continue to grow, and their multilingualism will continue to increase both in percentage of the population and in the quality of their use of the Tai languages. Increasingly more people will be able to participate in a full range of situational multilingualism. There is no indication that all children will cease to learn either the Northern Khmer or Kuy language within the next century although the respective territories may shrink somewhat because many individuals, families and villages on the edges may switch from the languages they speak now. At the point where enough children do cease to learn either of the languages it would become endangered (Kraus 1992:6).

Summary

Northern Khmer is the largest marginal regional language in Thailand. Together, it and Kuy—both Mon-Khmer languages rather than Tai—epitomize the strength of the lower ranks of Thailand's language hierarchy in its most perfect form. So well do these languages fit into the hierarchy that they go virtually unnoticed by the rest of the country. Northern Khmer, spoken by more than a million people, is inaudible to the rest of the people in Thailand until it is brought to their attention.

The area in which Northern Khmer is spoken has shrunk slightly over the past one hundred years, but the population speaking it has grown rapidly, and continues to grow. At the same time, multilingualism is increasing, so that in the larger centers many native speakers of Northern Khmer use two, three or four languages as a normal part of life.

The marginal status of Northern Khmer is irrelevant to its position and role in Thailand. Cambodia exerts no pull on its speakers, and is no hindrance to speakers of Northern Khmer participating in Thailand's national unity.

Kuy is not a regional language, but it fits into Thailand's language ecology just as well on another level. Its area has shrunk considerably more than that of Northern Khmer, and at the expense of Northern Khmer, but its population continues to grow.

10

Pattani Malay

Native speakers of Pattani Malay are the majority population in the central and eastern parts of the southern panhandle of Thailand from about the level of the town of Hat Yai to the Malaysian border. Their language constitutes the final marginal regional language in the country, covering the provinces of Yala, Pattani, Narathiwat, and the southern part of Songkhla (map III.1). Other Malay-speaking people also live west and north of that region, but the language does not function as a regional language in those locations.

Pattani Malay is critical to our consideration of linguistic diversity and national unity in Thailand because it is the only sizable language with speakers who have participated in a persistent secessionist movement for more than two decades. It is almost a countercase to what otherwise characterizes the language ecology of Thailand, and therefore throws light on the larger whole.

Language is pertinent to the conflict, but is not the most fundamental issue in it. Rather, Malay and Thai cultures differ strongly in worldview, attitudes and values. To begin with, most ethnic Malay are Muslim and most ethnic Thai are Buddhist. Beyond that, long-standing antagonisms between a conquered people and their colonizers continue to fester. Malay sultans ruled these southern provinces in the past. Pattani in particular had an illustrious history at times. Descendants of those sultans and of the elite around them still live in the area, some in Malaysia and some in Thailand.

The Pattani Malay-speaking population of Thailand is substantial. The 1980 census reported 836,119 people using Malay as the language of the home. That figure is certainly low, but information of other kinds in the census provides some cross-check because of the close (but not absolute) relationship between the religion of Islam and the Malay language in that part of the country. Taking such figures into account, and allowing for population growth, probably about one million people speak some form of Malay in Thailand as of 1989.

155

Somewhat less than that, perhaps 880,000, may be Pattani Malay
native speakers in the marginal regional language area itself. Some
additional non-Malay Thai are native speakers of Malay along with a
Tai language in that area as well, most having learned it growing up
as children there.

Pattani Malay in the Language Hierarchy

The Pattani Malay spoken in Thailand is not the Standard Malay of
Malaysia, although that is also used by some people, especially for
religious purposes. Many native speakers of Pattani Malay can understand broadcasts from Malaysian cities only with difficulty. Instead,
their Pattani Malay is similar to and mutually intelligible with Malay
dialects spoken just south of the border in Malaysia.

The total expanse of Malay in Southeast Asia, of which southern
Thailand is the northernmost edge, constitutes a mosaic of dialects
covering west Malaysia (the mainland part of the country), coastal
areas of east Malaysia, the countries of Brunei and Singapore, and
some coastal areas of Indonesia. In a standardized form Malay is a
national language in Malaysia, Brunei and Singapore, and in a somewhat different standardized form a national language in Indonesia,
where it is called Indonesian.

At the northern extent of the mosaic, on the east coast of the
peninsula in Thailand, the primary Malay historical and cultural center is Pattani. On the west coast, in Satun Province, other dialects are
spoken, significantly different from, but mutually intelligible with, the
Pattani dialects. There are reasons for distinguishing between Satun
Malay dialects and Pattani Malay dialects, as we shall see, but they
are all part of the same language (Maneerat 1981:123). The role of
Paktay is so great in Satun, however, that Satun Malay is probably
not a regional language there.

The term "Malay" for these people and this language in Thailand
is a problem for Thai officialdom. Official policy holds that they are
Thai, and should be called Thai. Officially, when this population
needs to be distinguished from the Tai-speaking peoples, they should
be called /thay 'ìsalaam/ 'Thai Muslim' as distinguished from /thay
phút/ 'Thai Buddhist'. But many of the Pattani Malay-speaking
people on the eastern side of the peninsula resent this terminology
deeply. They may live in Thailand. They may be Thai citizens. They
may not be antagonistic to such status. But they perceive themselves
as "Malay," ethnically Malay, historically Malay,[1] Malay in world-

view and values, Malay in language. This terminological controversy epitomizes the competition between these two peoples for the same ethnic and linguistic ecological place.

Part of the Thai definition of Thainess is knowledge of a Tai language, preferably native-speaker knowledge (chap. 18). In many situations Thai officials apply this requirement loosely, as they do with Northern Khmer who do not speak Thai or Lao, for example. Officials have no problem considering them Thai because they make no resistance to Thai, and their lack of a Tai language is seen as resulting from insufficient opportunity. But for some speakers of Pattani Malay identity centers around Malay culture and its language. They insist they are not ethnic Thai, which has meant that some have resisted learning any Tai language. At most, Standard Thai or Paktay may be useful to them because they live in Thailand, but Pattani Malay better reflects who they feel they are.

In spite of such Malay ideological resistance, however, the language hierarchy does describe very well much of the actual interrelationship between Pattani Malay and other languages. Pattani Malay is marginal to the country because it overlaps into Thailand from a neighboring country. It is a regional language because it is the dominant language in three provinces and the southern part of another. In those areas some non-Malay (Sino-Thai and others) learn it in order to operate within the language ecology of the area. But although Pattani Malay fits into the hierarchy as a marginal regional language, its speakers do not fit as comfortably into its being dominated by Standard Thai, although that discomfort is decreasing.

The Satun Malay Dialect Area

Such statements about competition between Pattani Malay and Standard Thai are much more true of the population on the eastern side of the peninsula than on the western side. Before the Thai conquest, Satun Province on the west side was at times under the political domination of the Malay Pattani State on the east side, but was never an integral part of it because communication across the mountains and jungle was formerly difficult (Fraser 1966:3). Linguistically the Satun Malay dialects are closer to adjacent areas of Malaysia than they are to east coast dialects, although they are also mutually intelligible with the latter (Anne Wilding personal communication).

Satun Province, furthermore, has long had extensive contacts with Tai language centers such as Songkhla, Hat Yai, and Phatthalung, so that much of the population is bilingual with Standard Thai and/or Paktay. In the more northern part of Satun Province, furthermore, many Malay speak a Satun dialect of Paktay characterized by large numbers of Malay borrowings. For some it is their native language (David W. Hogan, Anne Wilding personal communications).[2] In some places the ability to speak the Satun Malay dialect is even limited to older people (Court 1975), or those who speak it do so only for religious purposes (Arong 1985:5).

Separatist movements never captured the imagination of the people in Satun as much as they did of the people on the other side of the peninsula, either. Thai language and Thai education have been more fully accepted there much longer, too. So Satun must be excluded from the discussion of competition between Pattani Malay and the Tai languages, its speakers taking their place quite fully in the hierarchy as a marginal language (part 4), and conforming to the expectations created by it.

But Satun Malay-speaking people are nevertheless sometimes aroused by Muslim or nationalist sentiment just the same. In 1985 a large protest broke out against a new Ministry of Education policy requiring Buddha images to be displayed in elementary schools. This insensitive government move was received with something of the same feelings which Jewish communities would have on hearing that crosses were to be displayed in all public schools in the USA. The Thai regulation seems not to have been widely enforced, a common tactic of local officials all over Thailand when they understand the local situation better than bureaucrats in Bangkok, but it was implemented in at least one district. As a result, Muslim students there went on strike until negotiations were held with the protesting parents, who demanded the removal of the headmaster.

The Pattani Malay Dialect Area

How greatly knowledge of Thai and acceptance of it has increased in the Pattani Malay region can be seen from an example of extreme linguistic conservatism and rejection of Thai in a fishing village of one thousand people in Pattani Province in the 1960s. Only four adults could really use Standard Thai with facility although a Thai government school with four grades had been open for twenty years or more. Some young adults who had once been to school could not even pass the time of day in Standard Thai. Some children still in school were able to respond to simple questions, but after leaving they soon lost whatever facility they had gained because of lack of interest, lack of use, and rejection (Ismail Haji Daud personal communication).

Even at that time such a degree of difficulty with Thai would have been unusual for slightly less conservative rice-growing or rubber-tapping villages (Anne Wilding personal communication). In one such village in Yala Province in the early 1970s attitudes toward Standard Thai and the education which brought it had already changed radically among progressive-minded parents from earlier indifference and even hostility. No longer did they feel that Standard Thai was useless. With easy travel to the district and provincial towns people found that a knowledge of written and spoken Thai greatly simplified life for them. Television also came into the village by way of a set owned by the Sino-Thai shopkeeper, who allowed free viewing to anyone interested.

And if this acceptance of Thai has been increasing in small country villages, it is all the more advanced in populated centers. In the towns, Pattani Malay-speaking children have more exposure to both Paktay and Standard Thai, schools are stronger, bright pupils may reach secondary school, and Standard Thai is used in various forms of employment, so the quality of whichever Tai language is used by

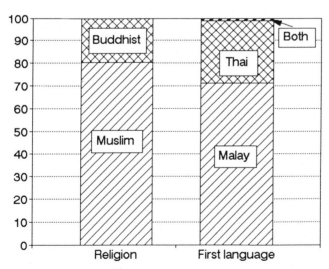

Fig. 10.1. Comparison of percentage of people who were Muslims and Buddhists, with those who spoke Malay and Thai as their first language, from a sample of generally educated people in Pattani Province (after Narong 1979:16-17).

native speakers of Pattani Malay is often high and the demand for it increasing.

How Pattani Malay is now fitting more into Thailand's language hierarchy is also shown in figure 10.1, where the percentages of Muslims and Buddhists in one sample[3] are in roughly the same proportions as in the general population. More people speak Thai as their first language than there are Buddhists, and more people are Muslims than speak Pattani Malay as a first language. The report does not distinguish between Paktay and Standard Thai.

People surveyed were also asked how often they used Thai and Malay. The combined totals for "often" and "very often" in the categories of speaking, listening, reading and writing are shown in figure 10.2. Strongholds in which Malay is especially used are the mosque, the traditional schools, the home, and "with Muslims" (Narong 1979:34-36). Malay predominated in dreaming and praying, but not as strongly in thinking, counting, or diary writing (fig. 10.3).

Bilinguals normally used Thai, the external language, when speaking with non-Malay, whether bilingual or not. And, of course, they used Pattani Malay with people monolingual in it. But when bilingual Malay spoke with each other, they exhibited a gradation of usage. In the home, for example, domestic matters were discussed in Pattani

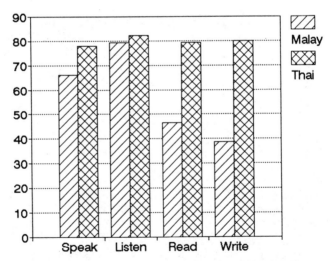

Fig. 10.2. Percentage of people who reported using Malay or Thai "often" or "very often" in various functions (after Narong 1979:42-43).

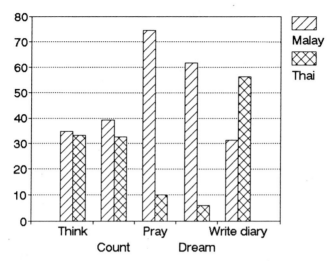

Fig. 10.3. Percentage of people who use Malay or Thai for various purposes when no other person is involved. The first language of respondents is Malay (after Narong 1979: 40).

Malay, whereas outside of the home they were discussed primarily in Pattani Malay, secondarily in Thai. In the home, school matters were usually discussed in Pattani Malay but might also be discussed in Thai. But outside of the home they were discussed primarily in Thai, although occasionally in Pattani Malay (Sukhuma-Vadee 1980, 1981). In rural areas, more remote from contacts with Thai, people who have had only four years or so of Thai schooling as children still often lose the ability to do much with it, or lapse into illiteracy even if they can still speak it (Patya 1974:57). And whether urban or rural, just as the person in northern Thailand uses Standard Thai and Kammüang in complementary situations, the bilingual Malay in the south uses unrelated Standard Thai and Pattani Malay in complementary ways.

The Roots of Competition

But although the language hierarchy increasingly structures communication patterns in the area, competition between the languages is nevertheless of long standing. The formerly independent Malay state of Pattani held varying amounts of territory on the peninsula at times from the fourteenth to the nineteenth centuries, becoming a major

Muslim center when its ruler was converted to Islam in 1474 (Kobkua 1988:5). At other times it was in varying degrees subservient to Thai kingdoms, often by recognizing greater Thai power through paying tribute, but maintaining local autonomy. Continuous direct Thai rule has been exercised since 1893 (Chavivun 1982:69-71; Wyatt 1984: 110-112, 172-173, 213; Surin 1985). Thailand replaced its tributary relationship by direct rule partly as a defense against British colonial expansion from the south (Kobkua 1988:208-214). The conflicts, therefore, are both political and cultural.

Thai Government Strategies

In general, Thailand has tried to rule the Malay population of the south much as it ruled the rest of the country, but its strategies have not always worked well with the Malay: '

1. A highly centralized bureaucratic hierarchy governs from Bangkok. Policies and their implementation are directed from the top down. Deep understanding of the local situation does not inform policy decisions, but upper- and middle-level officials are moved from post to post so that they do not develop an attachment or loyalty to the local situation. Low-level officials who know the situation best have little influence (Ladd 1970; Arong 1985:36-39).

At certain periods of great Thai chauvinism, particularly under King Vajiravudh in the early part of this century, and under Prime Minister Luang Phibunsongkhram (generally known as Phibun) during World War II and again in midcentury, the government attempted to force assimilation of the Malay and other minorities in Thailand. Not only did that not work, but it also aggravated the climate of mistrust which continues to plague present-day Pattani Malay-Thai relationships. The Pattani Malay often respond to the administration with the classical resentment many colonized people feel for their colonizers.

2. In another line of strategy the government seeks to promote acceptance and assimilation by enlisting the religious leaders of the subject people (Tambiah 1976; Surin 1985:166-215). With the Buddhist or animist populations of other parts of the country this has been largely successful. But with Muslims in the Pattani Malay region it has often been bitterly resented.

One major Thai measure, for example, the Patronage of Islam Act of 1945, sought to control Muslim religious leaders by extending assistance and protection after the alienation of the Phibun period. The responsibility of the King to be the sustainer of Buddhism was extended to all religions, and a Muslim official was appointed as the spiritual leader of all Muslims in Thailand, on the model of the Supreme Patriarch in Buddhism. A Central Islamic Committee of Thailand was established to advise the government on Muslim matters, but members of that committee were appointed and dismissed according to the advice of the Ministry of the Interior.

Whereas the act was generally accepted by Muslims in other parts of the country, the Pattani Malay were angered by government interference in their religious affairs (Surin 1985:102-109). They saw the act in much the same light Thai might have seen an attempt by the United Nations to appoint a Buddhist Supreme Patriarch, or Catholics would see an attempt by the Italian government to appoint the Pope.

3. Another government strategy has been to exert control over traditional Muslim schools, as it did over all other private schools in the country. We will discuss this later.

4. Thai officials, furthermore, often treat the Malay population with insensitivity and contempt, even behaving as though Malay people were foreigners and intruders in their own country. It is of no help to the Malay that government officials also often treat other marginal and enclave peoples badly, and even do so to lower-class speakers of Tai languages at times (Arong 1985:44-46).

This mistreatment often seems worse for the Malay because their customs and beliefs are so different. The government changed the Malay day of rest from Friday to Sunday, for example, and built a massive Buddhist statue outside Nakhon Si Thammarat, another extremely insensitive provocation. Officials who would respect a Northern Khmer Buddhist temple or shrine will sometimes walk into a Muslim mosque with their shoes on. Such an act of sacrilege, whether intentional or not, is analogous to a Western tourist climbing up on the head of a statue of the Buddha, an incident which incensed Thai people some years ago.

Brief training courses are available for Thai officials, who may spend a week or so learning about Malay customs. This may help a person of goodwill avoid some gaffes, but such superficial training is obviously tokenism. The cultures are profoundly, not just superficially, different.

And even people of goodwill may add fuel to the fire of resentment. A Thai may wear a Malay hat to show solidarity with the Malay, but unwittingly do so while eating in a Chinese restaurant where he is presumably eating pork, a gross insult (Tugby and Tugby 1971:15).

5. Thai police can be brutal in dealing with lower-class people, especially minorities, seriously disregarding civil rights at times (Arong 1985:53-60). Again, the Malay gain no comfort from sharing with others the honor of being beaten up by the police, and of being subject to extortion by officials. People among the Malay elite as well as peasants are sometimes subject to ignominy and injury.

6. The southernmost provinces of Thailand are economically depressed, and conditions are getting worse (Ladd 1970; Surin 1985: 18-22). The area has received less government attention to its economic problems than have some other parts of the country. The government has opened up resettlement areas for people to homestead, recruiting poverty-stricken people from other parts of the country to come to them. Such resettlement areas are open also to the Malay, but some Malay see the homestead opportunities as a government attempt to dilute the area with Tai-speaking peoples in order to weaken the Malay.

7. The government perceives the Malay to be a security problem, threatening to take away some Thai territory through secession, engaging in terrorism and violence. Communism and sheer banditry exist alongside Malay nationalism and secessionism, and are often not distinguished from Malay nationalism by government officials. So human rights and aspirations are often ignored in the attempt to further tighten Thai control.

Culture Clash

The Thai have no adequate strategy for learning to understand and communicate with the Malay. To do so would even be contrary to the worldview which sustains them in their relations with other peoples. In the Thai system superiors ideally offer protection to inferiors, try to provide for them if they are in need, try to make things easier for them, from the superior's point of view. In return, inferiors evince loyalty, support, subservience, even awe. Lower peoples must be passive, must acquiesce to the power of the superior.

In the Thai bureaucratic hierarchy the role and responsibility of each person is clearly set out by regulations. But the Thai understand how regulations can be bent or broken, and how concessions can be granted for many things as a part of the larger set of role relationships to which official and client belong. People in positions of power do favors for people who exercise less power in exchange for support of other kinds. Such support may be a bribe, but often also some other kind of reciprocal favor or concession instead, and it may not be an immediate repayment but a favor returned over time (Hanks 1962, 1975).

The Malay find it difficult to enter into such relationships which involve vague reciprocity based on a hierarchical social relationship. Their socioeconomic model is more individualistic, except with relatives and fellow villagers. So whereas the Sino-Thai in the south have become members of the "circles" of officials, gaining and giving favors in the process, the Malay have not. They not only do not know how to do it, and feel uncomfortable with the system, but individuals would also be strongly criticized by their peers if they did conform (Tugby and Tugby 1971).

The highly stratified Thai social structure, furthermore, has myriad verbal and behavioral ways of showing varying degrees of subservience and deference, according to the relative positions of the people interacting (chap. 3). Pattani Malay-speaking society is of a more egalitarian nature. People do not have, nor are they comfortable with, such elaborate signs of submission. So Thai officials are offended at not getting the symbols of respect due their position, and impute disrespect to the Malay. The Malay, in turn, are incensed that the Thai should insist on behavior which seems to them to range from bootlicking to the worship of pagan idols (Ladd 1970:152-153).

The few Malay who do have official positions live in Malay communities but work in Thai offices. At work they wear Thai uniforms, have Thai names, and speak Thai; at home they wear Malay dress, use their Malay names, and speak Pattani Malay. So far they sound like their parallels in any other part of the country. But at official dinners the parallel stops. Either they must eat Thai food with its taboo pork and liquor, sit at a separate table, or not go. Some may drink with Thai behind the scenes, but do not do so in public.

In any case many people in the community see such Malay officials as tools of the Thai, or as giving up their principles to make money. The individuals, in turn, will criticize the Thai strongly in the Malay community so as not to give the appearance of having sold out to the Thai (Tugby and Tugby 1971:17).

Some educated Malay, especially people who have not been fully alienated by Bangkok, do serve as a bridge between the cultures. A few of them have important official positions. But they never set policy; that always remains in the hands of superiors in the bureaucracy.

The Separatist Movement

So latent alienation is prevalent and persistent in the Malay population in these provinces, coming to the surface in demonstrations and anger on one occasion or another. In its most extreme form it is expressed in four small but tenacious separatist groups which seek to create a Greater Pattani Malay State. They are not united, but they agree that the Thai administration is a colonial power, and seek its overthrow. Some have, or have had, their headquarters in Malaysia and/or Saudi Arabia (Che Man 1990:98-112).

The separatism does not at present seem to have wide active support among speakers of Pattani Malay, but its potential is worrisome to the Thai. A charismatic leader could quickly attract alienated people. A more repressive Thai policy, such as has arisen at times in the past, could be the catalyst under which the movement might catch the imagination of the population.

For the moment the movement survives by terrorist acts, bombings, raids, killings of schoolteachers—all of the contemporary tools of alienated people who are too weak to get what they want. For a time, some of those in the movement ironically had relations with the anti-Malay Chinese communists who survive in the mountains along the border after having been driven out of Malaysia. They get sympathy, and sometimes actual support, from Arab countries in the Middle East.

Surin Pitsuwan ('Abdul Halīm Bin 'Isma'il), a Harvard Ph.D. political scientist at Thammasat University in Bangkok, who straddles the worlds of Pattani Malay discontent and Thailand establishment, makes this assessment (Surin 1985:216-217):

> The conflict threatens to involve foreign powers of various ideological shades and, if not effectively resolved, could adversely affect the good relations among . . . Thailand, Indonesia, and Malaysia. The Islamic bond among the peoples of Southeast Asia and those in the Middle East has frequently been invoked in order to attract moral and material support for the "oppressed Muslims under Thai rule" (PULO 1981).

Unlike the many other areas of the country where the Bangkok government meets the peoples of surrounding countries, the Pattani Malay-speaking area is an overlap zone between two radically different culture spheres. Thailand adjoins Buddhist countries at every point but this one. Even the Sino-Thai minority tends to be Buddhist, although of a different kind. The Thai also typically share the animistic outlook of many non-Buddhist minority peoples who speak marginal or enclave languages. The Christian minority is so small, so scattered over the country, and often so accommodating to Thai values, that it does not stand out as being radically different.

Non-Malay Muslims, in turn, come from a wide variety of different backgrounds. Some are members of Thai-speaking communities of Muslims with some features of a Thai worldview, rather than an orthodox Islamic one. They may be descendants of Thai converted to Islam or intermarried with Muslims (Burr 1972). Others are descendants of immigrants and refugees from India, Pakistan, or Iran. A few are descendants of Chams from Cambodia, or of Indonesians. Then again, Muslim Yunnanese Chinese have been added in the northern mountains (Scupin 1980; Forbes 1982). All of these other Muslims, with their various languages, seem to have accepted their places in the language hierarchy to a considerable degree, although differences of worldview do affect their attitudes (Scupin 1988). None of them, of course, are anywhere nearly as numerous as the speakers of Pattani Malay.

Nor do they live right next to another country of their same language and culture. Nor do they have the historical memory that their ancestors were citizens of an independent principality right where they are now living.

So the Muslim Pattani Malay are the only group within the country which the Thai have to face at a great cultural border. The confrontation is between Thai civilization rooted in India and Ceylon, developed in the Mon, Khmer, Burmese and Ayuthayan empires, and in Bangkok, eye to eye with Malay civilization, rooted in Arabia and the Middle East, developed in the Malay States and Indonesia (Arong 1985:5-12). The deep differences of worldview are overtly symbolized, furthermore, by behavior with strong ethnic associations ranging from religious practice to greetings to food taboos (Chavivun 1982:74-81).

The struggle has been unequal because Malaysia has kept out of it, Bangkok against a handful of religious leaders, intellectuals, and dispossessed elite. But if Malaysia or any Arab countries stepped in . . . That keeps Bangkok worried, and probably tempers the severity of its repression as well.

The Thai government sees itself as the constituted authority, and according to its assumptions all minority peoples presently in the country are to be assimilated to Thai in due course, to become a part of the great national cosmic order centered in Bangkok (chap. 6). But

Malay people who see themselves as conquered and colonized, held in
subjection against their will by superior military and police strength,
feel the bitterness of India and Malaysia under British rule, and of
Indonesia under the Dutch.

Thailand has frequently been called an open society, but it is so
only on its own terms. It is open to those who will take their place in
the hierarchical cosmology, of which the language hierarchy is one
reflection. The Chinese learned their place and accepted it, and so
have many Malay in Satun and elsewhere.

But Muslim societies are not typically open societies even in this
limited sense. Their ethnic categories have sharp boundaries (chap.
18). In the extreme, someone is either Muslim or Buddhist, and to be
Thai is to be Buddhist, so a Muslim cannot be Thai. For those Malay
who hold traditional values dearly and have the sophistication to think
about them, accommodation to the Thai hierarchical way of ordering
things is a denial of everything which is most important to them
(Scupin 1988). Allah does not bow to Bangkok. Only in an Islamic
state can a Muslim be free to follow Muslim law, to raise children in
Muslim (=Malay) ways.

Critical to this whole issue is the question of how much Bangkok-
centered cosmology is affecting Muslim self-understanding in areas
like Satun Province, where knowledge of Tai languages is widespread, where communication with Thai people has gone on for a
long time, and where Thai education has not been resisted. Critical,
also, is how much the Thai worldview is penetrating the young Thai-
educated Malay in the other provinces as well. The future receptivity
to Malay nationalist leadership in a time of crisis may well depend on
such factors as these.

Education in the Pattani Malay Areas

Outside of the three provinces of Pattani, Narathiwat and Yala, government schools have generally met with acceptance, and children in
Satun and elsewhere follow the same pattern we have seen in other
areas in the country, learning Standard Thai if they are able to stay in
school long enough. As elsewhere, the curriculum was designed in
Bangkok for the most part, and is often rather irrelevant to the students. But many thousands do get a little education, and some go
beyond the village schools to more substantial education. Some have
entered the civil service to become teachers or employees in the
government bureaucracy. A few have done well.

In the more resistant provinces, however, traditionalists fear the assimilative effect of the government schools and resist their Buddhist (="idolatrous") content (Arong 1985:22). In spite of steadily increasing acceptance of the first few years of education in the Thai public schools, some parents who are close enough to the border, or who can afford to do so, still send their children to school in Malaysia (Doomkum Lakhana personal communication). In one border town fifty students crossed the border daily (Daranee 1985).

The real educational struggle came, however, over control of the Malay Muslim schools. Traditionally a Malay teacher set himself up after he had gained an advanced level of education in a local Muslim school, or had been to Malaysia or even to the Middle East to study. Students then gathered around, supported by their families, who also made small contributions to the teacher, although the teacher's motivation was more religious than financial.

From the viewpoint of the Thai bureaucracy, the Pattani Malay schools were both inadequate and dangerous. The language of the traditional school was Pattani Malay, and Standard Thai was ignored. The teachers did not have the qualifications prescribed by the Thai school system, and the traditional schools were all terribly haphazard. Worse than that, they were not under the control of Thai officials, were suspected of being hotbeds of subversion, and certainly were not teaching Thai values. The power of the traditional schools far outweighed the influence of the government schools for most Malay.

As long as these schools maintained their influence, government efforts to assimilate the Pattani Malay were thus stymied on several levels. Even Thai efforts to recruit ethnic Malay teachers and other civil servants were being thwarted because only the Thai school system qualified people for these positions, and the Malay students were not going through the Thai schools.

For the Pattani Malay-speaking peoples, however, their schools were not just educational institutions. They were centers where the young could gather around holy men to be prepared for life as Malay Muslims. They were sacred communities "whose mission is to bring true Islam to the marginal society," that is, to purify the doctrine of the Muslim peasants whose emphasis was on rituals and animistic beliefs. This zeal to bring about the perfect Muslim society often led them into political activity (Surin 1985:179-180).

Students stayed in such schools as long as they could, and if they stayed long enough and were good enough they tutored those who were slower. There was no examination, no graduation. Some con-

tinued their education in Malaysia or Mecca before coming back to
set up their own schools (Surin 1985:184-186).

In 1949, when the Private School Act brought government control
to the Chinese schools and other private schools, the Pattani Malay
traditional schools were exempted because of their religious character.
But in the early 1960s the government began to try to transform them
into private schools under government control, allowing them to
include religious education but in effect changing them into secular
institutions (Surin 1985:180).

In 1968 the government then decreed that no new private schools
for Islamic education could be started, and handed down a new Thai
language curriculum for the ones which did exist. Teaching in the
Malay language would no longer be allowed. Students were not to be
admitted unless they had already been to Thai schools. The traditional
religious curriculum was reduced to make room for the Thai curriculum. Even the subject of ethics was to be taken directly from the
curriculum designed in Bangkok, with emphasis given to Buddhist
values. Regular examinations were to be administered, and students
were to be classified as in government schools. Teachers and administrators would have to meet Thai requirements, so few founders and
owners of the traditional schools were now "qualified" to operate
their own schools.

These government regulations broke the back of the traditional
schools as primary centers of Malay and Muslim culture, but part of
what the traditional schools did has not been lost to the Malay. Children have not stopped learning Standard Malay in Arabic script, as
they now study in part-time weekend schools and take instruction
before and after government school hours in programs which have
grown up to meet the need (Arong 1985:20).

But the government has accomplished its immediate purpose. Having earlier deposed the sultans, it has now deposed the traditional
intellectuals, depriving them of their base of operations and religious
leaders, their place of service and significance to the community. Thai
language and Thai education has received an enormous boost as a
result. It is not as clear, however, that the ultimate purpose of the
government was accomplished. Suddenly more students left for Malaysia and the Middle East, into centers of Muslim nationalism. And
the Pattani United Liberation Organization (PULO) was formed under
the impetus of these developments, becoming the most effective of the
secessionist movements in the south. Its leadership is in Mecca, Saudi
Arabia, where the eight thousand Pattani Malay students and other
residents from Thailand support it (Surin 1985:234).

But if we turn aside from the leaders who feel that they and their people have been culturally and linguistically raped, to relatively non-political Pattani Malay-speaking people living in Thailand, we can see what a strong effect Thai schooling is having since the changes were made. Many more children of school age attend government schools, and stay longer. Knowledge of spoken Standard Thai, and sometimes Paktay as well, has increased significantly among people whose native tongue is Pattani Malay. But perhaps most telling of all is the fact that unlike in earlier years, many Pattani Malay-speaking children in the regional language provinces now like their Thai education (David J. Clark personal communication).

Government Language Policies

As with other languages used in different parts of the country, the government does not interfere with nor object to people speaking Pattani Malay. In fact, it even broadcasts in it throughout the region, offering news and entertainment, and communicating the government point of view.

However, officials are often more nervous about writing languages other than Standard Thai and about people using writing systems other than Standard Thai script. No law prohibits writing minority languages, but strong official pressures have been exerted against doing so at times, especially against writing the languages of minorities in the north. Importing foreign-language publications (except English) has even been restricted at times. In Pattani Malay, where the Arabic script and Muslim religion are closely tied together, the government has not interfered with use of the script, although teaching it in the private schools has been curtailed since the government took control of them.

On the other hand, the government itself never takes seriously a language lower in the hierarchy than Standard Thai unless the people cause trouble, or seem to be a security risk in some way. Because of the unrest among Pattani Malay-speaking people, the government has at times encouraged officials to learn the language, even offering bonuses of some kind (Fraser 1966:52), but learning Pattani Malay is never a requirement, and never solidly implemented.

Other token efforts have also been made, as when Malay word lists have been published in Thai newspapers, and short seminars on Malay language and culture have been held sporadically. Some officials have studied Standard Malay at universities in Bangkok, but what they learn is both a different script and a different language (Queljoe 1971:xii). Officials who do study some Pattani Malay, furthermore, generally do not submit themselves to disciplined practice, and many pronounce it so poorly that they are unintelligible (Anne Wilding personal communication). Probably many would not want to sound too much like a Malay, anyhow! Learning it is contrary to the assumptions of the Thai language hierarchy.

Some Thai officials have tried to write Pattani Malay in Thai script, producing primers under the Department of Education and other agencies. But in the early stages, at least, this was an abortive effort by amateurs. It was inaccurate, inconsistent, and misleading, often based on errors Thai-speaking people made in hearing and recording (Anne Wilding personal communication). Furthermore, so far as the Muslims are concerned, it attacked the very sacredness of Arabic, including its script.

Pattani Malay and Standard Malay

In spite of Pattani's past as a Malay cultural and religious center, the Pattani Malay language itself is deprecated by many Malay themselves as a "backwoods" variety because it is different from the now more standard forms of Malay developed in the Malaysian nation and school system. This is so even though Pattani Malay is spoken by educated people and religious leaders in Thailand as well as by village farmers and fisher folk.

As is to be expected, differences from Standard Malay and from dialects farther south include pronunciation, grammatical structure and vocabulary. The conspicuous differences in vocabulary include large numbers of words borrowed from Tai languages in Thailand, and the absence of words which have been developed in Malaysia but have not spread to Thailand.

But the general feature which causes the greatest difficulty in mutual comprehension between Pattani Malay and Malay dialects to the south, including Standard Malay, is pronunciation. Pattani dialects have fewer final consonants, which makes intelligibility difficult for people who speak other dialects until they get used to the reduction (Graham 1924:124; Anne Wilding personal communication). Most notably, where Standard Malay has /p t k/ in final position, corresponding Pattani Malay words have only /'/, a brief closing of the vocal cords (glottal stop).

Standard Malay is itself known in varying degrees throughout the Pattani Malay area, however, written primarily in its traditional

Arabic script, and taught in connection with Muslim training. This makes it another important language in the southern border provinces of Thailand, as a part of the religious and cultural tradition. People aspire to know it, but preserve it apart from ongoing everyday affairs. The way in which it was used in the traditional schools is revealing. Students read the Arabic-script texts in Standard Malay, and these were then explained and discussed in Pattani Malay. Here is situational bilingualism again, with Standard Malay restricted largely to religious and literary use.

The Marginality of Pattani Malay

To Northern Khmer-speaking people, the fact that they are an extension of a much larger Khmer-speaking population outside of Thailand is of no particular significance. They consider themselves Thai. The Karen peoples in Thailand would rather be under the Thai than under the Burmese, where peoples who speak related languages are often fighting Burmese rule. So would the Tai Yai. By and large, these groups are Thai, want to be Thai, are glad for their education in Thai, raise their children as Thai.

So it is, also, with many Pattani Malay-speaking people, especially in Satun and in the more northern areas of the region. Some have even lost their Malay language. But for many others, their marginal status is of great significance. More than any other language group in Thailand, such people feel a sense of identification outside of Thailand. Some Pattani Malay are even illegally registered as citizens on both sides of the border. People, radio and television programs, goods and ideas cross the border with little more difficulty than they move about within Thailand. Separatists have found refuge on the other side of the border ever since the sultans were deposed.

And unlike the other border areas of Thailand, life across the border is attractive, peaceful and prosperous. Some goods are cheaper in Malaysia than in Thailand, so Pattani-speaking Malay cross over to go shopping if they live near enough. Thus the marginality of the Pattani Malay-speaking people in Thailand gets strong reinforcement.

That does not necessarily mean that separatist sentiment is widespread, or that the terrorist tactics of the separatists have wide support, but it does mean that Malay ethnicity is constantly being refreshed and renewed. It does not mean that the population will stop becoming more fully multilingual, but it does mean that the ethnic clash, the misunderstanding, the resentment is not going to disappear in the near future. Although communication between Thai and Pattani Malay-speaking people will improve with more knowledge of Thai on the part of the Malay, traditional behavior patterns on both sides will continue to offend the other.[4]

Although the number of people who are generally at home in both cultures is growing, it is still small. Two government schools with a heavy preponderance of Pattani Malay-speaking students, one rural, one urban, had a total of thirty-six teachers, of which only two were Malay (Sukhuma-Vadee 1980:23-24). Now that Thai education is more common, and more people are qualified for government positions, some Malay people nevertheless still find the stigma within their communities and the deterrent power of the terrorists too great to take government jobs. In spite of a government policy of incorporating qualified Pattani Malay-speaking people into government employ, the influx is very small.

The present position of Pattani Malay in the language hierarchy of Thailand is reminiscent of Chinese languages thirty-five years ago. Standard Thai was strong in the younger generation, many young people no longer speaking a Chinese language. Identification with Thailand was increasing. The private Chinese schools were no longer powerful. More Chinese believed that it was to their advantage to know Thai. But that sentiment had nevertheless not yet solidified. There were contrary voices, even a Chinese communist movement in the country, with terrorist tactics. But today that ambivalence has generally evaporated among the Sino-Thai (chap. 12).

The same thing may happen in the Pattani Malay area in the next thirty years. It is already well advanced in Satun. But even so some differences exist. For one thing, the Sino-Thai are being incorporated into Thailand on a generally higher socioeconomic level than the Malayo-Thai, which seems easier to take, for both sides. The Chinese had a lot to gain, economically, by life in Thailand, but the Malay not so much. Then too, the pragmatic Chinese worldview is more adaptable to a Thai perspective than the separateness of the Malay is to the incorporativeness of the Thai.

But changes are taking place, and much will depend on external history. Events in Malaysia and the Middle East may have an effect on the secessionist movement in the southern border provinces, one way or the other. As one example, in 1986 Libya's preoccupation with the United States and its own reduced oil revenues were suspected of having lessened funding for the Pattani Malay secessionist movement in Thailand.

Present trends being what they are, however, most likely the possibility of Pattani Malay fully taking its place in a non-competitive way in the language hierarchy of Thailand will depend most on the degree of Thai provocation. Thai language policy may have all but won the war, but Thai xenophobia could reignite long-standing latent Pattani Malay antagonism and distrust. Thai policy seems to be winning, but Thai officials could easily blow it.

Summary

At the present time Pattani Malay is close to being an important exception to the set of factors which create national unity within the linguistic diversity of Thailand. Pattani Malay is the most important language around which there remains a residue of resistance to the place of Standard Thai in the hierarchy. Secessionist activity has been strong at times in the past, and continues weakly at present. Most important, resentment is widely felt in the Pattani Malay-speaking population, although it is not now as intense as it was in the past.

Pattani Malay is the only marginal language in Thailand where the marginality is actually significant to national unity. Pattani Malay-speaking people in the border areas maintain easy ties across the border to Malaysia, which is an attractive alternative for them.

At the crux of the disunity is the gulf between Thai Buddhist and Malay Muslim worldviews. The differences are not just in religious practices, but penetrate to the very nature of social reality itself. Muslim ideology does not accept the kind of hierarchy on which Thailand is built. Muslim ethnic categories are sharply delimited, not allowing for the easy interpenetration which is generally characteristic of ethnic groups in the rest of Thailand.

However, although it has made many mistakes, and lost many battles, Thailand is slowly winning the war. Pattani Malay has significantly moved into the language hierarchy in the understanding and behavior of increasing numbers of its speakers. As with other populations, Thai control of the school system is bringing about change, although that control in itself is resented.

Part IV

Other Language Categories
Introduction

As we move down to the bottom of the Thailand language hierarchy (fig. II.1) the categories and the languages become more numerous. In this section we discuss only enough languages to illustrate the categories and show how they relate to linguistic diversity and national unity in the language ecology of the country.[1]

What the rather disparate languages on this level have in common is that adult speakers of other languages do not normally learn to speak them. Even that generalization has to be qualified, however, for the Chinese languages themselves have an internal hierarchy with Taechiu at the top, Mandarin, Cantonese, and the others following (chap. 12). However, in Thailand adults typically learn Chinese languages only if they are already speakers of another Chinese language, so the Chinese languages as a group are still at the bottom of the overall Thailand hierarchy.

Enclave Languages

Some of the categories of languages within this level are also less sharply demarcated than previous categories. All of them are enclave languages, for example, but we distinguish only one set of them by that name. Enclave languages in the broad sense are languages totally surrounded by other languages within the country. Their speakers are distributed in pockets, often small ones. Even different villages in which people speak the same language are often separated by areas in which speakers of other languages predominate. Speakers of these languages therefore occupy no contiguous areas of any size where their languages are dominant.

Some of these languages have other characteristics which are more important in Thailand's language ecology than are their enclave distributions, however, so we use other terms to classify them. Urban enclave languages we call the languages of Thai towns and cities. Displaced Tai rural enclave languages we call displaced Tai languages. Marginal enclave languages we call marginal languages. The remainder—those without other defining features—we call simply enclave languages.

Enclave status (in the narrow sense) sometimes makes language survival difficult, because it renders attrition easier. Some of Thailand's enclave languages are vigorous and growing, but a small number may be endangered, perhaps likely to become extinct. Which tendency wins out will depend on speakers' responses to the hierarchy. They may choose multilingualism, speaking languages above theirs along with their own, or they may choose assimilation, switching to languages above theirs exclusively.

Marginal Languages

Languages which overlap from larger populations in neighboring countries are marginal languages in our typology, and all of the languages on this level of the language hierarchy except the enclave languages (narrow meaning) are languages of that type. On this present level we find three categories of such languages differentiated by varying roles in the language ecology, and use other terms for some of them to focus on their central functions. Urban marginal languages we call languages of Thai towns and cities. Displaced rural Tai marginal languages we call displaced Tai languages. For the non-Tai rural remainder of marginal languages we use the unqualified term, marginal languages. We have already described the marginal languages Kuy and Phlong in other contexts.

In marginal regional languages we saw that being marginal may or may not be relevant to Thailand's unity within diversity. The marginality of Northern Khmer is of no political significance, but that of Pattani Malay is highly relevant. Similarly, the significance of marginality varies among the marginal languages here on the lowest level of the hierarchy. But that significance lies more in the perception of Thai officials than in the outlook and behavior of the marginal peoples. This was especially clear during the Vietnam War, when Thailand was an ally of the non-communist forces, and when some Hmong in Laos were fighting on the side of the communists there. That made Thai officials nervous about the marginal status of the Hmong in Thailand (chap. 14). The marginal character of the Kuy, on the other hand, is both tenuous and irrelevant to everyone.

Some marginal languages are newer to Thailand than most of the languages discussed so far, while others have been in the country for many centuries. For some groups the trickle continues, as those who speak them seek a more favorable life in Thailand than they had in Myanmar or Laos.[2] Some marginal languages like Kuy antedate the Tai peoples.

Languages of Towns and Cities

Thailand's towns and cities have significant populations of native speakers of languages from India, Pakistan, China, and other countries. Of these, Chinese languages have been especially critical to issues of diversity and unity. They are also somewhat anomalous in that although they are at the bottom of the Thailand language hierarchy, they rate high in world importance, and some of their speakers are at the top of the Thai economic scene.

Chinese marginality was troublesome to the Thai at certain periods in its history, but is no longer a significant issue. The fact that speakers of Chinese languages and other Sino-Thai people no longer demand their own schools to reinforce their languages is a major component in Thailand's present relative national unity.

Displaced Tai Languages

Standard Thai, the four major regional languages, and Tai Yai are not all of the Tai languages in the country. Several others are found in locations to which speakers have migrated from elsewhere. They are called "displaced" because unlike previous marginal languages they break into the expanse of the Tai regional languages as pockets of Tai languages not mutually intelligible with the regional Tai languages around them. The fact that they are Tai languages makes their role relationship to the regional languages slightly different from enclave and marginal languages.

Displaced Tai languages are not troublesome to national unity although they are significant components in the linguistic diversity of the country. The history of the development of the tone systems found in different Tai languages provides a backdrop for describing the relationship of these displaced Tai languages to the regional languages.

11

Development and Displacement
of Tai Languages and Dialects

Standard Thai, the four major regional languages of Thailand, and Tai Yai are all closely related, which means that they have much in common because of their descent from a common ancestor language. At the same time, their linguistic differences grow out of long-time processes of change in which their respective lines of descent evolved somewhat differently. Each of them is also manifested in numerous mutually intelligible local dialects because the same processes of change continue to work wherever the languages are spoken. That is why one village often has small or great differences in speech from neighboring ones.

The same sort of change experienced on a much wider scale and over a much longer period of time has also produced the larger Tai family of languages spread over much of Southeast Asia and South China (map 11.1). Speakers of any Tai language find that they understand at least some words and phrases of any other Tai language when they first encounter it, although those words are usually pronounced quite differently in any two languages separated by considerable space or line of descent. After a few days or weeks of listening and interacting such speakers understand more and more. Even when they do not find mutual intelligibility they may experience rapid adjustment, rapid learning, because of the systematic and sometimes minimal nature of many differences (chap. 17).

Early in this century, for example, the missionary William C. Dodd, writing from the perspective of Kammüang in northern Thailand, recorded traveling for months by elephant from Chiang Mai across northern Laos and into South China. He spent considerable time in a number of Tai-speaking villages and towns along the way, and achieved communication with each group:

Their dialect is so different that while we understood each other and could talk together freely after the first few days, there were comparatively few words that we pronounced alike. Their tones are in many cases entirely dif-

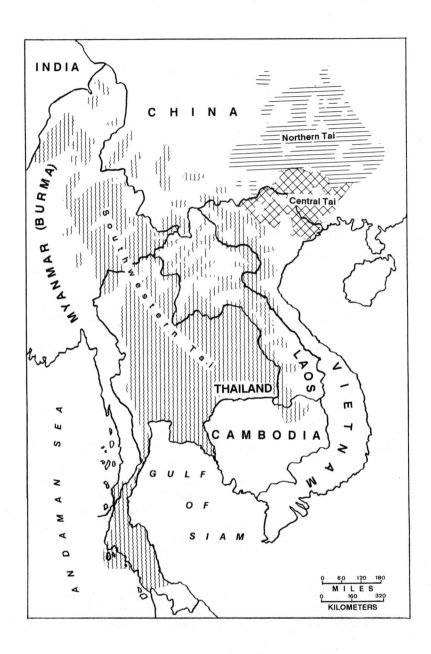

Map. 11.1. Distribution of Tai language families.

ferent. They make diphthongs out of some of our single vowels and single vowels out of some of our diphthongs. In some cases the initial consonant is the same as ours and the rest of the word entirely different, and in some cases vice versa.

Added to this, like other non-Buddhist Tai, these Yangtze Tai lacked all Pali terms. . . . For many of the connecting words in sentences these northern Tai use Chinese, although they know the Tai equivalents of most of them. Then there are some of the most frequently used verbs and nouns for which Chinese terms are used. There are also many terms that are distinctly Siamese localisms.

Yet the language is so essentially Tai that, by diligent search for substitutes for the missing Pali terms—generally finding Tai terms and in a very few cases using Chinese—in less than two months we found ourselves comparatively at home in the local dialect (Dodd 1923:38-39).

The several displaced Tai languages in Thailand need to be understood in relation to this dispersion of Tai languages and dialects and to their historic development. For that matter, so do the other Tai languages discussed earlier. In fact, the examples used to illustrate change in this chapter are taken from those larger languages.

To consider the processes of language change requires, however, that in most of this chapter we temporarily shift somewhat from the perspective of much of this book. Elsewhere we treat languages and dialects as relatively discrete entities, although we also point out that related languages shade into each other at the boundaries. Now we will look at Tai languages and dialects from a more fluid developmental perspective, gestalts in a large ever-shifting pattern of changing varieties with myriad small types of similarities and differences. We will see them more like the images in a giant kaleidoscope of many colors and textures at several depths.

Comparing whole languages and dialects for their patterns and the changes which cause them would be far too complex, however, so we restrict our discussion of language change to tone systems, as illustrative of the whole. The changing tone patterns are fascinating in themselves, and tones are crucial to the ways in which Thai people identify language and dialect differences.

Language Change and Tai Tone Variation

Foreigners find Standard Thai writing extremely complex, especially in how it represents tone, and are puzzled by some of the terminology used to talk about the spelling of tone. However, in its complexity the writing system provides a valuable key to understanding the tone changes which have helped produce much of the linguistic diversity in Tai languages.

In the Standard Thai writing system tones are not represented by unique diacritic tone marks—"accent marks"—alone, as they are in many languages and in the roman transcription we use for tone languages in this book. For example, each column below has the same Standard Thai diacritic— ˋ or ˊ, or nothing—but the tone pronunciations of the two words in the column are always different, as shown by the diacritics (or lack of them) in the roman transcription.

The display shows, in addition, that Thai falling tone, represented by /ˆ/ in the romanized transcription, is spelled with ˋ in the second column (second example), ˊ in the third column (first example) and no Thai diacritic at all in the fourth column (second example). It shows also that no Thai diacritic occurs in words with rising /ˇ/ or mid (no mark in the roman transcription) in the first column, low / ˋ/ or falling /ˆ/ in the fourth column, and low or high /ˊ/ in the fifth column. (The ˜ in the last column is a vowel sign, not a tone marker.)

ขา	ข่า	ข้า	ขาด	ขัด
khǎa	khàa	khâa	khàat	khàt
leg	galangal[1]	slave	lack	obstruct

คา	ค่า	ค้า	คาด	คัด
khaa	khâa	kháa	khâat	khát
embedded	cost	trade	to strap	be clogged

In spite of this appearance of randomness, however, the system does have a complicated logic to it. To see how it works you have to know that Standard Thai written consonants are divided into three groups, or classes, according to how they help to represent tone in the writing system. The traditional Thai names for these classes are /ˈaksɔ̌ɔ nsǔuŋ/ 'high consonants', /ˈaksɔ̌ɔ nklaaŋ/ 'middle consonants' and /ˈaksɔ̌ɔ ntàm/ 'low consonants', or High Class Consonants, Mid Class Consonants and Low Class Consonants. In the example above, ข is a High Class Consonant, and ค a Low Class Consonant, so although they both spell the same spoken consonant /kh/ they help symbolize different tones.[2]

But that is not the whole story either. The combination of consonant class plus tone mark, if any, plus final consonant, if any, plus length of vowel preceding the final consonant (columns 4 and 5) all work together to symbolize the tone. Part of that configuration will become clearer as this chapter progresses.

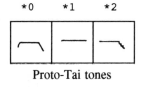

Each of these tones could occur
with any initial consonant

Proto-Tai tones

Fig. 11.1. Three postulated Proto-Tai tones, about A.D. 700
(Brown 1979a:113).

The whole system seems additionally complicated when the learner
finds no relation in Standard Thai between High Class Consonants and
high tone, or Mid Class Consonants and mid tone, or Low Class Consonants and low tone. What relationship between consonant class and
tone does exist is neither obvious nor simple, as the example amply
demonstrates.[3]

These consonant classes and their complex relationship to tone
arose as present Tai languages and dialects developed through processes of change from a common ancestor, generally called Proto-Tai,
sometimes Ancient Thai. No written records or other direct evidence
of Proto-Tai exists; it was not itself ever written. But linguists have
reconstructed something of what it must have been like by comparing
languages and dialects recorded at later times.[4]

According to such reconstruction, Proto-Tai had three different
tones, any one of which could occur on any syllable which ended in a
vowel,[5] as in figure 11.1. The labeling of the tones there as 0, 1, 2
anticipates the writing system developed later. The * before the tone
number indicates that the tone is postulated by linguistic reconstruction, not verified by observation. The shape of the line within each
box shows the presumed rise or fall of the voice during the pronunciation of the tone. The tops and bottoms of the boxes show the upper
and lower limits of the voice range. The ragged ending to tone *2
represents a "creaky" voice quality as the tone falls off, the vocal
cords being constricted a bit.

Seven hundred years later, the Khmer writing system was adapted
to the form of Tai then spoken in Sukhothai, one of the first great Tai
political and cultural centers within present-day Thailand. The language spoken at Sukhothai still had the three contrastive tones, but
due to changes in pronunciation since the time of Proto-Tai, each tone
now had three non-contrastive pitch variants. They were three
different pronunciations for each tone, a high, a mid and a low one,
depending on what type of consonant preceded it in a syllable. Al-

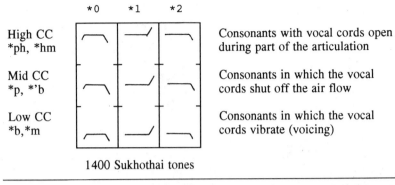

	*0	*1	*2	
High CC *ph, *hm				Consonants with vocal cords open during part of the articulation
Mid CC *p, *'b				Consonants in which the vocal cords shut off the air flow
Low CC *b,*m				Consonants in which the vocal cords vibrate (voicing)

1400 Sukhothai tones

Fig. 11.2. The three tones of Sukhothai in roughly A.D. 1400, each pronounced at three postulated different pitch heights as conditioned by High Class Consonants, Mid Class Consonants and Low Class Consonants, respectively (Brown 1979a:112-113).

though the three original tones were still contrastive, the variants of each were automatically and predictably governed by the preceding consonant, as described to the right of figure 11.2.

What *contrastive* means here can be illustrated by the following words in Standard Thai, which developed much later, of course.

> măa (rising tone) 'dog'
> maa (mid tone) 'come'
> máa (high tone) 'horse'

Because the only difference in pronunciation between these words is the tone difference, tone alone is enough to distinguish between the spoken words, so the tones are shown to contrast with each other.

In Sukhothai, however, although 'come' and 'horse' had contrasting tones, 'come' and 'dog' did not. There was a tone difference between the two, but at that time 'dog' was pronounced with a different consonant from 'come' and the tone difference was tied to the consonant difference, so that the tone difference alone never distinguished between those words or any like them. The tone indications in parentheses in the examples which follow refer to cells in figure 11.2, which show how the tones were pronounced.

> *hmaa (High0) 'dog'
> *maa (Low0) 'come'
> *maa (Low2) 'horse'

In other words, any High Class Consonant like *hm automatically caused whichever one of the three tone contours that directly followed it to be pronounced on a relatively high pitch, and any Low Class Consonant like *m automatically caused the tone which followed to be pronounced on a relatively low pitch. Thus, the tone pronunciation difference between 'dog' and 'come' was created automatically by the system, and was therefore not contrastive. Contrastive tones are separated by solid lines in the figures, while non-contrastive variants of what is structurally the same tone are not so separated.

This Sukhothai pattern of three tones, each with three variants, is no longer to be found in any Tai language because other major changes in pronunciation produced other tone configurations over the next four or five hundred years. Sukhothai, for example, had a series of consonant sounds in the High Class Consonant group which are technically known as voiceless nasals: [hm], [hn], [hñ] and [hŋ], represented by *hm in figure 11.2 and our previous examples. These sounded like the Low Class Consonant nasals [m], [n], [ñ] and [ŋ], except that they began almost as though they were whispered.[6] But over time the voiceless, whispered part was eliminated, so that they became indistinguishable from the voiced nasal sounds already included among the Low Class Consonants. In other words,

HCC	LCC
*hm → m	m
*hn → n	n
*hñ → ñ	ñ
*hŋ → ŋ	ŋ

In similar fashion, some of the Sukhothai Mid Class Consonant sounds, represented by *'b in figure 11.2, lost their feature of preglottalization—a closing of the vocal cords represented by [']—and became like [b] and [d], which already existed as Low Class Consonants.[7]

MCC	LCC
*'b → b	b
*'d → d	d
*'j → j	j

At the same time, the Low Class Consonants represented by *b in figure 11.2 gained a little puff of air (aspiration) after them, to become [pʰ], [tʰ], [cʰ] and [kʰ], in most cases duplicating sounds which already existed among the High Class Consonants.

LCC	HCC
*b → ph	ph
*d → th	th
*j → ch	8
*g → kh	kh

However, although these various groups of consonants came to be pronounced the same as consonants already existing in other classes, they did not change class membership. This meant that there were now High Class Consonants [m], [n], [ñ] and [ŋ], for example, in some words, and Low Class Consonants with identical consonant pronunciation in other words.

And while all of this was happening to the consonants, pronunciation of the tones was changing as well. Tones *0 and *1 merged (came to be pronounced the same) after High and Mid Class Consonants, so that any distinction between those tones following consonants of those classes was lost. Some of the other tone pronunciations were also modified.

The results of these complex changes can be seen in figure 11.3, the modern Paktay system which developed out of Sukhothai. Representations of the new pronunciations of the older consonants are shown between / /, and the new pronunciations of the tones are shown in the cells of the matrix. These changes were not merely shifts of detail, but created a different kind of tone system. Instead of nine pitch contours—nine tone pronunciations—there are now six or seven. And instead of three contrastive tones, there are now five, one or two of them having two pronunciations apiece.

While this line of tone development was taking place from Proto-Tai through Sukhothai to modern Paktay, other partially different changes from Proto-Tai were simultaneously occurring elsewhere as well. Thaiklang tones, for example, developed from Proto-Tai through the different dialect spoken at Ayuthaya rather than through Sukhothai. We do not need to go into the details of the development, but figure 11.4 shows some Thaiklang dialects, both reconstructed and modern, demonstrating that the solid lines of their matrices are in characteristically different positions from those of Paktay.

Thaiklang, for example, has no merger of Tone *0 and Tone *1 after any consonant class. Tone *0 has three tone pronunciations in three of these dialects, but Mid0 and Low0 merged in Bangkok. Tone *1 and Tone *2 first developed into two tones each (1400 Ayuthaya), but then High2 and Mid2 merged with Low1, so that two different kinds of falling tones became one. In figureld 11.4 the open link be-

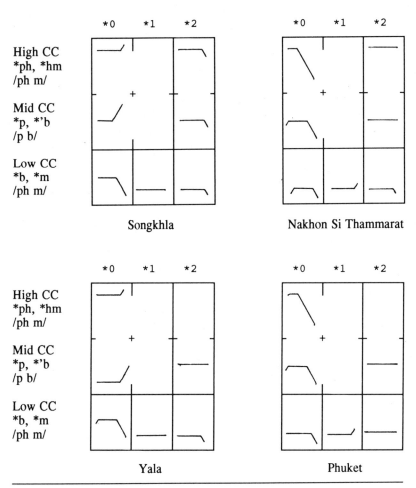

Fig. 11.3. Four representative Paktay tone systems from four provinces of southern Thailand (Brown 1965).

tween High2, Mid2, and Low1 in the three more modern matrices, with only one kind of falling tone, is a distinguishing characteristic of modern Thaiklang dialects and Standard Thai, as is the fact that High0 and Mid0 are not pronounced alike (Kalaya 1986).

In Bangkok still other important developments took place. For the first time in what has been presented so far, tones related to all three classes of consonants now contrasted with each other. However, none of the actual pronounced tone contours now resembled any meaning

of the terms "High," "Mid," and "Low," which nevertheless remained labels for the classes of consonants. The terms were now simply
labels for historical groupings of consonants which remained relevant
for the spelling of tones, but not for their pronunciation. The spellings, however, continue much as they were.

Meanwhile, in northeast Thailand and throughout Laos, another set
of changes was taking place to produce the Lao dialects. Figure 11.5
shows four modern Lao tone patterns. Unlike Thaiklang and Paktay,

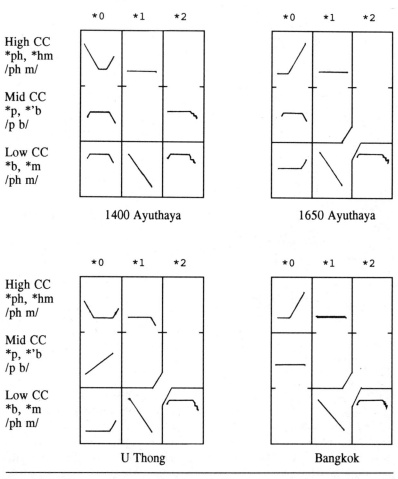

Fig. 11.4. Two reconstructed older Thaiklang tone systems followed by
two modern ones (after Brown 1965, 1979a).

none of the three Proto-Tai tones (the vertical columns) have merged at any point. A characteristic split has come, however, between High2 and Mid2. In different dialects, furthermore, Tone 0 has split between High and Mid or between Mid and Low. If Tone 1 has split at all, it has done so only between Mid and Low.

The same kind of association between changing consonants and tones was true of Kammüang as well, with additional complications. In the languages so far discussed, all consonants in any consonant

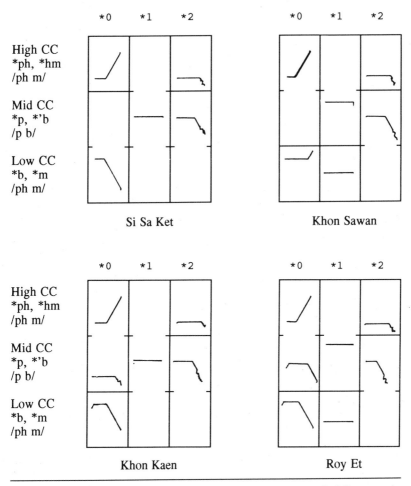

Fig. 11.5. Four dialects of Lao, showing resemblances and differences in their pitch pronunciation and tone systems (after Strecker 1979:198, 204-206; Brown 1965).

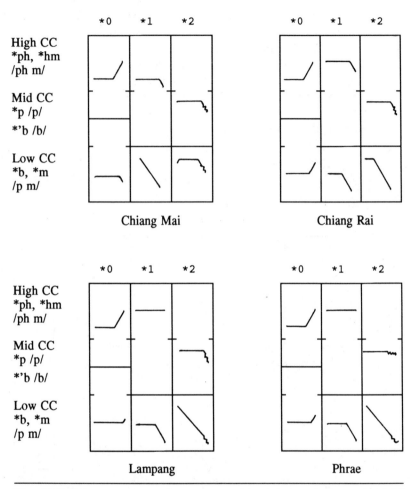

Fig. 11.6. The Kammüang tone system, with dialect variations. The Mid Class Consonants split into two classes in respect to Proto-Tai Tone *0, as shown by the solid line across the middle of the Mid0 cell (after Brown 1965).

class relate to tone changes in the same way. But in Kammüang two different sets of Mid Class Consonants affect Tone 0 differently, so that *p and *'b are associated with different modern tones. This means that the matrix we have been using has to be modified for Kammüang, as in figure 11.6. Another major Kammüang consonant difference from the other three regional languages, furthermore, is

that earlier Low Class *b, *d, *j, *g have changed differently from
how they changed in the rest of Thailand.

	Kammüang	Elsewhere
*b →	p	ph
*d →	t	th
*j →	c	ch
*g →	k	kh

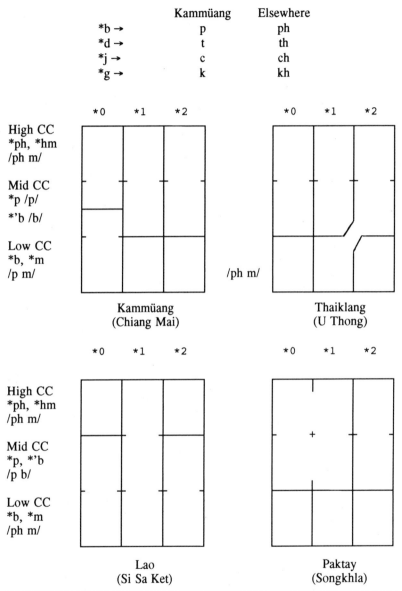

Fig. 11.7. Characteristic shapes of the tone systems of the four regional
languages of Thailand, each exemplified by the shape of the system in a particular dialect of the region (After Brown 1965; Strecker 1979a).

Examples of both tone and consonantal differences were given in chapter 5.

Figure 11.7, finally, compares the characteristic differences of tone patterning for each of the four Tai regional languages.

The Thai System for Writing Tones

So what became the Standard Thai writing system got started in Suk-hothai, but the Standard Thai language came through Ayuthaya and Bangkok (fig. 11.8). At some point the consonants with which the different pronunciations of each tone were associated came to be called High, Mid, and Low. The terms made sense for Sukhothai speech, and later for Paktay, but were not descriptive of the tones of Ayuthaya, so they became arbitrary labels there, and remained so when Standard Thai developed (Brown 1979a:113).

Because of some of the changes described above, two different consonant symbols derived from different ancestral sounds sometimes represent the same modern sound in the Standard Thai writing system.[9]

Spelling		Proto-Tai	Standard Thai
พ	(LCC)	*b	ph
ผ	(HCC)	*ph	ph
ท	(LCC)	*d	th
ถ	(HCC)	*th	th
ค	(LCC)	*g	kh
ข	(HCC)	*kh	kh
ม	(LCC)	*m	m
หม	(HCC)	*hm	m
น	(LCC)	*n	n
หน	(HCC)	*hn	n
ย	(LCC)	*ñ	y
หย	(HCC)	*hñ	y
ง	(LCC)	*ŋ	ŋ
หง	(HCC)	*hŋ	ŋ

In light of all these changes, figure 11.9 shows why Thai tone spellings like the following, which seem inconsistent on the surface, are actually quite regular.

    ผา (no tone mark) spells /phǎa/ 'cliff' (rising tone, High0 cell).

    มา (no tone mark) spells /maa/ 'come' (mid tone, Low0 cell).

    หมา (no tone mark) spells /mǎa/ 'dog' (rising tone, High0 cell).

    บ่า ({1} tone mark) spells /bàa/ 'shoulder' (low tone, Mid1 cell).

    พ่า ({1} tone mark) spells /phâa/ (no meaning) (falling tone, Low1 cell).

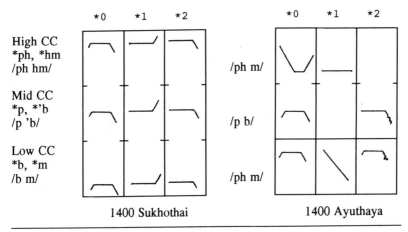

Fig. 11.8. Sukhothai and Ayuthaya tones at the time the writing system was borrowed from Sukhothai by Ayuthaya (Brown 1979a:113).

บ้า ({2} tone mark) spells /bâa/ 'crazy' (falling tone, Mid2 cell).
ม้า ({2} tone mark) spells /máa/ 'horse' (high tone, Low2 cell).

Two spellings for the same pronunciation are therefore possible when both High and Low Class Consonant symbols represent the same modern consonant phoneme, and when the syllable has a falling tone. Only one of them is the correct spelling for a given word, however. Thus, both ผ้า and ว่า (High2 and Low1) spell /phâa/ but only the first spells the word for 'cloth' correctly.

Language Patterns and Displaced Patches

Map 11.1 shows in a gross way how Tai languages range all over Southeast Asia and South China, as classified into three groups based on similarities within each (Li 1959, 1960, 1977; Strecker 1987). But a map of this kind is not nearly detailed enough to show the interlocking similarities and differences which are due to myriad changes such as we have been describing.

If it were possible to have a map of all the Tai languages and dialects of Thailand, one which plotted all of their different tone systems, vocabulary differences, and grammatical differences, it would show a great deal of shading from one pattern into another. Each bit of phonetic detail, each word, would be found over an area that was sometimes large, sometimes small. The area of one trait would not necessarily coincide fully with the area for any other, but the patterns would be intertwined. Some areas would be relatively similar, with transitional zones between them, but the areas of similarity would also have patterns of difference within them. We saw one example of such shading from one language to another in figure 7.1.

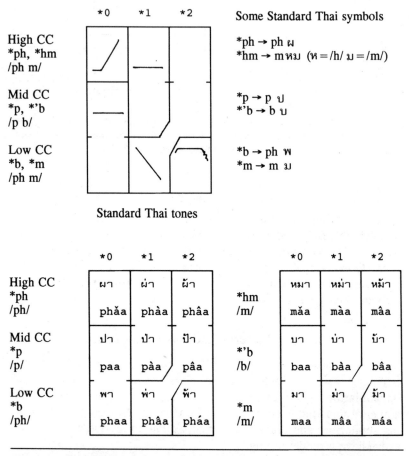

Some Standard Thai symbols

*ph → ph ผ
*hm → m หม (ห = /h/ ม = /m/)

*p → p ป
*'b → b บ

*b → ph พ
*m → m ม

Standard Thai tones

Fig. 11.9. Writing of Standard Thai tones. In the top matrix Standard Thai tones are shown together with consonant symbols representing the consonant classes. In the lower row these Thai consonant symbols are shown in the respective cells (together with a following vowel า /aa/) to demonstrate the tone phonemes which the combinations represent. The syllables used for illustration in these examples are not necessarily meaningful Thai words.

Such patterns are the effects of multiple changes in language as they spread. They have been likened to the crisscrossing ripples which radiate across the surface of water when pebbles are droped into it at different places and times. Nearby villages share most of the changes, but not all of them. The same change reaches some villages farther away, but not all of them. The kaleidoscope is created.

But if we did have such a detailed map of language and dialect traits, it would also show some pockets where the local language is unusually different from surrounding languages, as though the more general ripples had been inhibited in this spot, and a different set of pebbles caused a different set of ripples; or as though the primary pattern had been patched with a piece of pattern taken from some distance away. There are places in central Thailand, for example, where the map would show villages where dialects of Kammüang or Lao are spoken, with tone matrices considerably different from those of the Thaiklang-speaking people around them.

Such patches are created when Tai communities are displaced from their original locations. Their speech was part of a pattern in their former locations, but does not fit in as neatly with surrounding languages at their present locations. Sometimes the displacement is from another part of Thailand, sometimes from outside Thailand. Some of it is the result of wars long ago, when captives were brought in as laborers or to settle underpopulated parts of the country; some of it results from people having migrated on their own.

Saek

In Thailand the Tai language which is most different from all the others in this respect is Saek, found in scattered locations in Nakhon Phanom Province near the border of Laos in the northeast (map 11.2). Other Tai displaced languages in Thailand are all part of what is known as Southwestern Tai, but Saek belongs to the Northern Tai[10] group spoken mainly in southern China (map 11.1), although it varyies significantly even from that branch as well (David Strecker personal communication). Saek patches intrude into the area covered by Lao.

Groups of Saek people moved into Laos and Thailand from Vietnam two hundred years ago or more, and are located not far from each other on both sides of the border. The culture of the Saek people is now almost identical with that of the Lao around them, language being the key difference (Gedney 1970). And although Saek is not

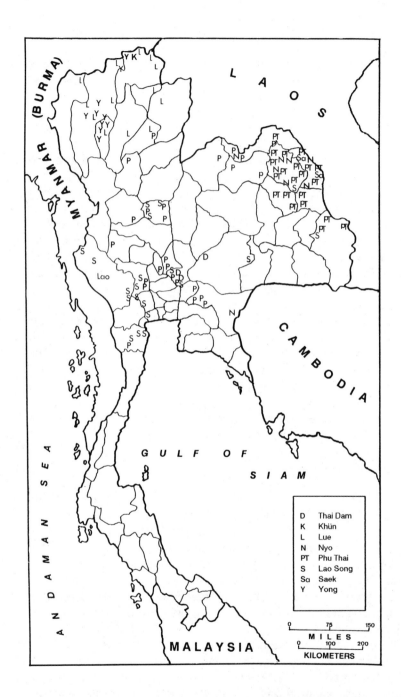

Map. 11.2. Distribution of some displaced Tai languages.

mutually intelligible with Lao or with Standard Thai, proximity to Lao villages and to the Nakhon Phanom provincial center and the universal presence of schools means that most Saek people in Thailand are multilingual.

In the 1960s older people still used Saek as the language of the village and home. Young people spoke it freely, with slang and other evidences of a language still alive and functioning, but they had a tendency to substitute many words from Lao or Thai in it. Younger children understood Saek, but replied in Lao when addressed in Saek. Older people were afraid the language would die out in a couple of generations (Gedney 1970:68). Sometimes such situations stabilize into multilingualism with different languages having different functions, as we have seen; sometimes they do not.

But for the present, at least, many Saek people move freely between three languages, Saek in the village, Lao as the regional language, and Standard Thai as the national language and language of official affairs and education. The Saek are thus unambiguously integrated into the language hierarchy of the country (fig. II.1).

Phu Thai

Another example of a displaced Tai language in Thailand is Phu Thai (Phuthai, Putai), spoken by over one hundred thousand people,[11] located primarily in the northeast (map 11.2). The Phu Thai entered Thailand during the first half of the nineteenth century from Laos (Kirsch 1966:371), where scattered groups still live, and probably ultimately from the Tai-speaking area of North Vietnam around the city of Dien Bien Phu. They tend to live on slightly higher elevations than the Lao, in higher valleys or at the foot of low-lying hills (Kirsch 1967:38, 49).

In earlier times the Phu Tai in the northeast had a semi-autonomous status in Thailand, and were ruled by at least one Phu Thai prince (Kirsch 1967:44). In the latter part of the nineteenth century, when King Chulalongkorn consolidated the national administrative structure of the country, the Phu Thai lost that degree of independence, and were absorbed into the Thai governmental system (Kirsch 1966:371). Small areas of Phu Thai are completely surrounded by Lao. Travel to and communication with their Lao neighbors is easy.

Phu Thai, however, is a separate language from both Lao and Thaiklang (Brown 1965:14). A Phu Thai speaking "pure" Phu Thai to a native speaker of Central Thai will almost certainly not be understood (A. Thomas Kirsch personal communication). A Lao is likely to understand more, but not perfectly.

At present as many as five Phu Thai tone patterns are to be found in different dialects, with additional variation in actual tone contours from village to village within some of them (Pojanee 1985). Considerable other dialect variation is also present in Phu Thai. Nevertheless, people say that speakers of the other Phu Thai dialects all speak essentially the "same" (A. Thomas Kirsch personal communication).

A shift has taken place in self-perceptions of the Phu Thai people in modern times. Earlier, to be Phu Thai was their highest level of identity, in contrast to Thai, Lao, and other groups. Now Phu Thai identity has become one kind of Thai. As a result, the Phu Thai see no incompatibility in using both Phu Thai and Thai languages, but see their increasing Thai characteristics as progress (A. Thomas Kirsch personal communication). This shift includes joining the language hierarchy of the country, primarily effected through the schools, the government, and the Buddhist administrative structure.

Virtually all Phu Thai men and many women claim to speak and understand Lao as well as Phu Thai. Young adults, local officials, teachers, young monks (and some older ones) often understand Thai-klang as well, and are able to speak it to varying degrees. But Kirsch (personal communication) has also commented that the primary mistake he made in his earlier analysis of the Phu Thai situation was in assuming that the communities would soon lose their Phu Thai language. Twenty-five years later, in spite of increased multilingualism, the Phu Thai language seemed as strong as it was in the 1960s.

Lue

Lue (Lü) is a third displaced language, this one scattered across the northern provinces (map 11.2). The heaviest concentrations of speakers are in Chiang Kham District of Phayao Province, Chiang Khong District of Chiang Rai Province, and in Pua and Nan districts of Nan Province (Moerman 1967b).

Two to three generations ago Lue-speaking people were much more extensively distributed through northern Thailand (Dodd 1923: 11; Seidenfaden 1958:25; Moerman 1965a:1222). Some of their descendants have been absorbed into the general Kammüang regional language, and no longer have any separate identity. Many others still remain a distinct group in spite of the fact that they have few characteristics other than language to distinguish them from the Kammüang population (Moerman 1965a, 1967b, 1967c).

The Lue began settling in Thailand as long as four hundred years ago, coming from around the ancient city of Chiang Rung in south China (Ruengdet 1980:27; Hartmann 1976:11). Some Lue in Thailand were brought in as war captives, or were otherwise persuaded to settle tracts of land left empty when previous raids by other states carried off large numbers of the local population (Kraisri 1965b; Moerman 1965a:1222). Others came by migration to escape war and other hardships (Moerman 1965b:168). The migration continues, as Lue refugees still trickle into Thailand from time to time (Wijeyewardene 1990:51).

The Lue in Thailand have the same traditional writing system as the Northern Thai, related also to the temple system of Lao. As with these others, it is now largely relegated to a religious function, known primarily by monks, and not by all of them.

The question of mutual intelligibility between Kammüang and Lue is hard to resolve because the speakers have had such extensive contact. Linguistically the languages are closely related. Dodd (1923: 62, 185) considered the difference between Lue and Kammüang to be about as great as that between a Bostonian and a Midwesterner in the USA, which is not much. Seidenfaden (1925:189) considered the varieties "practically identical." Similar statements have been made by others who have known the Lue (Freeman 1911:91; Moerman 1965a:1226). On the other hand, Moerman also wrote (1967b:513) that in his earlier work he had unduly minimized the reality of the Lue dialect. He had identified it too closely with Kammüang.

It seems to be a case where virtual mutual intelligibility exists between Lue and Kammüang, but although Kammüang people generally have only a little trouble understanding Lue who are speaking directly to them on the consultative level, they do sometimes have considerable difficulty understanding Lue talking to each other (Dorothy Uhlig, Melvert W. Byers personal communications). The disruption of the larger regional dialect pattern is therefore not as great where Lue is to be found as it is where Phu Thai speakers are located, or especially where the Saek are, but there is some.

But whatever the degree of mutual intelligibility between Lue and Kammüang, multilingualism is widespread among the Lue, most of whom speak Kammüang freely, sometimes Lao, and often Standard Thai as well. As in other multilingual communities, a conversational group in a Lue village may include people whose mother tongue is not the local one and people whose skill in languages other than their own varies. People speak one language or another according to their abilities and those of the people they want to include or exclude.[12]

Lue language remains a strong marker of Lue identity as one kind of Thai. As in the regional languages and the other displaced languages, Lue is changing to be more like the forms of Tai above it in the hierarchy. The breaks in the pattern are therefore becoming less distinct, which may or may not mean that they will disappear.

Summary

Tai languages and dialects have undergone a long history of fluid change which we have illustrated with the tone systems. Such change is always going on at different rates and in different parts of the language in different geographic locations. Pattern shades into pattern across the expanse of territory where the Tai languages are spoken.

Sometimes communities of speakers of one Tai language move to another location considerable distance away. Their language fit into the pattern of Tai languages in its original location, although it differed in small ways from the languages around it. But it is sharply different in some respects from the patterns of the language in the new location. The Saek or Phu Thai tone matrices, for example, do not match the Lao matrix of the new location. It is as though a patch of pattern from a predominantly blue area was placed in a predominantly green area. This is the phenomenon of displaced Tai languages.

Saek, Phu Thai and Lue are three examples of such languages in Thailand. They, like most other displaced Tai languages, function in some ways more like the marginal and enclave languages to be discussed in later chapters. They differ from those languages, however, in their close linguistic relationship and similarity to the regional and national languages around them.

The sound changes in Tai languages and dialects have produced much greater diversity than this chapter had room to recount, but in earlier chapters we also saw how the strong influence of Standard Thai causes some people to shift their language in the direction of the national language as well. Borrowing vocabulary is one notable way in which that is done. So along with the changes toward greater diversity which we have examined here, other changes diminish diversity. Language change can and does work both ways in creating language patterns.

12

Languages of Thai Towns and Cities: Chinese Languages

Bangkok streets, like those of any other densely populated city, are full of writing publicly displayed: signs, advertisements, store names, company names, brand names, notices, announcements, newspapers, magazines, books. On some blocks hundreds of such visual samples of language vie for attention.

In Bangkok such written language samples also come in a variety of languages and scripts. Signs giving the names of streets, for example, are typically written in Thai letters with smaller roman script underneath. Although these transliterations of street names only roughly approximate the sound of the Thai, they are essential for the many people from other countries who do not read Thai but do read a language written in roman script.

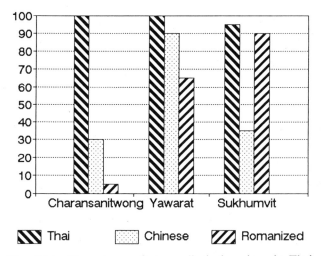

Fig. 12.1. Percentages of stores displaying signs in Thai, Chinese and romanized scripts. Many stores, of course, had all three.

Considerable English language writing itself is also to be seen on the streets of Bangkok. Sometimes an English word or phrase is conspicuous in an otherwise Thai advertisement or notice. T-shirts display English slogans. Many Western and anglicized Japanese brand names are used with or without Thai transliteration as well. English messages are directed at tourists and others from abroad: "Pattaya weekend" or "Currency exchange" or "Cheapest air fares."

Chinese signs are also common, frequently displaying the name of a shop or a business concern in Chinese along with Thai, and often along with an English name or a roman script transliteration of the Thai or Chinese name. Different stores and different areas of the city give prominence to one language or another by the size, position, and color of the writing.

Charansanitwong Road, for example, is in a part of town neither extremely Chinese nor extremely European, whereas Yawarat Road is in a strongly Chinese area, and Sukhumvit Road runs through a more Westernized section of the city. Twenty-two contiguous stores were checked for the languages used in each of those locations (fig. 12.1), revealing the not-very-surprising fact that the presence of a Chinese store name was clearly related to the "Chineseness" of the area, and the occurrence of romanized writing to the degree of Westernization. However, more romanized signs appear in the Chinese section of town than might have been predicted (table 12.1).

Table 12.1. Percentage of stores with names written in various combinations of language and script, Thai language in Thai script, etc. The four bottom rows indicate combinations of languages, such as a Chinese name plus the words "Limited Partnership" in Thai or English.

Language	Script	Charansanitwong	Yawarat	Sukhumvit
Thai	Thai	67.7	68.2	28.8
Thai	roman	0.0	9.1	3.0
Chinese	Thai	3.0	7.6	1.5
Chinese	roman	0.0	1.5	3.0
English	Thai	4.5	0.0	33.3
English	roman	4.5	6.6	63.6
Chinese & Thai	Thai	3.0	48.5	3.0
English & Thai	Thai	19.7	22.7	31.8
Thai & English	roman	4.5	21.2	18.2
Chinese & English	roman	0.0	1.5	1.5

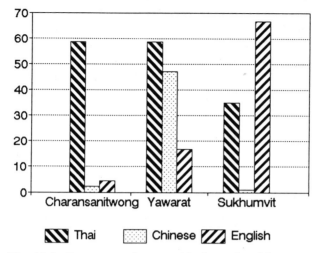

Fig. 12.2. Percentage of stores with signs advertising services in different languages.

On these signs the Thai script sometimes represents actual Thai
language, or sometimes Chinese or English transliterated into Thai.
Likewise, roman script represents English or a roman transliteration
of Thai or Chinese.[1]

As is also apparent from figure 12.2, virtually no stores had signs
announcing services in Chinese in the non-Chinese areas surveyed,
but 47% of the stores in the Chinese section had such signs. Signs
advertising services in English were also infrequent in the Thai section, but very common in the section where more Westerners live.
Stores advertising their services in Thai were much more evenly distributed.

Almost all people of Chinese ancestry in Thailand are Thai citizens
and should be able to read Thai, so far as government policy is concerned, so Chinese signs are not placed on government buildings.
They are more likely to be displayed by Chinese or Sino-Thai people
on their own establishments, where they serve as identity markers for
many such merchants and as communication media within the Chinese
community, especially with older people and newcomers who are not
able to read Thai.

The language of signs within buildings depends on the type of establishment and its clientele, as well as its ownership. Chinese does
not seem to be common except in Chinese or Sino-Thai establishments. Government offices do not normally have signs in languages

other than Thai, except for offices dealing directly with the foreign public, where some signs may also be written in English.

All over Bangkok, streetside stands which display newspapers and magazines for sale carry far more Thai titles than anything else, but one or two Chinese papers and one or two English papers are often for sale there also. In the heart of the Chinese district in Bangkok, eight out of ten newsstands had between one and five different Chinese newspapers, and three had two or three Chinese magazines.

In smaller Thai towns and cities not as much English or Chinese is to be seen, although English is increasing. Street signs, if any, are not as often transliterated as they are in Bangkok, and in the really small rural district centers frequently no signs are displayed at all on streets or on many stores. Presumably everybody knows the names of all the streets and stores anyhow—or doesn't need names. In larger towns Thai is still strongly predominant, but the larger the town the more Chinese signs to be seen. English is also common in towns like Chiang Mai where tourists come regularly, and roman-letter brand names are ubiquitous, even in remote areas.

Varieties of Languages in Towns and Cities

Even all the languages on signs and the other forms of visual communication in Thai towns and cities do not fully reveal the linguistic diversity of the urban areas, however, or how Thai towns and cities fit into the larger hierarchy of languages discussed so far. English is the primary language of Thailand abroad, and also the primary language of communication with and between foreigners within the country. Because foreigners concentrate mostly in the cities, especially Bangkok, English is used more there than anywhere else.

Standard Thai, the language of the nation, is also used most extensively in the cities, where the people with the most education are concentrated. The language of the region in which the city is located is used too, normally even more than Standard Thai.

When cities are located in one of the marginal regional areas (part 3), still another layer of language is present. The most common language on the street in the city of Surin, for example, is Northern Khmer. Pattani Malay is commonly heard in Pattani. And because people migrate to the larger cities from different parts of the country to find work, Lao, Kammüang and Paktay are also to be heard in the quarters of Bangkok where such people live.

From one standpoint, then, cities are but a denser and more complex projection of the language hierarchy of the part of the nation in which they are located. But the cities are different, too. Some languages have specialized roles to play as the languages of Thai towns and cities, their basic position in the hierarchy. Of them, the Chinese languages are by far the most important, but languages of south Asia like Hindi, Urdu, Panjabi, and Tamil are also spoken by some urban citizens of Thailand. Little information is available about their use or the people who use them, however. Hussain (1982) called his book *The Silent Minority: Indians in Thailand.*

Chinese People

People of Chinese background are the most numerous and powerful non-Tai ethnic minority in Thailand. In commerce and other business they are usually more powerful even than ethnic Thai, although politico-military power, which the Thai have, has generally succeeded in trumping economic power when it sought to do so. Typically, powerful leaders in both groups cooperate for their mutual advantage.

Relations between native Thai people and those of Chinese ancestry are much better than those between the Chinese and their host peoples in surrounding countries. This results partly from half a century of Thai policy toward Chinese immigration and education, which has been different from policy in other Southeast Asian countries and has kept Chinese power more fully under Thai control.[2]

Chinese immigrants and people of Chinese ancestry have lived in Thailand for a long time. Chinese discovered tin ore deposits in the peninsular section of the country and began developing them before Tai peoples ever reached that area. Chinese people were present in the early Tai kingdom of Sukhothai. Ayuthaya, the great kingdom where much Thai advanced culture was formed, had its Chinese quarter, and so did other towns of the time. When a king of Ayuthaya inaugurated royal trade monopolies, he called upon Chinese people to manage them.

After the fall of Ayuthaya, Taksin, son of a Chinese father and a Thai mother, defeated the Burmese with the help of Chinese from southeast Thailand, and set up the new Thai kingdom. King Rama I, the first king of the present dynasty, had a Chinese mother as well as a Chinese concubine. He established the capital at Bangkok, a Chinese port and trading center. Under the early kings of this dynasty, Chinese people were highly favored. Chinese immigration was encouraged; trading monopolies were given to Chinese; Chinese scholars were maintained at the court; Chinese commanders directed the Thai navy; some governors were Chinese; a few Chinese leaders were given titles of nobility. By the late seventeenth century, the Chinese had begun commercial vegetable and fruit production around the cities, a type of agriculture in which they still hold a virtual monopoly (Hafner 1983:35-40).

In the first part of the nineteenth century, the period just before Thailand began modernizing, Chinese settlements were to be found all over the central plains and Chinese people were major minorities or sometimes the majority in major towns. In this period the Chinese presence sometimes created great resentment and some violence. The Chinese, furthermore, were themselves divided between linguistic groups, and fought each other at times (Terwiel 1989:253-254).

Beginning in the latter part of the nineteenth century massive numbers of Chinese were imported to work as laborers in tin mines, on plantations, and in the construction of canals, roads, the railway system, and temples. Rates of immigration varied with events in Thailand and in China, and with two world wars, but generally heavy immigration continued until 1949, when a quota limiting immigration to two hundred people per year per nationality was legislated. Although the law was written to cover all nationalities equally, it was aimed particularly at curtailing Chinese immigration, and has notably done so.

But all of this immigration did not mean a corresponding net increase in the number of Chinese in Thailand. Many returned to China after making some money, and others married Thai women, especially as Chinese women did not immigrate in earlier years. The children of mixed marriages then often married Thai spouses. Successive generations therefore sometimes had weaker Chinese ethnic characteristics, and are more accurately called Sino-Thai. Some descendants of Chinese ancestors have completely assimilated, having no significant memory or trace of Chinese ancestry.

Assimilation continues, with different Sino-Thai families and individuals having abandoned Chinese traits to different degrees. Boonsanong (1971:11-19) compared three groups, all born in families where both parents were native speakers of a Chinese language. The first group consisted of people with little education and with jobs outside the government; the second group contained people with more education but still with jobs outside the government; the third group was made up of government employees. When asked about language, 24% of group 1, 45% of group 2, and 81% of group 3 reported speaking more Thai than Chinese at home. 68% of group 3 found it not very necessary to speak Chinese anywhere, whereas 27% of group 1 found it not very necessary to speak Thai at all.

Many ethnic Thai have some Chinese ancestors, which in some cases they may not even know about, or may consider just a historical fact with no bearing on their present situation or identity. Many other people are both Chinese and Thai, their "double identity" (Coughlin 1960) on the way to greater assimilation if present trends continue. However, the rate of assimilation may have slowed somewhat as the ethnic category of Sino-Thai has itself become firmly established (Szanton 1983). The mixture has different proportions for different people, a few individuals strongly Chinese, with relatively little Thai influence or identity, but many more the reverse (Jirawat 1973:99-100; Guskin 1968:56-60).

The Chinese and Sino-Thai populations which speak a Chinese language in the Thai towns and cities are most numerous in Bangkok, and most of this chapter is based on patterns there. However, Sino-Thai and even small Chinese populations are also located in all of the provincial towns and cities and in district centers as well. In district centers, the Sino-Thai merchant or rice mill operator or broker for local products may be married to a local woman; their children go to local schools and have largely local status. In the towns of a marginal regional area like the Malay-speaking area in the south or the Khmer-speaking area in the northeast, people of Chinese background may outnumber not only native speakers of Standard Thai but also speakers of the regional Paktay or Lao languages, respectively.

Scholars have had difficulty making accurate estimates of the "Chinese" population now in Thailand. The official census ignored the issue as a matter of policy in earlier decades, except for Chinese citizens who were counted until 1980 (table 12.2). Use of languages other than Thai is grossly underreported in the 1980 census. In 1980, for example, the Royal Thai Police Department listed 294,059 Chinese citizens registered in Thailand,[3] but the national census that same year lists only 90,500 people as speaking Chinese in the home.

Table 12.2. Percentages of alien Chinese in Thailand (Wyatt 1984:291; Royal Thai Police Department, reported by National Statistical Office personal communication).

1937	1947	1960	1970	1980	1989
3.6	2.7	1.6	0.9	0.6	0.5

Table 12.3. Indicators of Sino-Thai presence in a survey of household heads in rural, provincial, and metropolitan areas, in percentages (after Visit 1972: table 8).

	Rural	Provincial	Metropolitan
At least one Chinese characteristic	3.4	16.8	31.5
Language spoken in the home			
Thai and Chinese	0.9	14.0	26.2
Chinese	0.5	2.3	6.2
Total some Chinese language	1.4	16.3	32.4
Ethnic origin of name			
Both names Chinese	2.7	13.5	23.5
first name Chinese, family name Thai	0.6	1.7	0.5
first name Thai, family name Chinese	0.8	2.7	2.1
Total some Chinese name	4.1	17.9	26.1

It is extremely unlikely that less than one-third of the alien Chinese use a Chinese language as the language of the home, not to count any of the people of Chinese ancestry who are citizens. In the census, furthermore, Sino-Thai of whatever degree of assimilation are counted as Thai. Political problems inhibit separating them, and practically speaking, if the Sino-Thai were to be separately counted, up to what degree of assimilation would such people be classified separately? \

In table 12.3 "Chinese" includes all of the Chinese languages. "Characteristics" noted include such cultural features as the type of shrine in the home, presence of Chinese-language written materials, language spoken, dress, etc. The percentage figures for various Chinese indicators also perhaps understate the Sino-Thai population because people could have strong memories of Chinese ancestry and make regular visits to less assimilated relatives and friends, participat-

Table 12.4. Estimated Sino-Thai population, extrapolated from table 12.3, assuming a population of five million people in the metropolitan area and fifty million in the country in 1989. In each case the largest Sino-Thai indicator was used (*name* in the case of rural and provincial, *language* in the case of the metropolitan area).

	Rural	Provincial	Metropolitan	Country
Sino-Thai population percentages (table 12.3)	4.1	17.9	32.4	16.3
Population estimates			1,620,000	8,150,000

ing in Sino-Thai life without any of the Chinese characteristics noted for the survey.

Extrapolation from the percentages in table 12.3 produces the estimates of Sino-Thai population in table 12.4. A survey seven years later—one which did not distinguish provincial populations—showed slightly smaller percentages (Institute of Population Studies 1981: 21). Estimates of native speakers of the different Chinese languages in the towns and cities are

Teochiu	2,200,000
Hakka	580,000
Hainanese	379,000
Cantonese	275,000
Hokkien	150,000
Taiwanese	37,000
	3,621,000

Chinese Ecological Niche

In his study of the Mon (chap. 13) Foster (1973b:244-250; 1977:236-237) suggested a reason why successful major commerce is in the hands of minority groups in many countries where the dominant people are not as successful in business, even with government sponsorship and protection. In many societies the marketplace and commerce conflict with traditional values of assistance and mutual responsibility carried out through social networks. A person who is fully a part of village society must be generous in traditional ways to those in need, and the more a person has, the greater the obligation. To be an efficient merchant, on the other hand, such relationships have to be limited. Business relationships and village society relationships are to an important degree incompatible.

But people of another ethnic group may not be as tightly tied into the social network of a village, even though they live there. They can more easily set up a symbiotic relationship with a different set of obligations from traditional family-based obligations.

The implications of Foster's suggestion are that people of Chinese ancestry in Thailand are successful not only because they are capable, hardworking, aggressive, and have business aptitude and experience, as is the stereotype.[4] In fact, their ancestors were often poor rice farmers in China, many coming to Thailand because they were not successful in the homeland. Instead, Foster suggests that they are successful in Thailand partly because they are not ethnic Thai, that their

very ethnic difference has been significantly functional for the development of the country and will continue to be so wherever Thai still
live in face-to-face communities or operate under cultural norms
established in such communities.[5]

With Foster's comments in mind, it is enlightening to look again at
Boonsanong's figures on differential assimilation of the Sino-Thai,
quoted earlier. The people who were not government employees,
most of them in business, saw a greater need for maintaining and using a Chinese language. People who worked for the Thai government
saw much less need for it. They had more ethnic Thai friends, and
were more nearly full participants in Thai social networks.

Chinese Languages

There is one written Chinese language, but the Chinese people who
read this one written language speak several mutually unintelligible
languages. Chinese is a family of spoken languages with a single writing system. China is like another Europe, with a whole array of
related languages, but is unlike Europe in having only one set of reading materials.

In this book "Chinese" refers to a cultural tradition, to a written
language, and to a family of spoken languages. Individual Chinese
languages will be referred to by their individual names. Other writers
often call these languages "dialects," but they are sometimes as
different from each other as French is from Italian.

Teochiu (Swatow) is the most widely spoken Chinese language in
Thailand, or at least in the Bangkok area.[6] Teochiu-speaking immigrants came to Thailand from the Chinese coast opposite the island of
Taiwan, many of them from the area around the city of Shantou.
People of Teochiu ancestry are estimated to be 60% of the Sino-Thai
population, but the language is even more important than that. In
Boonsanong's survey (1971:14-15), 61.7% of the nine hundred respondents claimed Teochiu as their first language, but 81.5% could
speak it.

The next most important Chinese language in Thailand is
Mandarin, the official language of China, and the most widespread
there. The number of native Mandarin-speaking immigrants has been
small in Thailand, perhaps less than 1% in the cities,[7] but even
though none of Boonsanong's respondents knew Mandarin as their
first language, 19.9% could speak it, making it the second most
widely known Chinese language in this population. Knowledge of

Mandarin is found especially among older educated males in Thailand (Hjejle 1972:5-6).

In Boonsanong's sample, Mandarin was spoken by 27% of the better-educated respondents who were not government employees. This reflects both their orientation towards Chinese and their education, but even so, an even larger 32.3% of the same group spoke English. Among other respondents English was spoken by about half as many as spoke Mandarin.

The next two languages have approximately the same numbers of speakers (17% each in Boonsanong's survey) for different reasons. For Hakka it is because Hakka was their mother tongue. Few non-Hakka learn it. On the other hand, mother-tongue speakers of Cantonese are few in Thailand (8%), but other people learn the language because it is spoken in Hong Kong and is, therefore, one of the international trade languages of Chinese merchants. Hakka-speaking people came to Thailand mainly from an area just west of, and inland from, the area from which the Teochiu came. Cantonese-speaking immigrants came from the city of Canton in southeast China and from areas between it and the coast of China.

As for the remainder, Hainanese speakers (11% of the total) are descended from people who came from the island of Hainan south of China and east of Vietnam.

Hokkien[8] speakers (4% of the total) came from the coastal area around Amoy, north of the area of Teochiu origins.

Some Taiwanese (1%) make up the rest.

In some Chinese and Sino-Thai homes only a Chinese language is spoken, whereas increasingly in others the situation is mixed, a Chinese language being used by and with older people but not among the younger people. Ten years after Boonsanong's survey, in a study of 148 Chinese in Chiang Mai, Sumon (1984:84) found only 29.1% who spoke exclusively Chinese or mostly Chinese with their fathers, and 19.9% with their mothers. None spoke exclusively Chinese or mostly Chinese with their children. In some Sino-Thai homes, as we have seen, no Chinese language is used at all under normal circumstances.

On the other hand, Sino-Thai people who were not government employees gave such reasons for using a Chinese language as these:

It is more natural for me to speak Chinese in my family because we are Chinese.

My parents and older relatives do not like it when I speak Thai to them.

Chinese is the business language. If you do not speak Chinese how can you do business?

I try to speak to my children only in Chinese so that they can learn from me. If they do not know how to speak Chinese they will have very little future in business (Boonsanong 1971:17-18).

The emphasis on the language of business in these statements possibly hints again at the functional need to separate traders and merchants ethnically from the general population, as suggested by Foster. When actually selling, however, transactions with non-Chinese are done in Thai. Hawking of goods in the markets near Yawarat Road, in the heart of Bangkok's Chinese section, is done in Thai to reach a more generalized buying public than would be possible with any Chinese language. But for this group, business planning, discussion and decision are apparently done in a Chinese language.

An extensive variety of media serve the Chinese-speaking population. Chinese movies are imported into Thailand from Hong Kong and Taiwan, their dialog normally in Mandarin, Cantonese or Taiwanese. They are frequently dubbed in Thai, and some of them have Chinese subtitles for people who do not understand the language of the film, but can read Chinese. Broadcasts in Mandarin can be heard via shortwave from Beijing but no Chinese language broadcasts originate in Thailand. Four Chinese-language newspapers are published daily in Bangkok, while others are imported from Hong Kong and Taiwan as well. Several Chinese-language magazines are also published in the country, or imported. Books are also written in Chinese and published in Thailand from time to time.

Obviously, therefore, written Chinese and the spoken Chinese languages are still thriving among the languages of Thai towns and cities, but they are clearly no longer as important as Coughlin (1960: 159) described written Chinese to be in the late fifties:

Participation in the normal day-to-day life of the community requires that one know written Chinese, and conversely, a person's inability to read and write Chinese severely limits the range of his activities. Many shop signs are in Chinese characters only. Even to clerk in a Chinese store a boy must know written Chinese since most bills and notices . . . are in Chinese.

Thai Government Chinese Policy

The Thai government watched the growth of the Chinese community in numbers and power over the years with fluctuating reactions. Under some of the earlier kings of the present dynasty immigration was promoted as a source of labor and skills. Rama VI, on the other hand, sounded a nationalistic, anti-Chinese tone, playing on derogatory stereotypes. Again, after the revolution which reduced the role of the monarchy and introduced parliamentary government in the 1930s, a period of Thai nationalism with anti-Chinese overtones erupted under Prime Minister Luang Phibunsongkhram, generally known as Phibun. In the sixties a communism scare made some Thai officials suspicious of possible Chinese subversion.

However, although more Chinese may have immigrated into Thailand than into any other country of Southeast Asia, their assimilation into the host society is also the greatest (Amyot 1972:83). This is due to Thailand's policy and practice, and is fostered by Thai people's often easygoing lack of rigid exclusiveness, especially when strangers take on some symbols of Thainess.

Thailand's policy concerning acquiring citizenship has changed at various times, but for the most part since 1913 people born in Thailand, regardless of the nationality of the parents, are legally Thai citizens,[9] with exceptions such as foreign military and diplomatic personnel. Naturalization also takes place, but not in large numbers. It is expensive, and has numerous requirements like many years of continuous residence in the country, but some Sino-Thai people do become naturalized citizens (Amyot 1972:87-89; Khachatphai 1983). As a result of such immigration and naturalization policies, plus the growth of the non-Chinese population, the percentage of Chinese aliens in the Thailand population has dropped steadily (table 12.2).

From the language standpoint, however, the most important Thai government policy affecting the Chinese-speaking population is its educational policy. In 1937, 230 Chinese schools served the Chinese population. A Chinese language was the medium of instruction in each, and Chinese culture and values were emphasized. The schools were very much like the schools in China itself, from where teachers were recruited, bringing with them some of the shifting ideologies of China, including the communist movement, much to the alarm of Thai officials.

But these schools declined in ethnic importance after the government put all schools under the supervision of the Ministry of Education. Those which remain have become essentially Thai schools, most of them teaching Chinese only six to ten hours a week, while they teach Thai for twenty-five hours a week. Most of the teachers and all of the principals must be Thai (including Sino-Thai), must be educated in Thai, and must be qualified to teach under the Ministry of Education. Instructors in Chinese languages are exceptions, but they must at least be able to pass a Thai language examination. The government also controls the content of the textbooks (Pichai 1969; Amyot 1972:90). Attendance at a Sino-Thai school still fosters Sino-Thai group identity, and helps to slow the erosion of those Chinese values promoted at home and in the community, but does not give much of a Chinese education.

Thai policy, furthermore, relegates Chinese languages to the category of "foreign languages" even when the students are native speakers. At the upper levels, university majors and elective courses are offered in Mandarin as a foreign language. Teochiu is taught in some colleges and technical high schools as well, and one regular high school teaches both Mandarin and Teochiu (Pichai 1969).

Chinese-language kindergartens and night schools are still allowed, as are Chinese classes with less than seven students (Pichai 1969). This means that highly motivated individuals or the children of highly motivated parents can become literate in Chinese and can learn some Mandarin outside the regular school system. For traditionally oriented families, however, the only way to give their children a really Chinese education is to send them to a Chinese school outside Thailand: to China until disillusionment with the communist government set in, to Hong Kong, Taiwan or Singapore since then (Jirawat 1976:24).

It takes years to learn to read and write Chinese with any competence. The advantages of having a written form which can be read by speakers of any of the many Chinese languages come at a high cost in the individual effort required to learn it. Students have to memorize scores of characters and combinable parts of characters, more than can be accomplished in the token time allowed in the Sino-Thai schools. Among Chiang Mai Chinese respondents, 11.5% could read and write Chinese well, and another 24% could do so passably, but half of those who had learned to read and write well had spent five to ten years or more in the learning process (Sumon 1984:38). After completing Sino-Thai government-controlled school alone, therefore, most students can neither read nor write enough Chinese for practical use (Amyot 1972:90). Those who really do learn to read have supplemental training elsewhere.

In the 1950s Coughlin (1960:156) attributed the increasing sense of the importance of a Thai education in the Chinese community to the realization by Chinese parents that their future and that of their children lay in Thailand. Fluency in Thai and skill in negotiating in a Thai environment were seen to contribute to business success. People who had been sent out of Thailand as children to spend years on a

Chinese education now spent many more years getting the Thai education their parents had repudiated for them. Otherwise, they were handicapped in making a living in Thailand.

So, the net effect of Thai educational policy is that Sino-Thai young people are educated in Thai, in schools which systematically foster Thai characteristics (Guskin 1968), whether they go to a "Chinese" school or not. Students read and write Thai better than they do Chinese, if they read and write the latter at all. By the third generation most of them are more comfortable in Thai than in a Chinese language for communication not strictly related to the Chinese community. Some younger people are not much interested in Chinese at all. From their point of view, efforts which might have been expended on learning Chinese are more profitably spent instead on English, or even Japanese (Amyot 1972:90; Boonsanong 1971:14). Some Chinese Christian churches have services in a Chinese language for older people and in Thai for younger people.

Back in the late fifties Skinner (1957a:381) wrote:

The only third-generation Chinese who identify in most social situations as Chinese are those educated in Chinese schools, in Thailand or abroad. The only fourth-generation Chinese who *ever* identify as Chinese are likewise Chinese-educated. The implication is clear that *without a Chinese education* grandchildren of Chinese immigrants at the present time become Thai.

Now there are fewer immigrants to have grandchildren. The pressures for a Chinese education are becoming weaker, and use of a Chinese language is less of a requirement in marking what it means to be a person of Chinese ancestry in Thailand.

Assimilation Patterns

The Thai government policies outlined above have certainly been critical in leading to the present position of the Sino-Thai. But some of the same government policies could have been inflammatory. They might have been resisted bitterly as repressive if both groups had not recognized their interdependence and had not allowed this realism, in the long run, to win out over nationalistic chauvinism and over stereotypes and prejudices (Botan 1977; Consensus 1983).

In recent years wealthy Sino-Thai have had less hindrance in moving into the upper classes of Thai society. Supported by their wealth, they enter at least into the upper middle class through education, marriage, business and social contacts (Jirawat 1976:24). Other

Sino-Thai are a disproportionate part of the rapidly growing business and professional middle class in Thailand (Evers 1966).

The luck of timing has been crucial as well. Some years ago Chinese nationalism was strong in the Chinese community because the current government in China was seeking to expand its influence in Southeast Asia. Sentiments of people with Chinese ancestry could have grown to create greater separatism and conflict with Thailand. However, the excesses of the cultural revolution in China dampened nationalistic enthusiasm among them (Jirawat 1976:21).

Taking on Thai names is one linguistic measure of assimilation for Chinese in Thailand, as shown in table 12.3. In another sample in Chiang Mai, 77.7% of the Sino-Thai had both Thai first names and Thai family names; 14.9% had a Thai personal name but a Chinese family name. In only 4% of the cases were both names Chinese (Sumon 1984).

A diminishing number of the least assimilated people simply keep their Chinese names, transliterating them into Thai script when it is necessary to write them for non-Chinese purposes, as on government forms. Some people have a bona fide Thai name as well as a Chinese name, sometimes with the short Chinese name incorporated into the longer Thai name. Such adoption of a Thai name may be completely opportunistic, to improve business or social standing, or it may reflect a move into a "double identity," with a desire to be more like the Thai.[10]

For children in Thai schools and young people in universities the Thai name may be the salient name, with their Chinese name reserved for use in private life or even restricted to contacts with elders. If they do not go into business but into professional or government occupations, the Chinese name may become even less important, or may be given up entirely.

But while the forces for assimilation are strong, and the avenue of education in Chinese is less attractive, Chinese identity, culture and language are often implicitly and explicitly sustained in Thailand. Although weakening, the use of a Chinese language in some families is fundamental, and institutional supports exist as well.

One type of support is embodied in the many associations to which Chinese and Sino-Thai people may belong. Some of them further business interests within an explicitly Chinese context, specifying their Chinese ethnicity in their names, like the Chinese Insurance Association of Thailand and the Chinese Printing Association of Thailand.

Membership in another type of organization is based on language and ethnic origin in China, with an association for each of the major linguistic groups: Teochiu, Hokkien, Cantonese, Hainanese, Hakka and Taiwanese. As the largest of these, the Teochiu Association informs its members of issues relevant to them, operates a cemetery, supports sports and arts, runs a hospital and two schools, among other functions. Its schools cover the first four grades, and Chinese writing is taught ten hours a week. The hospital administers both traditional Chinese medicine and Western medicine.

Other support groups include family name associations, social associations, Buddhist and Taoist associations. The Sino-Thai schools also have school boards and alumni associations.

Reciprocal Influences of Thai and Chinese Languages

Two languages such as Thai and Teochiu, or Thai and any one of the other Chinese languages in Thailand, could not exist together for so long, with so much bilingualism, without mutual influence. It comes on several different levels and in different forms.

Sino-Thai people who learn Thai as adults, or as children in the Chinese community, or who use it much in the Chinese community, typically speak it with an accent. For example, a sampling of Teochiu speakers overheard dealing with Thai people in a market area showed a few rather consistent substitutions of one sound for another (from the Thai point of view). Most common was substitution of [ŋ] for [n] in final position. In the examples which follow tone marks and vowel duration are not included in the Chinese-influenced pronunciation because these features were not noted.

> [kiŋ] for [kin] 'eat'
> [toŋ] for [tôn] 'plant'
> [waŋ] for [wǎan] 'sweet'.

An analogous mispronunciation was [k] for [t], as in

> [lok] for [lót] {rót} 'car'
> [pek] for [pèt] 'duck'
> [mak] for [mát] 'tie'.

Fewer substitutions occurred in initial position, but [l] was notably substituted for [d], as in

> [liaŋ] for [dian] 'month'
> [lek] for [dèk] 'child'.

Teochiu, furthermore, has no distinction between vowels of short duration and those of long duration such as occurs in Standard Thai. Neither does it have Standard Thai vowels /i/, /ɛ/ or /ɔ/, either long or short. A Thai word with a vowel /ɨɨ/, as in /sɨɨ/ 'buy' may be pronounced in a Teochiu accent as [ɨɨ], [ɨ], [əə] or [ə] (Beebe 1977a, 1977b, 1981).

Thai has inevitably borrowed from Chinese languages as well. The largest number of words, according to one study of 463 such borrowings, have to do with food and its preparation. Slang words also make up an important part. Lesser categories included tools and instruments, religion, beliefs and values, commerce, professions, places, trees, plants, etc. Some of the borrowings are very common words like /kŭaytǐaw/ 'noodle dish', /seŋlíi/ 'make a big sale for quick profit', /suay/ 'to have bad luck, be accursed'. Of these words, 44% came from Teochiu, 24% from Hokkien, and others could not be identified with certainty or came from other dialects (Pranee 1983).

So Chinese languages and the major languages of Thailand have been inextricably linked in spite of their vastly different roles in the country. Their coexistence is a creative synthesis because of the immense importance of the respective roles. The Chinese languages are at the bottom of the Thailand hierarchy because their speakers need to learn the major languages around them to do business. But the economic position of the Sino-Thai people place them high on other scales.

Summary

No other languages can match the specialized place of the Chinese languages in Thailand's cities. Thailand's regional languages are rural as much as urban. Standard Thai is national, although more urban than rural. English is international. But although specialized rural Chinese languages are also to be found in Thailand, the most characteristic niche of the Chinese languages in Thailand is in the towns and cities, in the Bangkok-Thonbury metropolitan area most of all. Some other Asian languages belong to this category as well, but have nothing of the importance of the Chinese languages.

More Chinese people have migrated to Thailand over the years than to any other Southeast Asian country, yet their descendants are better accommodated to Thailand than are corresponding people in neighboring countries, except Singapore, where they are in control. In spite of their numbers, their conspicuousness, and their economic position, speakers of Chinese languages have adapted to their place at the bottom of Thailand's language hierarchy. They thrive in a dual Sino-Thai identity in which the part played by Chinese languages is sometimes large, sometimes small.

13

Marginal Languages in the Hierarchy: Mon, Pray, plus Non-marginal Mal

Thailand has long been a magnet to people in surrounding countries. Earlier underpopulation, economic opportunity, and traditional Thai laissez-faire attitudes toward immigrant peoples have all made the country attractive at different times. Troubled situations in the countries of origin continue to drive people as well.

A small group of Lahu people who moved into Thailand in the 1960s illustrates what can happen. It consisted of about 120 individuals, a small village in Myanmar. They had planned their move for months as the unsettled situation in their home area became intolerable. They were, for example, being forced to pay taxes to three competing military factions which "controlled" their area for brief periods of time and then moved on. In the end they sold what belongings they could to people staying behind, led as many pigs and dogs as they could lead, and carried their small children and some rice, along with as many chickens, pots and pans, clothes, and blankets as they could manage on their backs. They abandoned the rest.

It took them twenty days to make the trip on foot, hiding out during the day and walking through the jungle at night. Sometimes they had to stay hidden for several days at a time, away from the trails where troops of any faction might pass. A baby was born on the journey. In Thailand, border officials allowed them to move into a resettlement area. A Christian relief agency provided supplies until they could harvest their first crop for themselves.

Moving into Thailand like that is much harder now than it used to be. Until the middle of this century consciousness of any border was slight in the mountains, and governmental restrictions on immigration into mountain areas had not been established. Since the above incident, movement has become much more tightly controlled. But some people still come.

When people do move in, they settle in an existing village or form a new village which may necessarily be isolated from other speakers of their language. Or, their new village may be part of a small cluster of villages where their language is spoken. In any case, people who speak other languages live around them in every direction at varying distances.

But such new immigrants also continue to have relatives and friends in the country they left, and continue to keep sporadic contact with them. Individuals and small groups may go back occasionally to marry or participate in a funeral. And as long as new people occasionally keep coming in to join them they are reminded of their former life.

Although the immigrants start out speaking like the people in their former locations, their speech soon begins to diverge. Lewis (1985a) contains an illustrative list of fifty-eight words which are different in Lahu as spoken in Thailand, Myanmar, and China. The list ranges from words for things which are part of traditional Lahu culture, like 'child', to modern ones like 'bicycle'.

Over a few generations, contact with people in the former location lessens. In time nobody knows anyone back there any more; the reasons for visiting disappear. All the immigrants have left are stories about how they came from the former area, that they speak partly the same language and have partly the same customs. Marginality becomes more tenuous, as was described for the Kuy (chap. 9), so that the functional distinction between marginal language and enclave language weakens. This solidifies the place of the people in the language hierarchy.

In this chapter we describe two marginal languages which have been in Thailand for a long time, speakers of which have long since settled into their roles in the language hierarchy, and are treated accordingly by the Thai. The pecking order is established, understood and operative. Multilingualism is widespread, if not universal in such groups.

Then in the next chapter we will describe a less assimilated group, where language use is now being adapted to the hierarchy after years of existing in tension with it. The Phlong (chap. 8) lie between.

The languages of this chapter belong to the Mon-Khmer language family, descended from the same ancestral language as Northern Khmer and Kuy, while the one in the next chapter, and others like it, do not (chap. 17). Their difference in adjustment to Thailand is not due to language family, however, but to the length of time the group has been in the country, and to longstanding cultural traditions. The Tai-speaking peoples have dominated the speakers of Mon-Khmer

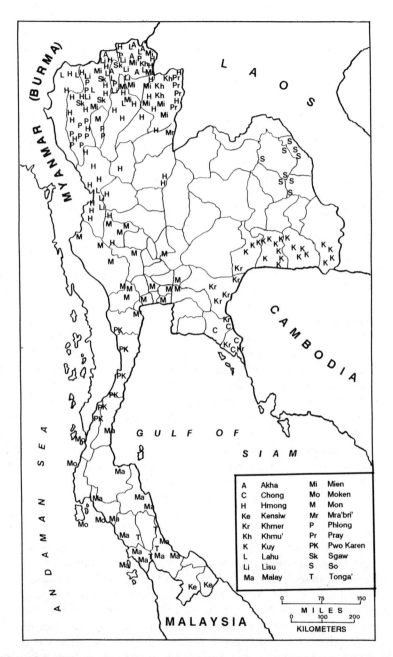

Map 13.1. Distribution of some marginal languages in Thailand. Marginal
regional languages are not shown, but some of the same or related languages are shown where they are to be found without regional function.

languages in Thailand and Laos for centuries, and patterns of behavior have long since been established.

Mon on the Plains of Thailand

Ancestors of the present Mon population came into Thailand in several migrations, perhaps beginning in the sixteenth century. Some came voluntarily or were stimulated by conditions in Myanmar, while others were forced to move by Thai war parties raiding that country. New Mon people still continue to come in small numbers (Halliday 1913; Foster 1973b:10; Sujaritlak et al. 1983:11-16; Bauer 1990: 22).[1]

In the first half of the nineteenth century, Mon people became numerous in the provinces around Bangkok. In fact, a belt of Mon settlements, along with those of other non-Tai peoples, served as a shield for Bangkok, with many Mon from those villages enlisted as soldiers. The Mon then living in Kanchanaburi Province, on the Burmese border, contributed likewise to Thai defenses against Myanmar. Thus the Thai capitalized on the fact that the Mon or their ancestors had left Myanmar and had no love for the Burmese (Terwiel 1989:85, 116, 150-151, 174, 253-254).

Currently the Mon in Thailand live primarily in these same areas, but are found elsewhere as well (map 13.1). According to one survey they live in seventeen provinces, in 403 villages, with a total population of just under one hundred thousand people, of which probably less than half still speak Mon (Bauer 1990:24-26, based on census by Su-ed Kochaseni 1969-1972). The concentrations range from over twenty thousand each in the provinces of Pathum Thani and Samut Prakan in central Thailand to seven hundred in Lamphun Province and one hundred in Tak Province in the north (Sujaritlak et al. 1983:23-34). Some Mon also live in the mountains of Kanchanaburi Province, near the Myanmar border.

This long-standing Mon population has been heavily assimilated, with extensive intermarriage between Mon and Thai. Some people of Mon descent have become high Thai officials, and some Mon ancestry is to be found even in the royal family.

In earlier times a number of Mon cultural characteristics were somewhat different from those of the Tai peoples around them. In addition to a different language, they had a different form of Buddhism, a different Buddhist hierarchy of monks, a different spirit cult with totem-like spirits, a different and colorful New Year's festival. They also had some less tangible features of ethnicity like an awareness of a different ancestry, history and place of origin, a sense of "Mon-ness" (Foster 1973a:210-213).

Most of this ethnic difference is gone, or nearly gone, or partially gone, at different places and with different Mon people, to the extent that some descendants of the Mon may not even be aware of their Mon ancestry or partial ancestry. Thus the Mon illustrate one extreme on the spectrum of marginal groups—the extreme of weak ties with the area they came from, partial loss of language, and very little to distinguish them from the people speaking the regional language around them (Foster 1973b:124-138).

Mon Language

The Mon language in Thailand has a typical range of dialects (Foster 1973b:19-20; Bauer 1981; Bauer 1982:vi-xii). The sound systems of Mon in Lamphun and Chiang Mai provinces in the north retain all of the features of Mon in Myanmar, but the southern dialects on the central plains of Thailand do not, and vary from place to place. The dialect differences, however, are not so great as to hinder communication. The differences between dialects spoken in Thailand and those spoken in Myanmar are greater in part because the Mon of Thailand have borrowed vocabulary from Thai. Mon in Thailand is nevertheless said to be mutually intelligible with Mon in Myanmar (Bauer 1990:23).

Adults who still use the Mon language in Thailand are all multilingual. Many such Mon speak Tai languages with a characteristic Mon accent, however (Bauer 1990:34), which Thai actors imitate in a stereotypic way when playing Mon parts. In some areas where Mon identity is preserved more fully than in others, children are often not yet fluent in a Tai language when they start school, but they soon become so (Foster 1973b:127).

The Mon language has been written for centuries, and a small number of Mon in Thailand, especially a few monks and older people, know how to read and write it. But Mon literacy is only marginally functional in Thailand, having been replaced by Thai literacy for most purposes (Bauer 1990:36-37). Like the traditional writing systems for Kammüang and Lao, Mon writing in Thailand is now restricted largely to religion and to attempts to record traditional culture. Mon literacy is taught for a few months from time to time in one Mon Buddhist temple or another as part of the training of novices

(Sujaritlak et al. 1983:129), but this is only a token effort largely restricted to learning the alphabet (Foster 1973b:127). Some people who recognize their Mon ancestry nevertheless do not even realize the language was ever written.

Some classical Mon literature is preserved in Mon temples in Thailand, and a small amount is still imported occasionally from Myanmar (Bauer 1990:36-37). A printing press which published Mon literature in Thailand in the earlier part of this century is no longer in use (Sujaritlak et al. 1983:130).

In all but a few areas, Mon spoken language is also diminishing in Thailand. It had virtually disappeared in two of the communities Foster studied near Bangkok, where only older people still spoke it. Even when adult use of the language was strong there, Foster would sometimes be told by parents that they tried to get their children to speak Mon, and spoke only Mon to them when they were small, but from the time they entered school they refused to speak it any more. They continued to understand it, but answered in Thai (Foster 1973b: 132-133; Bauer 1982:34).

In the other Mon village which Foster studied, however, even the few Thai and Sino-Thai who married into the village learned to speak

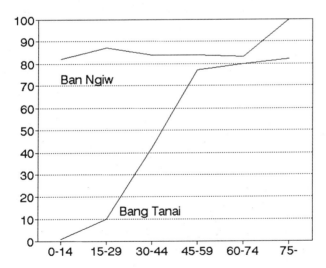

Fig. 13.1. Percentages of people who speak Mon at different ages in two different Mon communities, Bang Tanai in Nonthaburi Province and Ban Ngiw (Ban Klang) in Prathum Thani Province (after Foster 1973b:127).

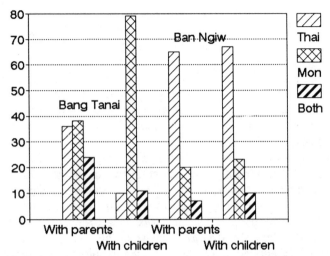

Fig. 13.2. Languages normally used with parents and children in two Mon villages (after Foster 1973b:138).

it. Comparison of the two types of situations can be seen in figures 13.1 and 13.2. In fact, the Mon in Ban Ngiw used even less Thai than the graph indicates because the survey included some Thai families also living in the village.

The expansion of the Bangkok metropolitan area swallowed up three formerly distinct Mon communities (Bauer 1990:21), but in spite of their overwhelmingly Thai and Sino-Thai environment, in 1972 Mon was still spoken by all adults among themselves in at least one of them. Adults and children likewise generally spoke Mon to each other, except when the children used Thai to express ideas learned outside the community. The children generally spoke to each other in Thai (Smithies 1972:308-309).

In these communities some other functions traditionally carried out in Mon had also been partially switched over to Thai. On every holy day, for example, the sermon was preached in Thai in the morning and in Mon in the afternoon, but the Thai service was better attended. The head monk, who spoke and read Mon fluently, said this was because of the time rather than the language. Some time earlier, when a radio station had an hour of Mon programming in the evening, every single house tuned in (Smithies 1972:317).

Foster's theory concerning why some Mon are not yet losing language and identity is what gave rise to our earlier discussion of the need for merchants to be ethnically alien in traditional Thailand and even in some modern situations. Foster found that it was the Mon farmers of Bang Tanai who did not use the Mon language, whereas the traders of Ban Klang did use it. As people engaged in commerce it was more profitable for them not to be absorbed into the network of Thai socioeconomic obligations.

The people of still a third village had also once occupied a special economic niche, making and selling pottery, but the business had been declining for a long time due to cheaper pottery made in more advanced plants elsewhere. Their commercial distinctiveness was becoming less clear. The knowledge of Mon manifested in that village was intermediate between the other two (Foster 1973b:231-250).

Ten years after his field work Foster returned to these villages and found his hypothesis strongly supported by intervening events. People who had left trading had turned to Thai, but the traders used Mon as extensively as before (Foster 1988:154-155). Thus Mon is shrinking in Thailand, but so long as some Mon remain engaged in trade their children apparently continue to learn it, and the language will probably not be endangered.

Ethnic Integration of the Mon

Foster (1973b:118-120) gives some interesting examples of multiple ethnicity among the Mon, which also show how thoroughly they are integrated into Thailand.

One young man of Mon ancestry . . . married a Mon girl from Bang Tanai, and now lives in his wife's parents' house. . . . He and his wife are fluent Mon speakers, but they speak mostly Thai together. He is in the Thai air force and commutes daily to work at the air base. . . . He was ordained in a Mon wat [Buddhist temple] and attends a Mon wat regularly.

A man had two Thai, one Mon, and one Chinese grandparents; he lived in a Chinese market town . . . on the site of an old Mon settlement and surrounded by Mon villages. He is a village headman (i.e. an officer in the Thai government) and is head of the legal department of a large insurance company in Bangkok. He speaks Thai plus some Chinese, Mon and English. He was ordained in a Mon monastery, can chant in the Mon style, and still regularly attends a Mon wat; but he is also active in the local Chinese temple. He drives one American and one English car and is reasonably at home eating in a western luxury hotel.

Pray in the Lower Northern Hills, plus Mal

The second marginal language to be discussed in this chapter belongs to a speech group, the other member of which may not be a marginal language, but enclave. They will nevertheless be discussed together because they are otherwise very similar, and in this instance marginality or lack of it is of no great significance to their place in the ecology. Like the Mon, their places are established in the language hierarchy of the country, but their speakers also manifest some significant differences from Mon.

The group speaking the marginal language calls itself /khram pray/ 'Pray people',[2] while the group speaking the other language calls itself /phyam maal/ 'Mal people'. Speakers of each language number some seven thousand, mostly in the Pua District of Nan Province, along the Lao border of northern Thailand. The marginal Pray population extends into Sayaboury Province in Laos (map 13.1), where they are called Phay.

The Mal and the Pray are sometimes lumped together by Thai as Lawa /lawáa/ and by Northern Thai as Lua' /lúa'/, terms sometimes applied to other non-Tai inhabitants as well (chaps. 8, 15). Mal and Pray are related to some of these other groups called Lawa/Lua', but they are entirely separate languages now. None of the groups called by those names has knowledge of the others, nor do the local Thai or Northern Thai in any area usually know that different peoples called by those terms live in other parts of the country (Filbeck 1976:239).

Thai people also refer to the Mal and Pray as Thin /thìn/ (also spelled Tin, T'in, Htin in English).[3] The Pray- and Mal-speaking people themselves have no such name to cover both groups, however, except as some adopt the term Thin or Lua'.

Culturally the two groups are similar, and occupy the same kind of relationship to other peoples of Thailand. The languages are closely related, although not mutually intelligible. The three primary Mal dialects are all mutually intelligible, and Pray likewise has at least five such dialects in Thailand (Filbeck 1973:10).

The Thin peoples are believed to have come into Thailand from Laos, beginning at least by the late nineteenth century (LeBar, Hickey, and Musgrave 1964:128; Dessaint 1981:111), but among the Mal, Filbeck (1978:8) found no memory of ancestors having lived anywhere but Thailand. On the other hand, the Pray in Thailand do know about the Phay in Laos. Dessaint states that groups have migrated back and forth across the border depending on economic factors and the attitudes of government officials.

In Thailand, the Mal and Pray traditionally lived on the lower altitudes of the mountains, at heights from three hundred to one thousand meters. Where possible, they chose the gentler slopes as places to build their villages, which were often not far from the villages of other mountain-dwelling ethnic groups, especially the Hmong and Mien, or from Northern Thai villages.

All Thin in Thailand speak the local dialect of Kammüang as well as Mal or Pray. They normally communicate in it not only with Northern Thai people, but also with Hmong and Mien peoples nearby. Children begin picking up the Kammüang which they hear used by their fathers or by visitors in the village almost as soon as they start talking Mal or Pray. Boys soon have greater facility in Kammüang than girls as they associate more with the men who deal with outsiders, while the girls tend to retire to areas where women congregate and so do not hear it as much. By the time they are twenty, men have good Kammüang rhythm and intonation patterns, but women of the same age speak more haltingly, with Mal or Pray intonation.

Typically, men use Kammüang whenever speakers of that language are present. Sometimes they will also speak Kammüang to each other when walking along a trail, although back in their village they would speak Mal or Pray. Perhaps they are speaking as though Kammüang speakers were present in this public place, in case they should be overheard (Filbeck 1973:12).

Mal and Pray men who have had sufficient education also have varying skill in Standard Thai. Women, again, speak it more haltingly. Both tend to have a strong Nan Province Kammüang accent. Once out of school, village people hear Standard Thai most often on the radio.

In the 1960s, in at least one Pray-speaking village surrounded by Mal villages, the people spoke Mal fluently in addition to their Pray. More typically Mal and Pray people do not speak each other's languages. A few Mal individuals with frequent contacts with the Hmong in the area also spoke some Hmong, most commonly when someone in the household was addicted to opium and dealt with Hmong suppliers (Filbeck 1973:11).

Mal and Pray self-esteem tends to be low. They are described as having a generally "despondent" appearance (Dessaint 1981:107). Like some other Mon-Khmer peoples in Southeast Asia, they have been at the bottom of the pecking order of peoples for generations.[4] Their economy and technology have not been as advanced as the Tai peoples of the nearby valley. They are almost the poorest people they know. Northern Thai often laugh at their language.

Swidden Agriculture

Thin economy has traditionally been based on dry rice, unirrigated, slash-and-burn (swidden) agriculture, supplemented in some cases by raising livestock and by *miang* production. The latter is a fermented or pickled tea-leaves preparation popular in northern Thailand as a mild narcotic (Filbeck 1973: chap. 2, 8-9; Keen 1978b). Food has also been available through gardening and hunting (Dessaint 1981: 112, 118-123). In the past thirty years, however, making a living by traditional means has become increasingly difficult as forest and other natural resources are being used up.

Swidden agriculture is practiced widely over Southeast Asia wherever the development of permanent irrigated rice fields is impractical, as on mountain slopes. It requires different strains of rice from those grown in irrigated fields as well as different agricultural techniques. Three types of swidden agriculture are practiced in northern Thailand with varying ecological implications (Kunstadter, Chapman, and Sanga 1978: 6-13; Keen 1983:294-301).

Northern Thai farmers living close to or in the hills supplement their wet-rice cultivation by the first type, a cycle with short cultivation followed by a short fallow period. This means that they clear an area of the scrub forest, burn off what they cut down, cultivate dry rice or other crops on the land for a year, or two at the most, and then let it lie fallow for a short period of four to six years before using it again. Under this system the forest does not get restored, the soil becomes depleted, and weed and grass infestation becomes heavy. Care is not taken, furthermore, to prevent fires from spreading into uncleared areas, which further inhibits rejuvenation of the land.

A relatively non-harmful system, on the other hand, has traditionally been practiced by groups like the Pray, Mal, and various Karen peoples. It involves short cultivation with a long fallow period. Under this system a plot is cleared, with careful attention to creating firebreaks to protect the uncleared forest. It is used for two to three years and then allowed to lie fallow for seven to ten years. The forest begins to grow up again; weeds and destructive grasses do not become established; fertility of the soil is restored. Under this second system swidden agriculture has provided a stable, long-lasting subsistence for some peoples living in the same area for generations.

The third system involves long cultivation, which then entails a permanent fallow state because the land is ruined for agriculture. It is practiced by the Hmong in opium production, as described in the next chapter. The same poppy field may be cultivated for ten years or more, but at the end it will not revert to forest because tough, dense *Imperata* grass has become so thoroughly established that the forest cannot get started. Peoples who follow this pattern keep moving their villages to areas where they can cultivate new land.

Except for opium poppy cultivation,[5] in swidden agriculture the ground is not softened or disturbed; the roots of the jungle vegetation are left intact in the ground, and the rice, corn or other crops are planted by simply dropping the seeds into a hole made with the point of a stick. Under this technique little erosion is created by disturbing the soil. However, when the fallow period is insufficient to restore the forest the root system disappears over successive years, and erosion begins.

With limited populations, with small villages widely scattered, the land can provide subsistence indefinitely with any of these swidden technologies. But over the last fifty years the population explosion has hit the hills in Thailand, and swidden technology cannot support it. This increase is due not only to the natural population growth among people like the Pray and the Mal who traditionally lived in the hills, but overpopulation of Northern Thai valleys has also forced some valley people into the hills as well. Northern Thai villages have been established, or sometimes Northern Thai people live in villages with marginal-language people. Marginal language-speaking people have also continued to trickle across the border from troubled Myanmar and Laos. At the same time, the commercial exploitation of timber has been increasing. Wholesale wasteful destruction of forest lands by clear-cutting loggers, legal and illegal, has been rampant.

Population increase and deforestation from lumber operations have inexorably destroyed swidden agriculture, even where it was stable. Too many people are now trying to live off the mountains. Fallow periods have grown shorter, often down to three years, even in traditionally long fallow areas. The result has been fertility depletion, erosion, loss of water-holding capacity, and the growth of resistant weeds in the mountains plus floods in the lowlands and silting in the rivers and reservoirs.

For centuries the people living in the mountains of Southeast Asia used the mountain land freely except as they recognized the right of prior use. That is, anyone who had cleared a plot earlier had the right to use it again when it was ready, but otherwise the land was unclaimed. But now the Thai government has enforced a claim to all "waste land" as property of the King, brushing aside ancient patterns of land use. Under the law, waste land means any land not permanently occupied or developed and registered as such. On this land logging is to be done only by license, and swidden agriculture is forbidden (Sophon 1978).

So for various reasons swidden agriculture, at least in its historic forms, is ultimately doomed. But the people who practice it usually see no alternative to it as they become poorer and hungrier. Such became the fate of the Pray and the Mal.

Pray and Mal Culture Contact

Before the 1960s the Thin had varying levels of contact with the outside world. Migrations to the lowlands were rare, but villagers who lived close enough to the market sold miang, vegetables, and the hides of such animals as deer, bears and tigers. In turn, they bought goods like rice, medicines, cloth, pots and pans, axes, sickles, and beads (Dessaint 1981:135-136). When dealing with Sino-Thai shopkeepers, many villagers were exploited, however, reinforcing avoidance of the outside world, which was frightening anyhow because it had spirits with which the Mal and Pray did not know how to deal. More isolated villages had even less frequent contact with the towns, although some lowland peoples did occasionally travel to such villages searching for miang or giving injections of powerful modern drugs to sick people.

Some intermarriage took place between the Thin and the Khmu', another marginal group much like them, or less often between them and Northern Thai. Pray and Mal people also occasionally hired themselves out to Hmong or Mien for agricultural work. More rarely, they became domestic servants for Northern Thai or Sino-Thai people (Dessaint 1981:125, 126).

During the same period, four villages within a ten-mile radius of each other illustrated differing degrees of assimilation to the dominant Northern Thai culture (Filbeck 1973, chap. 8:9-13). In the first the Mal dialect was the least changed from earlier forms of the language. The villagers were also the least fluent in speaking Kammüang. They had no school; nor was the village located near a Northern Thai village, or even on a main trail, so they encountered few outsiders passing through. The villagers also showed very little mobility. A few had gone to live in other Mal-speaking villages nearby, but apparently none had ever moved to a Northern Thai village, nor had a Northern Thai person ever moved to their village.

The second village showed more change on all of these counts. Greater movement to and from other Mal villages and to and from Northern Thai villages produced more intermingling with other peoples. A school existed, but sessions were held haphazardly. The Kammüang language was better known and contact with Northern Thai people was more frequent.

The third village was considerably influenced by the Northern Thai and Central Thai, including some Northern Thai people who actually lived there. It was on a major trail, at a place where traders stopped overnight on their trips. It had had a school for at least thirty years. People had come and gone, moving to other Mal villages or Northern Thai villages, or to cities for work. But some of the people who had moved out still maintained contacts with the home village. Money which they sent back from work outside allowed villagers to buy more goods. Mal was still spoken in the village as the mother tongue of everyone born and raised there, but many men preferred to speak Kammüang, which most knew well.

The fourth village was inhabited by people who came originally from several different Thin villages in the area. Their original languages included two Mal dialects and one Pray dialect, so many of them could not talk to each other except in Kammüang, which they used exclusively. Adults still claimed to understand their original languages, but insisted that they no longer used them and had not done so for so long that they could not carry on a conversation in them. Children said that they knew only a few words of Mal or Pray. Filbeck, in numerous contacts with people from the village, was never able to communicate effectively with any of them in Mal. Even traditional religious ceremonies had been dropped, as the village was on a mountain with a particularly powerful spirit which would not allow the practices.[6]

In the mid-1960s Buddhism, schools, army recruiting, and government projects were among the agents for change among the Thin (Dessaint 1981:134-135). The impact of each was limited, however. At one point government officials told the Thin they were Buddhists, so they were all labeled as such on their identity cards. The people called themselves Buddhists to outsiders, and sometimes had a poorly maintained Buddhist temple in the village, but did not practice Buddhism on a regular basis.

The period of mixed relative isolation and heavy contact with the outside world which we have been discussing was also a period of desperation because traditional means of livelihood were no longer sufficient, the distress coming to a climax in the second half of the 1960s. More and more land was being restricted by the forestry department; more and more other ethnic groups, including Northern Thai, had come in to occupy land the Mal and Pray would have used.

First a messianic movement broke out among the Thin in 1964, a symptom of a people undergoing severe hardship and cultural dislocation. It was led by a Lao prophet married to a Thin woman. He announced that everyone would live in prosperity if they followed the religious practices he prescribed, and that those who did not would die. A god, Chao Phu Bun, would come and bring development and prosperity. The prophet unified a large part of the Thin population around him for a brief period. Many Thin, lacking food, proceeded to eat their seed rice because the prophet told them that five liters of rice would miraculously increase to be enough to eat for five years. Many did not plant crops that year because they thought they would not need them. Domestic animals were killed under the prophet's orders.

The movement lasted only seven months, until the police arrested the prophet and some of his associates, charging them with being communist agents, the standard accusation for anyone rocking the boat at the time. Some of the prophet's relatives did then join the communist rebel group working in the area, but at this point they probably had no alternative. The prophet died in prison.[7]

Then in 1967 came a turning point in Thin relations with the government. Some Thin joined some Hmong in a rebellion (chap. 14). The Thai military were not prepared for a Mal and Pray insurrection, having long taken them for granted as a people who were assimilating well.

The insurgency among the Thin lasted altogether from 1967-1983, but had begun to peter out in the late seventies. Harsh repressive measures by the Thai army did not succeed with Mal and Pray insurgents, but the people did later respond to the promise of pardon, resettlement, and land located away from the mountains. Whole groups gave themselves up for that, and this time the promise was kept by the Thai government. Some who moved out of the hills have been satisfied and have not wanted to move back to their old villages, but others have returned under new economic conditions.[8]

As a result of this episode and of the Thai awakening to the situation, the Thin economy has been very much improved. In addition to the fact that part of the population was relocated on the plains and can grow irrigated rice there, paved roads which were built for military control in the mountains now permit transportation for economic purposes as well. Trucks pick up the corn grown by the Mal and Pray from large roadside shelters, and transport it to market. Some people have begun to use portable corn huskers. The Mal or Pray people can therefore sell agricultural produce much more readily than before in the markets of Northern Thai towns. With the cash they can buy rice, which reduces the need for swidden-grown rice. As a result of this economic activity much more money is available.

Many Thin now live in areas where they are in constant contact with other peoples. Schools are everywhere. Children are learning Standard Thai. Local people and strangers alike move freely, and do so easily on public transportation of different kinds. Many Mal and Pray therefore now live in a different world from their world before 1967. In Filbeck's estimation, this will lead to the eventual disappearance of the languages. Whether the languages are really endangered as a result of these changes may be a little too early to tell (chap. 17).

Summary

If we go back far enough historically, all but a few of Thailand's languages are immigrant languages. Even older forms of the Tai languages came from South China. Some of these languages are marginal, spoken outside of Thailand by more people than use them in Thailand. Some such languages have been discussed under various categories in previous chapters. The languages in this chapter are representative of the well-assimilated part of the remainder.

The marginal languages which are most fully assimilated to the Thailand language hierarchy are in the Mon-Khmer family of languages. People speaking such languages normally are not disruptive of national unity, but accept their place rather unquestioningly. The Pray-speaking people, together with the enclave Mal, became so desperate because of their economic decline, however, that they revolted for a while until Thai authorities corrected the situation.

The Mon language is shrinking in Thailand under the heavy cultural assimilation which its speakers have undergone, but still maintains remarkable resilience especially in communities which are engaged in commerce rather than agriculture. Having a separate language serves an economic function for Mon in such occupations.

14

Marginal Languages Adapting
to the Hierarchy: Hmong (Meo, Miao)

At the other end of the spectrum of peoples speaking marginal languages in Thailand lie the Hmong, Mien, Lisu, Lahu and Akha, who are not so fully adapted to the country as the Mon and the Pray. The Hmong, whom we will use as our example in this category, are just beginning to adjust a little, and in varying degrees.

Where the Mon were Buddhists long before coming to Thailand, and some Pray have taken on weak Buddhist trappings, the Hmong, with individual exceptions, have virtually no Buddhist overlay to their worship of the spirits of nature around them and the veneration of ancestors. Where the Mon live on the plains and along the rivers like the Thai, and the Pray live in the somewhat accessible lower hills, the Hmong traditionally live in the upper heights of the mountains. In appearance, in custom, and in language, furthermore, the Hmong are sharply and colorfully different from the Tai-speaking people of the valleys below them and from the rest of the country.

Such people speaking marginal languages and still adapting to the language hierarchy provide another near exception to the hypotheses advanced in this book, but in a somewhat different way from the Pattani Malay. Unlike the latter, the Hmong and others like them are relatively new immigrants, not already in place when colonized by the Tai peoples. Ethnic identity is of great importance to them, however, and they have not fully learned to function within the multiple identities implied in the hierarchy. More serious, perhaps, the Tai-speaking peoples have not accepted them into the hierarchy as readily as they now have the Mon or the Pray, perhaps because the Hmong are newer and less familiar, and have not conformed so completely.

Stages of Adaptation

Originally minority inhabitants of southwest China, the Hmong are now repeating in Thailand the stages of adaptation which they under-

238

went after thousands of them moved to Vietnam and Laos (Smalley 1985, 1986). These are not fixed stages, beginning and ending at discernible dates, but are configurations of relationship to the country and to the people already resident in it.[1]

Small numbers of Hmong are believed to have started moving into Thailand from Laos in the mid-nineteenth century (Mottin 1980a:55), initiating the penetration stage, and by 1929 Hmong were scattered thinly across the mountain ranges in the north, and along the mountain range between the Korat Plateau and the central plains (Cooper 1984:17, citing older sources).

Most of the Hmong came looking for land. Unlike the Mal and the Pray, or the Karen peoples, and unlike some of the other not-yet-integrated marginal-language peoples, their major cash crop is usually the opium poppy. This plant requires intensive cultivation by digging up the soil on the mountainsides, and a suitable plot is used for many years. As a result of such cultivation, however, once the soil is depleted of nutrients, Imperata grass usually takes over and keeps the forest from growing again, preventing renewal of the land and destroying it for agriculture as well. The Hmong, therefore, typically move their villages from time to time, sometimes over considerable distances, to find new jungle to cut. This is the "long cultivation, very long fallow" technique mentioned in the previous chapter.

Hmong movements have not been caused by cultivation needs alone, however. Population pressures and conflicts with the Chinese drove their ancestors out of China, and the years of warfare in Laos during the 1960s and 1970s stimulated some to move into the Thai border regions of Nan and Loei provinces. The Hmong also move because of severe illness or misfortune if they believe that the place where they live has proved to be inauspicious.[2]

In Thailand the Hmong ultimately reached the end of the sparsely inhabited mountains which are their habitat (maps 10.1, 13.1). Now they have nowhere else to go as population pressures increase, soil depletion becomes more critical, and conflicts occur with the Tai peoples and others.

From a communication standpoint, the classic Hmong penetration stage was generally characterized by weak contact with the peoples already in the country before them. Most Hmong could not speak the regional or national language, and were not familiar with the laws and customs of the country, so contact meant misunderstanding and conflict, ridicule and humiliation, which they sought to avoid. According to some Hmong refugees now in the United States, for example, country Lao people of northeastern Thailand came to the Ban Vinai refugee camp when it was first built in Loei Province, wanting to see the strange Hmong savages who had tails, as local rumor described them. Contact also meant being exploited by people who were more powerful.

So the Hmong who entered Thailand in earlier times stayed remote in the hills, in some cases making arrangements for the use of land with the Karen and Lavüa' or other peoples who were there before them, but preferring relative seclusion for the most part. They had their trading channels through Yunnanese merchants who regularly traversed the hills buying opium and selling trade goods. Some of the Hmong spoke Yunnanese Mandarin Chinese, and some of the Yunnanese spoke Hmong, so the Hmong did not yet need the Tai-speaking peoples or the urban Sino-Thai very much. Because population was sparse, considerable avoidance was possible, although it was never complete, of course.

The penetration stage was followed in time by a traditional stage, during which Hmong people still kept essentially to themselves and followed their traditional way of life, using their traditional trade patterns, but gradually moved a little into the orbit of other peoples in the area as well. They were now confident enough to visit market towns, which sometimes gave them an advantage in price over what they could buy or sell in the hills, and always gave them access to a wider range of goods.

When they turned toward the Tai-speaking peoples they generally did so at their own initiative. They came out of the hills when it suited them, and then returned to their distant homes where few Thai went. In this stage, when communicating with outsiders the Hmong primarily sought out people who spoke Yunnanese Chinese, and a few men in a village would serve as spokesmen for the group (Smalley 1985:249). But gradually more people gained a working knowledge of heavily accented Kammüang or Thaiklang. The Thai government introduced contacts as well, establishing a Tai language-speaking Hmong headman in each village as a government link.

Those trends begun in the traditional stage have now accelerated into the adaptive stage, which is just getting started for some Hmong in Thailand, but is well advanced for others. This stage is characterized by extensive multilingualism, some individuals even having gained advanced skills in the regional and/or national language. It is the stage of increasing education and acculturation. It is the stage most fully operative at the present time and is therefore featured in this chapter.

Not until the 1950s did the Thai public in general begin to notice the Hmong and other "hill tribes."[3] In the 1960s increasing population, increasing visibility as colorfully dressed people visited the market towns, increasing attention by linguists, anthropologists and missionaries from the West—all this drew their attention to the Hmong, Mien, Lahu, Lisu and Akha, as well as to longer-established peoples. In the early 1960s books began to appear, introducing educated Thai and others to the minority groups in the northern hills (Boon Chuey 1963a, 1963b; Young 1962).[4]

The Problem

By the late 1960s, however, the Thai government announced that Hmong from Thailand were being taken to Vietnam, indoctrinated and trained by the Vietnamese communists, and sent back to lead anti-government activities in the border areas of northern Thailand. Various elements in the Thai government now viewed the Hmong in particular, and others of the marginal northern groups as well, with alarm. Hmong across the border in Laos were fighting on both sides of the Vietnam War there, and were proving to be excellent guerrilla soldiers, so the thought that communist Hmong might bring insurrection to Thailand was a chilling one. Such fears were then realized in a small Hmong insurrection in the late 1960s and much of the 1970s, which stirred the Thai government to reconsider the Hmong and other marginal groups. Their very marginality—the fact that they were extensions of larger populations elsewhere—became central in the perception of officialdom.

At the same time, other problems associated with the Hmong, and to varying degrees with some of the other northern marginal groups, became more apparent. Of all the marginal peoples, the Hmong were the largest opium producers, cultivation of which was officially authorized by Thailand in 1946, but banned in 1959 under pressure from the USA and because of alarm at increasing heroin use inside Thailand itself (Tapp 1990:154, 160).

Moderate use of opium for medicinal purposes has been a traditional part of Hmong life back to their time in China. Men in their prime sometimes began using it as a narcotic as well. It created some problems of addiction in traditional Hmong society, but these were usually no greater than the problems of alcohol addiction in other societies. This pattern has changed, however, for under modern conditions of stress and economic scarcity, abuse of opium and heroin has taken on epidemic proportions among some peoples speaking marginal languages, including the Hmong (Lewis 1985b:41-55).

Although opium existed in China from antiquity, the British bear the blame for forcing China to accept enormous quantities imported from India and for requiring the development of a widespread market for it there in the nineteenth century. Peoples like the Hmong in southwestern China then increased their production as well, capitalizing on the increasing demand. Later in Laos opium was a French government monopoly, and the Hmong were encouraged, virtually mandated to cultivate it. In the last third of the present century the enormous American and European demand for illegal heroin, derived from opium, has made access to opium highly lucrative to opium warlords in the Golden Triangle, where Thailand, Myanmar and Laos meet. They and others buy raw opium from farmers at a tiny percent of what it will bring them.

For most Hmong opium is a product, a source of livelihood, virtually their only income. They are aware of some of the dangers of it, as are some people in the United States who grow tobacco or distill whiskey. They also see some of its social cost as the pressures to be described below are driving their own and neighboring peoples increasingly to its use and to desperation in order to maintain the habit. They are also subject to a barrage of information about its social effects in other parts of the world (Tapp 1989a:30). They get little money for their product, but what they do get is essential for survival. The income fluctuates, but in 1982, for example, in one place villagers received $100 for 1.6 kilograms, less than $30 per pound (Tapp 1989a:31).

The Hmong do know that opium growing is illegal in Thailand, and sometimes they suffer for growing it, as when Thai soldiers or police sporadically and unpredictably crack down with a highly publicized raid in which they destroy acres of poppy fields. They also know that normally their fields will be undisturbed if they pay bribes to the right officials, or simply because some government officials realize that many Hmong have no alternative to growing opium but starvation. The Hmong also know that after a crackdown the bribe required of those whose crops did not get destroyed may be higher, as may be the price received for opium not destroyed.[5]

Another problem associated with the Hmong is destruction of the forest, and even of the land, resulting from their type of swidden agriculture. Thai officials are naturally concerned about timber reserves, erosion, water runoff, and about the flooding and silting in the river valleys which can result (Keen 1978a). Occupation of unregistered land on hills and mountains is itself against the law in Thailand, as is occupying or destroying a forest. A license is even required to fell individual trees. Enforcement of the law has often been erratic and not very strict, however, because there are so few alternatives for the upland people (Sophon 1978). Strict enforcement tends to be concentrated in periods when the government is promoting and seeking to enforce resettlement onto the plains or to push people across the border at gunpoint, sometimes to be killed on the other side (Tapp 1990:161).

Furthermore, although most of the marginal-language peoples in the mountains are theoretically Thai citizens because they were born in Thailand, they are often not all registered as such, and therefore do not have proof of citizenship. Without it they cannot own land even where it is legal to do so, but in any case, obtaining registration without hefty bribes and endless painful dealing with unsympathetic officials is well-nigh impossible.

The hill peoples, furthermore, are often blamed for problems they did not create. Actually, four different kinds of groups are competing for the mountain lands in the north (Kunstadter 1978a; Cooper 1984: 5-25).

The first of these is the Forestry Department, representing the Thai government and responsible for preserving timber reserves and the watershed. Legally, most of the mountain land in Thailand belongs to the Crown, and the Forestry Department is responsible for it. It was formerly common land, for all to use but none to own.

The second group consists of logging interests, both legal and illegal. This group wastefully destroys enormous tracts of timber every year, creates erosion, and otherwise upsets the ecology. In fact, it sometimes destroys watershed stands of timber which swidden farmers of the stable type have carefully protected for generations in order to preserve the land. Those who cut timber illegally simply cut it in isolated places and pay bribes or kill off officials if necessary (Post 1985). Those who have licenses to cut timber legally do it openly. In either case the public which sees the devastation easily blames it on hill peoples like the Hmong, who have a reputation for cutting down the forests.

The third group is the rapidly expanding Northern Thai population, which is steadily pushing up into the hills from its traditional lowland locations. Northern Thai people near the hills have long practiced swidden agriculture to supplement their wet-rice cultivation (Judd

1964; Chapman 1978), but the practice is being widely extended. Northern Thai villages are being established along the roads which have been cut through the hills. Northern Thai families also sometimes live in Hmong villages, or those of other marginal peoples. Their extensive swiddens sometimes include opium as well as rice.

The fourth group with an economic interest in the hills consists of the minority-language people—marginal-language people like the Hmong, together with some marginal regional language people and some enclave groups. Although all of them together make up only a part of the problem, they are the least powerful of the four groups with an interest in the forest, and the most convenient scapegoats.

On the one hand the Forestry Department is notorious for its inability to see problems in human terms, and the timber industry has enormous profits at stake, as do officials who benefit directly and indirectly from those profits. On the other hand, the Northern Thai and the minority peoples are driven by the reality of becoming poorer every year, competing unequally for insufficient land but unable to move because there is nowhere better to go.

The Hmong are not a large group in Thailand, numbering some eighty thousand. Their numbers do not come near those of the Northern Khmer, the Pattani Malay, or the Karen peoples, although they are the largest of the northern marginal language groups presently adapting to the language hierarchy of the country. They are the fringe of a population numbering three hundred thousand in Laos (Yang 1975), perhaps an equal number in North Vietnam, and several million in South China (Cooper 1984:1).

But the Hmong, one-fifteenth of 1% of the population of Thailand, together with the other marginal and marginal regional language groups, jointly numbering less than one-half of 1% of the population of the country, have become the "Problem" upon which Thailand, the United States, other countries, the United Nations, and private agencies have lavished many millions of dollars, and enormous amounts of attention.

The Problem, and the people who are believed to have created it, have also drawn the attention of scholars, so that what were little-known groups before the 1960s have now been studied to the point where a much clearer picture of their languages and ways of life is beginning to emerge. Some of these studies deal directly with the Problem (Geddes 1976; Kunstadter, Chapman, and Sanga [eds.] 1978; Lee 1981; Cooper 1984; Tapp 1989a, 1990).

The Problem, from the Thai government standpoint, and that of outside agencies, no longer involves insurrectionist tendencies, but does include overpopulation in the hills, swidden agriculture, opium production, the need for alternative crops, destruction of the forest reserves, erosion, water runoff and silting. The Problem from the Hmong standpoint involves scarcity of resources, especially land, no place to move to, lack of alternative ways of making a living, harassment by villagers from other villages crowded too close, being treated with contempt or disdain, capricious enforcement of laws, corrupt government officials, uncertain citizenship, increasing poverty, increasing hardship.

And whereas the Mon, and even the Mal and Pray, blend into Thailand, the Hmong, in their black and brightly embroidered costumes, are highlighted on the landscape of diversity in the country. Their color is no longer communist red, but it is bright; in size they are only a speck, but the speck immediately attracts the attention of observers. Unlike the one million invisible Northern Khmer, the eighty thousand Hmong have the visibility of flashing beacons.

Hmong Language and Multilingualism

The group name Hmong (/hmɔ́ⁿ/ spelled {Hmoob} in the most widely used Hmong writing system in Thailand) is pronounced with an initial voiceless nasal [hm] (like English *Hm!*) or voiced nasal [m], depending on the dialect in which it is spoken. The {b} at the end of the Hmong language spelling does not represent a consonant, but the high tone of the word.

A Thai-based writing system has also been used by Hmong in Thailand (Smalley 1976d; Smalley, Vang, and Yang 1990:149-163). Only a small amount of written material is produced in Thailand in either system, largely by Christian groups.

Two major dialects of Hmong are spoken in Thailand, with many minor subdialects within each. In Thailand the larger dialect is Hmong Leng {Hmoob Lees} or Hmong Njua {Hmoob Ntsuab} (also spelled {Moob Lees} or {Moob Ntsuab}) 'Green/Blue Hmong'. The other is Hmong Daw {Hmoob Dawb} 'White Hmong'.[6] Speakers of the two dialects talk to each other readily, each often using their own dialect to do so, so the dialects seem to be mutually intelligible (Geddes 1976:39). Some people speak both dialects.

Some words in the two dialects are completely different, but more have the same historical source and any difference lies in pronunciation.[7] Most of this pronunciation difference is consistent, in that certain sounds or sound combinations in Hmong Daw will be automatically matched by corresponding sounds or sound combinations in Hmong Leng (Purnell 1970:46-64; Smalley 1976d:92-98). In other cases exceptions or correspondences do not seem as regular (Smalley 1976d:98-99).[8]

All clans have speakers of both dialects, but Hmong villages in Thailand tend to be made up of speakers from one dialect or the other, although exceptions occur (Cooper 1984:30-33). People from the two dialects sometimes marry, and under such circumstances Hmong Leng people tend to assimilate to Hmong Daw speech, rather than the reverse.

Hmong Leng and Hmong Daw are not closely related to any other languages in Thailand, although they are to some languages in China. The nearest relative in Thailand, but still quite distant, is Mien (Yao), another of the marginal languages in the north. Still more distantly yet, these languages are considered by some linguists to be related to the Tai languages (chap. 17).

Such a remote connection, even if correct, does not have any bearing on linguistic diversity and national unity in Thailand, however. Differences between Hmong sound systems and those of the Tai languages, for example, are enormous. Unless Hmong people learn Kammüang or Standard Thai early and well they tend to leave off the final consonants from each syllable when they speak these languages, in keeping with Hmong syllable structures. This often makes them difficult to understand.

Other than the Hmong language itself, the language most often spoken by Hmong coming into Thailand in older times was Yunnanese Mandarin Chinese, reflecting the main external trading contacts Hmong had elsewhere. A few Yunnanese Chinese merchants also live in Hmong villages (Geddes 1976:107, 223-226; Nusit 1976: 11-12).

People near the border of Laos, or ones who came into Thailand from Laos more recently, often speak some Lao. In keeping with the general hierarchical pattern in Thailand, Hmong in Sgaw marginal regional language areas sometimes speak Sgaw (Nusit 1976:12). A good knowledge of Kammüang or Standard Thai is still not extensive among Hmong, although it is growing rapidly now in this era of adaptation. Lesser knowledge, however, is widespread (Cooper 1984: 284; Kunstadter 1983a:26).

Education

The Kammüang or Thai learned by Hmong people in earlier stages was, for the most part, a mixture picked up in dealings with Northern Thai villagers, Thai officials, contacts with other marginal peoples, and sometimes the radio (Story and Story 1969a:3). Now some Hmong speak better Standard Thai than they do Kammüang because their primary exposure to a Tai language is through school.

The general level of education is still low, however, although rising rapidly. In a Tribal Research Centre survey (1978), less than 10% of Hmong adults could read and write Thai (Kunstadter 1983a: 26), a figure which would certainly be larger now, as schools have been established in Hmong villages only since the early sixties. Until recent years few Hmong saw any need for education, or for much language beyond rudimentary Thai. However, as early as the 1960s, some of those few showed high motivation for schooling, and occasionally small villages moved closer together in order to provide a population large enough for a school (Story and Story 1969a:3-4). Villagers now often cooperate also in building and maintaining village schools. More parents are now insisting that their children stay in school, a major sign of the adaptive stage.

Hmong children do not normally speak any Tai language before going to school, and it takes them two years of school just to begin to catch on to the Standard Thai language in which they are taught. For that and other reasons, education received in the village is minimal. The children who really learn Thai well go beyond the four to six years provided in the village school, and take additional years of education away from the village. In recent years a small number of Hmong have graduated from high school; some are in technical schools; a few have gone on to university; a very few have employment in professional positions, even outside the north.

Student hostels which have been established in a few towns are among the most important institutions for enabling a few marginal language young people to get more education than what is available in village schools. They were operated at first by Christian churches or missions, but now also by townspeople for profit, providing places for young people to live while attending school in town. Some take children from early grades; others limit them to upper levels.

Another source of education for a few Hmong young people has been the Buddhist monastery. Wat Si Soda, at the base of Doi Suthep 'Suthep Mountain' in Chiang Mai, for example, is a monastery which specializes in education for children from minority groups. Such opportunities have made a few years of education possible for some poor young people, but the quality of education in the monasteries is not generally as high as in the urban public schools.

Contacts with Tai Peoples

Regular contact with Tai-speaking peoples right in the Hmong villages themselves is also more common now than it used to be. Some Hmong villages, for example, now have Northern Thai people living in them permanently because of the population pressure in the valleys. In one village four such families were growing and dealing in opium and operating small shops (Cooper 1984:62).

More typically, Tai-language government medical or agricultural teams are now located in some Hmong villages, as well as school-teachers. In some cases these are dedicated people who develop good relations with the marginal-language people. In others they take their responsibilities lightly, even exploitatively. But their presence, in any case, helps strengthen multilingualism among the Hmong.

The many Hmong who sell their handicrafts at the night market in Chiang Mai or below the temple and palace on the mountain that overlooks Chiang Mai are also participating in the adaptive stage, no longer avoiding the larger population (Smalley 1985:246-251). Among them some older people speak very poor Standard Thai or Kammüang, knowing just enough to trade, aided by circumlocution and gesture. Increasingly, however, those doing business are more like one Hmong young man in 1986, a high-school graduate learning welding in technical school, and operating a large booth in the night market as well. His life manifested a string of radical changes from tradition: education, new skills, entrepreneurship. His use of Standard Thai sounded natural.

In Thailand, Buddhism has often been a strong assimilating force, but not with the Hmong. Thai Buddhist missionary efforts are too closely geared to assimilative purposes, and the worldview perspectives are too different (Tapp 1989a:85-91). These worldview obstacles might be overcome if the Hmong wanted to assimilate, and were free to do so at their own pace without coercion as they found it to be to their own advantage.

The adaptive stage involves profound shifts in the way Hmong people view the world and their place in it. In their traditional self-understanding they were an independent and self-reliant people, beginning in China centuries ago, and continuing in Vietnam and

Laos. They came to Thailand looking for a place to maintain that independence and self-reliance. But some of the characteristics which enabled them to survive earlier as a people make it difficult for them to adapt to a new situation where they have no more underpopulated mountains to move to. As they do adapt, however, their other qualities can probably be harnessed to ways more suitable for present conditions. So it was in Laos (Smalley 1985, 1986), and so it is becoming in Thailand.

Hmong Response to Change

As the traditional stage of Hmong life in Thailand is drawing to a close, and familiar ways have become more elusive, Hmong people respond in various ways. The majority have continued to eke out a declining subsistence by old patterns, even as the world has closed in around them. Those who respond in this way may see no reasonable alternative, but their course is doomed, and some of their increasing number of failures succumb to addiction or resort to begging.

Another response has been to try to bring in a golden age through a messianic movement such as has occasionally broken out among the Hmong at earlier times of stress (Tapp 1982a; Tapp 1989b:71-79; Smalley 1965; Smalley, Vang, and Yang 1990), and such as was described among the Mal and Pray in the last chapter. According to some Hmong a former Hmong king/deity will come back and reestablish the legendary Hmong kingdom. At one time in Laos and in Thailand he was believed by some Hmong to be waiting in a cave with all of the modern things Hmong lack: airplanes, cars, refrigerators, and plenty of food, not to speak of recognition and prestige. If the Hmong would do the right things he would come and liberate them.

A third response to the deteriorating situation has been to fight back. A small number of Hmong in Thailand, probably one thousand at most, participated in guerrilla actions against the Thai government in the late sixties and seventies. They were helped and trained by communist agents from Laos and Vietnam, thus threatening to widen that conflict. They probably had numerous sympathizers among the Hmong in Thailand, but the whole movement probably involved no more than 10% of the Hmong population at anytime (Tifveman 1972:11; Tapp 1989a).

But to the Thai, and to their American advisers, this insurrection, along with insurrections by other peoples in the northeast and the south of Thailand, was part of the effort of communist China and Vietnam to gain control over Thailand. The marginality of the Hmong loomed large at this point. So the Thai responded with all of the processes by which military types kill mosquitoes with sledgehammers. They bombed Hmong villages and burned them with napalm, and attempted forced resettlement of Hmong people into more secure areas (Mottin 1980a:58-59; Tapp 1986:38-39; Tapp 1989a). Of course such Thai action only made the situation worse, and the Hmong more desperate, more angry.

This insurgency, however, did eventually awaken the Thai government to think more realistically for a time about the needs and problems of the Hmong and of some of the other marginal-language groups like them. And in time a new and more sensible Thai policy of dealing with the insurrection did work: the Thai offered pardon, voluntary resettlement with schools, health and other services, and land. The Hmong rebels therefore began to give themselves up. The Thai were lucky in the timing of this change, too. China had become antagonistic to Vietnam and was seeking to become friendly with Thailand, so the threat of the dragon only one hundred kilometers (eighty miles) to the north of the Thai border did not seem so great. However, in the late 1980s and early 1990s Thai authorities seemed to be relying on more repressive measures once more (Tapp 1990:161).

In the fourth response to the changing situation, a few Hmong have adapted with increasing rapidity to the new circumstances in Thailand. They began to welcome Thai education, as we have seen. Some people began growing irrigated rice near their villages in the rare places where the land could be terraced (Cooper 1984:77-82, 148-176). Some began growing permanent crops like castor oil trees and peach trees in orchards, others vegetables for the market. Some Hmong have planted peach seedlings at strategic times in declining poppy swiddens. As a swidden petered out, the trees were maturing in the plot. The small, hard peaches are eaten pickled by the lowlanders (Keen 1983:303-304).

A few Hmong villages have also been promoted by tourist agencies as tourist attractions, with everything available to tourists from imitation crossbows to opium (Cooper 1984:119-121). Begging and the tawdry imitation of cultural artifacts, as well as of colorful cultural behavior, are the primary means through which some Hmong people can benefit from tourist exploitation. Thus contact brings out not only the loss of independence, but sometimes also the loss of dignity (Cohen 1983:318-324).

Not that all the goods Hmong prepare for the tourist trade are tawdry, however, by any means. Some beautiful work is being adapted to the needs and tastes of Westerners and Thai. Some of the women who do such sewing are justly proud of their work, but get only a fraction of its value when they sell it.

Tourists can shoot Hmong crossbows at targets outside the King's summer palace and at the foot of the temple on Suthep Mountain. Stores and market stalls for selling Hmong artifacts and craft products are open in Chiang Mai. But entrepreneurship of this kind is not possible for all Hmong, even for those who know enough Thai or Kammüang. Only the Hmong who have some economic resources left can profit by doing such things, and most Hmong have been getting poorer in Thailand for years. As a few Hmong families, furthermore, have been able to send their children to school, to develop irrigated rice, to set up little businesses, the gap between those who are better-off and the abjectly poor has become wider (Cooper 1984:177-212).

Assistance to the Hmong

Numerous agencies have been trying to help solve the Problem of the marginal-language people. Small Christian mission projects were the first, experimenting on a small scale with alternate crops and training people on a small scale to cultivate them. The Thai King and the royal family also began to show a direct concern for such people as part of their wider concern for the poor and underprivileged in the country. Their efforts, and the projects begun under their sponsorship, have continued over the years, becoming among the most extensive in the northern hills. The lot of marginal-language people would be very much worse were it not for them (Tapp 1990:154).

International concern, especially American concern about narcotics, brought numerous agencies to work on the Problem by the early 1970s. Many countries, as well as the United Nations, have organized programs in cooperation with various agencies of the Thai government. The Thai Narcotics Control Board, the Welfare Department, and the Forestry Department were all involved as well, some with one project and some with another. Since the policies of these different agencies differed on the Problem and on their treatment of marginal-language peoples, and since they were working with such a number of different foreign agencies, the programs were uncoordinated, and sometimes even contradictory (Tapp 1990:155-160).

The United Nations/Thai Crop Replacement Community Development Project, and its successors, is an example of such an effort

(Richard Mann personal communication; Thai/UN 1984). It started in 1972 with a charge to find ways of replacing the opium poppy with other crops. The main crops with which it has worked are kidney beans, coffee, potatoes, lettuce, cabbage, wheat, and fruits. It has also promoted rice subsistence improvement.

Unlike some of the other programs, this one did not try to replace swidden agriculture, but developed ways to make swiddens work under present conditions, for the time being at least.[9] It introduced a crop-rotation system for the swiddens, with rice, kidney beans, and legumes, along with the use of fertilizer, so that crops have been raised on some land for ten years. Steeper slopes are planted with tree crops.

An important part of the program has been to develop markets for the products, to the point where the private sector has taken over distribution of kidney beans. Sino-Thai merchants from the town go up into the hills with their trucks and buy the crops, shipping them to Bangkok. From there they are sent to Singapore, Europe, and Australia. Some of the coffee produced is processed and sold in Thailand.

Another feature of this project is organization of the farmers into cooperative groups to give them more leverage in sales, and to provide a mechanism for controlling credit for fertilizer. It remains to be seen how groups like the Hmong in Thailand, with no previous experience of this kind, will maintain such organizations.

Response to the project was very slow at first, and doubtless many of the projects like it are bumbling. Lee (1981:234-247) describes the unsatisfactory situation in one Hmong village from 1972-1978. While one of the agricultural projects in the hills was announcing great accomplishments, Lee was checking its reports in the village and finding the local reality less glowing. He quotes one village leader in a 1978 interview:

I don't think anything will be achieved. . . . We will just carry on living alongside the project staff without doing much with one another. So far, I don't see that they have succeeded in anything related to opium replacement. For sure, they have tried all kinds of crops . . . but nothing outstanding has come of all this effort. We still have to depend on opium like before (Lee 1981:234).

But since 1982, at least in some areas the response to alternatives has been increasing. Now that pressures from the Thai government are greater, many Hmong and others are taking the need for change more seriously. People have also had more time to accept new ideas, more opportunity to observe some of the experimental projects which have been successful. They also profit by the experience of those who changed earlier. More roads make transportation of crops to market possible, and more markets have been developed. Perhaps more people are ready for the adaptive stage, and the project provides the opportunity and model for change.

Hmong, like people elsewhere, cannot really be changed by outsiders except through brutally enforced deprivation. They make changes themselves, furthermore, only when the changes make sense to them. Some outside agency efforts are completely futile in the long run, but others provide ideas, alternatives, which may be adopted when the Hmong are convinced they are in their best interests. Ironically, in making such an independent decision to adapt in one way or another, the Hmong are surrendering their prized independence to market forces far beyond their control (Keen 1983:305-306). In 1985, for example, the market in the Mae Sariang area (Mae Hong Son Province) had become so glutted with cabbage raised in the hills that farmers found no more profit in cabbage.

Hmong Movement into the Hierarchy

Movement into the adaptive stage is still partial, slow—but accelerating—and often painful. It means that some Hmong who can afford to do so have begun to swim in the economic mainstream, and have in other ways decided to identify with Thailand. However, it does not mean that Northern Thai people or Thai officials have always decided to let them have a place, or have seen them as a legitimate part of the hierarchy of peoples which is Thailand. The Hmong who have made these moves toward adaptation are taking steps away from a traditional vision of isolation and independence toward precarious dependence within the hierarchy. This is enormously important for reducing the Problem, from both sides, but integration is a two-way process, and the marginal-language peoples are sometimes denied a place (chaps. 17, 19).

Thai people often look down on the Hmong and other marginal peoples as poor aliens, temporary residents and savages. The resettlement areas and the services provided are under the jurisdiction of ethnic Thai because the Hmong and other marginal peoples are not normally included in leadership above the village level. Positions in agricultural extension and in low-level teaching in village schools are open to them, but the Thai have been reluctant even to incorporate

Hmong in the Border Police. Many Thai are incredulous that some Hmong are university graduates, or that they might become doctors or lawyers. Suitable positions for brilliant Hmong university graduates are not easily forthcoming (Tapp 1989a:68).

Many Hmong, on the other hand, are unable to step more fully into the adaptive stage. People too old or too poor, people fearful of change, people without the necessary education—most such people continue to be caught up in the Problem, both from the Thai stand-point, and from their own. As the Thai military destroys acres of poppy fields, and as unmolested crops are insufficient to provide an adequate income, the farmers face greater hunger. In response, a few move more deeply into the mountains, to yet more inadequate land where they continue the downward cycle. Some lose themselves in opium. And some formerly proud and independent Hmong even go as far as Bangkok to beg in the streets. Only a few Hmong have the resources to overcome the odds. What happens now will be a measure not so much of the Hmong, as of the Thai.

Summary

Like the Pattani Malay, the Hmong epitomize the significance of marginal groups in their relationship to the language hierarchy. Recent Hmong immigrants find adjustment to Thailand difficult and Thai have been inclined to fear their ties to communist Hmong in Laos.

The deeper problems of the Hmong are not so much in their marginality, however, as in the fact that many are relatively recent immigrants, that they have not had time to learn to adapt to the Thai expectations expressed in the hierarchy of languages. Resources in their habitat cannot support all of the populations which need them or claim them, either.

The Hmong, furthermore, epitomize to the Thai all of the undesirable characteristics subsumed in the "hill tribes" stereotype. They grow opium, and do so with a non-regenerating style of swidden agriculture. They therefore tend to be made the scapegoat for forestry problems also created by Thai and Sino-Thai logging interests.

Some Hmong are adapting to their Thailand environment, while others face starvation and disintegration. Historically, they have proved to be a very resilient and creative people, however. Some of them, at least, will certainly find their place in Thailand.

15

Enclave Languages

Enclave languages constitute the remaining major category at the bottom of Thailand's hierarchy of multilingualism. These are minority languages wholly contained within the country, not overlapping the borders. They are scattered primarily around the margins of the country and in mountainous areas (map 15.1). Speakers of enclave languages are almost all multilingual. Populations are small, but not always smaller than marginal and displaced languages. Assimilation to the regional language and culture is often relatively advanced.

But although the enclave languages may have small populations they are not necessarily disappearing. In some cases present-day speakers of these languages are descended from people who were in the country before the Tai-speaking peoples came, and although their coexistence with Tai-speaking peoples has lasted for these many centuries, they remain viable communities.

Lavüa' Languages

Four Lavüa' /ləvɨə'/ languages constitute a language cluster including at least nine major dialects plus vowel and vocabulary differences from village to village. Often the speech of one village is not intelligible to people of another village two days' walk away, and villagers have to use Sgaw, the marginal regional language of the area, or Kammüang, the regional language, to communicate with people speaking another Lavüa' language (Kunstadter 1967:643). The difference between the Lavüa' of Bo Luang (Chiang Mai Province) and its nearest neighbors in Mae Hong Son Province is especially large (Schlatter 1976:237; Mitani 1978).

The differences in varieties of Lavüa' from one village to the next form patterns like the geographic distribution of Tai varieties (chap. 11), but the Lavüa' differences are greater than typical Tai differences. They have been in Thailand longer, and have therefore had more time for differences to deepen.

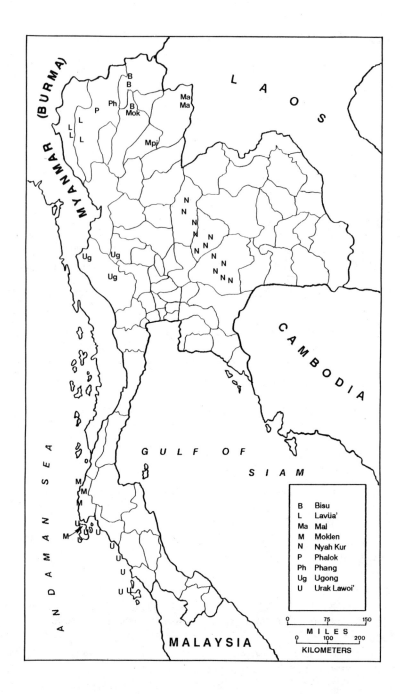

Map 15.1. Distribution of some enclave languages (after Gainey and Theraphan 1977; Wurm and Hattori 1981).

The Laviia' language cluster is part of a subbranch of the Mon-Khmer language family (chap. 17), to which branch also belong languages spoken in Myanmar and China, as well as the Lua' of Wiang Papao in Chiang Rai Province, Thailand. The people who speak Laviia' languages are located primarily in Mae Hong Son and Chiang Mai provinces, southwest of the city of Chiang Mai (map 13.1). Three of the four Laviia' languages are clustered around the villages of Umphai and La-up in Mae Sariang District, Mae Hong Son Province, and Bo Luang in Hot District, Chiang Mai Province. The fourth is located some distance north of them, in the northern part of Mae Chaem District, Chiang Mai Province. These different languages do not have different names except as identified by the names of the villages in which they are spoken (Donald Schlatter personal communication).[1] The Thai call the Laviia'-speaking peoples Lawa, the same term which they use for some of Thailand's other aboriginal peoples, and the Northern Thai likewise call them Lua'.

The Laviia'-speaking populations are small, with four thousand regularly speaking the La-up form of Laviia' in Mae Sariang District, and another fifteen hundred people there who are largely assimilated to Kammiiang, but who can still remember it. The Laviia' of La-up comprise the largest population, so the total number of people regularly using any Laviia' language may be approximately seven thousand (Schlatter personal communication), plus some ethnic Laviia' who do not speak it.

Some Laviia' live in the hills, others in the lowlands. The latter range from people who have recently moved out of the hills, some of whom may still be dressed in traditional costume and still speak their form of Laviia' language, to others indistinguishable from the Northern Thai people around them, speaking Kammiiang and having only a memory of ancestors who were Laviia' (Kunstadter 1964: 135).

Among the upland Laviia', almost all men and many women have long spoken Kammiiang in the southern part of the area, and Sgaw especially in smaller villages in the northern part (Kunstadter 1964: 15; Schlatter personal communication). Many people speak both regional languages, but not normally Tai Yai even though Tai Yai is more prominent as a regional language than Kammiiang in part of the area where Laviia' live (Peter Kunstadter personal communication). This extensive use of Kammiiang and Sgaw in upland Laviia' villages does not bring about any loss of Laviia', however.

People speak all of these languages with their children, joke in them, and even perform some religious rituals in them, apparently having done so for a long time. Lavüa' people sometimes look down on the Sgaw as inferior to themselves because they do not learn as many languages and are not as adept in speaking the languages they do learn.

In the more remote parts of the hills, however, Lavüa' and Sgaw people feel an affinity for each other in other ways, calling each other "relatives." According to a Lavüa' legend, the Lavüa' peoples and the Sgaw, along with others in the region, were born of the same family, Lavüa' as the oldest, Sgaw as the youngest (Sureeporn Yaysanga personal communication). Lavüa' and Sgaw recognize that they occupy the same ecological space, and the Sgaw sometimes even speak of themselves as "the Karen of Lua' country." They have many of the same skills, and common interests. Lavüa' identity is much more closely tied in with the land, however, than is the Sgaw. Moving away from the place where a person is born involves more of a change in identity for the Lavüa' (Kunstadter 1979:141-147).

Lavüa'-speaking people do occasionally become Sgaw, joining the people of that marginal regional language above them in the hierarchy. Whole families may move into a Sgaw village, wear Sgaw clothes, speak Sgaw and take on Sgaw ritual. When they do so it is usually because they are too poor to keep their expensive Lavüa' religious practices involving the sacrificing of animals (Kunstadter [ed.] 1967:34). Sgaw practices are not as demanding. A Sgaw, on the other hand, never becomes Lavüa' except by marriage, and that is rare (Kunstadter and Helm 1966:3-4). The Sgaw, furthermore, are taking over more and more land from the impoverished Lavüa' (Kunstadter 1967:660-661).

The importance of Kammüang as against Sgaw is increasing, however, as contacts with the valleys are increasing. With a growing network of roads through the hills, a few Lavüa' even own their own trucks. People therefore get out of the village and down to the Northern Thai towns in the valleys to trade more than they did before.

In the more fully Northern Thai environments of the river valleys, furthermore, use of Lavüa' is diminishing, although unevenly (Keyes 1968:16-17). Sometimes children learn Kammüang first and then learn their parents' language as they get older (Schlatter personal communication). In some long-settled villages in the valley only the older people still know Lavüa', and do not use it much. In cases of still longer settlement, even the older people may not know the language of their ancestors. When Lavüa' people settle permanently in Mae Sariang they may make a conscious effort to speak Kammüang exclusively in their homes so that their children will grow up speaking it, with little or no knowledge of Lavüa' or Sgaw (Kunstadter 1967: 646-648).

Former Lavüa' people sometimes move in order to change their identity to Northern Thai rather than keep their multiple identity, and their speech behavior then reflects their new place in the language hierarchy. This is very different from the behavior of Karen, Shan and Lue people living in the same lowland areas. They use their own languages and live apart from the Northern Thai, even when adjacent to Northern Thai villages.

Once the Lavüa' decide to become Northern Thai the transformation can be sudden. They talk and act like Northern Thai, living Northern Thai lives. To do this they must have been culturally assimilated before they made the move. They were already bilingual and bicultural individuals through observation of Northern Thai culture, aided by the fact that rural Northern Thai and Lavüa' cultures are very similar in many ways, so the changes in behavior that accompanied taking on a new identity are not difficult. The Karen peoples in the same area are unable to make the same kind of complete and immediate transition (Kunstadter 1969:20; Keyes 1979a:6).

The Lavüa', furthermore, are not in a state of cultural demoralization, the fate of some peoples in the face of rapid loss of their culture. They make the transition with straightforward adjustment. They do not meet with severe rejection by the Northern Thai, either, probably because they take on Northern Thai characteristics so completely, following the rules of the hierarchy so well (Kunstadter [ed.] 1967: 80).

Lavüa' knowledge of Standard Thai is also growing, with increasing numbers of Lavüa' children going to school. Those in Mae Sariang are reported to be better than average students, and some have done outstandingly well in classes by comparison with Northern Thai and Karen (Kunstadter 1967:647).

In some of the more remote mountain villages the young people may know as much or even more Standard Thai now than they do Kammüang because of the presence of the school and their distance from speakers of Kammüang. Some health workers, agricultural extension workers, and other government representatives now living in many villages are from the central plains, and their presence also increases Lavüa' contact with Standard Thai. Among valley Lavüa', however, Kammüang is far more prevalent than Standard Thai, just as it is among Northern Thai people themselves (Schlatter personal communication).

The Lavüa' have long used Thaiklang or Standard Thai for some specialized purposes. In the 1930s Lavüa' spirits had Thaiklang names in their ritual. "It may well be that the Thai language in the ears of the Lawa has the same effect as Pali in the ears of a Siamese, and is deliberately used for the nomenclature of superior beings." (Hutchinson 1935:158).

Lavüa' langages are still vigorous, but in some areas the old Lavüa' poetry is almost completely gone, replaced by transistor radios and other Thai forms of recreation. Adult men may listen to brief daily Sgaw radio broadcasts, and younger people tend to listen to music. For both older and younger people the radio often provides a background of noise which doubtless provides passive exposure to Thai and Kammüang language and music (Schlatter personal communication).

Missionaries introduced first a romanized, then a Thai-based writing system for the Lavüa' of La-up (Schlatter 1976). The switch from the romanized to the Thai-based system was made to enhance transfer between written Thai and written Lavüa', contributing more toward Lavüa' integration into the mainstream of Thailand (Smalley 1976a). Children in school, or other people literate in Thai, have little trouble learning to read materials prepared in this system. Reading material which has been prepared so far is primarily religious, with a few other publications such as health booklets.

Some Christians among the Lavüa' are motivated to read material written in Lavüa'. Some write letters in it, and church groups sometimes circulate newsletters. Among them some individuals even have their own typewriters. The writing system has also been used by non-Christians in the Pa Pae dialect, both in writing letters and for recording poetry (Suriya 1985:266). Some other Lavüa' show no interest, however, seeing no economic or other advantage in writing. Overall, the writing seems to have moved from the experimental stage to an established system, at least on a small scale (chap. 16), even though it has primarily religious use (Schlatter personal communication).

Lavüa'-speaking people have had contact with peoples who live in more complex social structures for centuries. The Lavüa' were already widespread inhabitants of the area when the Old Mon kingdom of Haripunjaya was established in Lamphun in the seventh century, and when the Tai kingdom of Lan Na was established in Chiang Mai in the thirteenth century. Some Lavüa'-speaking people were in contact with Old Mon civilization if not Old Mon rule for nine hundred years (Hutchinson 1935:180), and with the Tai peoples for seven hundred or more years.

For centuries Lavüa' people lived in the valleys where the Tai peoples now live. It is not known whether or not they also lived in the mountains in the early period (Kunstadter 1964:6-7). For centuries there was a close and mutually influential relationship between the two cultures, with many non-Buddhist concepts common to both peoples (Keyes 1968:15-16).

Over the centuries Lavüa' people were both absorbed and displaced by Old Mon and Tai-speaking colonizers, just as the Old Mon were absorbed by the Tai. Many present Northern Thai people from Chiang Mai westward are descended, or partially descended, from Lavüa' valley-dwelling ancestors, or from Lavüa' ancestors who moved out of the hills into the valleys at later stages.

In the nineteenth century, Lavüa' villages were formally incorporated into northern kingdoms (Kraisri 1965a). The rulers of Chiang Mai and Lamphun guaranteed them the right to continue control over the land they still used, and to continue to conduct their village affairs. They paid tribute to these princes, and ran a caravan route between Chiang Mai and the Burmese town of Papun (Kunstadter 1983b:137). As a part of their control over the land the Lavüa' were allowed in turn to collect tribute or rent (10% of the rice crop) from the Sgaw and other Karen who were increasingly coming into the area (Kunstadter 1967:640; Kunstadter 1979:128-129).

After the Thai from the central plains consolidated their control over the northern kingdoms, the lot of the Lavüa' declined. They now had to pay taxes in cash rather than provide tribute in produce, and they could no longer collect from the Karen peoples. As they were forced into the cash economy of the country some of them began working for lowland employers (Kunstadter 1983b:137). For a long time Lavüa' bachelors have worked in mines near Chiang Mai in order to earn money for the bride price they need to get married (Kunstadter 1967:653).

More recently the acculturation process has accelerated. People in some Lavüa' villages learned techniques from the Northern Thai and used them. They imported limited wet rice cultivation into the hills where there were flat areas with accessible water. New techniques sometimes spread from them to the Sgaw as well (Kunstadter 1967: 652). Education was enthusiastically received when first introduced in Border Police schools (Kunstadter 1976:662), and has continued to spread.

Now there are Lavüa' people, some from the hills but mostly from the valleys, who have advanced educations. Some have become teachers, or other government workers. Some of these teachers have disappeared from the area, having taken positions far away, but most have returned, although they are not necessarily assigned to Lavüa' village schools where they could do the most good. Instead they are moved from one position to another, with advancement seen as getting positions in the larger towns (Schlatter personal communication).

Government extension workers are often personally appreciated by the upland Lavüa', some even having learned a few Lavüa' words, which pleases the people even though what the workers know may not be enough to facilitate communication. Others, on the other hand, show their feelings of superiority and act like colonizers. In any case, the villagers do get some economic benefit from the presence of government workers, as they bring some money into the village (Schlatter personal communication). The presence of these workers also provides the opportunity to speak some Thai.

On the other hand, there seem to be limits on cultural assimilation in the hills, as opposed to the valley, and government extension workers have had little effect on Lavüa' life in the hills so far. Toilets, which are built at their urging, are not used, but simply rot away. Model agricultural plots are not imitated. Ethnicity and religion are strongly associated, and they have geographic correlates. Even though most hill Lavüa' consider themselves nominally Buddhist, many consider temples and saffron robes and merit-making activities to be valley activities. When people move to the valley they take on these activities, and young men become monks (Kunstadter 1983b:147).

There are exceptions to this attitude toward Buddhism, however. The upland Lavüa' of Bo Luang, for example, are strongly Buddhist, and Buddhism has a start in the Chang Mo area where six villages have Buddhist temples with monks from the outside. This Buddhism there is not deeply rooted, however (Schlatter personal communication).

And the association between location and forms of culture may be breaking down. Thai ways are gaining status and have become the "proper" ways for some Lavüa' young people with a little education. The desire for consumer goods from the Thai market is also increasing. As such expectations develop, young people spend more money and go into debt, a process which their elders resist, causing some younger people to lose respect for their parents, whom they consider to be old-fashioned.

Meanwhile, the same land and population pressures which affect the Mal, Pray, Hmong, and other northern marginal peoples have created severe difficulty for the enclave Lavüa' as well. When the land in the mountains was sufficient to support the existing population with swidden agriculture, the Lavüa' agricultural system was exemplary in its disciplined, regulated short cultivation, long fallow pattern (Kunstadter 1978b; Zinke, Sanga, and Kunstadter 1978). The Lavüa' traditionally preserved an area of forest around each village which was not subject to swidden rotation as well, and maintained unburned forest strips between swidden plots, to facilitate the return of the forest. They also used firebreaks to control the burning (Keen 1983: 297-298; Schlatter personal communication).

But Sgaw, then Hmong and finally Northern Thai peoples moved into the area, filling up the land. The hill population has been growing through reproduction as well. The area where the Lavüa' live is apparently doubling in population every generation, putting impossible pressures on the land (Kunstadter 1978b:74).

In spite of taking on limited wet rice agriculture, leveling paddy fields where it was possible to do so, people in the hills have been forced into short fallow periods of swidden agriculture and into dropping their ancient land conservation technology. Like other upland peoples dependent on swidden agriculture, the Lavüa' are therefore becoming poorer and turning increasingly to outside work. That process, plus the fact that their traditional religious practices in times of illness require great expenditures, makes moving out of the hills attractive. But the valleys, too, are saturated now, with Northern Thai people moving into the hills to find swidden land and other sources of income.

Cash crops have been introduced through government programs, but without much success for the Lavüa'. If the crop grows successfully then availability of the produce in quantities quickly drives the price too low to make a profit. The town of Mae Sariang does not provide a good market for fruits and some other crops, and transporting them all the way to Chiang Mai is too expensive.

When they can, Lavüa' people in the hills try to raise more rice, which is their best cash crop. Rice mills are now located in the hills, and rice is easily transportable to market by pickup truck. But with the shortage of land, rice cultivation cannot be expanded any farther (Schlatter personal communication). The land shortage is squeezing the ancient Lavüa' to death.

Nyah Kur

Predating the Tai peoples, and long before the present Mon population moved in to become speakers of a marginal language in various parts of the country, Old Mon extended into Thailand from its center in Myanmar. Its civilization in what is now Thailand was called Dvaravati, with primary centers at places like Nakhon Pathom and Lopbury, near present-day Bangkok, and outlying spheres of influence at Haripunjaya in the Lamphun-Chiang Mai area in the north, and on the northeastern plateau (Wales 1969).

This northeastern plateau is separated from the central plains by a range of mountains. Today in and near those mountains, close to the center of the former Dvaravati civilization, live a people whose language is closely related to the Old Mon language.

Like the Lavüa', the Nyah Kur are a people whose ancestors were already living in the country when the Tai peoples began trickling in. Unlike the Lavüa', they are a people whose ancestors were linguistically closely related to, if not actually part of, a civilization more advanced than that of those early Tai peoples. That civilization had writing and religion and social structures which the Tai peoples would emulate. The Tai peoples learned from the Old Mon, ultimately absorbing them all except for those left in that string of mountains running through the area of the ancient Dvaravati civilization (Diffloth 1984:1-11).

The Thai call this enclave group Chaobon /chaawbon/ 'highland people' or Lawa, the same name they apply to the Lavüa', Phrai, Mal and various other aboriginal groups. The people call themselves Nyah Kur /ñàh kúr/[2] 'hill people' or Niakuol, depending on the dialect.

One of the first to write in English about the Nyah Kur (and other minority peoples in Thailand) was Seidenfaden (1918).

In former days before the construction of the Korat railway, heavy traffic passed through this last pass, untold numbers of pack bullocks bringing down produce from Korat and returning with merchandise from . . . the nearest river ports to Bangkok. Nowadays all of this has been altered; the passes are rarely visited by man with the exception of some few cattle thieves or gendarmerie patrols. In the big mysterious forest all sorts of game abound. . . .

In these surroundings lived and hunted the Niakuols, planting their rais [swidden fields] with rice, Indian corn, tobacco and gourds and dwelling under primitive leaf shelters until some 60 years ago, when they were induced to come down from their mountain fastnesses to the plain and settle in orderly built villages like other people. . . .

. . . the whole tribe should number about 700 individuals, but the number of Niakuol-speaking is not more than 500 to 600, as these people are rapidly becoming assimilated by the surrounding Tai and losing their characteristic peculiarities. The children in some villages are already ignorant of the language of their parents, and for the rest most of the members of the tribe prefer now to be called Tai for fear of being termed "savage."

Whatever the accuracy of Seidenfaden's numbers at the time, there may be some three thousand speakers of Nyah Kur now (Theraphan 1985a: 38), and present-day descriptions of their assimilation to their Tai neighbors sound very much the same as those given by Seidenfaden nearly a century earlier. All Nyah Kur, including old people, are at least bilingual. Many speak both Lao (or Khorat Thai for some living in Nakhorn Ratchasima Province) and Standard Thai as well as Nyah Kur (Payau 1979:5; Theraphan 1984b:iii; Schlatter personal communication).

The Nyah Kur, even those not completely assimilated, have taken on many Thai ways. Roads lead to every village now. Schools have been established in the area for twenty years or more. Every Nyah Kur village has long had some ethnic Thai or Lao residents, many of whom are married to Nyah Kur-speaking people. Many Nyah Kur young people prefer to speak the local Tai language because it has more prestige than Nyah Kur, and children in some places often play with each other in a Tai language. There are communities where only a few older people still know any Nyah Kur (Theraphan 1984b:iii; Diffloth 1984:39). As with the more remote Lavüa', we have no way of knowing how many have passed into the Tai world over the centuries.

Urak Lawoi' and Moklen (Plus Discussion of Moken)

Down the western coast of Thailand, both along the shore itself and on the islands offshore from the peninsula, three little-known languages are spoken by sea-faring peoples. Two of these languages (Urak Lawoi' and Moklen) are enclave languages in Thailand; one of them (Moken) is actually marginal because its population extends over into Myanmar.

Collectively, these people have been called Sea Gypsies in older Western literature, Orang Laut 'sea people' in Malay, Chao Nam

/chaaw náam/ 'water people' or Chao Thale /chaaw thalee/ 'sea people' in Thaiklang, or Chao Le /chaaw lee/ 'sea people' in Paktay. Some Urak Lawoi' resent especially the term Chao Nam, and sometimes Chao Thale, and are called Thai May /thay mày/ 'new Thai' by Thai who do not want to give offense (Hogan 1972:206-207; Kannika 1985:13). The Moken in Myanmar are called Selung, with variant spellings. In their own languages these peoples call themselves Urak Lawoi' /'urak lawoc/, Moklen /məkleεn/ and Moken /məkeεn/, respectively.

The Urak Lawoi', Moklen and Moken speak Austronesian (Malayo-Polynesian) languages closely related to Malay. The Urak Lawoi' seems to be a Malay population which did not adopt Islam as its religion, and which therefore remained outside the mainstream of Malay historical development. The language is so close to Malay that they are almost mutually intelligible, but people from the respective languages do not understand each other at first meeting (David W. Hogan personal communication).

The Urak Lawoi' live in small communities on islands off the coast of four provinces of Thailand: Phangnga, Phuket, Krabi and Satun (map 13.1). Urak Lawoi' has two major geographical dialects, one spoken on Phuket Island and the other on islands in Krabi and Satun provinces east and south of there (Kannika 1985:1). Hogan also analyzes Phuket Urak Lawoi' as having two age-related varieties, which he calls "Old People's Dialect" and "Young People's Dialect" (Hogan 1985). These dialects have pronunciation differences and differences of vocabulary, but are easily mutually intelligible.[3]

Moklen live on the coastal strip of Phangnga Province and on offshore islands. The dividing line between them and the Urak Lawoi' comes at Phuket Island (Sorat 1981:47-48). Some of the Moken, on the other hand, are genuine sea nomads who live on boats which anchor at different points up and down the coast of southern Myanmar and Thailand. They may be remnants of a widespread boat culture among some of the peoples along the coasts of Malaysia, the islands of Indonesia, and the Philippines (Sopher 1977).

Moklen and Moken are similar to each other, and together form another language cluster more distant from Malay (Sudarat 1984; Sorat 1981). Moklen from Phuket and the Phangnga Province coast do not ordinarily understand speakers of Moken, but Moken and Moklen from the islands of Takuapa, where both groups are to be found, can talk with each other because of frequent contact (Hogan 1972:229). The primary reason for associating these two languages with Urak Lawoi' here is the general similarity of their place in the linguistic ecology of Thailand.

Native speakers of these languages are not as universally multi-lingual as are speakers of the previously described enclave languages. Urak Lawoi', Moklen and Moken men speak Paktay if they speak any Tai language. Some speak it fluently where contact with Paktay is more extensive, but in many communities use of Paktay is limited, and marked by strong interference from the speakers' own language, sometimes including a strong accent.

The same patterns occur in their use of the local dialects of Malay. On Phuket Island few of the Urak Lawoi' can speak any Malay; nor would their speech be understood by a speaker of Malay. However, farther south on Adang Island, the Urak Lawoi' have been in more contact with the local Malay language, so that many of them understand it and borrow vocabulary from it in their own language (Hogan 1972: 229).

In some villages on Lanta and Adang Islands, where few Paktay-speaking children live, the Urak Lawoi' children attend school regularly. Initial teaching is difficult as teachers and students do not share a language, but in the end most of the younger generation in those areas can read. However, in the village of Rawai on Phuket Island, where the Urak Lawoi' children are few in comparison with the Thai children, absenteeism is high. Children are embarrassed by their poverty which does not allow money for clothing and lunches.

Many Urak Lawoi'-speaking children, furthermore, cannot attend school because their parents never registered their births or simply do not insist that they go. Only a small percentage of those who start school complete four years, fewer yet six years, the official minimum. Of those adults who have been to school, few have ever reached the place where they read easily, and many are functionally illiterate.

In the last few years adult education has been tried in some areas. Some classes have been helpful for individuals with previous experience in school, but not of much help for those with more limited backgrounds. The lesson materials were prepared for typical Thai rice-growing communities, so are largely irrelevant for these people whose lives center around the sea (David W. Hogan personal communication).

A Thai-based writing system for Urak Lawoi' has been designed (Hogan 1976; Hogan 1985:137-144) and a few booklets have been produced in it, but Urak Lawoi'-speaking people have not shown much interest in that, either. The number of readers is small, although any Urak Lawoi' speakers who know how to read Thai could easily pick up Urak Lawoi' reading if they wanted to.

Speakers of all three languages lead a rather meager existence, with evidence of cultural disintegration. Among the Urak Lawoi' income is frequently inadequate. When fisher folk occasionally do get a large catch they may sell it for the equivalent of $40, but then most of them spend all of the money immediately, often on drink and gambling. Boating and boat-building skills are good, and Urak Lawoi' fishing boats go farther out to sea than Thai boats of the same size, but they cannot compete adequately with large mechanized fishing trawlers. The people are badly exploited by Sino-Thai fish merchants, to whom they sell their catch, and by Paktay and Sino-Thai fishermen for whom some of them work (Sorat 1981; Hogan personal communication).

The self-image of many of these people is very low. In contrast to the Lavüa' and almost any other group described in this book so far (with the possible exception of the Mal and Pray), the Urak Lawoi' are people whose sense of well-being has been destroyed through culture contact and the inability to cope with their present situation. They view themselves as fated for poverty. Although not Buddhists, they have accepted the Thai point of view that their present lot is due to their *karma*[4] and that nothing can be done about it. Some beg outside Buddhist temples at Buddhist festivals, but are embarrassed (Hogan 1972:223). Their Paktay neighbors, in turn, often regard them with contempt, as inferior beings and beggars. These mutually reinforcing perceptions make improvement in their situation very difficult indeed.

Ugong

In 1927 Kerr published an article with word lists from two "Lawa" languages. One was a Lavüa' language, as discussed earlier in this chapter, the other a language spoken by a small number of people in Kanchanaburi Province along the western border of Central Thailand in the area where Phlow is the marginal regional language.

Unlike Lavüa', Nyah Kur, Prai and Mal, which are also called Lawa, "Lawa of Kanchanaburi" is not a Mon-Khmer language, but Tibeto-Burman, related to the languages north and west of it in Myanmar, northern Thailand and China (appendix A). In the early years of the present Thai dynasty, up to two hundred years ago, Karen and Lawa were listed in its chronicles as having marched in processions of subjects. The northern groups called Lawa were not then under the effective control of the Bangkok government, but the "Lawa of Kanchanaburi" lived right along the strategic trade and invasion route to and from Myanmar (Bradley 1985:94).

Kerr described these people more than sixty years ago:

It is said that most of the Siamese-speaking inhabitants of these valleys are really of Lawa descent, but they have now quite given up their own tongue and speak only Siamese. Fortunately there are still some villages, in the upper parts of the valleys, where this Lawa is still spoken; but practically all those who speak Lawa can also speak Siamese. These people freely intermarry with their neighbors, whose customs and religion they have adopted. In a few generations their language will, in all probability, have disappeared (Kerr 1927:57).

About three hundred speakers of this language are left, not all of whom are in Kanchanaburi Province.[5] The name of the language in the village where its use remains strongest is Ugong /'ugɔ̀ŋ/. Variant but related names are used in the other areas according to people in those areas who still remember what their ancestors called themselves. Some present-day speakers and others who are descended from people who once spoke the language refer to it as Lawa, the Thai term. In general, descendants of this once widespread people, now speak Thaiklang, Lao[6] or Karen. Kerr's prediction of the disappearance of this language in a few generations is taking place. Unlike other languages we have discussed, whose disappearance was predicted fifty or sixty years ago but are still vigorous and even growing in numbers of speakers, Ugong is almost gone (Bradley 1978; Bradley 1985:94-98).

Ugong is now spoken in four primary locations, or remembered as having been used there in the past. These places are scattered in three provinces, Kanchanaburi, Suphanburi and Uthai Thani, at considerable distances from each other, apparently relics of a wide dispersion. And at that distance, over a long period of time with relatively little contact, extensive dialect differences have developed.

The strongest remaining use of Ugong is in the remote northwestern corner of Suphanburi Province, in a village which had been almost 100% Ugong until about 1965. The small number of non-Ugong inhabitants at that time consisted of Lao men married to Ugong women. Their children had been the first Lao-Ugong bilinguals in the community. In 1977, however, some other Lao and Thai people had moved in, and more intermarriage had taken place, and the Lao men who had married into the village more recently had not bothered to learn Ugong.

Three years later, enormous additional changes had taken place. A road now connects the village with the district town. Bus service is available a few kilometers away. Thai fruit-buyers have moved in with their trucks, establishing a cash economy. This has attracted a Thai shop, and a Lao-owned rice mill. The fruit trucks also provide regular transportation into and out of the village. A logging company had started to work in the area, employing villagers in its operation.

No school had yet been built in the village in 1980, however, although a few Ugong had gone out of the village to monasteries specializing in minority education. Many parents tend to resist education for their children as they are more concerned about their help in picking the fruit and vegetable crops which they grow for the cash market. They also seem reluctant to have their children Thai-ized.

No Ugong remain monolingual, and the quality of their Lao is now good. People are furthermore sometimes reluctant for non-Ugong to hear them speaking their language, and outside visitors would not at first realize that they were not in a Lao village because no Ugong would be spoken in their presence. So, in the past twenty years or so this village has changed from a virtually monolingual Ugong village to a bilingual one, but one in which Ugong identity is still strong.

In western Uthai Thani Province the Ugong presence was weaker. The village has had a road for a few years, and easy communication with the provincial center. Six times more Thai and Lao lived there than the one hundred or so Ugong-speaking people, with some Karen inhabitants as well. Sometimes Ugong men traveled as far as the village described above to search for wives. Relations between the Thai and the Ugong in the Uthai Thani village were generally good, and many of the Ugong worked for the Thai in their fields. The eighteen-year-old son of the Thai headman had an Ugong wife and spoke Ugong.

The village had no school, but some children walked to schools in nearby villages or were carried to them in pickup trucks daily. A few Ugong young people have had several years of education, and are literate in Thai. However, not all the Ugong sent their children to school as they could not afford the cost of uniforms. Nevertheless, the general level of Thai language spoken by the Ugong in the village was good.

Some of the Ugong there still married Ugong, and although cultural accommodation was advanced, they did not want to assimilate. However, the extent of contact, the availability of education, the multilingualism, all meant that any young person who did want to change identity from Ugong to Lao or Thaiklang could do so quite easily. Here again, people were shy about speaking Ugong when other people were around.

The third area is a radically assimilated formerly Ugong community in Sangkhlaburi District, Kanchanaburi Province, where a school has been in operation for forty-five years. The area has also been ethnically mixed for as long or longer. No marriage between two Ugong people has taken place in that village for fifty years, and no one under fifty years of age speaks the language. Bradley attributes the loss of the language to the opening of the school, but it seems more likely that the small size of the Ugong population in an area of extensive ethnic mix was more important. We have earlier seen areas where solid populations of minorities had schools which helped make the young people multilingual, but did not stop the use of the language.

In the fourth area, also in Sangkhlaburi District, even the memory of an Ugong past is almost gone. Bradley's search turned up only an individual here and there who knew even a few words of Ugong, whereas about fifty years ago the area had at least two Ugong communities. Bradley again attributes the decline to a school, but does not mention that the Phlow in the area also have schools, but that their language remains a marginal regional language of considerable strength.

Clearly, Ugong is no longer even remembered through most of its former extent, and the two enclaves in which it does still effectively remain are so small that they are barely viable. Kerr's prediction concerning the disappearance of the language "in a few generations" is coming true, so that now, three to four generations later, what he saw is virtually gone. Given the pattern of assimilation which has occurred in the past we would have to guess that Ugong will have also disappeared from the two villages where it is still used "in a few generations," although some other small enclave language minorities like that persist for a long time. But whatever the future, for the moment at least, Ugong remains a small enclave language in Thailand.

In light of the preceding discussion of Urak Lawoi', it is interesting to note that Bradley gives no hint of psychological disintegration among the Ugong as their language and culture is being overwhelmed by others around them. Like the Lavüa' and so many others, they have simply changed. Bradley gives evidence of some resistance to change in the rejection of education and the search for Ugong wives at some distance, but gives no hint of traumatic cultural stress.

Mla'bri'

In 1919 Seidenfaden published a note in the *Journal of the Siam Society* giving a third-hand account of a band of people called Kha Tong Lüang /khàatɔɔ ŋlĭaŋ/ 'yellow banana-leaf savages', who were said to go naked (Seidenfaden 1919). They were reported to be in the northern, more rugged part of the same mountain range in which the Nyah Kur are found. Such people were also mentioned in the *Journal* at various times over the subsequent years (Boeles 1963:157-158), not usually described as naked, but as moving about in small bands without permanent villages or agriculture. They lived by what they could find in the forest, consuming it themselves or bartering it.

Peoples matching this description were also known to the Tai-speaking peoples and others along that same mountain range, especially in the provinces of Nan and Phrae where they were typically called Phi Tong Lüang /phĭitɔɔ ŋlĭaŋ/ 'yellow banana-leaf spirits'.

The "yellow banana leaf" in these names referred to abandoned temporary shelters in the forest, lean-to constructions, often made with wild banana leaves spread out over rough frames of bamboo or wood poles. Hunters in the forest would find these uninhabited windbreaks, their banana leaves yellowed, but no other evidence of humanity. Some considered them to have been created by jungle spirits /phĭi/.

The term Kha /khàa/ is used in Standard Thai languages for mountain-dwelling peoples speaking Mon-Khmer languages and looked down on as inferior beings, or savages. But it was the term "Spirits of the Yellow Leaves" rather than "Savages of the Yellow Leaves" which caught on both in Thai and in English, and became the popular name for this elusive and virtually unknown people. A more accurate neutral Thai term also used of them is Khon Pa /khonpaa/ 'forest people'.

Two Western explorers each made contact with a band of such people, and travelled with them for a brief period in the mountains of Nan Province. Bernazik (1938) and Weaver (1956) thus documented their existence and described something of their life. Bernazik also provided a list of words from the language of the people he encountered, and stated that their name for themselves was Yumbri 'forest people'. People calling themselves by that particular name, however, have never been documented since.

In subsequent years, sightings and brief contacts with such people became more frequent as other populations became larger and as roads became more extensive. The people also became more frequent visitors in some Hmong villages, and at times developed a dependence on working for the Hmong in exchange for food.

In the early 1960s two expeditions from the Siam Society sought out such people in Nan Province and recorded as much as they could about them (Kraisri and Hartland-Swann 1962; Boeles 1963; Kraisri 1963; Velder 1963). The investigators reported that this particular band called themselves Mrabri also meaning 'forest people', a term confirmed by later researchers as Mla'bri' (Mlabri). The word list collected showed that Mla'bri' was related to Mal and Pray and Khmu'. It has later been shown to be the same language as Yumbri (Rischel and Egerod 1987:20-21,23).

In addition to their own Mla'bri' language, some of the people spoke Kammüang and Khmu' (Boeles 1963:134). The men spoke Kammüang to each other in the presence of the expedition members, but one spoke Mla'bri' to his mother (Kraisri 1963:180). Their Kammüang and Khmu' languages were strongly accented, and the Kammüang was spoken without tones. When checked on their ability to distinguish Kammüang words whose meanings were different according to the tone with which they were spoken, they could not do so except in context (Kraisri 1963:180-181).

The camp in which the Mla'bri' people lived at the time was located in a forest of dense virgin trees and bamboo. It consisted of lean-to windbreaks, rows of sleeping places (made by piling up leaves, bark, and/or woven palm branches), and rows of fires, between which people slept. There were sleeping places for seventy-one people, but some of them were not in use. The band itself consisted of about forty-five people (Velder 1963). They said there were other bands as well.

The people were dressed in loincloths and rags made from old discarded clothing obtained from the Hmong village with which they were in contact. They were shy and most of them would not come out from hiding in the forest while the outsiders were present. The only defense they have against human beings is flight, and the only defense against wild animals is fire.

Since the mid-sixties sporadic contacts have increased (Trier 1981). Most notably for our purposes, a team of linguists was able to investigate the language for eleven days, correcting the name to Mla'bri' and publishing information on the language (Rischel 1982; Egerod 1982; Egerod and Rischel 1987; Rischel and Egerod 1987).

In the meantime, the Mla'bri' situation has changed radically because of the massive and wasteful devastation of virgin forest by logging companies in the area where they live. Their natural habitat has been greatly reduced, and their dependency on the Hmong has increased as they are no longer able to subsist by what they can gather in the forest. They are still extremely shy, avoid contact with strangers, and where contact is established they often disappear without warning (Schlatter personal communication).

It is impossible to know whether the ancestors of the Mla'bri' always lived this way, or whether they were forced into this kind of life by some disaster. They are not the only non-agricultural hunting-and-gathering society in Thailand, for Negrito peoples in the southern peninsula still have a traditional life of that kind. But Mon-Khmer-speaking peoples do not typically live on such a primitive nomadic level.

Too little is known about the Mla'bri' even to guess whether the population is smaller than it used to be, and if so, what happens as the language slowly becomes extinct. Do people just die off? Do individuals enter Khmu' or Northern Thai or Hmong communities? If so, in what role, and how are they received? There may be no more than 150 Mla'bri' now (table B.1). The next few years will certainly be critical, as so much of their habitat has been destroyed.

Summary

The Lavüa' languages, Urak Lawoi', Moklen, Nyah Kur, Ugong and Mla'bri' provide a cross-section of the enclave languages in Thailand. Clearly the people speaking them are diverse. Many have been in the country a very long time, and have partially succumbed to assimilative pressures exerted by the Tai peoples for centuries. Some of them nevertheless remain linguistically viable and healthy to the present, but unlike almost all the languages above them and even on the same level in the hierarchy, even these most viable of the enclave languages show some signs of losing out. As long as the hierarchy continues to work, however, and as long as people are able to follow its rules, speakers of most enclave languages may have multiple identities or may pass to a higher language niche without serious cultural anomie or psychological stress as their own language is diminishing.

Small size, scattered locations, and extensive contact with more dominant peoples do cause disintegration when people do not follow the rules of the hierarchy of multilingualism. The hierarchy does not provide a linguistic ecological niche for groups or individuals who are inadequately multilingual and insufficiently bicultural. They are unable to pass into the next higher group when their situation becomes intolerable. They become a despised people, living in poverty and hopelessness, as seems to be the lot of the Urak Lawoi'. Such people, fortunately, are an infinitesimal part of the population of the country.

Part V

Trans-Language Issues
Introduction

Much minor detail makes up the linguistic diversity in Thailand, and large issues underlie the national unity which exists in the face of that diversity. The first parts of this book have majored on the detail, with reference to larger issues from time to time. In this section we take a broader look at a few of the larger issues. Earlier parts dealt largely with the *what*—what the situation is. Now we focus more on the *how* and the *why*. The questions raised in the introduction to this book are addressed most directly here.

The role of education has been mentioned frequently, but in this part the issue of using languages below Standard Thai in the hierarchy as media for education is also explored. Historical developments have come up in many chapters, but some of them are now sketched in a more integrated way. Language has repeatedly been tied in with ethnicity in what has gone before. Now their interrelation is explicitly amplified. And finally, the delicate interrelationship between ethnic Thai and the minority groups—the minority problem—is shown to be largely a Thai problem.

16

Writing and Education

As we have repeatedly seen in earlier chapters, education is one of the most important forces bringing unity to the language diversity of Thailand, especially in enabling millions of people to use Standard Thai along with their other languages. Through education also, children learn of the Thailand which exists outside the village, of Thai kings and heroes, of national values.

On a more individual scale, however, the educational system is wasteful. Thousands of youngsters spend varying lengths of time in school without understanding what is said. Many individuals do not become more than nominally literate, and many lapse into illiteracy even though they are counted in the national statistics as literate because they have attended school.[1]

On the one hand, the Thai educational system is improving in many respects. Over the past twenty years more schools have been placed in more remote places, and more parents want their children to attend. Teachers are generally more qualified, and some are deeply concerned for the education of the children. As a result, some minority children know more Standard Thai than they do a regional language because people who speak the regional language are not present in the village, but the school is. And some individuals are doing well.

On the other hand, the Thai educational system is elitist. Although six years of education is theoretically mandatory, even that much is scarce in rural areas, with education beyond the sixth grade restricted to towns. Young people who do not qualify by examination or bribe for places in higher-level schools are excluded. Only the luckiest, the brightest, or those with the most favorable backgrounds will go on. Elitism is furthered as parents who can afford to do so send their children to better private schools. The requirement that all education must be in Standard Thai strengthens the elitism.

Yet the elitism is sometimes partly softened as it is implemented. We have often seen that teachers will use the regional language, or even one on a lower level, to bridge the gap between their students and Standard Thai. And in the Pattani Malay region, strong unrest has caused the government at times to accept locally dictated modification in education.

Government educational policy is not only elitist but is also wasteful as it seeks to diminish the importance of languages other than Standard Thai rather than to capitalize on them. Implementing this policy is also partially self-deceptive when the regional languages are labelled dialects of Thai and teaching Standard Thai to speakers of regional languages is treated as a process of standardizing substandard speech.[2]

In the official Thai scheme of things, language is a critical national security matter, so the Ministry of Defense has the ultimate say on language policy. This Ministry tends to respond more to the perceived threat of minority unrest than to the needs of Thailand's peoples. Other ministries directly concerned with language issues are the Ministry of the Interior, the Ministry of Education, and the Office of University Affairs (Achara 1982:207-209; Noss et al. 1984:75-79). They sometimes show more concern for developmental issues than does the Ministry of Defense, but their efforts on these lines are usually small, sporadic, and temporary.

Special Educational Needs of Minorities

In a survey of education among non-Tai minorities in Thailand, Bradley (1982) pointed out some of the disadvantages which children experienced under public education in remote areas in spite of recent improvements. (1) Few of the schools even reach the legal minimum of six grades. (2) Often ad hoc arrangements have to be made to have a school at all, as few are provided in normal fashion by the central authority. (3) Buildings often have to be constructed by the villagers themselves. (4) Curriculum is entirely in Standard Thai, a foreign language. (5) Textbooks may be in short supply, even non-existent. (6) There are insufficient teachers, sometimes only one to a village. (7) Teachers may not be at the school full time, sometimes showing up only a few hours a month. (8) Supervisors do not come.

Another disadvantage, not the fault of the educational system, is frequent inadequate parental understanding of the nature and value of education, and therefore the inability to support children in it. Many parents tend, for example, to pull them out of school when they need their help in farming.

Nevertheless, some children do learn, and a few learn well. More than any one single institution, the schools have helped to establish the unity which exists in Thailand's diversity. They have not usually succeeded in replacing other languages, but have been remarkably successful in solidifying Standard Thai at the top of the language hierarchy, as the language of the nation (Smalley 1988a).

It would seem, though, that a more helpful educational policy could be developed for peoples speaking regional, marginal and enclave languages. One of several educational models could be applied: (1) education could be conducted in the vernacular while students are learning Standard Thai as a second language; (2) education could be bilingual, with more vernacular language at first, phasing into Standard Thai;[3] (3) education could remain in Standard Thai, but more sophisticated attention could be given to helping students learn Thai as a second language; (4) education could remain in Thai, but literacy in Thai could be taught through literacy in the vernacular. Some of these options involve writing local languages, one of the controversial issues impinging on linguistic diversity and national unity in the country.

In a departure from normal policy, and with the approval of higher authorities, experimental educational programs in the Northern Khmer and Kuy languages and cultures were being organized in their respective language areas of northeast Thailand in 1991-1992. Classes were to be conducted one or two hours a week on the lower secondary level (table 1.1). Thai-based writing systems designed and used by missionaries were employed (Smalley 1976c; Johnston 1976), and the textbooks were approved by the Department of Education in Bangkok (Beulah M. Johnston personal communication). Such a program is obviously not designed to help monolingual children entering the school system, where the use of the local languages is most badly needed, however.

Writing Thailand's Languages

Some Thai officials fear that writing Thailand's other languages would destroy unity, particularly if the writing is not in Thai script. Their perception is all the stronger when the writing is associated with religions other than Buddhism, like Arabic script for Islamic Malay, or roman script for some marginal and enclave language groups with Christian minorities.

Some years ago, the then Minister of the Interior called together leaders of all of the Christian missions in Thailand and told them firmly that with the exception of the Burmese-based Sgaw writing, no further materials were to be published in any of the minority languages in the country except in Thai script. He also hinted strongly that eventually no literature would be permitted in minority languages at all.

Marginal peoples who already had their own writing systems, and for whom these were important, were greatly upset. The regulation has never been enforced, and such policies often last no longer than the particular Minister who announces them, or even the meeting in which they are announced, but the event had a chilling effect on the development of some marginal and enclave language written materials. Of course this is what it was intended to do, but its wisdom is another matter.

A dozen or more writing systems of different kinds are to be found in Thailand, decidedly part of its linguistic diversity[4] and with implications for national unity, but sometimes in ways different from what government policy assumes. These systems vary in the characteristic shapes of their symbols and in the rules by which people read and write them. Chinese and English, for example, not only have different appearances, but also differ in what features of the respective languages they symbolize. The Chinese writing system represents syllables and morphemes[5] while the English system generally symbolizes sounds and morphemes.[6]

Even though English and Standard Thai writing both symbolize sounds, they too are different systems. In addition to their different scripts, they represent sounds in partially different ways. In English, for the most part, symbols are written in much the same order in which the sounds are spoken. In Thai, however, consonants are written in the order in which they occur in speech, but vowels have different fixed positions in an orbit surrounding the initial consonant or consonant cluster of each syllable. So, keeping in mind that ม represents /m/ in Standard Thai,

/maa/ 'come' is written มา, with the vowel after the consonant;
/mii/ 'have' is written มี, with the vowel above the consonant;
/mêɛ/ 'mother' is written แม่, with the vowel before the consonant (the ˙ is a tone mark);
/mûuk/ 'mucus' is written มูก, with the vowel below the consonant;
/mɨɨ/ 'hand' is written มือ, with the vowel above and after the consonant;
/maw/ 'to be drunk' is written เมา, with the vowel before and after the consonant;

/mia/ 'wife' is written เมีย, with the vowel before, above and after the consonant.

Another radical difference between English and Standard Thai writing is that Thai has spoken tones to be represented in writing, but English does not, and that Thai symbolizes its tones differently from any roman script system for writing tones (chap. 11).

Some of the writing systems used for Thailand's languages (table 16.1) are well established in the sense that native speakers regularly use them on their own initiative in Thailand or elsewhere. Others are experimental, with the initiative for their use still lying primarily with

Table 16.1. Languages classified by writing systems used in Thailand. Some appear in more than one category because of the variety of options available. The list includes only those systems which are intended for popular use, not ones designed for linguistic or anthropological purposes. The table is probably not complete (See also Theraphan 1985a:67).

Type of system	Established	Experimental
Thai-based	Standard Thai, Lao, Kuy, Lavüa', Mien, Northern Khmer, Pali	Kammüang, Paktay, Akha, Hmong, Lisu, Mal, Phlong, So, Urak Lawoi'
Lao	Lao	
Temple	Kammüang, Lao, Khün, Lue, Tai Yai, Lao Song, Yang, Yong	
Roman	English, Other European, Akha, Hmong, Lahu, Lavüa', Malay, Mien, Sgaw, Vietnamese	
Chinese	Chinese languages, Mien	
Mon-Burmese Mission	Sgaw, Phlong, Phlow	
Mon	Mon	
Mon-based Monastic	Phlow	
Leke	Phlow	
Arabic-based	Standard Malay, Pattani Malay	
Fraser Script	Lisu	
Indigenous from Laos	Hmong	

their promoters because they have not caught on extensively enough for native speakers to use them much on their own.

Thai-based Writing Systems for Minority Languages

Entirely aside from the dubious security issue, good reasons do exist for writing some of the other languages of Thailand in Standard Thai script (Smalley 1972, 1976a, 1976b). If the system is well devised, people who learn to read and write Standard Thai in school can also read and write their own languages with little additional effort. More important from the perspective of the hierarchy of multilingualism, a greater number of people can learn to read and write Standard Thai, and can do so more easily, through literacy in their own language.

People learn to read only once, even if they learn more than one language. Reading and writing involve learning to make an association between marks on paper and meaning, learning to communicate through hand and eye rather than mouth and ear. Learning to read a second language does not involve relearning this basic skill, but reapplying it, and possibly learning a different script.

Because learning to read means learning how to get meaning from the page, the skill is efficiently gained only when the student can easily understand the language in which the page is written. Without meaning the process descends to rote memorization of esoteric symbols. As has been repeatedly mentioned earlier, however, when small children go to school in regional, marginal, or enclave language communities, they often understand no Standard Thai at all. The first two years, in which they are beginning to learn Standard Thai, is otherwise generally an educational waste. With a well-designed curriculum for teaching them to read and write their own language during that time, along with the Standard Thai they are learning, they would become literate in Standard Thai earlier, and gain more in the limited time most of them have in school. The rather large lapse into illiteracy characteristic of many rural and remote regions might not be as great.

But along with the advantages of a Thai-based writing system for minority languages, come problems. For one thing, the system is complex and cumbersome when applied to some languages which are significantly different from Standard Thai. These complexities often impede learning to read tone languages in particular.

Sometimes no suitable Thai character seems to be available for a sound in another language. The Thai system therefore has to be adapted somewhat, and rarely used Thai characters have to be given other values than what they have in Standard Thai, just like some roman letters have different values in different European languages.

A third problem involves acceptability of a Thai-based system when the language already has an established writing system in some other form. People resent having their writing system tampered with or displaced. Even minor spelling reforms are impossible to bring about in English, and Sgaw-speaking people who read Sgaw in a Burmese-based script, and whose ancestors have done so before them, would be incensed if they were required to switch to Sgaw in Thai script. People not literate in traditional Sgaw writing might not care, however.

A fourth issue involves the need for standardized spelling between people who use any given writing system. In Thailand this is particularly a problem for individuals writing Tai languages in Standard Thai script. Such people often write impressionistically, without developing or understanding systematic spelling principles, so that two or more writers may not spell in the same way, or any one writer may not be consistent. No single source of written materials is strong enough to set a norm.

The fifth issue is the nature of the correspondence between the system developed for the minority or regional language and the Standard Thai system. This will probably be easier to understand if we take it up in connection with specific cases.

Tai Languages in Thai Script

There are theoretically two ways of writing Tai languages in Thai script, depending on how the language for which the writing system is being developed corresponds to Standard Thai itself. They are the sound correspondence approach and the earlier stage approach.

For most non-Tai languages anywhere in the world, when a writing system is being devised people follow a sound correspondence approach. That means that the symbols used represent as consistently as possible the structurally significant sounds of the language for which the writing is being devised, but in a way that corresponds to how those symbols represent similar sounds in some model language. Every /u/ (a vowel similar to that in English *soon*), for example, is consistently represented by the same symbol, whether the model symbol is {u} as in German, {ou} as in French, {oo} as in English (sometimes), or anything else.

When the sound correspondence approach is applied to Tai languages like Kammüang or Lao, however, it has serious disadvantages, some of which can be illustrated from the analogy of creole languages which are related to English. In Tok Pisin (a creole language also known as New Guinea Pidgin) *tupela han* is a sound correspondence spelling for what translates literally as 'two fellow hands', or 'two hands'. *Tu* (with {u} as in *tumor*) seems to many people who know English to be the wrong spelling for *two*, *pela* for *fellow*, and *han* for *hands*, even though the words are spelled as pronounced in Tok Pisin, and all sounds are consistently written with the same symbols wherever they occur.

In the same way, words in any Tai language which have the same meaning and the same or partially different sound from Standard Thai seem to be spelled wrong from a Standard Thai point of view, if spelled in a sound correspondence way. If we go back to some of the Kammüang examples in table 5.2 we get spelling examples as in table 16.2.

In the first place, the Kammüang /˜/ tone (high short fall in Chiang Mai) is simply different from and in addition to anything in Standard Thai, adding a sixth tone to Standard Thai's primary five. So to keep a sound correspondence system it would be necessary to make up a way of writing it. ´ is used in table 16.2. More importantly, a sound correspondence spelling produces results which are confusing for the Northern Thai person who knows how to read Standard Thai, because words which have the same meaning and similar sound in the two languages are spelled differently, as in all three examples.

Table 16.2. Problems with sound correspondence spelling for Tai languages. Each pair of words on the same line is assumed to have the same meaning although some of the words used as examples are made up to simplify the comparison. Tones are described in parentheses. ´ was adapted from another function to represent a Kammüang tone which does not exist in Standard Thai.

Standard Thai		Kammüang	
Pronunciation	Spelling	Pronunciation	Sound correspondence spelling
pâa (fall)	ป๋า	páa (high)	ป๋า
phâa (fall)	ผ่า	pâa (fall)	ป่า
pháa (high)	ผ้า	pāa (high short fall)	ป๊า

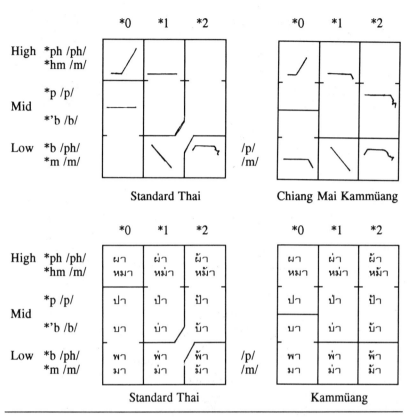

Fig. 16.1. The basis for earlier-stage writing. The two matrices at the top show how differently the identical spellings below would be pronounced. For a fuller explanation of this type of figure see chapter 11.

On the other hand, in the earlier stage approach these words would be spelled alike in both languages, even though pronounced somewhat differently. It is based on the fact that Standard Thai writing itself is a sound correspondence representation not of how words are pronounced now, but of how they were pronounced at an earlier stage. Both the language to be written in Thai script and Standard Thai are descended from the same Proto-Tai (chap. 11).

In figure 16.1 we first reproduce the chart of initial consonant classes and tones of Standard Thai and Chiang Mai Kammüang from chapter 11 and then place the examples of table 16.2 in them, along with others. Because of factors like the ones discussed in that chapter, it seems likely that the earlier stage approach should be the basis for writing all Tai languages in Thailand, and it is in fact often used to some degree by individuals who do write them in Thai script, but not consistently. Lao and Kammüang, at least, seem ripe for such a system to be normalized, in spite of the complications which would be encountered. An earlier stage system like this will obviously work only when the languages are nearly mutually intelligible and the writing system of the model language already consistently reflects an earlier stage in the sound system.

Writing Non-Tai Languages in Thai Script

Writing non-Tai languages does not involve an earlier stage spelling option because such languages do not share a common ancestry with Standard Thai, at least not close enough to count. Sound correspondence can work because there are not hundreds of words which are almost the same in both languages. Even so, the Thai system of writing tones creates severe problems for sound correspondence.

In 1976 a group of people who had devised Thai-based writing systems for some non-Tai marginal and enclave languages of Thailand published the results of their work (Smalley [ed.] 1976). It is useful now to look back at how they faced the issues and what modifications have had to be made in their proposals. Their writing systems have been more successful in some languages than in others.

Because writing tone is the most difficult problem in producing a Thai-based system for non-Tai languages, we will first take up the languages in these reports which do not have tones. They are Kuy, Lavüa' of La-Up, Northern Khmer and Urak Lawoi'. Two examples will show the types of technical difficulties which have to be solved when devising a way of writing these non-tonal languages in the Standard Thai system.

The first problem is writing consonants and vowels which do not occur in Standard Thai, such as Urak Lawoi' and Lavüa' /g/. In this case the rare Thai symbol ฃ is used in both languages, changing it from its Thai value of /kh/.

For the other example, some Standard Thai written consonants do not necessarily represent the same pronunciation in syllable-final position as in initial position (table 16.3).

But on the whole, for these non-Tai, non-tonal languages, the development of a practical, readable Thai-based system has gone well. Some tinkering with details has been necessary since 1976, but changes have been small.

Table 16.3. Written consonant symbols which represent different pronunciations in initial and final positions in Standard Thai, but no difference in Northern Khmer (Smalley 1976c:52).

Symbol	Thai		Northern Khmer
	Initial	Final	Initial and Final
จ	/c/	/t/	/c/
ฮ	/h/		/h/
ล	/l/	/n/	/l/
ร	/l/, /r/	/n/	/r/
ญ	/y/	/n/	/ñ/

However, writing tonal languages in a Thai-based script has sometimes been less successful in providing a quickly learned, easily read system which is not confusing. The basic problem is that some Standard Thai spoken consonants are spelled with two sets of written consonants which help differentiate the tones, a characteristic resulting from historical changes which have taken place in the spoken language without corresponding changes in the writing (chap. 11).

In the 1976 publication, the five tone languages and their proposed Thai-based writing systems were Hmong, Lisu, Akha, Phlong and Mien (Yao), all marginal languages. The authors assumed that the best way to provide a strong transfer between the minority language and Thai was to follow the Thai system as closely as possible. For example, if learning to read Phlong in Thai script was to help new literates learn to read Standard Thai itself, the spelling rules for tones in Phlong should be the same as in Thai. For that reason, a Thai-type consonant class system was invented for each language rather than using a direct representation of each spoken consonant by a single written consonant, and of each tone by a single tone symbol.

When the work on these writing systems was being done, the people who devised them knew that consonant class spelling was more difficult to learn than single consonant spelling would be. They reasoned, however, that people were able to learn it in Standard Thai, and that a single consonant system would seem wrong to native speakers literate in Standard Thai.

However, with further testing some of these people later found that even fluent readers of Standard Thai among minority-language speakers were confused by the consonant class spelling as applied to their own languages. It also took a long time to learn to read, and especially to write. It seems also that Thai people of limited education themselves do not generally understand the Thai system of writing tones, but learn the shapes and spellings of words by rote. If that is true, use of the single consonant spelling would not produce as great a loss of transfer value to the Thai system as formerly imagined.

What the difference looks like for Phlong may be seen in table 16.4. The two types of spelling apply only to the spelling of tones, consonants and vowels being spelled by sound correspondence except as alternate sets of consonant symbols help to represent the tones. In the second line of the consonant class spelling, note that ผ and พ both represent /ph/, but belong to different classes, as in Standard Thai. In the third line the ห before ม changes the class of the ม, as it does in Thai. The tone marks ˊ and ˘ do not always represent the same tones. /â/ and /á/ especially illustrate the problem (James A. Morris personal communication; Cooke, Hudspith, and Morris 1976:210-212).

So in Akha, Hmong and Phlong, people promoting use of the systems switched over to systems with single consonant classes, and felt that they worked better. Some who favored the change report that even people who already knew how to read Standard Thai learned the single consonant system more easily, and that it caused less confusion (Morris personal communication). It remains to be seen whether or not the single consonant system will ultimately be acceptable to bilinguals who are well educated in Thai.

The consonant class system is working well in Mien, on the other hand, where a concerted and sophisticated literacy effort supports it. Learning to read and write Mien in this system has proven to be a good bridge to Standard Thai.

Table 16.4. Comparison of consonant class spelling and single consonant spelling of tones in Phlong. Pronunciation of consonants and vowels (without tone indicators) is shown in the first column. The four remaining columns display the four tones, exemplified with the vowel า /a/.

	Consonant class spelling				Single consonant spelling			
	a	à	â	á	a	à	â	á
/pa/	ปา	ป่า	ป้า	ป๊า	ปา	ป่า	ป้า	ป๊า
/pha/	พา	ผ่า	พ่า	พ้า	พา	พ่า	พ้า	พ๊า
/ma/	มา	หม่า	ม่า	ม้า	มา	ม่า	ม้า	ม๊า

Cultural Integration of New Writing Systems

People devise writing systems for previously unwritten languages for various reasons. Sometimes the initiative comes from native speakers of the languages themselves, from people who may want to express themselves through writing their own mother tongues, in order to communicate with each other in writing, to facilitate remembering, or to record cultural traditions. If they do experiment with writing they normally base their system on one they already know in another language.[7] Sometimes their effort is successful, but often they do not know how to overcome the complications of the task, and their system cannot be widely used because it is too inconsistent or leaves out critical parts of the language. Sometimes such people conclude that the task is impossible, and that their language must therefore be inadequate for writing.

At other times outsiders may initiate a writing system. They may be officials in the government, or perhaps educators, or researchers of some kind. They may have motives ranging from the humanitarian to the political. Such people, however, usually lack training and experience in the complex skill of devising writing systems, and generally do not stay with the development long enough to see it through. Successful writing systems often take years to perfect, starting with analysis of the language, followed by testing and the steady production of small experimental publications to find out how well people can use the writing and how they receive it. In the meantime, simple, graded literacy teaching is required for people who do not already read another language.

Christian missionaries have prepared writing systems for far more languages in the world than has any other category of people. They usually do so to enable people to read the Bible as translated into the language, as well as to promote local development, lessen exploitation of the minority group, and respond to other humanitarian concerns (Sanneh 1989:88-156; Smalley 1976a:4-24; Smalley 1991:199-202). They tend to live with and work with a language group for many years, learning and using the language constantly. Only a minority of missionaries have the competence or technical skill for such a specialized task as designing a writing system, but those who do have accomplished much, and in modern times technical help or training is available from some mission agencies.[8]

To some Thai, on the other hand, missionary involvement in Thailand's writing systems is suspicious. They resent foreigners dignifying minority languages with writing systems, and making them vehicles to teach Christianity, which they also see as foreign. The language hierarchy makes it hard for them to believe that either Thailand or the minority peoples would benefit by reading and writing their own languages.

Native-speaker reception of newly devised writing systems, furthermore, varies widely from language to language. When first introduced, any writing of regional, marginal or enclave languages in Thailand is likely to have limited reception and use because the language hierarchy assigns the function of writing to Standard Thai. Some shift in cultural perspective is required to make writing on other levels seem desirable. In several languages like Kammüang and Mon people have already nearly given up their traditional writing systems. Speakers of smaller languages often see little reason to read and write at all. In Thailand experimental efforts at writing such languages have all been small, and where they have succeeded writing is used primarily for limited purposes like correspondence, memory enhancement and religion.

Reasons for New Writing Systems

But in spite of all of these qualifications, the education of beginning school children would be much stronger if they learned to read and write their own language in Thai script in the first two years of school, along with learning Standard Thai. Monolingual Mien children flounder in school in the early years before they learn to understand Standard Thai, and their resulting education is weak. Like other marginal peoples they usually have to go back a grade when they enter a higher-level school. But Mien children who have learned to read and write Mien in Thai script under a well-organized, educationally competent mission program enter much more quickly into the Thai educational process. They are ready for Thai education in a way in which others are not, and they frequently excel from its early stages on (Jennings 1986).

Students in parts of northeastern Thailand are notorious for their poor showing on national standardized exams because of the language gap, among other things (Kaeota and Banchong 1980). The Northern Khmer-speaking area, with its thousands of children who do not know Thai when they go to school, would therefore seem like an ideal place for a pilot project to teach Thai literacy through Northern Khmer literacy. A writing system is available, and people have been experimenting with its use for years. Northern Khmer-speaking teachers could easily learn to teach children to read in Northern Khmer. What is lacking, in addition to a change in policy, is a set of professionally designed reading primers and reading materials for young children, both to teach literacy and to teach the transfer of the skill to reading Standard Thai.

For people lower in the hierarchy than Standard Thai to read and write their own languages would, of course, add to the functions available to their languages on the lower levels, but would still not realistically make them competitive with Standard Thai. For Northern Khmer or Kuy people to write letters and read materials of local interest in their own language will never be enough for full participation in the nation any more than their local speech is enough. They will continue to need the language of the nation. The opportunity to read and write lower-level languages would enrich the hierarchy, however, and learning to do so before tackling Standard Thai would reduce the educational waste in the present system.

Summary

Thailand's elitist educational system has been remarkably successful in spreading advanced knowledge and use of Standard Thai among an upper crust of the people who have other languages for their native tongues. It has also been successful in spreading limited knowledge of Standard Thai widely throughout the country.

The system is a sink-or-swim system, however, for those children who do not speak some dialect of Thaiklang when they start school. It is inefficient and frustrating because it assumes the life, culture and language of central Thailand, no matter where children live or what they speak. It requires many children to lose two years in school before they can follow well what is going on in class.

Several minority languages have been written, some of them using Standard Thai symbols and varying aspects of the Standard Thai system. Others could also be written. If children had the opportunity to learn to read and write in their own languages they would move ahead in the Thai system with less difficulty and greater success.

Because of the complexity of the Standard Thai system, however, devising ways of writing regional and lower languages in it is not a simple task, especially when the language to be written has tones. Some form of sound-correspondence writing has to be used for non-Tai languages, but earlier-stage writing seems more suitable for Tai languages.

17

Change and Development

Human beings have lived in the area which is now Thailand for many thousands of years (table 17.1). The territory was part of a huge ecological/cultural zone extending from the Yangtze River of China south to the tip of Malaysia, and from the mountains of northeast India eastward to the coast of Vietnam (Bayard 1980). In this vast and sparsely settled expanse of mountains and plains, virgin jungle and rivers, lakes, marshes and seacoast, people learned from experience and from each other for many millennia, gradually developing some common cultural characteristics which would underlie all of the later different cultures of the area. By two thousand years ago they had an area-wide "common, distinctive, and advanced civilization" (Wyatt 1984:4) with a great deal of local differentiation as well.[1]

Much of present-day Thailand was underpopulated up to the middle of this century. People could move on to more promising locations when theirs became crowded, and until the present century armies brought back whole villages of people from vanquished areas to increase the human resources under their control. Such movement contributed to the intermingling of languages.

Both swidden rice cultivation and irrigated rice cultivation go back five thousand years, although which came first is debated (Bayard 1980:103-105). Wet rice cultivation eventually won out throughout the plains and river valleys because the same land could be cultivated each year, enabling it to support larger settled populations.

An early culture trait important to the dynamics of language diversity was a widespread distinction between *müang* 'town' (/miaŋ/ in Standard Thai) and countryside /bâan nɔ̀ɔk/. The latter was dotted with villages without much social stratification among their inhabitants, except for kinship and age. The former had social classes, a ruling military elite, and a chieftainship. Some towns later became petty kingdoms, a few of which eventually grew into the centers of the great classical empires in what are now Cambodia, Laos, Myanmar

Table 17.1. Appearance of significant early cultural traits at archeological sites in present-day Thailand (after Bayard 1980; Sujit 1986). Wyatt (1984:3) places some of the dates earlier.

B.C.	Cultural Feature Present
500	Beginning of Indianization
	Centralized towns
1600	Ironworking
3000	Extensive trade networks
3500	Bronze metallurgy
	Domesticated rice
	Domesticated cattle, dog, maybe pig
10,000	Horticulture
	Pottery
	Swidden (slash and burn) agriculture
	Hunting and gathering
700,000	Stone tools

and Thailand. Today Bangkok is the supreme development of the müang in Thailand.

Characteristic of those formative years also was the universal worldview that all nature is populated with a wide range of spirits which affect human life on every level. Such animism still underlies religion throughout the area, absorbed into the folk Buddhism which later became dominant in the major cultures north of Malaysia. To this day, animistic belief and practice provide a shared element of worldview onto which Buddhism is grafted when non-Buddhist minority groups become Buddhist in the process of assimilating to Thai culture.

So some of the roots of current Thainess go back into prehistory, and continued to be formative throughout the historical period as well. But of language fifteen hundred and more years ago we know nothing directly. We can only assume that different groups spoke languages that are the ancestors of some of those now in the area, and perhaps others of which no descendant language remains.

The earliest direct evidence of specific languages in what is now Thailand consists of inscriptions on stone (Bauer 1990:17-19). Thailand's recorded history thus begins with Old Mon in the central plains, the northeastern plateau, and up to the city of Haripunjaya (Lamphun) in the north (table 17.2). Very little is known of this civilization, but it is part of the cultural foundation on which the Tai peoples built. Descendants of these Mon-speaking peoples eventually replaced the Old Mon language with Tai languages, except for present speakers of Nyah Kur, who are bilingual. Modern Mon, on the other hand, came into Thailand from Myanmar more recently.

As the Old Mon civilization was fading, the Khmer extended their power and cultural influence from their centers in what is now Cambodia, but Khmer-speaking peoples probably lived in parts of the area of present-day Thailand before then. The Tai-speaking peoples also learned a great deal from the Khmer, whose empire they eventually displaced, and many of whose people they absorbed.

Tai-speaking people emerged after the Khmer civilization was well established, but were living in the area long before the Ramkhamhaeng inscription, which is traditionally considered the oldest example of Thai writing to have been preserved. Carved on stone at Sukhothai in 1292, it describes an established situation. Tai languages were probably present in what is now Thailand over a thousand years ago (Chamberlain 1972).

Certainly speakers of other languages lived there in early times as well. Ancestors of the Lavüa' lived in the Chiang Mai area before any speakers of Old Mon or of any Tai language, and other Mon-Khmer

Table 17.2. Epochs when speakers of Old Mon, Khmer and Tai became dominant over areas of present-day Thailand (after Wyatt 1984).

A.D.	Old Mon	Khmer	Tai
1782			End of Ayuthayan kingdom
1300		End of Khmer era in Thailand	Ramkhamhaeng inscription
1200			Beginning of classical Tai kingdoms in Thailand
1100			
1000		.	
900	End of Dvaravati		Tai-speaking people emerge on fringes of Khmer influence
800		Beginning of Khmer era in Thailand	
700			
600			
500	Beginning of Dvaravati era		

languages were doubtless scattered around, too. Ancestors of Malay-speaking peoples also lived in the southern parts of present-day Thailand before Tai-speaking people came that far south.

Language Families

Figure 17.1 shows the probable relationships between most of the Tai languages in Thailand. This figure ignores Tai languages outside of Thailand, including a whole branch called Central Tai (map 8.1).[2]

This display of language relationships is based on linguistic assumptions, some of which were made explicit in earlier descriptions of Tai tone changes (chap. 11).[3] As people spread out, their speech changed gradually in different ways in different areas. These different ways of speaking always gave rise to minor, but sometimes also to major dialects, and ultimately in some cases became great enough so that a speaker from one area could no longer understand a speaker from another.

Non-linguists, however, sometimes misunderstand language relationship. Some people say, for example, that Thai "comes from" Khmer or from Sanskrit, or from Pali (the language of classical Buddhism, itself descended from Sanskrit). They base such statements on similarities which exist because Standard Thai borrowed vocabulary extensively from those languages, and because the Thai writing system is derived from Khmer writing, which itself was developed from the writing of languages of India. But Tai languages were spoken long before words borrowed from Khmer and Indian languages were incorporated into them, and long before any Tai language was written. Thai, Khmer and Sanskrit/Pali, in fact, belong to three different language families descended from different ancestor languages. Sanskrit and Pali are distantly related to English rather than to Thai.

Along with other perspectives, figure 17.1 and others in this chapter help clarify some aspects of linguistic diversity when the languages or dialects are closely related. Issues we have met earlier, such as bilingualism, passing from the use of one language or dialect to another, and multiple identity of the individual or community, become easier to understand where differences between the languages have arisen recently enough to be still rather transparent, so that speakers of the respective languages or dialects can readily adjust to them as they hear them a few times.

However, when the separation of the languages took place many hundreds or even many thousands of years ago, when the intervening

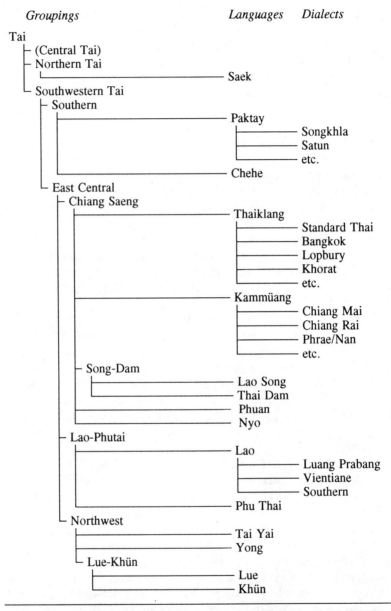

| Groupings | Languages | Dialects |

Tai
- (Central Tai)
- Northern Tai
  - Saek
- Southwestern Tai
  - Southern
    - Paktay
      - Songkhla
      - Satun
      - etc.
    - Chehe
  - East Central
    - Chiang Saeng
      - Thaiklang
        - Standard Thai
        - Bangkok
        - Lopbury
        - Khorat
        - etc.
      - Kammüang
        - Chiang Mai
        - Chiang Rai
        - Phrae/Nan
        - etc.
      - Song-Dam
        - Lao Song
        - Thai Dam
      - Phuan
      - Nyo
    - Lao-Phutai
      - Lao
        - Luang Prabang
        - Vientiane
        - Southern
      - Phu Thai
    - Northwest
      - Tai Yai
      - Yong
      - Lue-Khün
        - Lue
        - Khün

Fig. 17.1. Language family model of most of the Tai languages in Thailand together with illustrative dialects of some of those languages (after Grimes [ed.] 1988:597-604. See also Li 1960, 1977; Brown 1965; Chamberlain 1972, 1975; Strecker 1987, personal communication). A grouping in parentheses is not found in Thailand. Some displaced Tai languages listed in appendix A could not be included here for lack of information.

changes have been very great, and when native speakers cannot easily see a resemblance, relationship becomes more important for historical reconstruction than for understanding contemporary patterns of language use. Relatedness no longer facilitates learning or communication. Such is the case with the postulated ancient relationships of the Tai language family with Hmong, Mien, and Malay (fig. 17.2). Such a superstock, or very large extended family of languages, carries farther back in time behind figure 17.1 to a more hypothetical and more distant ancestor language. This one is even disputed among specialists, who are still working to verify or disprove aspects of it.

The relationship between Malay, Urak Lawoi', Moken and Moklen, on the other hand, is close and easily noticeable to users or observers. The relationship between Hmong Daw and Hmong Leng is so close that speakers understand each other, but the relationship between Hmong and Mien is not close enough to be readily noticeable.

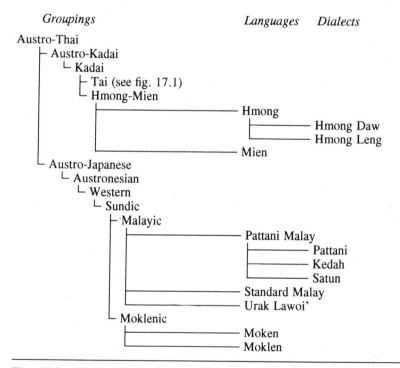

Fig. 17.2. The hypothetical Austro-Thai superstock of which the Tai family is one part, showing only those branches and languages which are to be found in Thailand (Bright [ed.] 1992, 2:380-381; Thurgood 1985:4).

Groupings   *Languages*   *Dialects*

```
Mon-Khmer
  ├ Northern
  │   ├ Khmuic ───────────────── Khmu'
  │   │   ├ Mal-Prai
  │   │   │             ┌─────── Mal
  │   │   │             ├─────── Pray
  │   │   │             └─────── Mla'bri'
  │   └ Palaungic
  │       └ Western
  │           ├ Waic
  │           │   ├ Bulang
  │           │   │        ┌──── Phang (Samtau)
  │           │   │        └──── Plang
  │           │   ├ Lawa ─────── Wiang Papao
  │           │   │   └ Lavüa'
  │           │   │         ┌─── Bo Luang
  │           │   │         ├─── Umphai
  │           │   │         ├─── Pa Pae
  │           │   │         ├─── La'up
  │           │   │         └─── Phae
  │           │   └─────────── Phalok (Khalao)
  │           ├ Lametic ─────── Lamet
  │           └ Angkuic ─────── Mok
  ├ Eastern
  │   ├ Khmeric
  │   │        ┌────────────── Northern Khmer
  │   │        └────────────── Other Khmer
  │   ├ Katuic
  │   │   └ West
  │   │          ┌─────────── Kuy
  │   │          │                ┌── Kuuy
  │   │          │                └── Kuay (Surin)
  │   │          ├─────────── Kuay (Suphan)
  │   │          ├─────────── Bru
  │   │          ├─────────── So
  │   │          ├─────────── So Tri
  │   │          └─────────── Nyoe
  │   ├ Pearic
  │   │        ┌────────────── Chong
  │   │        └────────────── Samre
  │   └ Bahnaric
  │       └ Brao-Kravet ────── Brao
  ├ Viet-Muong ─────────────── Vietnamese
  ├ Monic
  │        ┌─────────────────── Mon
  │        └─────────────────── Nyah Kur
  └ Aslian
           ┌─────────────────── Kensiw
           └─────────────────── Mos
```

In addition to this Austro-Thai superstock, with its Tai, Austronesian and Hmong-Mien branches, parts of two other great families of languages are also found in Thailand (figs. 17.3, 17.4). Again, only the lower levels of difference are particularly pertinent to this book.

Beyond these three sets of language relationships, Indo-European is also important in Thailand, although languages of that family are not spoken natively by many people (fig. 17.5). Except for the languages of immigrants from India, Pakistan and Bangladesh, Indo-European languages in Thailand more often have specialized functions like religion or external communication. Such languages include Pali (the Buddhist religious language of Thailand), Sanskrit (the classical language on which much Thai elegant vocabulary is built), and English (the primary external language of the nation), followed by French and German and other languages of Europe.

Language Homelands and Language Spread

Those language families which are uncontroversially pertinent to the language ecology of Thailand are Tai, Mon-Khmer, Chinese, Austronesian, Karen, Lolo-Burmese, Hmong-Mien, and in a more specialized way, Indo-European. Of these, Mon-Khmer is the oldest still-existing language family in the area (Shorto 1979). This assumption about the antiquity of Mon-Khmer is bolstered by Old Mon and then Old Khmer inscriptions, the oldest to have been found, but even these are not the strongest evidence. Inscriptions depend on the existence of a writing system and the practice of carving stone. Language families more ancient than Mon-Khmer could have existed without writing, or without stone inscriptions.

The linguistic evidence for the antiquity of Mon-Khmer starts instead with the fact that Mon-Khmer languages are more diverse in the area than are languages of other families. Whereas most Tai languages are close to being mutually intelligible no matter how far apart they are in the country, the Lavüa' languages are more different although located close together. If the Tai languages in the country had

---

Fig. 17.3 (opposite page). Some languages of the Mon-Khmer language family in Thailand (Diffloth and Zide 1992; Bright [ed.] 1992, 1:118-119, 3:125; Diffloth 1980, 1992, 1992a). See also Theraphan 1985a; Thomas and Headley 1970; Bradley 1985; Ferlus 1974; Huffman 1976; Matisoff 1983; Mitani 1978; Gainey 1985; Oranuch 1984; Pailin 1980; Grimes (ed.) 1988; Paulsen 1992.

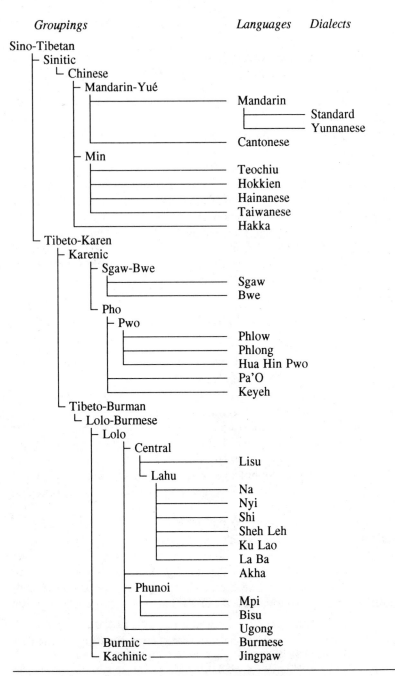

Fig. 17.4. Sino-Tibetan superstock, or family of language families, show-ing some of the languages to be found in Thailand (Ruhlen 1991; Jones 1961; Matisoff 1983; Bradley 1985).

been changing over as long a period as the Mon-Khmer languages they would be much more diverse than they are. The Austronesian languages in Thailand—Malay, Urak Lawoi', Moken, Moklen—are likewise also fairly similar to each other, with Malay dialects extending south into Malaysia without the strong differentiation which would be indicative of as long a presence in the area as Mon-Khmer.

The other side of that coin is that the area of greatest diversity for Tai languages is in North Vietnam and southeast China (map 8.1). That is where the upper levels of the superstock apparently divided (fig. 17.2), as did also the Northern, Central and Southwestern Tai branches of the Tai family.[4]

That area of great diversity among Tai languages contrasts with their relative similarity within present-day Thailand, indicating again that the Thailand area was settled more recently. This is analogous to the greater proliferation of English languages and dialects in tiny

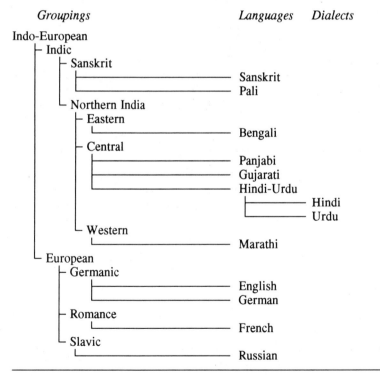

Fig. 17.5. Language families of sample languages in the Indo-European language family used regularly in Thailand (Ruhlen 1991).

Great Britain than in the broad expanse of the United States and Canada. The more recently settled New World, with its relatively short history of change in its English language, does not have as much language diversity as the original homeland, with its much longer time for changes to have taken place.

The third kind of linguistic evidence for the greater antiquity of Mon-Khmer comes from the geographic dispersion of Mon-Khmer languages in relation to those of the other families. Map 17.1 shows where present-day Mon-Khmer languages are located across mainland Southeast Asia and into Bangladesh, with other related languages also in India (including the Nicobar Islands). The most solid present concentration is obviously in Vietnam and Cambodia, together with some immediately contiguous areas.

Otherwise, Mon-Khmer languages appear in patches surrounded by other language families. Even these patches are broken up by fingers and enclaves of other languages, mostly Tai languages, penetrating within them.

The simplest explanation for this language distribution, supported by the evidence cited in the preceding paragraphs, is that Mon-Khmer languages once blanketed this entire area, but were displaced in major parts of it by Tai, Tibeto-Burman (like Burmese and the Karen languages) and Austronesian languages (like Malay). As a result, Mon-Khmer languages are left where the other languages did not reach— most of Vietnam and Cambodia, and also mountainous, less accessible, and less desirable locations through the rest of the territory.[5]

Of existing language families, then, Mon-Khmer languages were to be found in the greater mainland Southeast Asia area first, with Austronesian and Tai languages coming in later, the latter before the tenth century. Chinese people filtered in as well, but did not become established in the same way. Tai and Austronesian languages met in what are now the southernmost provinces of Thailand, while Mon-Khmer was eventually relegated to the edges of the expansion, and to the less accessible mountain regions. Then Karen and Lolo-Burmese languages came into Thailand primarily within the last two or three hundred years, having previously spread extensively through parts of Myanmar. Hmong-Mien languages also made their appearance at the southern fringe of their spread from China.

To say that the earliest Tai languages developed in China is different, however, from saying that "the Thai" came from China. Obviously, Tai languages did not move from one place to another

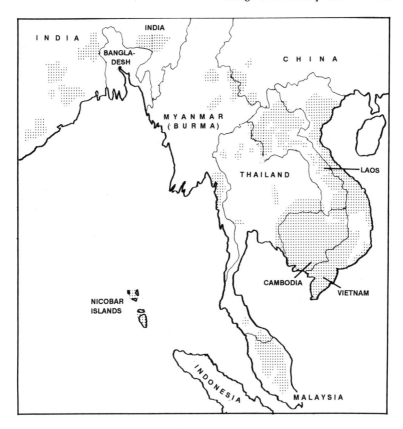

Map 17.1. Dispersion of Mon-Khmer and related languages.

without people to take them, but any present-day Thai individual is
not necessarily descended genetically from people who spoke a Tai
language in China; nor is Thai culture necessarily imported from
China. Those are partially separate issues. Many people who spoke
Mon-Khmer languages long ago in the territory which is now Thailand were ancestors to people who speak Tai languages now. There is
no automatic association between any pool of genes and the Tai
languages, or between any major culture traits and Tai languages
(Bayard 1979).

A movement in Thailand itself emphasizes that Thai culture was
developed within Thailand, and not imported from China or India.
The title of one book, for example, is *The Thais Were Always Here*
(Sujit 1986), and a great deal can be said for many of the points made

there. But the book does not acknowledge the linguistic evidence that the extensive cultural developments in the area before the present millennium, and some of those during this millennium, must have been by peoples speaking Mon-Khmer or other languages before the ascendance of Tai-speaking people.

All that raises the question of how the Tai languages ultimately did become dominant, how languages once spoken by small and isolated groups became widespread, relegating Mon-Khmer languages largely to enclaves and margins in Thailand.

The Dynamics of Language Spread

For a language to grow in a new area some group of people must first speak it there, which normally means that the group migrated there, permanently or temporarily. That is how Spanish, French and English got started in the New World, and how the Chinese languages, the Karen languages, Hmong, Malay and English got started in Thailand. And we assume that is how Tai languages got started there as well, although it is not the only possible way it could have happened.

Once a language is introduced into an area, it may eventually die out because it is not sufficiently reinforced, or has no long-lasting function, or its function is supplanted by another language. Ugong appears on the verge of becoming such a language.

Or the language may remain a minority language for a long period of time, oblivious to predictions that it will "die out in a couple of generations." In so doing it may or may not increase in population and/or territory. Kuy, Pattani Malay, the Karen languages, Northern Khmer and others are among the many examples in present-day Thailand.

Occasionally the no-longer-new language may outgrow its minority status, as did English and Spanish in the new world. The Tai languages as a group grew larger than Mon-Khmer languages in Thailand a long time ago. This growth in the number of speakers may be from within, through births in the community, or through other people learning the language, their descendants sometimes replacing their original language with it (Dressler 1977). We have seen both patterns in the growth of Northern Khmer at the expense of Kuy, of Tai languages at the expense of almost everything else, and of Thai-klang/Standard Thai at the expense of other Tai languages. Growth and attrition may go together, with the Kuy-speaking population in Thailand growing in numbers overall as well as losing speakers in areas of interpenetration with Northern Khmer and Lao.

Growth in numbers of speakers may be due to different causes. Some people learn languages because those languages are spoken around them and with them, as when children learn the languages of the children they play with or those of the adults with whom they talk. Thus some Tai-background people in the Pattani Malay-speaking border provinces have spoken Pattani Malay from childhood, and the children of people from the center of Thailand now living in the northern region speak Kammüang, and will continue to know it as adults if they stay there. Sgaw-speaking children living in a hostel in Mae Sariang and going to school there learn Kammüang in the same way, although Standard Thai is taught in school.

Unlike children, adults for the most part learn to use only those languages which they feel to be of advantage to them, and the perception of advantage often changes over time. In recent years almost all people of Chinese background in Thailand, plus large percentages of Malays and northern marginal peoples like Hmong, Mien and Lahu, have come to believe that it is to their advantage to know a Tai language, especially Standard Thai. Native speakers of Standard Thai, on the other hand, working and living in a community where another language is spoken, do not generally bother to learn more than a few token words of other languages.

The language hierarchy discussed throughout this book is a representation of community assumptions about what languages are advantageous to learn. For a community on any level, languages above them in the hierarchy are the languages which are perceived to provide the group or individual with wider communication, economic opportunity, prestige, and greater protection against exploitation and injustice. Nationally, Standard Thai is the most advantageous of all the languages. But languages in the hierarchy between a people's own language and Standard Thai may likewise provide important advantages, and with them people may accomplish things for which Standard Thai is not so useful, like communicating with their regional neighbors.[6]

Kinds and Degrees of Multilingualism

Dependent and Independent

Perceptions of the nature of multilingualism and of the process of learning another language differ from group to group in Thailand and elsewhere, leading to different learning strategies (Smalley 1986). The person brought up and educated in Bangkok, in a Standard Thai-speaking family, may see the acquisition of other languages as a difficult academic task, normally accomplished in school. When typical Lavüa' people grow up from infancy speaking Kammüang, Sgaw, and Lavüa' in their own villages and elsewhere, they do not associate this multilingualism with school at all, but with general community life. On the other hand, they may associate learning Standard Thai with school.

Learning language in school often leads to dependent multilingualism, where one language is filtered through another to varying degrees.[7] The dependent multilingual may have a "foreign accent," pronouncing Standard Thai in some respects as though it were Lavüa' or Kammüang. Meanings of many words tend to be learned and remembered as translations of words in the native language. Thinking is done primarily in one language and then at least partially translated into the other.

The Lavüa'-Kammüang-Sgaw type of multilingualism, on the other hand, is more likely to be independent multilingualism, where people have often learned their languages at the same time, or at any rate in childhood, and in the natural settings where they are used. Thus the Lavüa' person speaks Kammüang or Sgaw or Lavüa', each without much distortion by the others. One language is not filtered through another as they are all native or near-native languages for the speaker.

Often independence operates on some topics of discussion but the speaker is more comfortable using one language than the other on other topics, creating an interdependent multilingualism (Larson and Smalley 1972:14-15). Typically for a Hmong, for example, traditional religion is best discussed in Hmong but schoolwork in Standard Thai.

If widespread bilingualism exists, whether dependent, interdependent or independent, one or both of the languages may be affected by it in different ways. Bilinguals typically borrow vocabulary from one language to another, for example. More than that, what began as a dependent, filtered pronunciation with interference from the native language—Paktay pronounced in a Malay way by dependent bilinguals of Pattani Malay background—may end up as the established conventional pronunciation of an area or a class of people. Thus the children of Malay background, on the way to being independent bilinguals, or even monolingual in Paktay, learn this Malay-influenced pronunciation in their environment, so that Satun Paktay is the result.

Widespread independent bilingualism may cause languages to become more alike and to fuse in some aspects until differences of sound, grammar and vocabulary mask a more underlying similarity of meaning structures and thought processes. The person from north Thailand who is a native speaker or near-native speaker of both Kammüang and Standard Thai, who processes messages in both languages in the same brain, who uses one language under one set of circumstances, the other under another—such a person is probably contributing to an amalgamation of the two on the level of underlying patterns and the structure of meaning. At the same time, the sound processes and vocabulary may remain distinct, or partially so, as in Educated Paktay.

Communication Distance

In addition to language relationship, language spread, and the various types of multilingualism, communication distance also affects language ecology. Communication distance is the actual degree of difficulty people have communicating with each other, or learning to do so, in a multilingual community (Blair 1990). It has two primary components, intelligibility and comprehension. Intelligibility results from the degree of difference between the language varieties, and comprehension from the relevant language experience of the speakers. Some varieties may be so different that a speaker of one understands nothing when first exposed to the other, yet so similar that such a speaker can quickly get used to the differences. The variety to which that person is newly exposed ceases to be absolutely unintelligible after a few days or weeks of hearing it used. The difference in the languages makes them mutually unintelligible, but the experience of hearing them over time leads to comprehension (Blair 1990:1).

Mutual intelligibility (nest 1 in table 17.3) exists when speakers of two dialects can immediately understand each other over a wide range

Table 17.3. Scale of communication distance. The numbered nests are discussed and illustrated in the text of the chapter.

Degree of similarity	Mutual	One-way
Intelligibility	1	2
Decodability	3	4
Learnability	5	6
Recognizability	7	8
No recognizability	9	10

of social distances and non-technical topics even when neither has had previous experience hearing the other dialect. So the Thailand dialects of Lao are mutually intelligible, and are mutually intelligible with Lao in Laos, but are not mutually intelligible with Thaiklang. Intelligibility is caused by the similarity of the language varieties, unaffected by the user's previous experience.

One-way or non-reciprocal intelligibility (nest 2) refers to cases in which speakers of one variety can understand speakers of the other under the conditions outlined in the previous paragraph, but not vice versa. I do not know of any one-way intelligibility in Thailand although one-way comprehension is common, as when educated people and many others in all of the regions understand Standard Thai, but native speakers of Standard Thai do not fully understand the regional languages.

Intelligibility is a scale, not a fixed point, and it shades into decodability, the next category. This is the ability to get some of the meaning, to get the drift, to figure out some communications. Almost all Tai varieties in Thailand which are not mutually intelligible are mutually decodable. If a person from central Thailand and one from the northeast meet, although they do not fully and immediately understand everything the other person says on all non-technical levels, they can generally figure out what the other person means by context and asking questions of each other, each speaking their own variety.

There are traps in this, however. Often the languages are so similar that people sometimes think they understand when they do not. Words which sound alike may have somewhat different meanings. In most cases people get the general drift when they decode, but are not clear on all details.

One-way decodability (nest 4) between Pattani Malay and Standard Malay is partly due to structural differences between the languages. For one thing, a series of different final consonants in Standard Malay all correspond to the same glottal stop in Pattani Malay. So speakers of Pattani Malay find it easier to figure out Standard Malay than the reverse because of the greater phonological information. Even here, however, experience is probably more important for most people.

Decodability, in turn, shades into learnability. Here the languages are so different that decoding cannot occur, but so similar that people do not take long to learn to hear the other language with understanding, even without much conscious effort, if they have the opportunity and are motivated to do so. Some Mon-Khmer languages like Kuy and Khmer, for example, are at greater communication distance than Lao and Thaiklang. The decodability interaction between them does not work because of the amount of difference, but speakers of each can quickly pick up the other because of the similarity, given the opportunity and motivation.

Finally, recognizability is characteristic of those pairs of languages where the similarities are still less, where the languages are unrelated, or only distantly related, but where extensive borrowing has taken place, or both languages have borrowed from common sources. A speaker of Standard Thai cannot understand Northern Khmer, but recognizes vocabulary and expressions because Thai borrowed them from Khmer or Khmer from Thai, or both from Sanskrit, or from a Chinese language, or from English. Northern Khmer therefore sounds vaguely familiar in places. The speaker of Standard Thai does not get the same impression of familiarity when listening to Vietnamese or Standard Malay, where there is little if any recognizability (nest 9).

Because Standard Thai has borrowed vocabulary extensively from Sanskrit, the educated speaker actually experiences considerable recognizability also with languages of north India, unrelated to Thai but related to Sanskrit. A little recognizability exists also with Chinese languages because of borrowing and long contact.

To different degrees, decodability, learnability and recognizability make another language seem manageable, not distant and difficult like Vietnamese or Russian. They make it seem part of the natural environment and easier to learn.

Stages in Assimilation

As a result of the various developments described in this chapter, the Tai languages and dialects spread, and gained ever more speakers over the centuries. Overall, the changes which took place in each of them increased differences. At the same time, some of them were spoken by people whom others wanted to emulate, and so they borrowed vocabulary or copied aspects of the other languages. Some languages therefore became more alike in such respects. Today, therefore, we see languages not only manifesting processes of differentiation but also processes of assimilation, especially to Standard Thai, which exerts great influence on almost all languages in Thailand. Some of the current Tai varieties can be arranged into a typological continuum of stages in assimilation to Standard Thai, each example of which was discussed in its respective chapter:

1. Standard Thai (standardized)
2. Thaiklang (on which the standard is based)
3. Korat Thai (assimilated to Thaiklang through vocabulary borrowing)
4. Educated Paktay (remains Paktay because the tone system is classified as such by native speakers, although the vocabulary is largely Thaiklang)
5. Normalized Lao (prestigeful Standard Thai-influenced variety widely used in urban areas of the northeast)
6. Chiang Mai Kammüang (prestige dialect of a regional language)
7. Chiang Rai Kammüang (subregional dialect of a regional language)
8. Mae Sariang Kammüang (low-status subregional dialect of a regional language)
9. Ban 'village' X Kammüang (any rural dialect of a regional language)

Note that this scheme, although it correlates at points with parts of the language hierarchy of the country, is not the same as that hierarchy. It includes only Tai varieties, and it attempts to portray a developmental typology, not the patterns and dynamics of language choice on which the hierarchy is built.

Language Position and Language Attitudes

Not all languages are suitable for the top of the language hierarchy in a country (Ferguson 1968). The characteristics required of a modern national and official language can be developed over time in any language, of course, and a great deal of language planning in many countries is carried out to broaden the range of functions of a local language which is needed for an official capacity. Standard Thai began such development long before the many languages which first became official in different parts of the world after World War II.

To be the language of a modern nation, for one thing, a language must be written, preferably with a well-established and widely accepted writing tradition. Ancestor dialects to Standard Thai have been written for hundreds of years.

By definition, Standard Thai has also undergone standardization, without which a national education system is difficult and a fully national linguistic identity is weakened.

Standard Thai is rapidly undergoing modernization, an adaptation to other languages, which makes it easy to talk and write about nontraditional things learned from other cultures (Coulmas 1989). This is the process of "joining the world community of increasingly intertranslatable languages recognized as appropriate vehicles of modern forms of discourse" (Ferguson 1968:32). Modern scientific concepts, world affairs, Western philosophy, Japanese business, current developments, are all being discussed in Standard Thai, with constantly increasing efficiency.

Such discussion involves much borrowed vocabulary, primarily from English, but pronounced in a Thai way, even by people who speak English with little or no Thai accent. New ideas are expressed in other ways as well, however, including newly coined vocabulary and new expressions built out of traditional linguistic resources, like Sanskrit roots. Some grammatical patterns and styles of communication shift as well, like the development of Thai passive forms over the last two hundred years. An interesting question is whether or not continuing modernization of Standard Thai will accelerate reduction of its dimensions of social rank and social status, and of its sacred range.

But most languages lower in Thailand's hierarchy have not gone through as many of these stages of development, or are not as advanced in them. Some have been or are being written. Some regional ones have been somewhat normalized, which is a kind of incipient standardization. All languages in Thailand are being adapted toward Tai languages, especially toward Standard Thai, just as the latter is being adapted toward European languages. Minority languages are never likely to be modernized as much as Standard Thai, however, because people who need to engage in extensive discussion of the outside world do so mostly in Standard Thai. Mandarin is an exception to such generalizations, however, because it has undergone all of these processes in China.

Language Persistence and Language Death

Some languages have certainly disappeared from the Thailand area over the hundreds of years since the Tai languages began to grow there. Those languages were doubtless largely Mon-Khmer languages, from what we can estimate now. We have no way of knowing whether any other family of languages preceded them.

Few languages in Thailand seem to be dying at present, however. One common way of predicting language death is to compare the use of the language in a previous time with its use today. Old Mon was widespread over the center and north of the territory centuries ago, but its descendant, Nyah Kur, is now limited to three thousand speakers in tiny enclaves. Seidenfaden saw Kuy as shrinking in territory, and predicted its demise in a couple of generations. We have seen, however, that shrinkage in territory is not a good predictor of death, for more people speak Kuy now than did in Seidenfaden's time. And Nyah Kur is not dead yet.

A better way of predicting the future of a language is through learning patterns.[8] When all children stop learning the language of their parents the language may be considered moribund, a candidate for language death. This is only possible in any absolute sense when parents do not use the language with their young children, and seldom use it in their presence. Even there, the prognosis is not certain, however, because moribund languages are sometimes revived. In some cases young children refuse to speak a language, but understand it perfectly well, and use it when they get older.

We have not noted any truly moribund languages in this book, but in a few cases the possibility did not seem remote. This was most nearly true in Ugong, but a couple of communities remain where children still learn the language. In Saek we saw that children understood the language but did not like to use it. In some Mon villages the language is moribund, but the language as a whole is not, a pattern we saw in a few other languages as well.

A step up from moribund languages are those which children may stop learning during the coming century, and which then would become moribund. These may be called endangered languages. Accurate prediction is impossible, and should always be tempered with the realization that such predictions have usually been wrong in Thailand. However, we have seen some endangered languages, most notably those which are almost moribund now. Historically, languages have disappeared from the central plains more readily than from other areas, which may mean that the powerful spread of Standard Thai to other regions is introducing a danger to some languages which survived for centuries when they were more isolated from it. Languages with small numbers of speakers are more likely to become endangered than those with many speakers. Languages at the bottom of the hierarchy are more likely to become endangered than those above.

Other languages are presumably "safe." Certainly Standard Thai with its official status and position at the top of the hierarchy is safe. The languages with large numbers of speakers, like the regional languages, are safe. And if smaller languages are above the lowest level of the hierarchy, if they are being learned by speakers of other languages, they are safe, too.

From this perspective, the future of some languages is more easily predictable than of others, but the loss of more than two or three languages in Thailand over the next hundred years is unlikely.

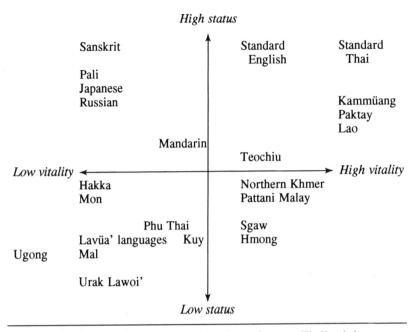

Fig. 17.6. Comparative status and vitality of some Thailand languages (model adapted from Ryan, Giles, and Sebastian 1982:9-11).

A third way of looking at potential language persistence and death is by weighing language status and vitality. Standard Thai is an example of a language with both great status and great vitality throughout the country. Its status is high both among people who speak it and those who do not know much of it. Its vitality is shown in its large and growing number of speakers, its use in various media, the many functions it serves, its place in the hierarchy, and the supreme power associated with it. Other languages rank at different places along these scales of status and vitality, as illustrated impressionistically in figure 17.6.

Languages in the lower left quadrant of figure 17.6 are the most likely candidates for extinction, other things being equal—which they never are. However, such a statement is again a statement of relative probability. Most of these languages are not dying out.

Summary

Of present language families in Thailand, Mon-Khmer languages were the first in the area, with the Tai languages and others coming in later. The language diversity and the language hierarchy in the country have come to exist through many long-standing forces at work. Migrations, the development and growth of cultures, cultural rivalries, military conquests, new ideas, ideas learned from other peoples, the normal processes of language change—these and much more have played their parts.

These forces produced different kinds of language interrelationship and language use. Multilingualism has necessarily been extensive since antiquity. Some people have been independently multilingual from childhood. Others learned their additional languages as adults, and lately in schools, so that the second language was built upon and dependent on the first.

Dialects which developed were first mutually intelligible, but some became less so over time. They passed then through a state of decodability, in which speakers of another dialect could partially figure out what was meant with some time and persistence. Many of the unrelated languages, in turn, manifested recognizability because so much vocabulary was borrowed back and forth, or from common sources.

Different languages developed different degrees of prestige and influence. Of these, Standard Thai emerged as the pinnacle in this century. Other regional and local prestige languages and dialects followed. Even among the smaller languages, however, ones with little vitality, with no prestige, there is usually little evidence that they are dying out. Thailand's linguistic diversity will continue to develop and change, but does not seem likely to diminish.

18

Language and Ethnicity

In this book so far we have not defined or discussed the nature of ethnicity, as though it were an obvious concept, whereas actually it is extraordinarily complex and variable. Neither have we directly discussed the relation between ethnicity and nationalism in Thailand (Edwards 1985:5, 23-46). So we need now to ask what it means to call someone a Thai, or Khmer or Malay or a member of any ethnic group. How can a member of such a group be identified? How does someone change from belonging to a minority group to becoming Thai? What part does language play in all of this?

Cultural Identity

The basic model of ethnicity used here is of a people who identify with each other in having a common culture because they perceive themselves to be descended from common ancestors and/or to have a common territorial "homeland." They likewise perceive other ethnic groups as having different ancestry and/or territoriality, and believe that some of the differences between themselves and the others are due to their different histories.

To amplify a bit, *culture* consists of the shared foundational ways in which people think and feel, the learned cognitive and emotional bases on which they pattern their behavior, including their use of language. People carry their culture within themselves, but reveal it in their behavior, including their talk about it. It is a group phenomenon because they share much of their cultural norms within their group and transmit them to their children. Individuals vary within such groups to some degree, of course, but too much variation (however the group defines that) is not tolerated. The culture of any group is nevertheless always changing, although some aspects are more impervious to change than others, and individuals vary in how much change they can tolerate.

317

Ethnicity, of course, is not anyone's only identity, not even any-one's only cultural identity. People have identities as individuals, as members of subgroups within ethnic groups, and often with groups which transcend major ethnic groups. Thus, the individual named Chai Lee is Hmong (a major ethnic group), Hmong Daw (White Hmong, a subgroup of Hmong with its own characteristic culture and dialect), and a leader in a Hmong subgroup which uses a writing system invented by a Hmong prophet and which has numerous other differences from some other Hmong (Smalley, Vang, and Yang 1990: 122-125). On the supra-ethnic level he is also a member of the Lee clan, which is a Hmong clan but which recognizes Chinese and Mien members of their Lee clans as distantly part of the same clan.

Nor are all cultural differences seen as ethnic. Citizenship may correlate with ethnic differences to some degree, and certainly does with territoriality, but is a legal classification, and in most countries like Thailand people of various ethnic groups are citizens of the same country. Likewise, major differences in economic level or education tend to be perceived as class rather than as ethnicity. People who are rich or poor, educated or uneducated, may all have a common Thai ethnicity. Differences in physical appearance of certain types, like skin color, hair form, and facial features are racial rather than ethnic, although racial characteristics become cultural symbols for and mark-ers of ethnicity in many situations. Non-ethnic differences also occur between age groups, interest groups, occupational groups, and others. So the fact of cultural difference, even in combination with identity, is not enough to create ethnicity.

Inheritance and Territoriality

For identity and difference to be perceived as ethnic they are most often accounted for by beliefs about inheritance, that the perceived distinctiveness was passed down from ancestors (Fishman 1977). Such inheritance may be historically true or partially true, or may be a modern rationalization of the past (Keyes 1981:6-7; Anderson 1983). Thus, millions of people in Thailand assume that their ances-tors were Tai, and for many that may be partly true, but typically their ancestors were or included Mon or Khmer or Chinese or Laviia' or Ugong.

Along with inheritance, ethnicity is often founded on territoriality. People who speak marginal languages in Thailand, for example, are sometimes conscious of their roots in Myanmar, Laos or China, which they may see as the locus of their ethnic differences. It is no accident that ethnic groups are often called by the place where they live: Thai, Northern Thai, or Northeasterners.

Most often these two ways of rationalizing difference occur together, so that ethnicity for most Paktay people is attributed to having inherited their culture from their parents, who learned it from their parents, all of whom did so in the southern region of Thailand. Thus, in effect, ethnicity is rationalized on the basis of a people's perceived history.

However, ethnicity sometimes also exists where people are known not to have common inheritance and/or territoriality. In spite of the assumption of inheritance, children born in a Khmu' family may be adopted into Hmong families and raised as Hmong, and their children considered Hmong. And Sgaw may leave Myanmar, their home location, to live in Thailand. So ethnicity often actually transcends inheritance and territoriality for individuals in spite of the fact that they remain at the core of how it is perceived. People who are accepted as having joined the cultural group in a legitimate way are included without actual inheritance.

Ethnicity as Cultural Contrast

Essential to ethnicity is also a sense of difference, of separateness from other groups, a sense that other people have a different inheritance or territoriality. Along with this go ways of identifying individuals according to the group to which they are assigned. Western newcomers to Southeast Asia are often puzzled when friends identify strangers as "Chinese" just by looking at them. The newcomers do not know the cues by which the judgment is made, but if ethnicity has high saliency in a particular situation people learn at least the stereotypes by which strangers are identified.[1]

Sometimes culturally interpreted bodily forms, colors or textures are among the most obvious cues to recognizing ethnic identity in others. Race plays a relatively insignificant role in Thailand, but it does frequently help people identify the ethnic category of a stranger. Facial form, for example, sometimes contributes to identifying people of Chinese background and also marginal people whose ancestors came from China. Darker skin helps to identify some Mon-Khmer-speaking peoples like the Northern Khmer, and also Malay-speaking peoples. Obviously racial clues are not precise guides, as they are often falsified by all of the intermingling and passing between ethnic groups which has been going on for centuries, as well as by the normal range of variation in any population.

Often behavioral cues to ethnicity are more important than racial ones in Thailand. One category of such cues consists of bearing and posture. The low-status poor rural Thai farmer often has a humble appearance, looks deferential, and avoids assertiveness when approaching a higher-class person, whereas Mien of the same position in life will often appear self-assured, and behave assertively.

Traditionally costume, jewelry, tattoos, beard styles and other ornamentation have been markers of some ethnic identities. Although more rare now than they used to be in Thailand, they are nevertheless still important, for example, among some Malay, some of the marginal peoples of the north, some elderly Chinese, or Sikh men.

Examples of other cues which may be evident on occasion include food preferences like pork for Thai but no pork for Malay, or glutinous rice for Northern Thai and Northeasterners but non-glutinous rice for the people of central Thailand.

Language is unquestionably the most important single marker of ethnic identity in Thailand, and often elsewhere (Weinreich 1953:91; Fishman 1977:25; Lieberman 1981:4, 7; Giles and Johnson 1981: 202-206). Almost nobody uses the lower languages in the hierarchy except people born to them. In higher-level languages which native speakers of lower-level languages also learn, differences of accent sometimes reveal that the speaker has another ethnic identity. When people lack the normal range of usage controlled by native speakers, others assume that they did not grow up with the group that speaks the language.

But more than marking the speaker, language is also the principal medium by which a generation passes its culture along to another, and by which people in the same area build their shared perceptions. That often means that people sense emotional affect in their native language more fully than they do in languages learned later, no matter how well they have been learned. The best jokes, the most powerful poetry, and most moving expression for them are often in the language of their original ethnic group.

Names are another linguistic clue to ethnicity. Nguyễn-văn-Vạn is Vietnamese; Soob Lwj Yaj is Hmong; Kukrit Pramoj is Thai. But, of course, people in Thailand sometimes do change their names, especially into Thai names, or have names in two languages corresponding to dual identities. In addition to personal names, ethnic groups also normally have both a name for their own group and names for the various other groups which they perceive as distinct.

Many other cultural differences are not easily detected by outsiders, like the ways in which people view reality, their understanding of how to think and behave, the covert institutions which organize their lives. Behavioral differences often manifest these deeper differences, but the connection may not always be obvious. People in one ethnic group often make mistakes dealing with those of another when such assumptions, and the behavior which stems from them, are not understood.

But no individual differences like these by themselves are sufficient cues to ethnicity. People judge by configurations of cues seen in context. If someone is speaking good Standard Thai but wearing a Mien vest, the vest will likely be more telling than the language in signalling ethnicity. That is true unless the cues are conflicting, as when the person is standing in front of a stall where Mien vests are sold to Thai tourists in the night market at Chiang Mai. And all of this is complicated by the fact that most ethnic groups are culturally diverse, as with ethnic Thai who range from village farmers to King Bhumibol.

Ethnicity, therefore, is enormously elastic, a configuration or gestalt without objective criteria, its content differing from society to society. People in all societies apparently sense it, however, and respond in some degree to perceived differences in culture which they associate with inheritance and/or territoriality. In many cases their own ethnicity is the soil in which their whole being is nourished, the foundation of their sense of belonging.

But the fact of ethnicity alone is not what gives it great power in so many situations. Rather, the meaning and function which people ascribe to it provide its moving force. In the following sections of this chapter we go on to look at some of the dynamics of ethnicity and ethnic interplay in Thailand, especially those that relate to language.

Thai Ethnicity

Modern Thailand makes a distinction between legal citizenship /sǎn-châat/ and ethnic background /chîachâat/.[2] This is somewhat parallel to the distinction made in the West between "state" and "nation." Legal citizenship is theoretically unambiguous, as by law anyone is either a Thai citizen or not a Thai citizen. The citizenship of many people whose ethnic background is not one of the Tai peoples is actually unclear, however. If a person is a citizen the fact is supposed to be officially recorded as such, but some who were born in Thailand, and are therefore theoretically citizens, do not have the papers to prove it. Their parents did not register them because they did not know enough to do so, did not care, were intimidated, could not pay a bribe, or for some other reason.

Ethnic background is also registered, along with citizenship, on an individual's identification card. But deciding when someone should be registered as ethnically "Thai" as against their parents' "Chinese" ethnicity, for example, is often arbitrary, if not capricious. One million Northern Khmer-speaking people are counted as ethnically "Thai," but nearly a million Pattani Malay-speaking people are ethnically "Muslim" in the official view, and ethnically *Khaek* /khèɛk/ ('person of South Asian, Middle Eastern, or Muslim ethnic background') in the popular view.

And, as we have seen, "Thai" includes speakers of many language varieties such that some cannot understand others. Furthermore, Lao-speaking people south and west of the Mekong River are ethnically "Thai," while those north and east of the river are ethnically "Lao" in the official position, although citizenship clearly overrides ethnic judgment here.

People who are perceived as unambiguously "Thai" from the Thai point of view are often referred to as "real Thai" /thaythɛ́ɛ/. In an interview, former Prime Minister Kukrit Pramoj commented on the recognizability of such Thai.

A Thai is not a person who is born by blood. . . . if you do something to yourself, then you become a Thai. [This] means you accept Thai values, Thai ideals, mostly you become a Buddhist. You worship the Lord Buddha, his teaching and the holy order of monks. And you respect your parents, you respect your teachers, . . . you are loyal to the king and . . . to the Thai nation, and you accept all kinds of ceremonies, you wear amulets around your neck, figures of the Lord Buddha, you get ordained as a Buddhist monk, you add the Thai ceremonies at home whether wedding or anniversary or things like that. You enjoy life in the Thai way and you have the same sort of Thai escape mechanisms when trouble arises (Vilas and Van Beek [eds.] 1983:203).

But in the very next paragraph, apparently unaware of the contradiction, Kukrit changed to a different position on religion, counting people of other religions as true Thai:

The Thais know each other. [We know] whether or not another person is a Thai . . . regardless of . . . skin color or religious belief. Because the various religions like Christianity and Islam have been established in this country for centuries and the people of those two religions including the Taoists from China . . . became Thai because they accepted all kinds of Thai values, ideas and customs even though their religious beliefs remain as in the beginning (Vilas and Van Beek [eds.] 1983:203-204).

Official Core of Thai Ethnicity

Part of the cultural configuration which symbolizes "Thainess" preoccupies the Thai school system, which is charged with homogenizing the country. The curriculum emphasizes three symbols: the King, the nation, and the Buddhist religion. It uniformly uses the Standard Thai language to do so. These focal symbols, which lie deep in Thai history and culture, were made overt in the pronouncements and policies of King Chulalongkorn in the nineteenth century, and were incorporated into the Thai constitution (Murashima 1988). A huge majority of the population agrees with the formulations, and in the idealized perception of many the three are virtually inseparable. To them, you are not really Thai unless you are loyal to all three.

Of these, the King is the symbol most universally acceptable to less fully assimilated peoples in Thailand. He and most other members of the royal family are loved and revered even among some people whose knowledge of any Tai language is minimal, and where few or none carry cards identifying them as Thai citizens. The monarchy, furthermore, bolsters the legitimacy of the other components in Thainess.

The requirement of adopting Buddhist religion, on the other hand, is clearly the most divisive of the major symbols, especially for the Muslim Malay-speaking majority population in the southernmost provinces, but also at times for the small Christian and Muslim minorities elsewhere. The King is by law the guardian of all religions, and the country grants religious freedom, but in the initial gut perception of the ordinary Buddhist Thai person, including the typical Thai government official, not to be Buddhist is un-Thai.

Buddhism is not monolithic or unitary in Thailand, however, any more than Christianity and Islam are there or elsewhere. Reform movements seek to "purify" it or adapt it to the perspective of people now part of the rapidly growing urban middle-class culture (Zehner 1990). A core of theoretical Buddhism is known well and followed closely by only a minority who have especially studied it, with gradations from it in one direction to animistic folk belief, and in another to materialism and secularism. Both animism and secularism, however, are masked with Buddhist symbolism even where contradictory to much of the core of theoretical Buddhism, a phenomenon which occurs in other religions as well. Almost any aspect of worldview characteristic of the area, and many area religious practices, are incorporated comfortably into Thai Buddhism if they allow a few symbols like a temple, merit-making activity, and a statue of the Buddha. Some core ideas in the Buddhist worldview, furthermore, have been very powerful in forming the social, political and linguistic reality which is Thailand today (chap. 19; Tambiah 1976; Keyes 1978:30-37)

Nation is not as controversial as religion for Thai ethnicity, but it includes several dimensions. One of these is the state, the legal political entity, with defined geographical boundaries established by treaties with other countries, plus citizenship. But within this territorial expanse comes a gradation of significance for assessing "Thainess." Thai territory is organized around centers, of which the supreme is Bangkok (Tambiah 1976:102-158). Bangkok is the core of the country, and in it "Thainess" is most perfectly expressed. The farther you get from Bangkok, the more peripheral the area, the less perfectly Thai. Peripheral areas are expected to imitate, to follow Bangkok.

Another component in the category of nation is the government, the social structure and processes of the state. It has a triple hierarchy consisting of the civil bureaucracy, the military (especially the army), and the organization of Buddhist monks. All are centered in Bangkok; all dominate in their respective spheres throughout the country. This strongly vertical national social organization correlates also with the territorial gradation mentioned above.

The third component in nation consists of the Thai people, one of whose main features is speaking a Tai language. Many varieties, some of them mutually unintelligible, are lumped together in the Thai understanding of "Thai." With Standard Thai at the peak, then the regional and displaced Tai languages ranging underneath, all Tai languages are "true Thai" in the ethnic sense, but again, Standard Thai from Bangkok represents the epitome.

The Thai population is also organized into elaborate social structures which are strong features of Thai ethnic belonging (chaps. 3,4) and which have to be learned by those who would become culturally Thai. That learning may be painful and degrading, however, as when the proud, independent Mien feel that they have to become obsequious with elaborate deferential behavior to become Thai. Mien culture does not have the same kinds of social gradations, and people do not express the social gradations they do have in the same way.

The third important characteristic of the population, in self-definition of its Thainess, is its worldview, including its perception of history, of how it came to be as a people and a nation, its ethnic inheritance. The Thai schoolbooks tell and retell the stories of the major kings, and of the events which are considered to be pivotal in the formation of the country. People who are Thai relate themselves to a common perception of history, even if it is not clearly formulated, and for that matter sometimes not "historical" in the academic sense.

Table 18.1 outlines these components of Thai identity which have been highlighted by official policy. The categories are general, but in the Thai context they have specific referents. Allegiance is to a specific king, to the Theravada Buddhism as practiced in the area, to the legal-political entity called /mianthay/ 'the country of the Thai'. The lower triads of characteristics are each amplifications of the last characteristic of the preceding triad. So powerful are some of these components that although a Thai woman with a Ph.D. in linguistics from an American university and teaching at prestigious Chulalongkorn University is in many ways more like her counterpart at the University of California, Berkeley, than she is like a peasant woman farmer with four years of long-forgotten schooling in northeast Thailand, nevertheless she perceives some kinds of similarities with the Thai peasant woman, and differences from American counterparts, which represent Thai identity. More importantly, she identifies herself with a lineage and history of location which she perceives to be in contrast with those of her American counterparts.

Table 18.1. Some components in overtly expressed Thai identity.

Allegiance to the monarchy
Allegiance to the religion
Allegiance to the nation
    Including territory
    Including government
    Including people
        Sharing language
        Sharing social structures
        Sharing worldview
            Common perception of history
            Common perception of similarity/difference
            Common perception of identity

Ethnic Identity: the Structures of its Meaning

The ethnic identity of the Malay, the Sino-Thai, the Mon, the Khmer, the Hmong, the Sgaw, and other peoples in Thailand may also have traits such as some of those in table 18.1, along with others. The Sino-Thai have historical perceptions which relate to ancestors in China, the Mon to ones in Myanmar, the Malay to ties with Malaysia. For the minority of Malay separatists the concept of their "nation" involves a Pattani Malay state in what is now the southern border region of Thailand, a different country from that of which they are now unwillingly a part.

In earlier times, and still among some less-assimilated marginal language-speaking communities, categories in the upper part of the table had no relevance. Monarchy, organized religion and political nation have little significance for Hmong identity as imported from Laos and ultimately from China, for example. Language, social structure and worldview, on the other hand, have been relevant to being Hmong in all stages and places (Smalley 1985, 1986). Now that they live in Thailand and move in the direction of being Thai, some of the upper categories become increasingly significant to emerging Hmong-Thai identity. Among them, Hmong people attach their allegiance first to the monarchy.

As a group becomes more Thai, the upper part of the scheme in table 18.1 is likely to change faster than the lower part, which continues to be the center of their residual difference. Assimilated Mon who have lost their Mon language and any distinctive Mon social structure may still have legends of ancestors who came to Thailand from Myanmar, and of earlier Mon kingdoms of which their ancestors were a part (Foster 1973a). And although their behavioral differences from their non-Mon Thai neighbors are infinitesimal, some symbolic differences may be maintained, like the Mon New Year celebration. The historical memory may be preserved over generations, but if these perceptions die the group ceases to be ethnically distinct.

For nearly forty years social scientists have been trying to understand the fluidity, the change, the lack of clearcut and objective markers of ethnic identity in Southeast Asia.[3] The debate has revolved around questions like "What is the significance of ethnic categories when some people change them so easily, like Lavüa' becoming Northern Thai almost overnight?" and "What is the significance of ethnic distinctions when they are not really differences at all?" One of the characteristics of Hmong culture often cited, for example, in contrast to Thai, is that the Thai grow irrigated rice and the Hmong non-irrigated mountain rice. In fact, however, some Hmong grow wet rice, and some Northern Thai grow their rice in swiddens (Judd 1964; Chapman 1978). Enormous similarity in rural culture is to be found among all peoples throughout mainland Southeast Asia, even those who consider themselves to be different peoples.

In all this discussion the semantic factors have not been studied very much, but when people call themselves Thai or Kuy or Phlong or Malay they are using a word, a linguistic term. They are performing a linguistic act, using language, so we need to look at the issue of ethnic identity linguistically, as well as in other ways. This involves not only what *Phlong* means, but also how people create the meaning of *Phlong*.

Hierarchies of Meanings

Many ethnic labels used by people referring to themselves in their own language also mean 'person' or 'human being', and therefore can refer to people in other ethnic groups as well. In Khmu',[4] for example, /khmu'/ [kɨmMmu'] means 'person' in contrast to 'animal' or 'bird' or 'spirit'. As such it can refer to a Thai or a Westerner as well as to a Khmu'. On the other hand, *Khmu'* also means 'ethnic Khmu' in contrast with /je'/ 'Lao', or /falaŋ/ 'Westerner', or other ethnic labels. In other words, if you were walking along the mountain trail with a Khmu' person and met a mixed party of traders, the Khmu' person might describe it as consisting of four *khmu'* 'people' and eight horses, or as three Yunnanese Chinese and one *Khmu'* 'ethnic Khmu'.

Vocabulary relationships in any language have structure, and one kind of structure which this example illustrates is a hierarchy of inclusion. The difference between Khmu' and English in this part of their respective vocabularies is pictured in figure 18.1, with *khmu'* on more than one level. It has both a generic 'human being' and a specific 'ethnic Khmu' meaning, each contrasting with a different set of words.

This phenomenon is not at all unusual in language. For example, the English word *animal* includes 'human being' on one level, in contrast with plants and minerals: "Human beings, like other animals, reproduce themselves." But on another level, *animal* in English excludes human beings: "She is a person, not an animal" (fig. 8.2).

When assimilation begins to take place in a multiethnic area, hierarchical meaning structure may shift for both the assimilating group

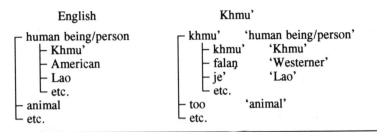

Fig. 18.1. Comparison of a small part of the domain of 'person' in English and Khmu', showing the term *khmu'* used on two levels of the domain.

and the group to which it is assimilating, as illustrated for the former in figure 18.3. The figure suggests that in the first stage Khmu' see themselves and Thai as different kinds of people, like other non-Tai people when they first migrate into Thailand.

In the second stage they see themselves as different from Thai in some ways, but in other ways one kind of Thai. People in this stage may be Thai citizens; they may revere the King. But the sense of difference also remains strong. This is the stage at which we find many of the Sgaw and some of the more recent marginal-language immigrants.

In the third stage people see themselves as one kind of Thai, no matter what their differences, the term *Thai* becoming a generic term which includes them. This is clear in the Tai-speaking peoples all over the country, and also in the Northern Khmer, the Kuy, the Lavüa', the Mon, and in many Sino-Thai people.

In the fourth stage any distinction on any level has disappeared. This is the stage of the descendants of the Old Mon and of many early

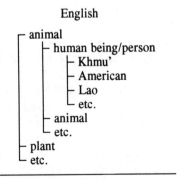

Fig. 18.2. *Animal* on two levels of English semantic structure.

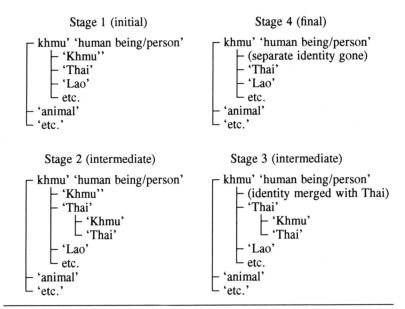

Fig. 18.3. Hypothetical steps in the change of a semantic structure of ethnic categories. Words in single quotes stand for the Khmu' words.

Chinese immigrants and other groups all over the country. The Ugong, also, have almost completely passed into this stage.

Of course, not everyone in the same ethnic group is necessarily in a given stage at the same time. Some older, recently immigrated Hmong individuals may be in stage 1, while in the same village or in the village next to it many people may be in stage 2. Some Hmong young people with education and experience in Chiang Mai are in stage 3.

And the actual situation is much more complicated yet because the levels of "Thai" include both the nation and the region, at the very least. Most groups assimilate to the region more easily than to the nation, as we have repeatedly seen, but in some ways to become Northern Thai or Lao or Paktay is also to become Thai.

Some individuals, on the other hand, become "one kind of Thai" without regional identification because they learn primarily in school. For example, some children going to mission-sponsored schools for upland peoples in northern Thailand have relatively little contact with Kammüang-speaking children or Northern Thai culture. The language of instruction is Standard Thai, which is what they come to use among themselves because they are from diverse language backgrounds like Lahu, Akha, Lisu and Hmong (Paul Lewis personal communication).

When such people go on to high school in the provincial centers of the north, or even to the University of Chiang Mai, they may then also learn more Kammüang. Contacts with their peers from the northern region may become intense. But their regional assimilation comes after their Thai assimilation gets a good start (Sakda Hasuwan personal communication). In a few cases they never use the regional language very much.

Bounded and Centered Meanings

Another way in which the structure of meaning affects ethnicity is in the distinctiveness of categories symbolized by ethnic labels. The meaning boundaries between some words in a language are relatively sharp (Hiebert 1978; Smalley 1988a; Giles 1979:275-280). A referent—the actual person or thing or event or abstraction in real life to which the term refers in a given context—belongs to one category or another, but not both, and the distinction is strongly recognized in the culture. Such are the meaning components of 'male' vs. 'female' in English words like *man* vs. *woman*, *boy* vs. *girl*, and *father* vs. *mother*, in their most typical uses. When the identity of an actual person, say a transvestite or homosexual, seems ambiguous in respect to such sharply bounded categories as these, other people often feel cultural discomfort. Emotional reaction may be strong.

An extreme illustration of the effect of a strongly bounded category on an individual's interpretation of events was observed in Japan. An American stopped to ask directions in Japanese of a rural Japanese, who responded in Japanese. Then the Japanese ran into her house calling out excitedly to her family, "I can speak English!" Apparently, so strong was the boundary of 'Japanese', and so unshakable the assumption that Westerners cannot cross to speak it, that she assumed the interchange must have been in English (Carol J. Smalley personal communication).

In contrast to such sharply bounded categories, borders are fuzzy and meanings are centered for some other categories in a language. In a color spectrum, for example, it is impossible to find a sharp boundary between blue and green, or between yellow and orange. A high percentage of speakers of English, for example, would agree that some shades of color were "yellow" and others "orange" with little controversy, but between the two colors on the color chart they would disagree on what to call the shades. The same individual, furthermore, would be inconsistent in labeling one of the intermediate shades as one color or another.

Ethnic labels tend to be taken as representing bounded categories by some peoples and as centered by others. The same people may also consider some ethnic categories bounded and others centered. If an ethnic category is strongly bounded, for someone to change ethnic identity may even be seen as traitorous. If ethnic categories are centered, change of ethnic identity may not be an emotional matter, and multiple ethnicity—one category under some circumstances, another category under others—may seem normal. Individuals, also, may differ within an ethnic group as to whether their ethnic categories are bounded or centered, especially in diverse societies.

Westerners and, I assume, Bangkok Thai find the following incident to be strange. Kunstadter (1979:158) noticed an adolescent girl in a Karen swidden chewing on a piece of red soil.

"Why are you eating soil?"

"Because I am Lua' [Lavüa']."

"What do you mean by that? I thought you and your parents were Karen?"

"We are, but I have Lua' relatives, and Lua' women eat soil like medicine, and so do I."

"Do Karen women do that?"

"No, only Lua' women."

"Would you like to marry a Lua' boy?"

"No!"

"Why not?"

"They're too dirty, and I don't want to get married!"

This incident illustrates that if people use ethnic labels with meanings of a centered category type, they may consider themselves to be partially of whatever ethnic category they perceive their behavior to be. So when a Lavüa' can become Northern Thai overnight by moving into a Northern Thai context and behaving like a Northern Thai, this does not imply moving across a sharp categorical boundary, but rather conforming to a slightly different configuration of characteristics. It is perceived not like changing from male to female, but like changing from a yellow shade of orange to an orange shade of yellow. And, in different circumstances, such people see themselves sometimes as members of one and sometimes of another ethnic group, like yellow in some lights, orange in others.

Of course, in order to shift like this, a person or a group of people must have learned the constellations of behaviors which are held to be significantly symbolic of the other group. The Lavüa' who become Northern Thai could not easily become Hmong, or Sino-Thai or American. The opportunity and/or motivation for learning the essential traits of the other culture is not there. In some sociopolitical situations they are probably not learnable (Edwin Zehner personal communication). Nor does the same sense of identification with the second culture become manifest.

Part of the reason why both assimilation and non-competitive diversity have been characteristic of Thailand is no doubt that all concerned, Thai and most others, have tended to see many ethnic categories as centered rather than bounded. A great deal of that meaning structure still remains, and contributes to the lack of competition between languages in Thailand. But at the same time, Thai nationalism from the time of King Vajiravudh, early in this century, has increased the sense of boundedness in ethnicity, especially by modernized and Westernized Thai people higher in the language hierarchy and strongly influenced by Bangkok values. For them someone is now more likely to be Thai or something else, not both, and not as often sometimes one and sometimes the other, depending on circumstances.

Nationalism is ethnic identity with political ramifications. It grows more freely where ethnic boundaries are sharp, so when boundaries are centered, leaders of nationalist movements seek to sharpen them. Such was the tactic by which chauvinistic Thai leaders earlier sought to diminish the power and position of the Chinese population and other "alien" groups, establishing greater control by Thai over a perceived threat to their own ethnicity.

Historically Pattani Malay people tend to have bounded ethnic categories. Earlier nobody could be a Malay Muslim faithful believer and a Thai apostate at the same time. The categories were mutually exclusive, a contradiction in terms. But in recent years some Pattani Malay are becoming Thai while remaining Malay and Muslim, so for them definitions are clearly becoming more centered.

Thai officialdom, furthermore, which in this case also generally operates with bounded categories created by nationalism on a Western model, has officially become willing to accept the Muslim component but not the Malay component, and has used the term Thai-Islam to reflect that distinction. Officialdom rejects a term like Malayo-Thai,[5] seeing it as implying dual nationality. By rejecting the Malay component, however, it has probably retarded bringing the Malay into the mainstream of Thai life. The policy may have contributed to confrontation between peoples and their defense of category boundaries rather than the softening of them. On top of that, many nationalistically minded Thai people, especially bureaucrats dealing with the Pattani Malay, do not really accept the Muslim component as included by official government policy; their bounded category of "Thai" includes only Buddhism as its religious component.

But the Thailand hierarchy of languages and peoples, with its relatively centered rather than bounded categories, also leads to nationalism. The top level, the Standard Thai level, the Bangkok level is seen as at least potentially all-inclusive of the people of Thailand, a national level. It is perceived to be distinct from other nation-states all over the world. And as we have seen, for most of the people of Thailand, however multiple their ethnicity, this is the way it should be. In this blending of the modern concept of nationalism with ancient, centered, hierarchically ordered categories lies the national dimension of the relative unity in Thailand's diversity.

Salient Features of Meaning and Underlying Configurations

Some features by which ethnic groups are identified, furthermore, may be perceived as though they defined the group or were diagnostic of it, whereas they are not really so at all. To use an analogy, we can tell the difference between a male lion and a male tiger by the lion's mane and the tiger's stripes. Yet we also believe that if we spray-painted the tiger black it would still be a tiger, and if we shaved off the lion's mane it would still be a lion. The mane and the stripes are typical, obvious, easily identified characteristics in normal situations, but they are not truly diagnostic of "lionness" or "tigerness." The latter are determined instead by whole configurations of characteristics, most of them known only to biologists.

Lee (1986:55-59), himself a Hmong, defined Hmong distinctiveness as follows:

To a Hmong, what distinguishes the Hmong from other people is their Hmong way of life. This way of life centered around shifting agriculture, a language with mutually intelligible dialects, a strong belief in ancestor worship and animism, a division of labour according to family membership and sex, a social structure based on kinship ties through the patrilineage and clan systems, a patrivirilocal pattern of residence, a history of migration from southern China and a long tradition of being stateless. . . .

No Hmong lifestyle is possible without subsistence farming, supplemented by foraging, hunting, some fishing and handicrafts. Agriculture . . . is closely related to the Hmong's religion through such practices as ritual offerings to appease field spirits and "first fruit" ceremonies for the dead members of one's lineage in order to seek their spiritual protection.

Lee went on to discuss the fact that many of these characteristics which "distinguish" the Hmong cannot be carried over into Australia or the USA by refugees from Laos. What is more, he himself happens to be an anthropologist, not a swidden farmer. He also does not mention the fact that many of these characteristics, taken individually, are not exclusively Hmong, either. They are just as true of many other peoples in Southeast Asia. Whereas many Hmong in the USA, or some Hmong in Chiang Mai, do few of these things which Lee says distinguishes them as an ethnic group, some other non-Hmong Southeast Asians regularly do them. Such contradictions in the compiling of defining characteristics for ethnic groups lead some scholars to throw out the baby with the bath and conclude that categories like Karen are not "real" (Hinton 1983).

But the continuing reality of their Hmong ethnicity is very marked to Hmong refugees from Laos in the USA, where they do few of the things Lee mentions. Many feel threatened because they cannot do them, but they do not doubt they are Hmong (Dunnigan 1986). Forms of life and agriculture turn out to be the mane on the lion or the stripes on the tiger of Hmong identity.

In other words, these characteristics are salient, visible, symbolic in one stage of the history of many thousands of Hmong in Southeast Asia, but when they are stripped away people do not cease to be Hmong. The core of the reality of Hmongness is in their self-perception, their sense of identity—and in their contrasting perception of others—even when the conspicuous symbols are lost. However, it does often become difficult to preserve the reality of a particular group when traditional symbols are gone if people do not develop powerful new replacements for what was lost. Because language is frequently the most salient of all symbols of ethnic identity, when language is lost a separate identity frequently weakens, although it does not necessarily disappear, as shown by many Mon or Sino-Thai in Thailand.

Core perceptions, too, are subject to change. Under conditions of dislocation, intense culture contact and rapid assimilation, they may change quickly. Sometimes they change in ways which sharpen boundaries, as happened to many Thai during periods of anti-Chinese political agitation. At other times they change to accommodate assimilation, which is the more normal pattern in Thailand.

Insider and Outsider Perspectives

The structures of meaning for ethnic categories are further complicated by differences of perspective, particularly the perspective of the insider as against the outsider. The perception of "Malay" by a government official from Bangkok is very different from that of a Pattani Malay religious leader.[6]

And, of course, neither insiders nor outsiders are homogeneous in their perceptions. The Malay separatist engaged in terrorism, the conservative Malay religious leader, and the young Malay college student hoping for a government job often have different, though related, perspectives. There are degrees and circles of "insideness."

People may be trapped, furthermore, by the perspectives of powerful outsiders. Such has happened to those people called "hill tribe" /chaawkhǎw/ 'mountain people' in Thai. With many Thai people this is now a generic term for non-Tai peoples in the rural north, at least some of whom live in the hills.

As such, it includes relatively recent immigrants speaking marginal languages like the Hmong, Mien, Lahu and Akha, as well as people like the Lavüa', speaking enclave languages, whose ancestors were there before any Tai-speaking peoples appeared in the area. It also includes people like the Sgaw and the Phlong, many thousands of whom have not lived in the mountains for generations, although other thousands do. While it does not include the people speaking the Chinese languages and other languages of Thai towns and cities, it does sometimes include the Yunnanese Chinese from southwest China, who trade in and have settled in the northern hills, and it is even used sometimes to refer to Taiwanese-related Kuomintang troops living near the border of Myanmar. To many Tai people all of these may seem vaguely like one group, but that view is decidedly not shared by the diverse people within it.

Groups or individuals have difficulty surmounting the stereotypes of powerful outsiders. One Thai educational administrator who knows a great deal about minority peoples in northern Thailand, and who has done enlightened work to foster their education, nevertheless assumed that although the "hill tribe" high school graduates would be able to go on to learn to be teachers and agricultural officials, they would never become doctors or lawyers. "Hill tribe" students in universities frequently encounter amazement and disbelief that they are able to do university work. Thai people who saw "hill tribe" people interviewed on television have registered surprise at their good use of Thai.

Yet, because ethnic categories in Thailand tend not to be sharply bounded, minority peoples do rise above the stereotype more easily than in many countries, if they are given the opportunity to prove themselves. The problem is in getting that opportunity, for the stereotype often causes them not to be seriously considered in any selection process.

Differing Attitudes toward Ethnic Status

In spite of universal ethnocentrism, ethnic groups differ in whether they see their own ethnic identity in a positive or negative light, and in whether they count themselves as superior or inferior. We have seen repeatedly how the native speakers of Standard Thai look down from their position at the top of the hierarchy with the assumption that their way is best, their language is best, they are the best in the country. At the other extreme we saw the Urak Lawoi' manifesting malaise, cultural disintegration, and feelings of inferiority.[7]

The Urak Lawoi' respond to their negative self-perception with anomie, drink, begging, and shame, but these are not the only ways in which a negative ethnic self-perception may manifest itself. For a long time Lao people in northeast Thailand have had a rather negative self-perception when comparing themselves with the people of central Thailand, believing themselves to be backward and poor. Unlike the Urak Lawoi', however, their ethnicity remained vigorous, and now some Lao are responding with cultural revitalization (Linton 1943; Wallace 1956; Smalley, Vang, and Yang 1990:10-13) by giving value to traits which had been stigmatized. Even some members of a widely dispersed language group like the Phuan are regaining ethnic pride, even maintaining their own newspaper (Snit and Breazeale 1988:224-225).

Some Malay, powerless and frustrated in the face of the Thai presence, have responded with confrontation, attempts at secession, and terrorism. Their ethnicity has been aggressively defended even in their subordinate position.

The language hierarchy described in this book, along with institutions like the priesthood, the military and education, provide mobility—yet another way of responding to negative ethnic self-assessment or subordinate position. If individuals can learn the language and the primary cultural symbols of the group with which they compare themselves unfavorably they can often escape from any ethnic identity which is a problem to them.

Evaluations of ethnic differences, positive or negative, may be lightly held, or may be virtually unshakable. The unquestioning ethnic superiority felt by the educated people of Bangkok, for example, is reinforced in many ways. Their status, the power and control exercised by their group, its large size, their location in the heart of the country, their position at the top of the language hierarchy, institutions such as the government, education, the media, the dominant Buddhism, economic growth, relative political stability—all of these support a positive view of their ethnicity and a sense of their superiority.

The weaker Mon ethnic vitality, on the other hand, is probably due in part to a longtime lack of supporting power, position and institutions. The forces to which they are subjected tend to minimize their Mon characteristics and enhance their Thai ones.

Differing Individuals in the Group

Ethnicity has been discussed so far as an identity shared by people in a group. However, this emphasis on societies needs to be complemented by allowance for individual differences. Some people approximate ethnic norms more closely than others, and feel ethnic identity more deeply. Circumstance and opportunity account for some of that difference, but other psychological/personality factors are also at work.

Individuals can be pictured as floating in social space with dimensions such as those in figure 18.4. Their positions in their social group lie somewhere from high to low status and from core to edge involvement. Core people are tightly integrated, participating as solid members in the group's characteristic behavior. They are the pillars of society. Such people are more likely to manifest traditional values, inclined to resist change which is not in keeping with traditional group expectations for change. They are likely to know the languages and dialects which are characteristic of the group, and not to learn others. Government officials from Bangkok epitomize one type of core Thai person.

Individuals on the edge through circumstance or personal inclination fit the group more loosely. They are not the primary carriers of the tradition, and may even be critical of elements of core behavior.

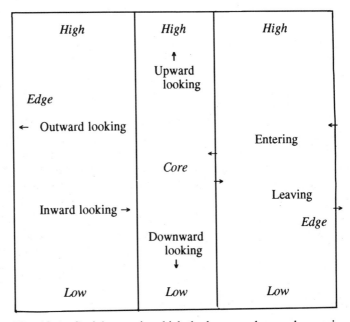

Fig. 18.4. Social space in which the language learner has position, posture, and the possibility of movement, elements in the dynamics of individual multilingualism (after Larson 1984; Smalley 1985:268).

They accept change more readily, if they see it as being in their interest, or in the interest of the group. They are more inclined to learn languages beyond the edge, to learn Kammüang or Lao, when living in the north or northeast, even though they originated in the center of the country.

Some strongly edge individuals are regarded with suspicion by core people. They may seem to threaten core interests. Some such Thai have been imprisoned, like Sulak Sivaraksa, the noted intellectual, others forced to flee, like Khamsing Srinawk, the writer.

Position in social space is always accompanied by posture. A person may be at the edge in some respects, but may also be inward looking, core-oriented, more interested in the core than the edge, aspiring to move to the core. Thus, many Northeasterners may seek to emulate Bangkok and downplay their Northeastern characteristics. On the other hand, someone at the core may be outward looking, toward and/or beyond the edge, interested in the edge as well as the core. The great Thai kings Mongkut, Chulalongkorn and Bhumibol have been outstanding examples, as was Puey Ungphakorn, the former rector of Thammasat University.

When posture is not the same as position the difference can affect multilingualism. A person on the edge may sometimes aspire to core language values. Lower-status people who are upward looking may try to emulate upper-class language. But if people are at the core of their lower-status position, and are not upward looking, they may strongly resist changing to upper-class language.

In addition to position and posture, a person may be relatively stationary or relatively mobile in the society—up or down, toward the core, toward the edge. And in some cases, people are entering the society, or leaving it, or entering or leaving the core. A person may be motivated to learn other languages at one point in life, but not at others.

The channels of vertical mobility discussed earlier, available in spite of the stratified social system, are also opportunities to move toward the core, toward Bangkok, toward Standard Thai, toward being more perfectly "true Thai." The language hierarchy, with its generalizations about who learns what language, reflects one part of that mobility. On the other hand, for some core individuals education and wider experience provide impetus to develop an edge-oriented posture.

So diversity includes individual diversity within group diversity, and individual diversity involves psychosocial characteristics which linguists are not well equipped to deal with. But linguists do have to deal with the results of that individual diversity in the language performance of different individuals, and groups of individuals. It is all part of the language ecology in Thailand and of the multivariate ethnicity of which language is itself a part.

Summary

Thailand's national unity in the face of linguistic diversity is intertwined with ethnicity. Ethnicity is a sense of shared culture based on perceptions of common ancestry and/or territoriality. As such, it provides categories of distinctions between groups of people perceived to be the same or different. People have names for the ethnic group with which they are familiar.

The primary overt and official symbols of Thai ethnicity are the King, the nation, and the Buddhist religion. The vast majority of Thai accept these with no question, but among the minority groups less fully assimilated to Thai ethnicity, the King is the symbol with which they identify first. Buddhist religion, however, is sometimes divisive as an ethnic symbol.

Ethnic labels reflect the structure of ethnic reality, and help to organize it. They come in semantic hierarchies, and the process of assimilation to Thai ethnicity is in part a process of reorganizing the hierarchies of meaning so that a formerly separate ethnic category becomes included within Thai. Ethnic categories, furthermore, tend to be centered rather than bounded in Thailand, which facilitates passing from one to another or having multiple ethnicity. One of the exceptions, the strongly bounded ethnic category of "Malay," contributes to the most serious ethnic conflict in the country.

Individuals differ in how tightly they fit their ethnicity, ranging from core people to edge people within the ethnic group. They may be narrowly oriented toward the group and its norms or open in varying degrees to other groups.

The language hierarchy in Thailand is one dimension of a larger ethnic hierarchy, and language is one of the most significant elements in ethnicity there. Because people accept the linguistic and ethnic hierarchy, on the one hand, and soften its levels with porous linguistic and ethnic boundaries, Thailand's unity in diversity becomes possible.

19

Minority Problem as Thai Problem

This book started by asking how Thailand can have eighty languages yet almost appear to have only one, an anomaly heightened by the fact that the one language is the mother tongue of a minority of Thai. It also asked what made Thailand linguistically more unified than many other countries in spite of all of its languages.

Part 1 set the stage by dealing with diversity within Standard Thai itself, both as variation in what people use as standard, and in the dimensions and ranges which reflect its social ecology. Although the details are often different, Standard Thai variation is generally similar to variation in other major languages in the world, which also manifest the complexity of the modern societies that use them.

However, sharp differences between Thailand and some other countries emerged in part 2, which covered the four major regional languages most Thai people speak as their respective native tongues. Unlike Thailand, in many countries speakers of regional languages fight for official recognition of their languages, for schools in which their languages are media of instruction, and for other manifestations of equality for their languages.

In Thailand regional languages have a symbiotic relationship with Standard Thai instead. They have functions different from it, are used for different purposes, and are appropriate in different situations. They are non-competitive with Standard Thai because they are complementary to it. Just as one speaker uses different varieties of Standard Thai as appropriate to different situations, speakers of the regional languages may switch between their respective languages and Standard Thai under similar social circumstances. At the same time, speakers of such regional languages do not compete linguistically with each other, either, because all accept their geographical complementarity as well.

None of the regional languages is as diverse as Standard Thai in varieties related to social use but each is more diverse in varieties correlated with geographical spread. That is, diversity in dialect is greater in any regional language than in Standard Thai, but diversity in dimension or range is not as great.

In part 3 we dealt with the marginal regional languages. They are much smaller than the marginal languages, and most of them are not Tai languages, but they serve the same functions as the marginal languages on a lower level of the hierarchy. They are the dominant languages in their areas, the languages which people learn if they are native speakers of languages still lower yet.

Part 4 described the remaining categories in the linguistic ecology of Thailand, the languages other people do not learn. The linguistic symbiosis of earlier chapters extends to the Chinese languages used in the cities, to marginal languages of different kinds, and to enclave languages. Much the same division of function as occurs between regional languages and Standard Thai also holds between Teochiu and Thai, and between Lavüa' and Thai. A similar relationship occurs also between these languages and the regional languages near which their speakers live. Each language has its place, and the places are not usually competitive. Thus the hierarchy of Thailand's multilingualism became apparent, the social structure by which linguistic diversity and national unity is organized.

In part 5 the perspective shifted to trans-language issues like education, writing of minority languages, language change and development, and ethnicity. We mentioned some of the historical mechanisms which produced and extend the diversity and some of the cultural context for the hierarchy, generalizing from the individual types of languages previously discussed in their respective ecological places.

In all of this we found many reasons for national unity in the linguistic diversity which is Thailand, including historical and cultural ones, as well as government policy. In this final chapter some of these reasons will be summarized and Thailand sometimes compared with the world around it.

Cultural Causes

Thailand's hierarchy of multilingualism is a cultural phenomenon, part of an implicit understanding of how things are and ought to be. It is effective for unity because it is shared by most ethnic groups living in the country. But this hierarchy in itself is neither unique to Thailand nor enough to account for the ethnolinguistic situation described in this book (Grillo 1989). In fact, a language pecking order is nearly universal in the world, as measured by what languages people tend to learn in order to live successfully in their circumstances.

The World Hierarchy of Languages

Looking at linguistic hierarchy more broadly than just its manifestation in Thailand, English has become a world language, the top of the hierarchy. More people in more parts of the world learn English than learn any other single language except their mother tongue. For many countries, as for Thailand, English is the most important language for communication with the outside world, and is a significant one in all other countries as well.

However, this sense of need for English is not reciprocated by a corresponding desire for other languages on the part of English-speaking people at the top of the world hierarchy. Except for those who grow up bilingual from childhood because they live in situations where English and other languages are regularly spoken together, native speakers of English are normally monolingual, although circumstances and individual perspectives create exceptions.

Next down in the world language hierarchy come the international languages used by the people of various countries for communication with parts of the outside world, especially regions of the world. They are English, French, Spanish, Mandarin, Russian and Arabic. Where these languages are important outside their homelands they were usually instituted originally by colonial governments or by cultural forces like Islam. They are still maintained in many former colonies because elites were educated in them and use them for communicating within the parts of the world which speak them. Only one international language is usually important in any one area or any one country except that English as the world language may also be used along with another.

On the next level down, multinational languages are official languages used as languages of internal as well as external communication in more than one country. They are often drawn from international languages, like Spanish in Latin America, or Arabic in the Middle East, or English, the world language. But more limited multinational languages exist as well, like Malay, Urdu, Hindi, Swahili, Portuguese and German.

Below multinational languages in the world pecking order often lie national languages, of which Standard Thai is one example. They are local languages which have either been given official status or else are commonly accepted as the internal language of a particular country. Sometimes one or more multinational languages are official languages along with a national language in a country. Thus, tiny Singapore has four multinational official languages—English, Mandarin, Tamil and Malay—of which Malay has also been designated the national language. Other countries have either a multinational language or a national one as their official language, but not both.

This is one point in the hierarchy where language conflict arises in countries like India, where some people resent English as the most widely used official language, while others consider it essential. Some people likewise resent Hindi as an official national language, while others defend it strongly. People speaking regional languages not listed as official languages in the Indian constitution, furthermore, often want their languages so counted (Khubchandani 1983; Brass 1974).

On the next level down, many countries have regional languages, but these often fill partially different roles from the regional languages in Thailand. Javanese and Sundanese in Indonesia, for example, have not lost their literary function, or their traditional scripts, in contrast to Thailand where any literary use of the regional languages is now very small. These languages of Indonesia are not considered different forms of Indonesian, either, in the way that the regional languages of Thailand are considered different forms of Thai. In India some regional languages are official languages used in state government and in education.

In some African countries where the official language is English or French, or another multinational language, no national language has been selected from among various regional or "tribal" languages within the country because raising one over the others would create or exacerbate rivalry (Fishman 1968:45-46). Indonesia selected Malay, a foreign language, on which to build its official language rather than risk the divisiveness of using one of its internal languages. The Philippines, however, selected Tagalog, one of its regional languages, creating resentment among some speakers of other regional languages. In Thailand, Standard Thai is based on the Thaiklang regional language without question.

Below regional languages, populations are usually smaller and the ecological niches occupied by their languages more varied. Thailand's categories, like the languages of towns and cities, marginal regional languages, marginal languages, and enclave languages, are by no means all of the ecological types which exist.

So Thailand is tied in to the world-wide hierarchy of languages by its use of English as its international language, and below that its hierarchy shows similarities to language hierarchies elsewhere, but is also relatively independent of them.

Cultural Contexts for Thailand's Hierarchy

But although Thailand is not unusual in having a hierarchy to structure its multilingualism, some of the undergirding for its hierarchy is less common. Hierarchical organization, for one thing, is one of the most fundamental principles in the Thai worldview, including Thai self-perception. It has explicitly and implicitly structured Thai civilization ever since the Ayuthayan kingdom adapted it from the Khmer (Akin 1975). Thai individuals sense strongly their hierarchical position in relation to everyone else, based on age, family, birth, patronage, education, occupation and other circumstances like those which govern the linguistic ranges and dimensions of part 1. Even twins born a few minutes apart are indelibly categorized as older and younger siblings in Thailand, and behave accordingly. Within such a worldview, hierarchy promotes unity because it structures and rationalizes the inequalities of life. More egalitarian worldviews found in some societies are intrinsically more divisive because people lower in a social pecking order find their actual position at odds with the egalitarian ideals of their culture (Paz 1979; Horowitz 1985).

Along with its social hierarchy, Thailand also has a geographic hierarchy in the form of concentric circles. Bangkok is at the center, with major provincial subcenters in other parts of the country, the areas around them relating through them to Bangkok. The King, at the peak of the social hierarchy, has his seat in Bangkok, the center of the geographic hierarchy.

Thus, language hierarchy is one manifestation of a much wider Thai cultural perspective on the way things are and ought to be, on the shape of reality. Accordingly, it only seems right and proper that the language of the King and of the Bangkok elite forms the language of the nation, and other languages take their respective subordinate places around them.

The Thai Buddhist world view, furthermore, helps legitimize hierarchy, fostering acceptance of the place in which people find themselves and others. Whether low or high on the scale, a person's position depends on merit generated in past incarnations, so that whatever fate people experience is the fate they deserve. Some people are higher than others not so much because they are more powerful, more wealthy, or more talented, or more fortunate, but because they are more meritorious. This view of reality does not prevent people from improving their situation in any way they can, but it does provide them with an explanation for inequities, and helps reduce any inclination to question them seriously. As a corollary, low-status people are seen to be inherently powerless, and derive even the ability to work effectively on communal efforts from the greater power offered by the leadership of higher-status people (Rubin 1973). They cannot presume to understand, or legitimately criticize, or make suggestions to their superiors (Zehner 1991:161, 165-166).

Such a worldview contrasts sharply with the more egalitarian Muslim worldview also found in Thailand. Even partially assimilated Muslims who are native speakers of Thai in central Thailand resist or are uncomfortable with Thai forms of hierarchy (Scupin 1988), the more so Pattani Malay-speaking Muslims in the south.

But Thai hierarchies are not rigid and inexorable either, at least not on the lower levels where most people live. Among built-in ways of achieving upward mobility are the monkhood and the army. Education plus some talent and luck also enable a few villagers to move up to the middle class. And language, too, is a channel of social mobility for many. Standard Thai gives people who know it the possibility of rising to a position above where they started, as do regional languages for people who start below them. For upward mobility to take place language must be coupled with other symbols of the status to which they are changing, such as Buddhism or clothing or occupation, depending on the circumstances.

The mobility is limited, of course (Keyes 1978:30-37). Commoners cannot become royalty; it is very hard for poor people to become wealthy. As elsewhere, native ability and circumstances are major factors. A significant number of people do move up the hierarchy, however, at least a little. Language and ethnic differences, furthermore, are sometimes easier to overcome than economic ones because of the inclusiveness of the upper categories of the hierarchy.

Lubricating all of this, linguistic and ethnic categories in the semantic systems of people considered native to the country are generally centered rather than bounded, so ethnic boundaries are not only porous, but also non-exclusive. People are simultaneously or sequentially members of more than one language-speaking group, and do not feel that they are making a radical change as they slip from one set of ethnic characteristics to another. Theoretical Buddhism accentuates this perspective, standing in contradiction to the sharp ethnic/caste boundaries of India, in which it arose (Premasri 1988:44-47).

On the other hand, the Thai understand some linguistic and ethnic categories in the country to be bounded, notably English and Malay.

English as a bounded category creates no problem in Thailand because no native speakers of English try to usurp for it the place occupied by Standard Thai, but Malay has been a problem precisely because of ethnic and linguistic competition in the border provinces of the south. Pattani Malay people, in turn, perhaps perceive all ethnic divisions to be bounded. Religion and such customs as eating pork make the Thai completely alien, if not repugnant, to many Muslims.

On the other hand, the semantic categories of the speakers of Chinese languages have apparently switched significantly from bounded to unbounded over the past thirty years or so.

So around Thailand's hierarchy of multilingualism other cultural characteristics serve to minimize conflict and competition. The hierarchy organizes the diversity in a rational fashion, and the cultural perspective on hierarchy, the worldview, and the semantic system generate ways of feeling, thinking and behaving which create Thailand's national unity within linguistic diversity.

Cultural Processes

Accepting a formerly alien people as Thai involves processes either of incorporation or of accommodation. These can be illustrated by patterns of religious acculturation in Thailand.

After language, Thai popular Buddhism is probably the next most salient evidence of Thai ethnicity. Orange and green temple roofs soar over the villages, and stupa spires punctuate both city and countryside. Amulets hang from many people's necks, and pictures of the Buddha or of important monks frequently adorn taxis and buses. Monks in their conspicuous saffron robes walk the streets or ride public transportation. Squares of gold leaf stuck above the doors of many buildings are left from the time when the buildings were blessed by the monks. Somewhere on almost every plot of inhabited land is a little house for the spirit of the land.

Thai people often suggest that Buddhism is the reason for Thailand's unity, but Myanmar is Buddhist, and interethnic strife is very serious there (chaps. 8, 18). So strong is the feeling that Buddhism is central that many Thai find linguistic diversity easier to accept within Thai ethnicity than religious diversity. The King is the patron of all religions, although the official religion is. Buddhism; but nobody protects any language other than Standard Thai.

Official government policy, however, is the reverse. Buddhism won out in Thailand by providing an overarching world view, and also by absorbing into itself many of the existing smaller-scale world views and religious practices of the people it incorporated (Tambiah 1970, 1976). Thus, for many Thai the symbols of Buddhism legitimize folk beliefs and practices which have much older roots in Southeast Asia. Of course these also get considerably modified through the influence of the Buddhism which incorporates them.

As the influence of Bangkok has extended over the other regions of Thailand, furthermore, the government has successfully incorporated the respective Buddhist organizations of the outlying regions into the Bangkok-centered Buddhist structure (Keyes 1971; Tambiah 1976: 230-261). Thus a centralized Buddhist ecclesiastical organization now controls Buddhist observance throughout the country.

This process of incorporating existing systems continues as non-Buddhist ethnic groups become Buddhist in modern times. Folk religion, widespread in the area and often classified by Westerners as "animism," is not counted officially as religion /sàatsanǎa/ in Thailand. When people from minority groups register with the government for the first time, they are asked their religion so that it can be entered on their identity cards. If they answer that they "worship the spirits" /thǐiphǐi/ they are told that is not a religion, and are listed as Buddhist by default.

So incorporation is the primary way of unifying the diversity of language and ethnicity, but where incorporation is not possible, the Thai alternative has often been accommodation. Thailand does not incorporate Islam and Christianity into Buddhism but has found ways of coexisting with them. In Chiang Mai and some other northern cities, for example, the Thai Christian community is prominent because it includes many professional people relative to its small total size, and because its schools and hospitals are greatly appreciated. Thai Buddhists who know established Thai Christians under such circumstances do not question their Thai identity, although when occasional other individuals convert to Christianity from Buddhism they may suffer accusations of being unpatriotic and of having repudiated their Thai heritage. Christianity has thus not been incorporated, and seems alien to Buddhists, but has nevertheless been accommodated in Thailand.

Except in the Pattani Malay area, Islam has also generally received much the same kind of more-or-less tolerant accommodation. Like Christianity, it is perceived as a foreign religion, but most Tai-speaking Muslims are recognized as Thai. On the other hand, in some of the Pattani Malay-speaking area where a concentration of Muslims is resistant to being a part of Thailand, the efforts of Thai officialdom

have oscillated between enforced incorporation and reluctant accommodation. The bureaucracy has sought to control, to diminish, to
limit, to eliminate the perceived threat, to divorce Muslim religion
from Malay nationalism, to incorporate the leadership structures of
the Muslim community into the Thai sphere of influence (Surin
1985). Officialdom cannot seem to bring itself to follow more completely those accommodation patterns which have worked for it elsewhere.

On the whole, Buddhism is a centered category, not a bounded
one, with respect to the folk religions of peoples in Thailand, and
centered categories lend themselves to incorporating. On the other
hand, Buddhism is a bounded category with respect to Islam and
Christianity, although a strategy of accommodation allows Thai identity to extend to non-Buddhists who show evidence of being Thai in
other ways than religion.

Incorporation and accommodation apply in language relationships
as well. Standard Thai is the official language of Thai identity, and
the whole official system is geared to promoting it and spreading it
throughout the country. As such, it is accepted as unquestioningly as
Buddhism is accepted, but many people who speak no Standard Thai
are nevertheless unquestionably Thai. The other Tai languages are
simply incorporated into "Thai," while the non-Tai languages are
accommodated by allowing them their local role in the language hierarchy. So long as the minority people do not want to use the minority
language in the functions reserved for Standard Thai, accommodation
is almost universal. Perhaps when Thai officials oppose attempts to
write minority languages in script other than Thai script, they are also
attempting incorporation, unwilling to accommodate an alien script.

Thai incorporation and accommodation of languages other than
Standard Thai is different from its incorporation and accommodation
of religions other than Buddhism in at least one important way,
however. Recognized religions are officially protected, while other
languages are only tolerated. The King is the patron of Islam and
Christianity but not of languages like Pattani Malay or Khmer or Mon
or Kammüang or Lao. And the bureaucracy is highly impervious to
adopting anything which would seem to promote or encourage them,
even when Standard Thai would be strengthened in the long run.

Political Contexts for Thailand's Hierarchy

Historically Tai-speaking peoples gradually expanded in the valleys
and plains of present-day Thailand, becoming dominant over peoples

already there. They accommodated and then incorporated those people to their hierarchy by oaths of allegiance, tribute, and support in
war. In doing so they also incorporated Buddhism along with the
Mon, and court culture along with the Khmer.

Peoples lower in the hierarchy, whether Tai-speaking or not,
pledged their loyalty to the prince of a müang, a city-state, and he
became their patron. In return he became, in principle, responsible
for their well-being. When he was a rascal or a tyrant his patronage
did not help much, of course, but it was often significant.

Fealty based on centered categories, however, was easily trans-
ferred:

About sixty years ago we were conquered by the Central Thai. We offered
them candles and flowers [signs of respect and loyalty]. They became our
caw naj ['officials, rulers'] and we pay them taxes. . . . We are the common
people; what happens to officials does not concern us. If there is a war, we
must leave for a while in order to avoid vandals and stray bullets. Whatever
side wins, we will return and call them our leaders (sentiments of Lue villagers in Moerman 1967a:403).

In earlier times there was also plenty of land. If people had trouble
with the lord of the müang to which they were attached they could
often move elsewhere, declare allegiance to another prince, and perhaps be better off. The prince generally left outlying peoples alone if
they fulfilled their obligations of tribute and other support, reciprocat-
ing with protection and help when needed.

In addition to this essential fealty to the lord of the müang, minority peoples often had relationships with individual patrons, often merchants who bought their produce, sold them goods and loaned them
money or credit until the next harvest. When lower-level people were
in trouble, their patron might use influence on their behalf.

Membership in Thai society was voluntary, at least theoretically
so, not only from the perspective of low-level villagers, as quoted
above, but also from the perspective of the center:

Thai society was the group of high officials allied to the king, together with
their followers and the followers of the followers on to the outermost
fringes of society. Then it was not *prathet thai* or Thailand *rachanachaksa-*
jam or "circle of the Siamese king's authority." Instead of being the authorized ruler of a certain mass of people, society consisted of the king at the
center of an organized network of voluntary allegiances. To enter society
required a petition to join the service of some one who was already linked

to the king. To be accepted was a privilege, and hence belonging to society was a privilege which might be renounced at any time (Hanks 1965:87).

The whole complex of shifting states and peoples consisted of "small umbrellas under the protection of larger and larger umbrellas which in turn were under those still higher and larger" (Lauriston Sharp quoted in Fraser 1960:vii). Or that at least is an apt image of one aspect of the ideal structure. However, the little people under all those umbrellas were still the most exposed, still lived in the most precarious position because they had the least power.

Changes Due to Modernization

The umbrella system of hierarchical patronage still exists in Thailand, but important changes began with the modernization instigated by King Chulalongkorn in the last part of the nineteenth century. For one thing, the place of the müang has diminished from semi-independent city-state to provincial center directly under Bangkok. Nationalism, an emphasis on obligatory loyalty to the state within a bounded geographic area symbolized by the King, the Thai language and Buddhism, replaced the flexibility of loyalties to local princes, who also lost their power. Bureaucracy in the form of government ministries replaced the human faces of earlier times (Riggs 1966).

Within these changes came also a rather rigid centralized language policy. As it was worked out over time this policy had two very powerful thrusts: (1) Tai languages in Thailand were classified as one single language, "Thai," which included mutually unintelligible varieties, even ones which had earlier ranked as different languages associated with different scripts and different places. (2) All education was conducted in the emerging Standard Thai based on the speech of the elite in Bangkok.

Under the first of these policies, the great regional languages and all other Tai languages except for the speech of the Bangkok elite were officially incorporated into Thai by being relegated to the place of substandard local varieties; and under the second no schools could be maintained in any Chinese language. These policies were remarkably successful in accomplishing what was intended, and in helping to shape Thailand's hierarchy of multilingualism into the form it takes today.

Many of these changes were part of a complex of development from traditional centered states with loose and variable frontier regions between them to modernized bounded states with sharply defined borders (Giddens 1985:50; Rajah 1990:122). The worldview change involved is still not complete in all sectors of the population in Thailand, although strongly upheld by the bureaucracy and the military.

From Legal to Cultural Status

Citizenship is, of course, one political factor in the Thai treatment of minority peoples. But change in legal status from alien to citizen is less significant for unity than gradual change in cultural status to Thai. Years ago in Thailand an unincorporated minority group, although alien in its citizenship from the Thai point of view, was allowed to be quasi-independent in the vague frontier areas. Thus people moving into the hills of northern Thailand from Myanmar or Laos a hundred years ago could build their villages, make their rice fields, trade with people in the area from which they came, rather than with the Thai, and not have intense dealings with officialdom.

Virtually no such degree of independence can be found in Thailand now. The tiny bands of Mla'bri' may be the closest to it, together with Kensiw and Mos, analogous groups in southern Thailand. When the Thai presence becomes too oppressive, as when the army destroys opium fields, some individual villages of other groups still try futilely to regain greater independence by moving into jungle areas as remote from the Thai as they can, seeking frontier areas which scarcely exist any more.

When the government does exert its authority with force, the alien minority is reduced to deeply resentful subject people. Government seems autocratic, capricious, incomprehensible to the governed. People in the minority group do not know Thai ways of getting around officialdom. Important parts of the Pattani Malay-speaking population still feel like subjects of the Thai, as do some people among the more recently arrived marginal-language Mien, Lahu, Lisu, Akha and Hmong.

The age-old pattern of patronage still helps in some cases to lead people eventually out from feeling like subjects, however. It mitigates some of the harshness of social hierarchy and often of oppressive government, as seen from the low-status person's point of view. People can attach themselves to a higher-status person, give that person loyalty, service, help in emergencies, gifts (tribute), votes, or whatever may be appropriate, in return for protection, connections, cutting of red tape, knowledge of the system, and clout (Hanks 1975).

Client-patron relationships can no longer be established with the prince of the city, but can sometimes be made with the headman of a nearby Thai village, a sympathetic official (or one who sees some profit in the relationship), a merchant, a schoolteacher, or a monk. They require individuals in the minority group to communicate with the patron or the patron's representative, which sometimes makes merchants and missionaries more likely to be sought out as patrons than government officials and teachers who have not learned the minority language. More enculturated members of minority groups become patrons in turn for their less-enculturated neighbors. People who have been away to school and have their patrons in Thai society can serve as brokers and patrons for other people back home, especially as they become older and more established.

This picture of patron-client relations is idealized, however. People in Tai-speaking villages are themselves fearful of officials and try to avoid them whenever possible. The headman of the village often reluctantly serves as the major link between the villagers and the officials above them when necessary in extreme cases. The situation is even worse for many minority peoples (Blimes 1980).

With patronage, the boundaries between ethnic categories become less rigid. Relations become more cooperative, reciprocal, hierarchically ordered, rather than confrontational and coercive. The fact that this relationship has only developed slowly in the Pattani Malay region contributes to the tension there.

But alongside patronage lies the possibility of another relationship, that of multiple identity (Coughlin 1960). Here interethnic communication has advanced so much that the minority group does not seem or feel so alien, so separate. Minority people participate in the life of the region without serious disadvantage because of their ethnicity. They are different, but the difference does not make much difference. They may be stereotyped, but they are not seriously hindered. They are Thai as well as whatever else they may be: Chinese and Thai, Phlong and Thai. Multilingualism is high.

Beyond such multiple identity comes integration. The minority group is now a new kind of Thai. Symbols of difference are muted and Thainess has expanded. Such is the position of many Northern Khmer, Kuy, the Lavüa', and all the Tai-speaking displaced peoples in the country.

The final relationship is assimilation. All distinction is gone. No functional relic of being a separate group remains. At most there remains the memory that ancestors were not Thai, but even the memory does not significantly affect self-perception or the perception of others. Such are millions of people in Thailand with Old Mon or Khmer or Chinese ancestors. Such also are people with Lao or Northern Thai ancestors, but who are themselves now Central Thai, or with Phu Thai ancestors, and who are themselves now Lao, or with Lue or Tai Ya ancestors, who are themselves now Northern Thai.

Thailand's "Thai Problem"

If these cultural and political factors have worked so well to produce Thailand's level of national unity in linguistic diversity, why does Thailand today have a "minority problem"? Thai military leadership is often concerned about security on the borders, fearing some of the marginal people. People sometimes worry about Malay separatism. Some people resent minority peoples, resent the King and the royal family paying what they consider to be a disproportionate amount of attention to the "hill people." The newspapers and television report friction between government officials or Tai-speaking villagers and people in groups farther down the hierarchy.

The regional Tai-speaking peoples like the Lao are considered, and consider themselves Thai, but they too sometimes experience unrest and dissatisfaction. A small insurrection mainly by people of the northeast continued for many years, fueled by poverty and a sense of unjust treatment. But language was not an issue.

In this century, those cases where language has been a significant ingredient in dissention, or even division, have primarily involved speakers of Chinese languages, speakers of Pattani Malay, and a small number of newly immigrant groups in the north.

Of these, the "Chinese problem," as the Thai government once saw it, seems to be over. Created both by Chinese nationalism and by chauvinistic Thai political figures long since gone, it melted away over the years for many reasons. Such forces combined with Thai processes of incorporation and accommodation to integrate the Chinese languages and peoples fully and remarkably harmoniously into Thailand's hierarchies of multilingualism and ethnicity.

Greater barriers still divide the other two types of peoples from the rest of Thailand, however. The Pattani Malay-speaking people in the extreme south and the small groups epitomized by the Hmong in the north have both had semantic systems in which language and ethnic categories are bounded, and for neither of them does hierarchy provide an immediately significant rationalizing structure in their worldview. They often find the elaborate deference which accompanies the Thai social hierarchy to be offensive. People in each group have also wanted to gain or preserve their independence, and pass it along to their children.

But although such cultural differences are major, they have been lessening, especially for people who have been educated in Thai schools. At most, the Pattani Malay and the marginal people of the north add up to no more than 2% of the population of the country, and dissent from the language hierarchy is by no means unanimous among them.

Actually, what Thai people see as the "minority problem" does not have linguistic or cultural foundations as much as it has demographic, ecological, economic, and military ones. We have earlier described population growth, destruction of the forest, opium production, and other deeply troublesome issues.[1]

The "minority problem" is in part a manifestation of a breakdown in ancient relationships between Tai peoples and others, an emerging incompatibility between aspects of an ancient worldview and modernization. Population growth and modernization have shifted radically the traditional position of unassimilated minority peoples in relation to the dominant Tai-speaking peoples. Although loyalty to the king of Thailand remains strong, in their actual relations with the Thai government minority peoples are forced to go through the lowest officials in the bureaucracy. These officials often lack any understanding of the needs and problems of people with a different culture and language, often treating them with contempt. Instead of paying tribute to a prince as their patron they must pay bribes to low-level officials who have nothing to gain by their well-being, and who exploit them as much as they dare (Tapp 1989a:52).

Higher government officials are often bureaucrats and military people from central Thailand, particularly from Bangkok, who do not understand the hierarchy of multilingualism because they view it from the top, and who substitute bounded linguistic and ethnic categories copied from the West for those which have been at work in Thailand for several hundred years. They see no need for any other language but Standard Thai, no need for any cultural systems than those of central Thailand. Some of them do not seem to understand incorporation or accommodation so much as suppression.

Their solution to the "minority problem" is sporadically to force Standard Thai and Bangkok perspectives on people in arbitrary and severe ways. Unaware of how the language hierarchy has contributed to harmony by offering languages of wider communication as privileges to be gained and by accepting people who learned them with relatively little hostility, some bureaucrats have wanted to substitute the harshness of linguistic totalitarianism. Such people constitute a "Thai problem" which interferes with the incorporation or accommodation of remaining peoples into the hierarchy.

The form of Thailand's modern bureaucracy is difficult for all people in the lower reaches of the language hierarchy to deal with, no matter what their ethnic identity. All of the ministries are centralized in Bangkok, far from the outlying parts of the country where people live. Almost all decisions of importance are made at the center, and all communication comes down from the center. Anyone on the periphery who has a problem at all out of the ordinary has to wait while the request goes up through levels of offices until a decision is made in Bangkok, and that decision comes down again through the levels.

Government ministries do not generally cooperate with each other, either, and may have conflicting policies enforced on clients at the bottom by their respective agents. In the 1960s when the Border Police was almost the only government agency in the hills, the non-Tai people of the north found this main contact with the government relatively understanding and helpful. As other government agencies have penetrated farther into the hills more recently, however, a range of sometimes conflicting government pressures is now exercised over people, who see a few of them as benign, others as irrelevant, and many as harsh and onerous.

The government presence in the hills of the north which has been most valued by the hill peoples of all kinds is its growing medical assistance. After that comes the gradually spreading and improving school system. The part of the government resented the most is the Forestry Department, which in the opinion of many inhabitants of the hills administers an arbitrary, capricious and even genocidal control over the forests from which the hill peoples get their livelihood. Thai bureaucratic and military treatment of the Pattani Malay-speaking minority in the south has likewise seemed destined to increase resentment and antagonism.

Basically, the sharp edge of the "Thai problem" is that there is no longer any buffer space for those peoples who are not yet ready to accept an expected place in the hierarchy, who do not yet want to give allegiance to the Thai center. The frontier has become a border. They can no longer live remote and semi-independent until they find it to their advantage to be accommodated according to the Thailand pattern. The Thai see those people who do not accept their place as alien, sharply separate. Many such people do find it to their advantage to join the hierarchy in spite of the "Thai problem" when they see involvement to be to their advantage. But the execution of modernized Thai policies often seems calculated to drive the remaining minorities into resentful antagonism.

Thailand in Contrast

But even with these tensions, Thailand's relative linguistic harmony is outstanding when compared to Myanmar, Malaysia, India, and some others of Thailand's neighbors. In pre-colonial days what is now Myanmar had a long series of wars between different ethnic groups, as did Thailand at the time, and when the British took over the area that became Myanmar there was still no equilibrium among the ethnic groups within it (Hall 1960; Hall 1961:343-354, 536-555). Beginning not long after that, however, in Thailand the great kings Monkut and Chulalongkorn worked at consolidating the hierarchy of multi-lingualism and ethnicity which is so important today (Wyatt 1984:181-222).

In spite of fighting between states, the pre-British peoples of Myanmar had much the same kinds of attitudes toward ethnic differences as those in Thailand did. In the larger, more elaborate states the people on the fringes, those out of power, were looked down on, but such people could easily become residents of the states and be considered to have become a new type of human being (Renard 1988:87-89).

The British stopped the interethnic fighting, but fostered concepts of linguistic and ethnic groupings as bounded categories. They believed people were Kachin *or* Shan (Tai Yai) *or* Burmese in spite of considerable reality to the contrary (Leach 1954; Lehman 1963). They believed, furthermore, that people speaking different languages should have equal opportunity for education and for participation in the lower levels of the British-controlled government. The Shan States were semi-independent of the Burmese when the British took over, so for them and many other peoples the British were the rulers, and the Burmese were just another ethnic group in the country (Bastin 1967: 97-98).

The language of government in British Myanmar was English, and so was the language of choice for education. An English-speaking elite, drawn from the numerous languages of the country, ran the government services. At the same time, many people migrated into Myanmar from British-controlled India, and Hindustani became the language of commerce in the cities. Burmese and all other local languages were thus of less political and economic importance than either English or Hindustani.

When the British left, the Burmese first made alliances with various ethnic groups in the country but then took control, substituting Burmese for English, and driving out the Indians. Many of the non-Burmese peoples revolted, along with the Burmese Communist Party (Silverstein 1980). Not only were ancient hostilities awakened, but the worldview in the minority groups had become more egalitarian, and in their view the Burmese treated them like dirt. On top of that, the government of Myanmar severely restricted some of the freedoms they had enjoyed, while its policies resulted in severe economic deprivation.[2]

The legacy of European colonialism was different in each of the other countries around Thailand, as was the policy of the government which took control when the colonial power left. The reactions of minority peoples to each such government also differed. But in Southeast Asia only Thailand significantly maintained patterns built up over generations as the core of present-day relatively harmonious relationships.

Around the world, people follow a few characteristic patterns as they try to deal with situations where one native tongue is subordinated to another (Liberman 1981:2). One of these ways is by sharpening boundaries between peoples through out-migration of the minority group, or its expulsion, or separatism, or revolution by the subordinate group. We have seen little of such an attempted solution in Thailand, although recently Thai administrations have sometimes harshly expelled refugees, forcing them back into Cambodia and Laos.

A second way is for the dominant group to reduce the hardships of the subordinate one by reforming social institutions like education, providing political processes, reforming economic injustice or establishing political states for the minority. Thailand has officially done very little of this, either. It has extended education, but only on its own terms. In fact, it has strongly prohibited minority-language or even regional-language schools. On the other hand, the official harsh line is ameliorated unofficially in the many ways we have examined. And the hierarchy of multilingualism with the other concomitant cultural and political forces we have described greatly softens the government line. Thailand unofficially often gives back much that it officially takes away.

A third predominant way found outside Thailand is for the minority group to assimilate into the dominant one, giving up its native language and reducing or eliminating its identity. Assimilation takes place in Thailand, but more often with multiple ethnicity and multilingualism. The Northern Khmer are Thai who speak Northern Khmer. They are Thai and Northern Khmer. Their number is regularly increasing even though many individuals have assimilated to monoethnicity.

In spite of its widespread acceptance of its linguistic diversity, Thailand is not a pluralistic society, however. Linguistic diversity is a descriptive term, referring to a characteristic of the world and of most of the nations on its surface. Pluralism is a state of mind, a policy by which diverse people seek to live together in reasonable harmony and mutual respect (Haugen 1987:53). The ideal of the dominant central Thai is homogenization rather than pluralism.

Yet, as we have seen, Thailand's languages co-exist remarkably well on the popular level, in comparison to many other countries which do not have a pluralistic ideology either. The covert ideology of language diversity in the country is "integrated and unequal," but much of what takes the sting out of the inequality is the fact that functional subordination, hierarchical inequality, is so widely accepted as a normal state of affairs.

So Thailand is a place where the harshness of interlanguage relationship frequently found elsewhere as well is tempered in various ways. And that tempering is what makes possible its national unity in the face of its linguistic diversity, even, at points, in spite of its official policy.

The great irony in all of this, however, is that if that unity is now in jeopardy to any significant extent, as is sometimes feared by some of Thailand's Bangkok leadership, such deterioration will occur because those same leaders do not capitalize on what has already been largely won. In their modernized splintered xenophobia some of Thailand's leaders could themselves create the disunity they fear, enforcing on Thailand's people some of the perspectives of the European colonizers against whose political control the country carefully and successfully defended itself for so long. People who have controlled society for a long time tend to believe that their power is the natural state of affairs, and abuse it (Royce 1982:156-158). What was once—and still significantly is—a society in which membership was attractive to people on the fringes, is in danger of becoming one in which membership is forced.

Appendix A

Languages in the Hierarchy

The following list of language names is organized by their places in the language hierarchy of Thailand. It is close to complete, except for languages originating in South Asia and Europe, which are only sampled.[1] A few Tai languages and some extremely small non-Tai languages may have been overlooked, some perhaps never even having been reported. Some languages appear more than once in the list because they function in more than one way in the hierarchy under special circumstances. An asterisk indicates that a listing is other than the primary listing for that language.

The complete hierarchical model of languages around which the listing is organized was shown earlier in figure II.1. For language family relationships see chapter 17. For population estimates see appendix B. N, NE, C, and S refer to the northern, northeastern, central and southern regions, respectively.

External languages of Thailand

Primary
    English (chap. 1)
Secondary
    Arabic (Semitic)
    European languages other than English (Indo-European)
    *All marginal languages
    *All marginal regional languages
    *Cantonese
    *Languages of India
    *Lao
    *Mandarin
    *Other Chinese languages
    *Standard Thai

Internal language of the nation (part I)

Standard Thai (chaps. 1-4)

Regional languages (part II)

Kammüang (chap. 5)
Lao (chap. 6)
Paktay (chap. 7)
Thaiklang (chap. 7)

Marginal regional languages (part III)

Northern Khmer (chap. 9)
Pattani Malay (chap. 10)
Phlow (chap. 8)
Sgaw (chap. 8)
Tai Yai (chap. 8)

Displaced Tai languages (part IV)

Chehe (Tak Bai) (S)
Kaloeng (NE)
Khün (N)
Lao Dan (C)
Lao Kao (NE, N, C)
Lao Khrang (N, C)
Lao Ngaew (NE, N, C)
Lao Song (C)
Lao Tai (N, C)
Lao Wiang (NE, N, C)
Lue (chap. 11)
Nyo (NE, C)
Phuan (NE, N, C)
Phu Thai (chap. 11)
Saek (chap. 11)
Tai Dam (NE, N, C)
Tai Ya (N)
Thai Wang (NE)
Yoi (NE)
Yong (N)

*Kammüang (C)
*Lao (C)

Languages of towns and cities (part IV)

Cantonese (chap. 12)
European languages (Indo-European)
Hainanese (chap. 12)
Hakka (chap. 12)
Hokkien (chap. 12)
Languages of India, Pakistan, and Ceylon (Indo-European,
    Dravidian)
Mandarin (chap. 12)
Taiwanese (chap. 12)
Teochiu (chap. 12)

Marginal languages (part IV)

Akha (Lolo-Burmese / N)
Brao (Mon-Khmer / NE)
Bru (Mon-Khmer / NE)
Chong (Mon-Khmer / C)
Hmong (chap. 15)
Jinghpaw (Kachin) (Tibeto-Burman / N)
Kensiw (Orang Asli) (Mon-Khmer / S)
Keyeh (Kayah, Bwe, Karen) (Tibeto-Burman / N)
Khmu' (Mon-Khmer / N)
Kuy (chap. 11)
Lahu Ku Lao (Lolo-Burmese / N)
Lahu La Ba (Lolo-Burmese / N)
Lahu Na (Lolo-Burmese / N)
Lahu Nyi (Lolo-Burmese / N)
Lahu Sheh Leh (Lolo-Burmese / N)
Lahu Shi (Lolo-Burmese / N)
Lamet (Mon-Khmer / N)
Lisu (Lolo-Burmese / N)
Mien (Hmong-Mien / N)
Mla'bri' (chap. 15)
Moken (chap. 16)
Mon (chap. 14)
Nyoe (Mon-Khmer / NE)

Pa'o (Karen) (Tibeto-Burman / N)
Phalok (Mon-Khmer / N)
Phang (Mon-Khmer / N)
Plang (Mon-Khmer / N)
Phlong (Karen) (chap. 10)
Pray (chap. 10)
Pwo Karen of Hua Hin (Tibeto-Burman / C)
Pwo Karen of Phrae (Tibeto-Burman / N)
Samre (Mon-Khmer / C)
Sgaw (Karen) (chap. 8)
So (Mon-Khmer / NE)
So Tri (Mon-Khmer / NE)
Tonga' (Mon-Khmer / S)
Vietnamese (Mon-Khmer / NE, C)
Wa (Mon-Khmer / N)
Yunnanese Mandarin Chinese (Sino-Tibetan / N)
*Languages of India and Pakistan
*Lao
*Other Chinese languages
*Tai Yai (chap. 8)

Enclave languages (part IV)

Bisu (Lolo-Burmese / N)
Kuay of Suphan Buri (Mon-Khmer / C)
Kuay of Ubon Rachathani (Mon-Khmer / NE)
Lavüa' of La-up (chap. 15)
Lavüa' of Umphai (chap. 15)
Lavüa' of Pa Pae (chap. 15)
Lavüa' of Bo Luang (chap. 15)
Lavüa' of Phae (chap. 15)
Lua' of Wiang Papao (chap. 15)
Mal (chap. 13)
Mok (Mon-Khmer / N)
Moklen (chap. 15)
Mpi (Lolo-Burmese / N)
Nyah Kur (chap. 15)
Ugong (chap. 15)
Urak Lawoi' (chap. 15)

Appendix B

Language Population Estimates

Language population figures listed here do not include all the people who speak the different languages, but only native speakers who learned them as the languages of their home and play.

Standard Thai and Thaiklang are separated in the tables because of their different functions even though they are mutually intelligible, and constitute a single language.

To produce these estimates I compared all of the sources I could find, including the 1980 census, and often made new calculations. Confidence factors in table B.1 indicate how far off I think the estimates could be. They are based on the age and reliabililty of the sources, the agreement between different sources which are not simply quoting each other, and the amount of guessing I had to do in arriving at the estimates.

Languages for which I had no information on which to base any estimate are not listed. Such populations were generally counted as speakers of "Thai" in the 1980 census, or combined under other languages, if their speakers were counted at all.

Table B.1. Estimated language populations in Thailand, in alphabetical order.

Language	Estimate (1989)	Percent	Confidence
Akha	33,500	.0629%	10%
Bisu	200	.0004%	40%
Brao	200	.0004%	40%
Bru	10,000	.0188%	40%
Bwe	1,500	.0028%	40%
Cantonese	275,000	.5161%	75%
Chong	4,000	.0075%	40%
English	2,000	.0038%	75%
Hainanese	379,000	.7113%	75%

Table B.1—*continued*

Hakka	580,000	1.0886%	75%
Hmong	82,000	.1539%	10%
Hokkien	150,000	.2815%	75%
Hua Hin Pwo	2,500	.0047%	40%
Jingpaw (Kachin)	1,000	.0019%	40%
Kammüang	4,800,000	9.0090%	30%
Kensiw	300	.0006%	40%
Keyeh	2,000	.0038%	40%
Khmu'	18,000	.0338%	30%
Kintao	100	.0002%	40%
Kuy	275,000	.5161%	10%
Lahu languages	60,000	.1126%	20%
Lamet	100	.0002%	40%
Languages of India	7,000	.0131%	75%
Lao	12,200,000	22.8979%	30%
Lao Song	25,000	.0469%	40%
Lavüa'	7,000	.0131%	10%
Lisu	25,000	.0469%	10%
Lue	30,000	.0563%	40%
Mal	7,000	.0131%	10%
Mien	36,000	.0676%	10%
Mla'bri'	150	.0003%	75%
Moken	500	.0009%	20%
Moklen	1,500	.0028%	20%
Mon	40,000	.0751%	40%
Mos	300	.0006%	40%
Mpi	2,000	.0038%	40%
Northern Khmer	1,100,000	2.0646%	10%
Nyah Kur	3,000	.0056%	20%
Nyo	30,000	.0563%	40%
Nyoe	500	.0009%	40%
Other European	225	.0004%	75%
Other Karen	1,400	.0026%	40%
Other Khmer	14,000	.0263%	40%
Pa'o (Taungthu)	600	.0011%	40%
Paktay	4,300,000	8.0706%	30%
Palaung	500	.0009%	20%
Pattani Malay	1,000,000	1.8769%	10%
Phalok	100	.0002%	40%
Phang	750	.0014%	20%
Phlong	50,000	.0938%	30%
Phlow	40,000	.0751%	30%
Phu Thai	100,000	.1877%	40%
Phuan	75,000	.1408%	40%
Pray	7,000	.0131%	10%
Sgaw	252,000	.4730%	30%

Table B.1—*continued*

So	40,000	.0751%	40%
So Tri	5,000	.0094%	40%
Standard Thai	10,400,000	19.5195%	30%
Teochiu	2,200,000	4.1291%	75%
Tai Yai	40,000	.0751%	40%
Taiwanese	37,000	.0694%	75%
Thaiklang (not St. Thai)	14,400,000	27.0270%	30%
Ugong	300	.0006%	10%
Urak Lawoi'	3,000	.0056%	10%
Vietnamese	88,000	.1652%	40%
Wiang Papao Lua'	7,000	.0131%	10%
Yunnanese Chinese	30,000	.0563%	30%
Rounded off	-3,225	-.0061%	
Totals	53,280,000	100.0000%	

Table B.2. Estimated language populations by areas where regional languages are spoken.

Language	Estimate (1989)	Percent
Nation-wide languages		
Standard Thai	10,400,000	19.5203%
Teochiu	2,200,000	4.1293%
Hakka	580,000	1.0886%
Hainanese	379,000	.7114%
Cantonese	275,000	.5162%
Hokkien	150,000	.2815%
Taiwanese	37,000	.0694%
Languages of India	7,000	.0131%
English	2,000	.0038%
Other European	225	.0004%
Languages of the Thaiklang-speaking area		
Thaiklang (not St. Thai)	14,400,000	27.0280%
Phuan	75,000	.1408%
Mon	40,000	.0751%
Phlow	40,000	.0751%
Lao Song	25,000	.0469%
Other Khmer	14,000	.0263%
Chong	4,000	.0075%
Hua Hin Pwo	2,500	.0047%
Ugong	300	.0006%

Table B.2—*continued*

Languages of the Lao-speaking area		
Lao	12,200,000	22.8988%
Northern Khmer	1,100,000	2.0646%
Kuy	275,000	.5162%
Phu Thai	100,000	.1877%
Vietnamese	88,000	.1652%
So	40,000	.0751%
Nyo	30,000	.0563%
Bru	10,000	.0188%
So Tri	5,000	.0094%
Nyah Kur	3,000	.0056%
Nyoe	500	.0009%
Brao	200	.0004%

Languages of the Kammüang-speaking area		
Kammüang	4,800,000	9.0093%
Sgaw	252,000	.4730%
Hmong	80,000	.1502%
Phlong	50,000	.0938%
Lahu languages	60,000	.1126%
Tai Yai	40,000	.0751%
Mien	36,000	.0676%
Akha	33,500	.0629%
Lue	30,000	.0563%
Yunnanese Chinese	30,000	.0563%
Lisu	25,000	.0469%
Khmu'	18,000	.0338%
Lavüa'	7,000	.0131%
Mal	7,000	.0131%
Pray	7,000	.0131%
Wiang Papao Lua'	7,000	.0131%
Keyeh	2,000	.0038%
Mpi	2,000	.0038%
Bwe	1,500	.0028%
Other Karen	1,400	.0026%
Jingpaw (Kachin)	1,000	.0019%
Pa'o (Taungthu)	600	.0011%
Palaung	500	.0009%
Bisu	200	.0004%
Mla'bri'	150	.0003%
Lamet	100	.0002%
Phalok	100	.0002%

Languages of the Paktay-speaking area		
Paktay	4,300,000	8.0709%
Pattani Malay	1,000,000	1.8769%

Table B.2—*continued*

Urak Lawoi'	3,000	.0056%
Moklen	1,500	.0028%
Samtao	750	.0014%
Moken	500	.0009%
Kensiw	300	.0006%
Mos	300	.0006%
Kintao	100	.0002%
Rounded off	-3,225	-.0061%
Totals	53,280,000	100.0000%

Table B.3. Estimated language populations in descending numerical order.

Language	Estimate (1989)	Percent
Thaiklang (not St. Thai)	14,400,000	27.0270%
Lao	12,200,000	22.8979%
Standard Thai	10,400,000	19.5195%
Kammüang	4,800,000	9.0090%
Paktay	4,300,000	8.0706%
Teochiu	2,200,000	4.1291%
Northern Khmer	1,100,000	2.0646%
Pattani Malay	1,000,000	1.8769%
Hakka	580,000	1.0886%
Hainanese	379,000	.7113%
Cantonese	275,000	.5161%
Kuy	275,000	.5161%
Sgaw	252,000	.4730%
Hokkien	150,000	.2815%
Phu Thai	100,000	.1877%
Vietnamese	88,000	.1652%
Hmong	82,000	.1539%
Phuan	75,000	.1408%
Lahu languages	60,000	.1126%
Phlong	50,000	.0938%
Mon	40,000	.0751%
So	40,000	.0751%
Tai Yai	40,000	.0751%
Phlow	40,000	.0751%
Taiwanese	37,000	.0694%
Mien	36,000	.0676%
Akha	33,500	.0629%
Lue	30,000	.0563%
Nyo	30,000	.0563%

Table B.3—*continued*

Yunnanese Chinese	30,000	.0563%
Lao Song	25,000	.0469%
Lisu	25,000	.0469%
Khmu'	18,000	.0338%
Other Khmer	14,000	.0263%
Bru	10,000	.0188%
Languages of India	7,000	.0131%
Lavüa'	7,000	.0131%
Mal	7,000	.0131%
Pray	7,000	.0131%
Wiang Papao Lua'	7,000	.0131%
So Tri	5,000	.0094%
Chong	4,000	.0075%
Nyah Kur	3,000	.0056%
Urak Lawoi'	3,000	.0056%
Hua Hin Pwo	2,500	.0047%
English	2,000	.0038%
Keyeh	2,000	.0038%
Mpi	2,000	.0038%
Bwe	1,500	.0028%
Moklen	1,500	.0028%
Other Karen	1,400	.0026%
Jingpaw (Kachin)	1,000	.0019%
Phang	750	.0014%
Pa'o (Taungthu)	600	.0011%
Moken	500	.0009%
Palaung	500	.0009%
Nyoe	500	.0009%
Kensiw	300	.0006%
Mos	300	.0006%
Ugong	300	.0006%
Other European	225	.0004%
Bisu	200	.0004%
Brao	200	.0004%
Mla'bri'	150	.0003%
Kintao	100	.0002%
Lamet	100	.0002%
Phalok	100	.0002%
Rounded off	-3,225	-.0061%
Totals	53,280,000	100.0000%

Table B.4. Estimated number of native speakers in each major language family.

Language	Estimate (1989)	Percent
Tai	46,400,000	87.0871%
Sino-Tibetan	4,120,000	7.7327%
Mon-Khmer	1,629,400	3.0582%
Austronesian	1,005,100	1.8864%
Hmong-Mien	116,000	.2177%
Other	9,500	.0178%
Rounded off	-3,225	-.0061%
Totals	53,280,000	100.0000%

Table B.5. Estimated number of native speakers in each category of the hierarchy of languages.

Language category	Estimate (1989)	Percent
International language	2,000	.0038%
National language	10,400,000	19.5195%
Regional languages	35,700,000	67.0045%
Marginal regional languages	2,420,000	4.5420%
Languages of towns and cities	3,628,000	6.8093%
Marginal languages	838,250	1.5733%
Displaced Tai languages	260,000	.4880%
Enclave languages	31,250	.0587%
Other	500	.0009%
Totals	53,280,000	100.0000%

Appendix C

Symbols

Four different types of symbolization are used to transcribe non-English terms in this book. Their respective characteristics and functions are first described here and then the correspondences between them are displayed in tables C.4–C.6.

Anglicization. In this book Thai place names are generally cited in a normalized roman letter transcription based on their pronunciation, as in the spelling of *Chiang Mai* and *Surin*. The most important exceptions are place names whose usage has already been established in English in another form. *Bangkok*, for example, is not even the Thai name for the city, which would actually be anglicized as *Krung Thep*; *Thailand*, likewise, is a partial translation of the Thai name for the country, which would be anglicized as *Muang Thai*.

The Royal Institute (1968) system of place name anglicization[1] used here does not distinguish all of the significant pronunciation contrasts, however, because some are too different from English. Thus, tone transcription is omitted entirely, and some sound distinctions are symbolized by the same roman letter. For example, /udɔɔn/ and /ubon/ (spoken with different vowels) are anglicized as *Udon* and *Ubon* (written with the same vowel symbol).

Anglicization of the Thai personal names in this book is less consistent. They are spelled in whatever way people write their own names in English. When I do not know the preferred spelling I have anglicized the name according to its pronunciation.

Language and ethnic names follow still another pattern. They have been anglicized according to whatever spelling is used in English language publications, if there is any consensus, and if some serious problem with the spelling does not make it unacceptable. Examples of regularly used acceptable spellings include *Thai*, *Lue*, and *Hmong*.

To be acceptable for this book, however, anglicizations must be based on native speakers' own names for themselves or for their language, not on usage in another language. Thus I use *Lavüa'* rather than the Thai name *Lawa* or the Kammüang name *Lua'*, both of which are more commonly used in English language discussions (chap. 15). Anglicizations must also not be too misleading for the English reader. For example, *Kammyang* is more frequently seen than the *Kammüang* used in this book for /kammian/, but readers are misled by the former anglicization into trying to pronounce the *y* as a consonant.

Phonemic transcription. A second type of roman transcription is used to cite words and phrases which illustrate or clarify some point in a language. All distinctive sounds (phonemes) are symbolized in this transcription, and each sound is represented by only one symbol in each language.[2] A single phonemic symbol may be made up of more than one letter, however, as in the case of /ph/. Tone is usually shown phonemically by a system of diacritics above the vowel when it is a distinctive part of the sound system, as in Standard Thai (table 3). Whenever the sounds of other languages are similar to ones in Standard Thai the same symbols are normally used for those sounds in both languages. Additional symbols are then required for sounds not found in Standard Thai (table C.7).

Phonemic transcription is graphically distinguished from anglicization by slant lines when it occurs in running text, although not normally in tables. Compare *Mae Sariang* to /mêɛsalian/ or *Ayuthaya* to /'ayútthayaa/.

In some contexts the roman symbol for a Standard Thai phoneme may be used to represent the Standard Thai spelling rather than the pronunciation. When that is the case the symbol is enclosed in braces, as in a sentence like "{r} is usually pronounced [l] in Bangkok." {r} there refers to ร, a Standard Thai non-roman symbol for /l/ (chap. 2).

Phonetic transcription. Sometimes more phonetic detail is required for the discussion than is clear from the phonemic transcription. Such phonetic transcription is enclosed in brackets. For example, "Some Bangkok speakers use [Θ] (as in English *think*) rather than the more common [s] for /s/ in a word like /sǎam/ 'three'." In other words, /sǎam/ is pronounced [Θǎam] by some people and [sǎam] by others.

Standard Thai transcription. The core of the Standard Thai writing system includes symbols which correspond rather closely—but not fully—to the Standard Thai phonemes (chaps. 11, 16). These consonants and vowels are shown in tables C.4–C.6, along with the other transcription systems. Non-core Standard Thai consonant symbols, many of which were introduced into the language for transliterating words from other languages, duplicate the core consonants in their representation of Standard Thai sounds.

Symbols for Standard Thai

The Standard Thai phonemes (distinctive sounds), as typically spoken in Bangkok, are shown in tables C.1–C.3. Organization of the tables schematizes the relationships between the sounds according to the position in which they are made in the vocal apparatus.

Part of the Standard Thai system of tone symbolization was described in chapters 11 and 16, and the rest is too complex for this presentation.[3]

Table C.1.   Standard Thai consonants.

Labial	Alveolar	Palatal	Velar	Glottal
p	t	c	k	ʾ
ph	th	ch	kh	
b	d			
f	s			h
m	n		ŋ	
	l			
w		y		

Table C.2.   Standard Thai vowels.

Long vowels			Short vowels		
Front	Central	Back	Front	Central	Back
ii	ɨɨ	uu	i	ɨ	u
ee	əə	oo	e	ə	o
ɛɛ	aa	ɔɔ	ɛ	a	ɔ
ia	ɨa	ua			

Table C.3.   Standard Thai tones, shown with the vowel /o/. The mid tone is not marked. The phonemic status of the lower-high tone is in dispute.

Symbol	Description	Symbol	Description
ó	High	ǒ	Rising
o	Mid	ô	Falling
ò	Low		
õ	Lower-high		

Table C.4. Four transcription systems for syllable-initial Standard Thai consonants. Not all rare Standard Thai consonants are shown. "HCC/LCC" refers to high and low class consonant pairs (chaps. 11, 16). The order of the symbols roughly follows table C.1.

Phonemic	Phonetic	Anglicized	Standard Thai	English analogue	Notes
p	p	p	ป	spill	
ph	p^h	ph	ผ/พ	p̄ill	HCC/LCC
ph	p^h	ph	ภ		non-core
t	t	t	ต	still	
t	t	t	ฏ		non-core
th	t^h	th	ถ/ท	till	HCC/LCC
th	t^h	th	ฐ/ฒ/ฑ		non-core
c	c	c	จ	Jill	voiceless, palatal
ch	c^h	ch	ฉ/ช	c̄hill	HCC/LCC, palatal
ch	c^h	ch	ฌ		non-core
k	k	k	ก	skill	
kh	k^h	kh	ข/ค	k̄ill	HCC/LCC
kh	x	kh	ข/ค		chap. 5
kh	k^h	kh	ฆ		non-core
'	'		อ	ill	glottal stop
b	b	b	บ	b̄ill	
d	d	d	ด	d̄ill	
d	d	d	ฎ		non-core
f	f	f	ฝ/ฟ	fill	HCC/LCC
s	s	s	ส/ษ	s̄ill	HCC/LCC
s	Θ	s	ส/ษ	thin	chap. 3
s	s/Θ	s	ศ/ซ		non-core
h	h	h	ห/ฮ	hill	HCC/LCC
m	m	m	ม	m̄ill	
n	n	n	น	n̄ill	
n	n	n	ณ		non-core
ŋ	ŋ	ng	ง	si̱ng	
l	l	l	ล/ฬ	L̄il	chap. 2
l	l	l	ฬ		non-core
l	r	r	ร		chap. 2
l	r̃	r	ร		chap. 2
l	ř	r	ร		chap. 2
r	ř	r	ร		some dialects. chap. 2
w	w	w	ว	wi̱ll	
y	y	y	ย	y̱ell	
y	y	y	ญ	y̱ell	

Except for tones, the four systems for transcribing Standard Thai in this book are compared in tables C.4–C.6. The column of English analogues, based on my dialect, gives rough approximations of some of the sounds. English dialects vary, however, so these examples are not always safe guides for any individual English-speaking reader. The Standard Thai pronunciation represented is that of Bangkok.

Table C.5. Four transcription systems for syllable-final Standard Thai consonants. Not all rare Standard Thai consonants are shown. The order of the symbols roughly follows table C.1.

Phonemic	Phonetic	Anglicized	Standard Thai	English analogue	Notes
p	p	p	ป/บ/ผ/พ/ฟ	si<u>p</u>	
t	t	t	ต/ด/ฏ/ฐ/ฑ ฒ/ช/ส/ศ/ษ ธ/ฐ/ท/ฒ	si<u>t</u>	
k	k	k	ก/ข/ค	sic<u>k</u>	
n	n	n	น/ณ/ญ/ล/ร	si<u>n</u>	
'	'		ะ		glottal stop. cf. C.6
w	w	w/o	ว	so<u>w</u>	cf. C.6
y	y	y/i	ย	bo<u>y</u>	cf. C.6

Table C.6. Four transcription systems for Standard Thai vowels. Some of the symbols incorporate final consonant sounds as well. In the Standard Thai column a consonant symbol อ is included to show the position of each vowel. - indicates that a consonant follows.

Phonemic	Phonetic	Anglicized	Standard Thai	English analogue	Notes
ii	ii	i	อี	b<u>ee</u>t	
i	i	i	อิ	b<u>i</u>t	
ɨɨ	ɨɨ	ü/ue	อื		
ɨ	ɨ	ü/ue	อึ		
uu	uu	u	อู	b<u>oo</u>m	
u	u	u	อุ	b<u>oo</u>t	
ee	ee	e	เอ	b<u>a</u>ne	
e	e	e	เอ็-/เอะ	b<u>ai</u>t	
əə	əə	oe	เออ		
ə	ə	oe	เอิ-/เออะ		
oo	oo	o	โอ	b<u>o</u>ne	
o	o	o	โอะ	b<u>oa</u>t	
ɛɛ	ɛɛ	ae	แอ	b<u>a</u>n	
ɛ	ɛ	ae	แอะ	b<u>a</u>t	
aa	aa	a	อา	b<u>a</u>lm	
am	ʌm	am	อำ	b<u>u</u>m	

Table C.6—*continued*

ay	ʌy	ai/ay	ไอ/ใอ	bite	
aw	ʌw	aw/ao	เอา	bough	
a	a	a	อะ		before /'/ or final
a	ʌ	a	อ̆–	but	elsewhere
ɔɔ	ɔɔ	o	ออ	bong	
ɔ	ɔ	o	ออ/เอาะ	bought	
ia	iʌ	ia	เอีย	see a	
ɨa	ɨʌ	üa	เอือ		
ua	uʌ	ua	อัว/อว–	to a	

Miscellaneous Other Symbols

As much as possible, the above symbols for Standard Thai are used for corresponding sounds in the other languages discussed in this book as well. A few additional symbols are required to represent other distinctions in those languages, however, as shown in table C.7.

Table C.7. Symbols for other languages.

Phonemic/ phonetic	Anglicized	English analogue	Notes
ñ	ñ	canyon	
j	j	Jill	voiced counterpart of [c] (table C.4)
g	g	gill	voiced counterpart of [k] (table C.4)
ɽ	r	run	retroflexed [r]
r̩	r	butter	syllabic [r]
a	a		low back vowel
x	ch		voiceless velar fricative
́			clear vowel (Nyah Kur)
̀			breathy vowel (Nyah Kur)
'b	b		preglottalized [b]
'd	d		preglottalized [d]
hm/M	hm		voiceless [m]
hn	hn		voiceless [n]
hny	hny		voiceless [ñ]
ⁿ	ng/n		nasalized vowel precedes

Notes

Introduction: Thailand's Sociolinguistic Anomalies

1. In Thailand people commonly refer to each other by their first names, even when they use titles. Thus Professor Patya Saihoo is normally called "Professor Patya" rather than "Professor Saihoo." In this book, including the references, we follow Thai practice when we cite Thai authors and other Thai individuals. Thai authors are also alphabetized under their first names in the references.

2. The spelling *Tai* denotes a family of related languages which is spread over several countries, whereas *Thai* refers to the Tai languages of Thailand, and *Standard Thai* to officially accepted varieties and ones used by educated and upper-class people.

Chapter 1: The Languages of Thailand at Home and Abroad

1. The Thai script is uniquely Thai in spite of some experiments in which people have used it to write other languages (chap. 16; Smalley [ed.] 1976). Like Pali-language Buddhist texts which are transcribed in Thai script, these writing systems are only for Thailand, used by ethnic minorities of Thailand.

2. Other more obscure languages like Tai Yai (Shan), Lahu, and Sgaw Karen also have cross-border functions on a different cultural scale.

3. In its anti-colonial stance Myanmar repudiated education in English for years, but has moved back more recently toward allowing a place for it.

4. Brackets [ ] enclose representations of pronunciation (appendix C).

5. Slant lines / / enclose transcription which represents the structurally significant sound units of the language (appendix C).

6. Achara 1982 describes Thai educational policy and practice.

7. Foreigners must pass a sixth-grade Thai language proficiency test if they teach in Thailand for any length of time.

Chapter 2: Standard Thai: Variations about a Norm

1. In this book we make no attempt to describe the grammar of Standard Thai or any other language. The focus is on the roles which languages play, not on the rules by which they operate. Gedney (1967) provided a survey of

379

both Thai and Western contributions to the study of the Thai language. CIEL (1977) and Pranee and Piansiri (1984) have followed with bibliographies (see also Huffman 1986). The most comprehensive, reliable published description of Standard Thai in English is Noss 1964. Haas 1964:xi-xxii and Hudak 1989 are brief summaries of some of the major grammatical characteristics of the language. Haas 1964 is an excellent Thai-English dictionary. The best published language course for English-speaking people learning Standard Thai as a spoken language seems to be Brown 1967, 1968, 1969, 1979a, 1979b. Diller 1985 and 1988 deal with issues concerning Standard Thai as discussed in Thai publications.

2. Diller (1988) describes some of this process for Standard Thai.

3. The * indicates that the word is hypothetical, not actually spoken in this form.

4. Braces { } enclose symbols which represent letters, not sounds. As noted in the previous chapter, brackets [ ] enclose representation of pronunciation and slash lines / / enclose representation of phonemes, or structurally significant sound units.

5. The linguistic status of this {l r} distinction in Standard Thai has been discussed frequently in the technical literature on Thai, as summarized in Beebe 1974: 63-70.

Chapter 3: Social Dimensions of Standard Thai

1. Writers do so also, but the present discussion is generally restricted to speech.

2. Terms which are affectionate when spoken to intimates, but insulting, demeaning, or coarse when spoken to non-intimates, are widespread in European and other languages as well, of course. The pronominal aspect of this phenomenon has been discussed in Brown and Gilman (1960) and in numerous articles stimulated by theirs.

3. Standard Thai doubtless has more than these three varieties in the dimension of social distance, but these three are distinct and very obvious. Other discussions of the phenomenon of social distance, using other terms, include Joos (1962), Gleason (1965:358-361) and Wonderly (1968:13-17). Social distance varieties are frequently called "registers" (Halliday, McIntosh, and Strevens 1964:87-94), but that term includes other dimensions as well.

4. Additional possibilities both for this official and for other combinations of relationships can be found in Cooke 1968, Angkap 1972 and Hatton 1978.

5. One kind of English analogy would be a mother switching from calling her young son "Chuckie" at one moment to "Charles James Peterson" at the next.

6. Although most status particles are often called "polite words," and some do have such a function, /wā wâ/ in the same group are not "polite words" (Noss 1964:217), and /yā yâ/ are impolite (Amara 1972:37-38).

7. The use of /wã wâ/, etc., also involves the social value dimension to be discussed in the next section.

Chapter 4: Multidimensional Varieties: Ranges and Media

1. Examples of different kinds of irregularities in the Thai writing system are outlined in Haas 1956:76-81. Haas 1964 marks dictionary entries with * when writing does not correspond with pronunciation. Manit 1965 and some other Thai dictionaries give a kind of guide to pronunciation, using Thai letters in unambiguous ways when the pronunciation is not completely predictable from the spelling.

Part II: Major Regional Languages: Introduction

1. Not included in these figures are the estimates for native speakers of Standard Thai who are not also native speakers of any other internal language or dialect of Thailand, even though Standard Thai is linguistically a dialect of Thaiklang (table B.1). We are here discussing the nature and function of regional languages, and Standard Thai is not such a regional language.

Chapter 5: Kammüang (Northern Thai)

1. For the meaning of /miaŋ/ in Thailand see chapters 17, 19.

2. The names used for the various languages and dialects of Thailand are sometimes numerous and confusing. In the text we normally use an anglicization of the name which the speakers of the language themselves call it, often followed by a term in parentheses commonly known to others. For the spelling of Kammüang and a few other cases the use of *ü* to represent spoken [ɨ] is somewhat unconventional. However, it seems more likely to suggest something like the correct pronunciation in English than the more common spellings, *Kammyang* or *Kammuong*.

3. The figure is too strong to be pressed very far. All languages are influenced by dominant languages around them in various ways. Many displaced Tai languages, however, maintain their identity for long periods of time in spite of such influence.

4. Standard Thai does have a limited sixth tone /˜/, the linguistic interpretation of which is disputed, used on some words as a variant of the rising tone /ˇ/.

5. In addition to the degree of social distance, whether a northerner uses Kammüang or Standard Thai may depend on factors like the speaker's knowledge of Standard Thai, the degree of urbanization, and the presence or absence of outsiders.

6. The latter term is used by Wonderly (1968:26-27) in a slightly wider sense than the former, which comes from Ferguson (1964). Ferguson's definition fits the Kammüang situation very well, however: "*Diglossia* is a relatively stable language situation in which, in addition to the primary dialects of the language [i.e., in our case, the dialects of Kammüang] . . .

there is a very divergent, highly codified (often grammatically more complex) superposed variety, the vehicle of a large and respected body of written literature, either of an earlier period or in another speech community, which is learned largely by formal education and is used for most written and formal spoken purposes but is not used by any sector of the community for ordinary conversation" (Ferguson, 1964:435). For a discussion of the concept of diglossia in relation to Standard Thai see Diller (1985).

7. A conference was held and a report published in an attempt to get an agreement on the form of transliteration (Songsak [ed.] 1986), but not everyone follows the recommendations (Ronald Renard personal communication).

Chapter 6: Lao (Northeastern Thai)

1. However, see Sulak's (1986) assessment that such changes have not brought "improvements" in the more basic conditions of the poor in the northeast or elsewhere in Thailand.

2. The spelling and pronunciation with *s* in Western languages does not occur in Lao or Thai.

3. At least one other dictionary of Lao terms with definitions in Standard Thai has also been produced (Wirawong 1972).

4. Kammüang and Lao are nearly mutually intelligible, closer than Kammüang and Standard Thai or Lao and Standard Thai. This near intelligibility is greatest between Kammüang and the Luang Prabang-Loei dialect of Lao.

5. For a moving fictional picture in English of a tiny Lao rural school in a poverty-stricken village in the 1960s, and of its teacher, who lived in a different world from the villagers, although he was physically present with them, see Pira 1983b. The little collection of short stories in which it is included (Pira 1983a) portrays the lot of people generally at the bottom of the social scale in different aspects of northeastern life.

Chapter 7: Paktay (Southern Thai) and Thaiklang (Central Thai)

1. Chehe /chehĕe/ spoken in Tak Bai at the very southern tip of the east coast of Thailand is not a part of this southern continuum, but is another Tai language, unintelligible to speakers of Paktay or Standard Thai (Brown 1965:69; Brown 1968b; Anne Wilding personal communication).

Part III: Marginal Regional Languages: Introduction

1. Yunnanese Mandarin Chinese and Lahu are widely used for communication between individual language groups in the north, often for trading purposes, but for other reasons as well. They are not regional languages in the sense described here, however.

Chapter 8: Tai Yai (Shan), Sgaw (Karen), Phlow (Karen) plus Non-regional Phlong (Karen)

1. Rajah (1990) analyzes some of the reasons why Karen in Thailand show little interest in joining the Karen nationalist movement in Myanmar.

2. Such were the names assumed when they gained Thai citizenship. Everybody knew them, however, as Benny Gyaw and Lah Say.

3. Phlong technically belongs in a later chapter, but because of its similarity to Phlow will be included here for convenience of discussion.

4. Yawalak (1985) sampled 270 Sgaw people in the community, school children and their parents.

5. On the complex issues of Karen ethnic identity, and those of other groups in Southeast Asia, see Keyes (ed.) 1979, and chapter 18, below.

Chapter 9: Northern Khmer plus Non-marginal Kuy

1. Most of this chapter is based on a survey, the results of which are partially reported in Smalley 1964b, 1976c and 1988b. Members of the survey team included John Ellison, Randolph Brock, sixteen Northern Khmer-speaking canvassers and informants, and myself. Ellison has spoken a dialect of Khmer from within Cambodia from childhood, as well as having learned Northern Khmer as an adult.

2. The lack of mutual intelligibility on a conversational level is confirmed by Dhanan (Dhanan and Chartchai 1978:iii). David Thomas (1990) and Jenner (1974) support the conclusion that Northern Khmer is sociolinguistically a separate language. Thomas explains the issues in rebuttal of Huffman (1970) and Bauer (1989), who do not consider it separate from Khmer in Cambodia.

3. That numerical position is often ascribed to Pattani Malay (chap. 10), perhaps because of its greater visibility to observers.

4. In this book we do not include refugee populations or others encamped on both sides of the Thai border waiting for the opportunity to return to Cambodia.

5. Johnston (1976: 259) referred to Kuy Kuy (which she later called Kuy Noa) and Kuy Mla (or Mloa). According to Van der Haak and Wykos (1987), Johnston's terms are those used by the Kuuy to refer to the two dialects. Oranuch (1984) seems to be the only explicit previous reference to Kuay, which is unintelligible with the related Kuay language in Suphan Buri Province of central Thailand (Pailin 1980). Taweeporn (1980) describes Nyeu /ñəə/, a language in Si Sa Ket which is at least closely related to Kuy, and which some native speakers report is mutually intelligible with Kuy, but which perhaps is a separate language in the terms of this book. Another closely related language is So.

Chapter 10: Pattani Malay

1. On the historic consciousness of Pattani Malay-speaking people see Arong (1985:8-12).

2. Some of these reports sound as if this may be a Paktay/Malay pidgin or creole language.

3. Generally urban people with some education in Pattani Province (Narong 1979).

4. For a description of the situation in reverse, misunderstanding between Malay and Thai communities in Malaysia, see Kershaw (1979).

Part IV: Other Language Categories: Introduction

1. A listing of languages by categories is included in appendix A.

2. In this book we do not include the hundreds of thousands of people who are living in refugee camps or other such restricted areas in Thailand (Smalley 1985, 1986).

Chapter 11: Development and Displacement of Tai Languages and Dialects

1. *Alpina sp.*, an aromatic rhizome used in cooking and medicine (Haas 1964:56)

2. Examples of Mid Class Consonants were not included because none of them spell /kh/.

3. The discussion of the development of the Tai consonant class system which follows is based on Brown 1966; Brown 1975; Brown 1979a:107-115. Not all of Brown's theory is accepted by all Tai specialists, but it is the most comprehensive and coherent published explanation for the complex facts, and the general scheme provides a good way of clarifying causes for existing phenomena. Other treatments include Chamberlain 1972, 1975; Gedney 1972; Hartmann 1976, 1980; Strecker 1979. See also Li 1977.

4. How linguists reconstruct ancestor languages is beyond the scope of this book. In this case the reconstructed tones shown in figure 11.1 are somewhat strange from the standpoint of what is known about tone languages in that all are postulated to occur on the same general level of pitch.

5. Syllables which end in consonants, and have other complications, are omitted from further discussion to keep it as simple as possible. Also omitted are occurrences of tone which have been borrowed into Tai languages from other languages.

6. English *Hm!* is a non-linguistic example of the pronunciation of [hm].

7. Brown considers these preglottalized sounds to have been nasals rather than stops: ['m], ['n] and ['ñ]. That would not affect the merger which resulted.

8. Apparently High Class [ch] did not exist in Sukhothai.

9. Other duplications in the writing system are due to the way in which borrowings from Sanskrit were spelled.

10. Northern Tai and Central Tai are not the same as Northern Thai and Central Thai although the respective terms are pronounced the same. The former are the names of branches in a huge language family with many members. They are parallel in meaning to Southwestern Tai, the language family of which most of the Tai languages of Thailand are a part (map

11.1). Northern Thai (an alternate name for Kammüang) and Central Thai (an alternate name for Thaiklang) are names for regional languages in Thailand, parts of the Southwestern Tai family.

11. Pojanee 1985 claims that 60,290 Phu Thai live in one district alone.

12. Recorded samples of such interchanges in a Lue village have been published in Moerman 1988:70, 125-173.

Chapter 12: Languages of Thai Towns and Cities: Chinese Languages

1. Suriporn Yaysa-nga, who conducted the survey, could not read Chinese, and so could not tell when the Chinese characters might have represented something foreign to the Chinese language.

2. Some of the studies of the Chinese in Thailand are Boonsanong 1971; Coughlin 1960; Deyo 1974; Guskin 1968; Jirawat 1973; Landon 1941; Preecha 1979; Purcell 1965; Skinner 1957a, 1958. An insider's view, in the form of a novel, is Botan 1977.

3. Figures supplied by Population Survey Division, National Statistics Office.

4. Botan 1977. See Deyo (1974, 1975) on the considerable inaccuracy of the stereotype for Thai and Sino-Thai clerical workers. See Fry (1977:185) on the finding that occupational success is due more to a higher socio-economic background and urban environment than to Chinese ancestry *per se*.

5. Kirsch (1975) sees Thai Buddhism as predisposing Thai males against business activity and as facilitating the assimilation of Chinese people.

6. The following percentages, which are from Bangkok, do not necessarily apply to any other location. Skinner (1957a:209-210), for example, estimated only 20% Teochiu in the south (Hokkien predominating with 32%). Hakka predominated in some northern provinces, and Hainanese was most common in some northeastern provinces.

7. Since this is a chapter on the languages of Thailand's towns and cities, we are not including three other Chinese populations in Thailand: the Yunnanese Chinese (Haw), traditional traders in the hills of northern Thailand; the Taiwanese-related Kuomintang army group and their families (mostly Yunnanese Chinese) on the Myanmar border in northern Thailand; and the rural Chinese of southern Thailand who work in the mines there. These populations live in ways which differ from the Chinese populations we are discussing. However, the first two groups speak dialects of Mandarin.

8. Coughlin (1960:7) implies that Teochiu and Hokkien are not mutually intelligible, but Skinner (1957a:35) states categorically that they are, and Purcell (1965:570) groups them together. They are considered the same language in some discussions of Chinese languages. Informants from both groups in Bangkok said, however, that they could not understand the other.

9. Actually, in more remote areas such as the hills of northern Thailand, parents of children born in Thailand often find it difficult or impossible to register their children as Thai.

10. In the view of one (apparently) Thai writer, this can be overdone: "[They] research sophisticated dictionaries to find lengthy Thai names and surnames in order to appear more Thai, with the result that now one can recognize really true Thais only by their short surnames" (Consensus 1983).

Chapter 13: Marginal Languages in the Hierarchy: Mon, Pray, plus Non-marginal Mal

1. Old Mon kingdoms predated Tai speakers in Thailand, and a Mon civilization predated even the Khmer civilization in Southeast Asia (Wyatt 1984:21-24, 322). Their populations, however, were ultimately absorbed by the Tai peoples. The Mon we are describing came into Thailand after Tai-speaking peoples had become dominant there (Foster 1973b:8).

2. Unless otherwise indicated, information on the Mal and Pray are from Filbeck (1973, 1976, personal communication).

3. The initial consonant is an aspirated [tʰ], as in English *tin* or *Thai*, not a [Θ] as in English *thin* or *thigh*.

4. See Smalley 1956 for the description of a similar phenomenon among the Khmu' in Laos.

5. Differences created by opium production will be discussed in the next chapter.

6. For a somewhat similar situation with a Khmu' group in Laos which had abandoned the Khmu' language, and where there were religious considerations, see Smalley 1956; Smalley 1964a:113.

7. Filbeck 1973, chap. 8:14-27; Cholthira 1990:91. Cholthira also reports previous messianic movements which led to revolt by the Thin, Khmu', Hmong and Yao in various combinations.

8. On Thai military policy and politics see Suchit (1987) and Chai-Anan, Kusuma, and Suchit (1990).

Chapter 14: Marginal Languages Adapting to the Hierarchy: Hmong (Meo, Miao)

1. Because thousands of Hmong immigrated to Western countries as refugees from Laos after the Vietnam War, they have become one of the most widely studied minority groups of Southeast Asia, although a high proportion of that study has to do with their resettlement outside the area. Two important bibliographies are Olney 1983 and Smith 1987.

2. As elsewhere in this book, we do not deal with the tens of thousands of war refugees who came into camps in Thailand, beginning in 1975.

3. The point has frequently been made, but must be repeated here, that peoples like the Hmong in Thailand are not "tribes" in any political sense. They are ethnic groups without any stable political structure above the village level.

4. The best general survey volume on the marginal upland people in northern Thailand is Lewis and Lewis 1984, and a corresponding Thai edi-

tion. It has the most complete and reliable descriptions of any of the many survey books available, plus scores of outstanding pictures in color.

5. On the cultivation, trading and effects of opium among Thailand's hill peoples, as well as the Thai and Sino-Thai who profit from it, see Lewis 1985b and Tapp 1982b, 1986. On the perspective which Hmong villagers have on government intervention see Tapp 1989a:51-56.

6. For an inventory of names of subgroups see Smalley 1976d:86, amplifying Heimbach 1969 and Bertrais 1964.

7. Several dictionaries of Hmong Daw and Hmong Leng have been published. Bertrais 1964, compiled in Laos, and Heimbach 1969, compiled in Thailand, were the pioneers in French and English, respectively, both recording Hmong Daw. Both authors spent many years living in Hmong villages as missionaries, and their works remain the best for many purposes. Lyman 1974 is on Hmong Leng, but is less useful. Suriya wrote two works, one in Thai (1972) and one in English (1976). Yang 1980, on Hmong Daw, is by a Hmong scholar writing in French. Xiong et al. 1984 is the first dictionary produced by Hmong refugees from Laos in the USA, and it records Hmong Leng.

8. Studies of Hmong grammar include Lyman 1979 on Hmong Leng and Mottin 1978. At present, analysis is being carried out on the language of Hmong refugees in the USA, some of the results of which are listed in Olney 1983 and Smith 1987.

9. For the range of possible agricultural systems in upland areas see Kunstadter 1978a.

Chapter 15: Enclave Languages

1. Schlatter (1976) and Jiranan (1985) describe La-up; Suriya (1985) describes the dialect of the village of Pa Pae, as do Suriya and Lakhana (1986); Mitani (1978) compares four major Lavüa' languages/dialects. See also Sureeporn (1985).

2. /'/ represents clear voice quality and /ˋ/ breathy voice quality.

3. Hogan's work is based primarily on Phuket, Amon's (1979, 1984) on Adang Island in Satun Province, to the south, and Kannika's (1985) on Lanta Island in Krabi Province. Veena (1980) has described Moken.

4. Buddhist belief that the degree of merit accumulated in previous incarnations governs the condition into which one is born. With this understanding, the miserable condition of the Urak Lawoi' is proof that they did not gain enough merit in earlier lives.

5. This section on Ugong is based on Bradley (1978, 1985).

6. There is a displaced-language population of Lao Dan in this area (Bradley 1985:97).

Chapter 16: Writing and Education

1. The 1980 national census, which lists 88.81% as literate (National Statistics Office 1980:39), did not count "hill tribes" or mobile fishing

groups, where literacy is low, and included as literate many people who have lapsed into illiteracy, although they went to school at one time.

2. For a summary of Thai government educational policy, see Achara 1982.

3. For notable success in bilingual education see Larson and Davis (eds.) 1981.

4. Kloss and McConnell (eds.) 1978-1989 is an extensive survey of written languages, their roles and status, in several parts of the world.

5. Morphemes are meaningful elements which are not necessarily full words, illustrated in English by *boy* and *-ish* in *boyish* or *un-* and *mistake* and *-able* in *unmistakable*.

6. Such spellings as {two}, {too}, and {to} for the same pronunciation show how the combination of sound and morpheme rather than sound alone is sometimes represented in the English writing system.

7. A Hmong man devised efficient writing systems for Hmong and Khmu' in Laos although he was not previously literate in any language (Smalley, Vang, and Yang 1990).

8. On the religious reasons why Christian missionaries have concerned themselves with writing systems much more widely than have the followers of other religions, see Sanneh 1989:1-6, 28-34, 50-54, 211-234.

Chapter 17: Change and Development

1. For a critical summary of archeological thinking about the prehistory of the area see Bayard (1980). For a collection of articles on different aspects of that prehistory see Smith and Watson (eds.) (1979). For a Thai statement about the development of Thai culture as a part of general Southeast Asian culture, absorbing but not derivative of Chinese and Indian cultures, see Sujit (1986).

2. For a brief description of the whole Tai family see Strecker (1987). Some linguists would combine Central Tai and Southwestern Tai into a single branch (Chamberlain 1975).

3. For a simple explanation of some of these assumptions see Ruhlen (1987).

4. Chamberlain (1972, 1975). The earlier theory that the ancient kingdom of Nan Chao in Yunnan, China, was the original homeland of the Tai peoples (D. G. E. Hall 1961:144) has been seriously questioned, and is not followed in Wyatt (1984:14-15) or Sujit (1986).

5. Supporting this linguistic evidence that Tai languages are more recent are many of the oral history accounts and early chronicles of Tai-speaking peoples now in Thailand, which often refer to a homeland in North Vietnam or in south China (e.g., Chamberlain 1972:237).

6. What is advantageous may be understood differently by different people. Some people learn languages simply to be sociable, to enter into the life of the other community, or children learn them to play with other children. Others do so because of goals like trade or political influence. The first motive has been called "dealienation" by Larson and Smalley

(1972:29-36). Gardner and Lambert (1972:11-15) call the two motives "integrative" and "instrumental."

7. Larson and Smalley (1972:13-15). Dependent multilingualism is frequently called "compound" and independent multilingualism "coordinate" (Weinreich 1953:8-9; Ervin and Osgood 1954; Fishman 1966:431-434).

8. The categories in this section are from Kraus (1992:4-10).

Chapter 18: Language and Ethnicity

1. The typology in the following paragraphs is based on Horowitz (1985:46-47).

2. Keyes (1976:206-207) discusses the differences in implication between the Thai terms, rooted in Buddhist worldview assumptions, and their English "equivalents."

3. The work which precipitated the discussion was Leach 1954. Lehman 1967, Moerman 1974, Keyes 1976, some of the articles in Keyes (ed.) 1979, and in Wijeyewardene (ed.) 1990 give a good representation of where the discussion has gone. The phenomenon is not restricted to Southeast Asia. Numerous other studies on the puzzle of ethnicity, there and in other parts of the world, have been published. See for example Barth (ed.) 1969; Banks (ed.) 1976; Brass 1974; Edwards (ed.) 1984; Giles (ed.) 1977; Giles 1979; Hildebrandt and Giles 1983; Jessel 1977; Keller 1983; Keyes (ed.) 1981; Khubchandani 1983; Nash 1989; Spickard 1989; Tapp 1989a; Wu (ed.) 1982.

4. Smalley 1961. The dialect cited is that of Luang Prabang, Laos, but Khmu' is also to be found in Thailand as a marginal language.

5. Dual Sino-Thai identity, however, is not seen to imply any serious sense of contradiction at the present time. Formerly there was sometimes a tendency for Thai nationalists to see Thai and Chinese as more fully mutually exclusive (chap. 12).

6. Larson and Smalley 1972:29-36, after Pike's (1967) categories of "emic" (insider) and "etic" (one kind of outsider) perspectives.

7. This section was stimulated by ethnolinguistic identity theory (Giles 1979; Giles and Johnson 1981; Hildebrandt and Giles 1983:442-444).

Chapter 19: Minority Problem as Thai Problem

1. McKinnon and Vienne (eds.) 1989 discusses aspects of the "minority problem" in the northern hills from a variety of perspectives.

2. My understanding of modern interethnic relations in Myanmar comes primarily from discussions with former participants in the Karen rebellion against the Burmese.

Appendix A: Languages in the Hierarchy

1. The other most complete and up-to-date listings of languages in Thailand are Grimes (ed.) 1988:597-604, and Theraphan 1985a:33-40.

Gainey and Theraphan 1977 and Wurm and Hattori (eds.) 1981 are the most detailed and complete maps.

Appendix C: Symbols

1. In spite of the Royal Institute attempt to introduce some consistency, anglicization of place names is not widely standardized in Thailand. Most of it, furthermore, is based on Standard Thai spellings rather than on pronunciation.

2. The system used here for Standard Thai is an adaptation of the one developed by Mary Haas (1956, 1964).

3. For fuller descriptions of the Standard Thai writing system see Haas 1956; Smalley (ed.) 1976e; Brown 1979a, 1979b.

References

Names of Thai authors are alphabetized by first name, in keeping with Thai convention. Dates in the format [BE 2525] are Buddhist Era dates used in Thailand.

Abdullah, Taufik, and Sharon Siddique (eds.). 1986. *Islam and Society in Southeast Asia*. Singapore: Institute of Southeast Asian Studies.

Abramson, Arthur S. 1962. *The Vowels and Tones of Standard Thai: Acoustical Measurements and Experiments*. Bloomington: Indiana University Research Center in Anthropology, Folklore, and Linguistics.

Achara Wangsotorn. 1982. Thailand. In Noss (ed.) 1982:177-212.

Achara Wangsotorn et al. 1981. *A Survey of Societal Needs for Using English*. Bangkok: Language Institute, Chulalongkorn University.

Adjamian, Christian. 1976. On the Nature of Interlanguage Systems. *Language Learning* 26:297-320.

Akin Rabibhadana. 1975. Clientship and Class Structure in the Early Bangkok Period. In Skinner and Kirsch (eds.) 1975:93-123.

Amara Bhamoraput [Prasithrathsint]. 1972. Final Particles in Thai. Master's thesis, Brown University.

Amara Pongsapich et al. 1985. *Traditional and Changing Thai World View*. Bangkok: Social Research Institute and Southeast Asian Studies Program, Chulalongkorn University.

Amara Prasithrathsint. 1983. The Thai Equivalent of the English Passive in Formal Writing: A Sketch of the Influence of Translation on the Target Language. *Working Papers in Linguistics*, Department of Linguistics, University of Hawaii 15:47-68.

———. 1985. Change in the Passive Constructions in Written Thai During the Bangkok Period. Ph.D. dissertation, University of Hawaii.

———. 1988. Change in the Passive Constructions in Standard Thai from 1902 to 1982. In Smalley and Amara (eds.) 1988:363-93.

Amara Prasithrathsint and Kalaya Tingsabadh. 1985. The Use of Address Terms in Thai during the Bangkok Period. Paper read at the 18th International Conference on Sino-Tibetan Languages and Linguistics.

Amon Saengmani [Taweesakdi]. 1979. Phonology of Urak Lawoi Language: Adang Island. Master's thesis, Mahidol University.

Amon Taweesakdi. 1984 [BE 2525]. *The Chaw Lee (Urak Lawoi') Language*. In Thai. Bangkok: Institute of Language and Culture for Rural Development, Mahidol University.

Amyot, Jacques. 1972. *The Chinese and the National Integration in Southeast Asia*. Bangkok: Institute of Asian Studies, Faculty of Political Science, Chulalongkorn University.

Andersen, T. David. 1987. Pwo Karen Language Survey: Interim Report. Manuscript.

Anderson, Benedict R. O'G. 1983. *Imagined Communities: Reflections on the Origin and Spread of Nationalism*. London: Verso.

Angkap Palakornkul. 1972. A Sociolinguistic Survey of Pronominal Strategy in Spoken Bangkok Thai. Ph.D. dissertation, University of Texas.

Arong Suthasasna. 1985. The Muslims in Thai Polity. In Regional Workshop 1985.

Ayal, E. (ed.). 1978. *The Study of Thailand: Analyses of Knowledge, Approaches, and Prospects in Anthropology, Art History, Economics, History, and Political Science*. Athens, Ohio: University Center for International Studies.

Ba Shin, Jean Boisselier, and A. B. Griswold (eds.). 1966. *Essays Offered to G. H. Luce. Artibus Asiae* Supplementum 23. Leiden: E. J. Brill.

Bailey, Richard W., and Manfred Görlach (eds.). 1982. *English as a World Language*. Ann Arbor: University of Michigan Press.

Banks, David J. (ed.). 1976. *Changing Identities in Modern Southeast Asia*. The Hague: Mouton.

Barth, Fredrick (ed.). 1969. *Ethnic Groups and Boundaries: The Social Organization of Culture Differences*. Boston: Little, Brown.

Bastin, John. 1967. *The Emergence of Modern Southeast Asia: 1511-1957*. Englewood Cliffs, New Jersey: Prentice Hall.

Bauer, Christian. 1981. Mon Language and Literature in Thailand. Final report submitted to the National Research Council of Thailand.

———. 1982. Morphology and Syntax of Spoken Mon. Ph.D. dissertation, University of London.

———. 1989. [Khmer Epic Recitatives]: Inherited Form or Adaptation? *Journal of Language and Culture* 8:61-89, 9:107-30.

———. 1990. Language and Ethnicity: The Mon in Burma and Thailand. In Wijeyewardene (ed.) 1990:14-47.

Bayard, Donn. 1979. Comment. In Smith and Watson (eds.) 1979:278-80.

———. 1980. The Roots of Indochinese Civilization: Recent Developments in the Prehistory of Southeast Asia. *Pacific Affairs* 53:89-114.

Beebe, Leslie M. 1974. *Socially Conditioned Variation in Bangkok Thai.* Ann Arbor: University Microfilms.

———. 1975. Occupational Prestige and Consonant Cluster Simplification in Standard Thai. *International Journal of the Sociology of Language* 5: 43-61.

———. 1976. Social Conditioning of Grooved and Flat Fricatives in Thai. In Gething et al. (eds.) 1976:13-27.

———. 1977a. The Influence of the Listener on Code Switching. *Language Learning* 27:331-39.

———. 1977b. The Dialect Code-Switching of Bilingual Children. *CUNY-forum* 3:141-58.

———. 1979. Initial Consonant Cluster Reduction as a Function of Age Group in Bangkok Thai Speakers. In Gething and Nguyen (eds.) 1979: 11-35.

———. 1981. Social and Situational Factors Affecting the Communicative Strategy of Dialect Code Switching. *International Journal of the Sociology of Language* 32:139-41.

Beer, William R., and James E. Jacob (eds.). 1985. *Language Policy and National Unity.* Totowa, New Jersey: Rowman and Allenheld.

Benchawan Suntharagul. 1963. Phonemes of the Chiang Mai Language. In Thai. Master's thesis, Chulalongkorn University.

Benedict, Paul K. 1975. *Austro-Thai Language and Culture, with a Glossary of Roots.* New Haven: Human Relations Area Files.

Bernatzik, Hugo Adolf. 1938. *Die Geister der Gelben Blätter* [Spirits of the Yellow Leaves]. Munich: F. Bruckmann.

Bertrais, Yves. 1964. *Dictionnaire Hmong-Français.* Vientiane, Laos: Mission Catholique.

Binney, George A. 1968. *The Social and Economic Organization of Two White Meo Communities in Northern Thailand.* Washington: Advanced Research Program Agency.

Blair, Frank. 1990. *Survey on a Shoestring: A Manual for Small-scale Language Survey.* Dallas, Texas: Summer Institute of Linguistics and University of Texas at Austin.

Blimes, Jack. 1980. Why do Thai Villagers Break the Wood Laws? *Human Organization* 39:186-89.

Boeles, J. J. 1963. Second Expedition to the Mrabri ('Khon Pa') of North Thailand. *Journal of the Siam Society* 56:133-60.

Boon Chuey Srisavasdi. 1963a. *The Hill Tribes of Siam.* Bangkok: Khun Aroon.

———. 1963b. *Mountain People in Thailand* [in Thai]. Bangkok: Odeon Store.

Boonsanong Punyadyana. 1971. *Chinese-Thai Differential Assimilation in Bangkok: An Exploratory Study.* Ithaca: Southeast Asia Program, Cornell University.

Boonterd Aratan. 1983 [BE 2526]. *The Chinese 200 Years under Royal Patronage.* In Thai. Special Edition of *Economic Line.*

Botan. 1977. *Letters from Thailand.* Susan Fulop Morell, trans. Bangkok: D. K. Book House.

Bradley, David. 1978. Identity, Dialect and Sound Change in mBisu and 'ugǒ̱ŋ. *Working Papers in Linguistics,* University of Melbourne 4:37-46.

―――. 1982. Traditional Minorities and Language Education in Thailand. Report to the National Research Council of Thailand. Duplicated.

―――. 1983. Identity: The Persistence of Minority Groups. In McKinnon and Wanat (eds.) 1983:46-55.

―――. 1985. Traditional Minorities and Language Education in Thailand. In Bradley (ed.) 1985:87-102.

Bradley, David (ed.). 1985. *Language Policy, Language Planning and Sociolinguistics in South-east Asia.* Canberra: Linguistics Department, Australian National University.

Brass, Paul R. 1974. *Language, Religion and Politics in North India.* New York: Cambridge University Press.

Breivik, Leiv Egil, and Ernst Hakon Sahr (eds.). 1989. *Language Change: Contribution to the Study of its Causes.* Berlin: Mouton de Gruyter.

Bright, William (ed.). 1992. *International Encyclopedia of Linguistics.* New York: Oxford University Press.

Brown, J. Marvin. 1965. *From Ancient Thai to Modern Dialects.* Bangkok: Social Science Association Press of Thailand. Reprinted in Brown 1985: 69-254.

―――. 1966. The Language of Sukhothai: Where Did it Come From? And Where Did it Go To? Reprinted in Brown 1985:1-4.

―――. 1967. *AUA Language Center Thai Course,* Book 1. Bangkok: The American University Alumni Association Language Center.

―――. 1975. The Great Tone Split: Did it Work in Two Opposite Ways? In Harris and Chamberlain (eds.) 1975:33-48. Reprinted in Brown 1985:18-36.

―――. 1976a. Thai Dominance over English and the Learning of English by Thais. *Pasaa* 6:67-85.

―――. 1976b. Dead Consonants or Dead Tones? In Gething et al. (eds.) 1976:28-38. Reprinted in Brown 1985.

―――. 1979a. *AUA Language Center Thai Course: Reading and Writing, Text (Mostly Reading).* Bangkok: The American University Alumni Association Language Center.

————. 1979b. *AUA Language Center Thai Course: Reading and Writing, Workbook (Mostly Writing)*. Bangkok: The American University Alumni Association Language Center.

————. 1985. *From Ancient Thai to Modern Dialects, and Other Writings on Historical Thai Linguistics*. Bangkok: White Lotus Co.

Brown, Roger, and Albert Gilman. 1960. The Pronouns of Power and Solidarity. In Sebeok (ed.) 1960:253-76.

Burr, Angela. 1972. Religious Institutional Diversity—Social Structural and Conceptual Unity: Islam and Buddhism in a Southern Thai Coastal Fishing Village. *Journal of the Siam Society* 60:183-215.

Chai Podhisita. 1985. Buddhism and Thai World View. In Amara et al. 1985:25-53.

Chai-Anan Samudavanija, Kusuma Snitwongse, and Suchit Bunbongkam. 1990. *From Armed Suppression to Political Offensive: Attitudinal Transformation of Thai Military Officers Since 1976*. Bangkok: Institute of Security and International Studies, Chulalongkorn University.

Chalida Rinprom. 1977. The Phonemic System of the Korat Dialect. In Thai. Master's thesis, Chulalongkorn University.

Chamberlain, James R. 1972. The Origins of Southwestern Tai. *Bulletin des Amis du Royaume Laos* 7-8:233-44.

————. 1975. A New Look at the History and Classification of the Tai Languages. In Harris and Chamberlain (eds.) 1975:49-66.

Chao, Yuen Ren. 1943. Languages and Dialects in China. *The Geographical Journal* 102:63-66.

Chapman, E. C. 1978. Shifting Cultivation and Economic Development in the Lowlands of Northern Thailand. In Kunstadter, Chapman, and Sanga (eds.) 1978:222-35.

Charuwan Pumpruk. 1982 [BE 2525]. Pronominal Usage of the Academic Community in Lopburi Province. Master's thesis, Mahidol University.

Chavivun Prachuabmoh. 1982. Ethnic Relations Among Thai, Thai Muslim and Chinese in South Thailand. In Wu (ed.) 1982:62-83.

Che Man, W. K. 1990. *Muslim Separatism: The Moros of Southern Philippines and the Malays of Southern Thailand*. Singapore: Oxford University Press.

Cholthira Satyawadhna. 1990. A Comparative Study of Structure and Contradiction in the Austro-Asiatic System of the Thai-Yunnan Periphery. In Wijeyewardene (ed.) 1990:74-101.

Chula Chakrabongse. 1960. *Lords of Life: The Paternal Monarchy of Bangkok*. New York: Taplinger Publishing Co.

Chulalongkorn University. 1983. *Chinese in Thailand, with Supplements on the Chinese Haws and the Kuomintang Chinese: An Annotated Biblio-*

graphy. Bangkok: Social Research Institute and Academic Resource Center, Chulalongkorn University.

CIEL. 1977 [BE 2520]. *Bibliography of Tai Language Studies*. Bangkok: Central Institute of English Language.

Clarke, Samuel R. 1911. *Among the Tribes of Southwest China*. London: China Inland Mission.

Coedès, Georges. 1967. *The Making of Southeast Asia*. H. M. Wright, trans. Berkeley: University of California Press.

Cohen, Eric. 1983. Hill Tribe Tourism. In McKinnon and Wanat (eds.) 1983:307-25.

Comrie, Bernard (ed.). 1987. *The World's Major Languages*. New York: Oxford University Press.

Consensus. 1983. The Chinese Connection in the Matter of Money. *Bangkok Post* (Oct. 10).

Cooke, Joseph R. 1968. *Pronominal Reference in Thai, Burmese, and Vietnamese*. Berkeley: University of California Publications.

Cooke, Joseph R., J. Edwin Hudspith, and James A. Morris. 1976. Phlong (Pwo Karen of Hot District, Chiang Mai). In Smalley (ed.) 1976.

Cooper, Robert. 1984. *Resource Scarcity and the Hmong Response: Patterns of Settlement and Economy in Transition*. Singapore: Singapore University Press.

Coordination Center. 1965. *Comprehension in the Rural Northeast of Thailand*. Bangkok: Coordination Center for Southeast Asian Studies.

Coughlin, Richard J. 1960. *Double Identity: The Chinese in Modern Thailand*. New York: Oxford University Press.

Coulmas, Florian. 1989. Language Adaptation. In Coulmas (ed.) 1989:1-25.

Coulmas, Florian (ed.). 1989. *Language Adaptation*. Cambridge: Cambridge University Press.

Court, Christopher. 1971. A Fleeting Encounter with the Moken (The Sea Gypsies) in Southern Thailand: Some Linguistic and General Notes. *Journal of the Siam Society* 59:83-95.

———. 1975. The Segmental and Suprasegmental Representation of Malay Loanwords in Satun Thai: A Description with Historical Remarks. In Harris and Chamberlain (eds.) 1975:67-88.

Daranee Krisnapan. 1985. The Phonology of Taba Malay. Master's thesis, Mahidol University.

Dassé, Martial. 1976. *Montagnardes, révoltes et guerres révolutionnaires en Asie du sud-Est continentale*. Bangkok: D. K. Book House.

de Silva, K. M., Pensri Duke, Ellen S. Goldberg, and Nathan Katz (eds.). 1988. *Ethnic Conflict in Buddhist Societies: Sri Lanka, Thailand and Burma*. Boulder, Colorado: Westview Press.

Dessaint, William J. n.d. [mid '60's?]. The T'in or Mal. Duplicated.

———. 1973. The Mal of Thailand and Laos. *Bulletin of the International Committee on Urgent Anthropological and Ethnological Research* 15:9-25.

———. 1981. The T'in (Mal), Dry Rice Cultivators of Northern Thailand and Northern Laos. *Journal of the Siam Society* 69:107-37.

Deyo, Frederick C. 1974. Ethnicity, Organization and Work Values: A Comparative Study of Thai and Chinese Industry. Ph.D. dissertation, University of Chicago.

———. 1975. Ethnicity and Work Culture in Thailand: A Comparison of Thai and Thai Chinese White-Collar Workers. *Journal of Asian Studies* 34:995-1015.

Dhanan Chantrupanth and Chartchai Phromjakgarin. 1978. *Khmer (Surin)-Thai-English Dictionary*. Bangkok: Indigenous Languages of Thailand Research Project, Chulalongkorn University.

Diamond, Stanley (ed.). 1960. *Culture in History: Essays in Honor of Paul Radin*. New York: Columbia University Press.

Diffloth, Gérard. 1980. The Wa Languages. *Linguistics of the Tibeto-Burman Area* 2:1-182.

———. 1984. *The Dvaravati Old Mon Language and Nyah Kur*. Bangkok: Chulalongkorn University.

———. 1992. Austro-Asiatic Languages. In *Encyclopaedia Britannica*, 22:719-721.

———. 1992a. On the Bulang (Blang, Phang) Languages. *Mon-Khmer Studies* 18-19:35-43.

Diffloth, Gérard, and Norman Zide. 1992. Austro-Asiatic Languages. In Bright (ed.) 1992,1:137-42.

Dil, Anwar S. (ed.). 1972. *The Ecology of Language: Essays by Einar Haugen*. Stanford, California: Stanford University Press.

———. 1981. *Language Diversity and Language Contact: Essays by Stanley Lieberson*. Stanford, California: Stanford University Press.

Diller, Anthony V. N. 1976. Toward a Model of Southern Thai Diglossic Speech Variation. Ph.D. dissertation, Cornell University.

———. 1979. Tones, Segments and Thai Regional Society. In Theraphan et al. (eds.) 1979:60-93.

———. 1985. High and Low Thai: Views from Within. In Bradley (ed.) 1985:51-76.

———. 1988. Thai Syntax and "National Grammar." *Language Sciences* 10:273-312.

Dodd, William C. 1923. *The Tai Race*. Cedar Rapids, Michigan: Torch Press.

Downing, Bruce T., and Douglas P. Olney (eds.). 1982. *The Hmong in Transition: Observations and Reports*. Papers of the 1981 Hmong Research Conference, University of Minnesota. Minneapolis: CURA, University of Minnesota.

Dressler, Wolfgang. 1988. Language Death. In Newmeyer (ed.) 1988:184-92.

Dunnigan, Timothy. 1986. Processes of Identity Maintenance in Hmong Society. In Hendricks, Downing, and Deinard (eds.) 1986:41-53.

Durrenberger, E. Paul. 1983. Changes in a Shan Village. In McKinnon and Wanat (eds.) 1983:113-22.

Edwards, John R. 1985. *Language, Society and Identity*. New York and London: Basil Blackwell and André Deutsch.

Edwards, John (ed.). 1984. *Linguistic Minorities, Policies and Pluralism*. Orlando, Florida: Academic Press.

Egerod, Søren. 1958-1959. Swatow Loan Words in Siamese. *Acta Orientalia* 23:137-56.

―――. 1959. Essentials of Khün Phonology and Script. *Acta Orientalia* 24:123-46.

―――. 1961. Studies in Thai Dialectology. *Acta Orientalia* 26:43-91.

―――. 1982. An English-Mlabri Basic Vocabulary (Preliminary Version). *Annual Newsletter of the Scandinavian Institute of Asian Studies* 16:14-20.

Egerod, Søren, and Jørgen Rischel. 1987. A Mlabri-English Vocabulary, *Acta Orientalia* 48:35-88.

Enninger, Werner, and Lilith M. Haynes (eds.). 1984. *Studies in Language Ecology*. Weisbaden: Franz Steiner Verlag.

Ervin, Susan, and Charles Osgood. 1954. Second Language Learning and Bilingualism. In Osgood and Sebeok 1954:139-46.

Esman, Milton J. 1990. Language Policy and Political Community in Southeast Asia. In Weinstein (ed.) 1990:185-201.

Evers, Hans-Dieter. 1966. The Formation of a Social Class Structure: Urbanization, Bureaucratization and Social Mobility in Thailand. *American Sociological Review* 31.4.

Faculty of Arts. 1980 [BE 2523]. *Research Report on Levels of Thai People's Language Proficiency: Errors in Usage in the Thai Language of Chula Arts Students*. Bangkok: Faculty of Arts, Chulalongkorn University.

Farouk, Omar. 1986. The Origins and Evolution of Malay-Muslim Ethnic Nationalism in Southern Thailand. In Abdullah and Siddique (eds.) 1986:250-81.

Ferguson, Charles A. 1964. Diglossia. In Hymes (ed.) 1964:429-39.

————. 1968. Language Development. In Fishman, Cooper, and Conrad (eds.) 1968:27-35.

Ferlus, Michel. 1974. Les langues du groupe austroasiatique-nord. *Asie du Sud-est et Monde Insulindien* 5:39-68.

Filbeck, David. 1971. The T'in of Northern Thailand: An Ethnolinguistic Survey. *Behavior Science Notes* 6:19-31.

————. 1973. *T'in Culture: An Ethnography of the T'in Tribe of Northern Thailand*. Chiang Mai: Department of Anthropology and Sociology, Chiang Mai University.

————. 1975. *Culture of the Mal Hilltribe*. Chiang Mai: Phayap University.

————. 1976. Mal (Thin). In Smalley (ed.) 1976:239-57.

————. 1978. *T'in: A Historical Study*. Canberra: Department of Linguistics, The Australian National University.

Fishman, Joshua A. 1966. *Language Loyalty in the United States: The Maintenance and Perpetuation of Non-English Mother Tongues by American Ethnic and Religious Groups*. The Hague: Mouton.

————. 1968. Nationality-Nationalism and Nation-Nationalism. In Fishman, Ferguson, and Das Gupta (eds.) 1968:39-51.

————. 1977. Language and Ethnicity. In Giles (ed.) 1977:15-57.

Fishman, Joshua A. (ed.). 1968. *Readings in the Sociology of Language*. The Hague: Mouton.

Fishman, Joshua A., Robert L. Cooper, and Andrew W. Conrad (eds.). 1978. *The Spread of English: The Sociology of English as an Additional Language*. Rowley, Massachusetts: Newbury House.

Fishman, Joshua A., Charles A. Ferguson, and Jyotirindra Das Gupta (eds.). 1968. *Language Problems of Developing Nations*. New York: John Wiley and Sons.

Forbes, Andrew J. W. 1982. Thailand's Muslim Minorities: Assimilation, Secession or Coexistence? *Asian Survey* 21:1056-73.

Foster, Brian L. 1973a. Ethnic Identity of the Mons in Thailand. *Journal of the Siam Society* 61:203-23.

————. 1973b. Ethnicity and Economy: The Case of the Mons in Thailand. Ph.D. dissertation. Ann Arbor: University Microfilms.

————. 1977. *Social Order of Four Mon and Thai Villages*. New Haven: Human Relations Area Files.

————. 1982. *Commerce and Ethnic Differences: The Case of the Mons in Thailand*. Athens: Ohio University for International Studies.

————. 1988. Changing Ethnicity and Social Resources in a Thai-Mon Village, 1971-1981. In Rambo, Killogly, and Hutterer (eds.) 1988:143-60.

Fraser, Thomas M., Jr. 1960. *Rusembilan: A Malay Fishing Village in South Thailand*. Ithaca: Cornell University Press.

————. 1966. *Fishermen of South Thailand: The Malay Villagers*. New York: Holt, Rinehart, and Winston.

Freeman, J. H. 1911. Personal communication to Samuel R. Clarke. In Clarke 1911:91-94.

Fry, Gerald Walton. 1977. The Educational Correlates of Occupational Attainments: A Bangkok Case Study of Large-Scale Organizations. Ph.D. dissertation, Stanford University.

Fuller, Theodore D., Peerasit Kamnuansilpa, Paul Lightfoot, and Sawaeng Rathanamong-Kolmas. 1983. *Migration and Development in Modern Thailand*. Bangkok: The Social Science Association of Thailand.

Gainey, Jerry. 1985. A Comparative Study of Kui, Bruu and So Phonology from a Genetic Point of View. Master's thesis, Chulalongkorn University.

Gainey, J. W., and Theraphan L. Thongkum. 1977. *Language Map of Thailand and Handbook*. Bangkok: Central Institute of English Language, Office of State Universities.

Gandour, Jackson T. 1979. Tonal Rules for English Loanwords in Thai. In Theraphan et al. (eds.) 1979:94-105.

Gardner, Robert C., and Wallace E. Lambert. 1972. *Attitudes and Motivation in Second-language Learning*. Rowley, Massachusetts: Newbury House.

Geddes, William Robert. 1976. *Migrants of the Mountains: The Cultural Ecology of the Blue Miao (Hmong Njua) of Thailand*. Oxford: Clarendon Press.

Gedney, William J. 1947. Indic Loan-words in Spoken Thai. Ph.D. dissertation, Yale University.

————. 1961. Special Vocabularies in Thai. In Zarechnak (ed.) 1961:109-22.

————. 1967. Thailand and Laos. In Sebeok et al. (eds.) 1967:782-814.

————. 1970. The Saek Language of Nakhon Phanom Province. *Journal of the Siam Society* 58:67-87.

————. 1972. A Checklist for Determining Tones in Tai Dialects. In Smith (ed.) 1972:423-37.

Gething, Thomas W., Jimmy G. Harris, and Pranee Kullavanijaya (eds.). 1976. *Tai Linguistics in Honor of Fang-Kuei Li*. Bangkok: Chulalongkorn University Press.

Gething, Thomas W., and Nguyen Dang Liem (eds.). 1979. *Tai Studies in Honour of William J. Gedney*. Canberra: Department of Linguistics, The Australian National University.

Giddens, Anthony. 1985. *The Nation-State and Violence*. Berkeley: University of California Press.

Giles, Howard. 1979. Ethnicity Markers in Speech. In Scherer and Giles (eds.) 1979:251-89.

Giles, Howard, R. Y. Bourhis, and D. M. Taylor. 1977. Towards a Theory of Language in Ethnic Group Relations. In Giles (ed.) 1977:307-48.

Giles, Howard, and P. Johnson. 1981. The Role of Language in Inter-Ethnic Relations. In Turner and Giles (eds.) 1981:199-243.

Giles, Howard (ed.). 1977. *Language, Ethnicity and Intergroup Relations*. London: Academic Press.

Gleason, H. A., Jr. 1961. *An Introduction to Descriptive Linguistics*. New York: Holt, Rinehart and Winston.

———. 1965. *Linguistics and English Grammar*. New York: Holt, Rinehart and Winston.

Goody, Jack (ed.). 1968. *Literacy in Traditional Societies*. Cambridge: Cambridge University Press.

Gosling, L. A. Peter, and Linda Y. C. Lim (eds.). 1983. *Identity, Culture and Politics*. Vol. 2: *The Chinese in Southeast Asia*. Singapore: Maruzen Asia.

Graham, W. A. 1924. *Siam*. London: Alexander Moring.

Grillo, Ralph D. 1989. *Dominant Languages: Language and Hierarchy in Britain and France*. Cambridge: Cambridge University Press.

Grimes, Barbara F. (ed.). 1988. *Ethnologue: Languages of the World*. 11th ed. Dallas: Summer Institute of Linguistics.

Gunyarat Punthong. 1979. An Analysis of Lexical Change among Three Generations in Kam Muong Dialect. Master's thesis, Mahidol University.

Gupta, Anthea Fraser. 1985. Language Status Planning in the ASEAN Countries. In Bradley (ed.) 1985:1-14.

Guskin, Alan Edward. 1968. Changing Identity: The Assimilation of Chinese in Thailand. Ph.D. dissertation, University of Michigan.

Haarmann, Harald. 1986. *Language in Ethnicity: A View of Basic Ecological Relations*. Berlin: Mouton de Gruyere.

Haas, Mary R. 1956. *The Thai System of Writing*. Washington: American Council of Learned Societies.

———. 1964. *Thai-English Student's Dictionary*. Stanford: Stanford University Press.

Hafner, James A. 1983. Market Gardening in Thailand: The Origins of an Ethnic Chinese Monopoly. In Lim and Gosling (eds.) 1983:30-45.

Hall, D. G. E. 1960. *Burma*. London: Hutchinson University Library.

———. 1961. *A History of South-East Asia*. London: Macmillan and Co.

Hall, Edward T. 1966. *The Hidden Dimension*. New York: Doubleday.

———. 1968. Proxemics. *Current Anthropology* 9:83-108.

Halliday, M. A. K., A. McIntosh, and P. D. Strevens. 1964. *The Linguistic Sciences and Language Teaching*. Bloomington: Indiana University Press.

Halliday, Robert. 1913. Immigration of the Mons into Siam. *Journal of the Siam Society* 10:1-14.

Hamilton, James W. 1963. Effects of Thai Market on Karen Life. *Practical Anthropology* 10:209-15.

————. 1965. Ban Hong: Social Structure and Economy of a Pwo Karen Village in Northern Thailand. Ph.D. dissertation. Ann Arbor: University Microfilms.

Hanks, Lucien M., Jr. 1958. Indifference to Modern Education in a Thai Farming Community. *Human Organization* 17.

————. 1962. Merit and Power in the Thai Social Order. *American Anthropologist* 64:1247-61.

————. 1965. Two Visions of Freedom: Thai and American. In Siam Society 1965, vol. 1:85-90.

————. 1975. The Thai Social Order as Entourage and Circle. In Skinner and Kirsch (eds.) 1975:197-218.

Hanks, Lucien M., Jane R. Hanks, and Lauriston Sharp. 1965. *Ethnographic Notes on Northern Thailand*. Ithaca: Southeast Asia Program, Cornell University.

Harris, Jimmy G., and James R. Chamberlain (eds.). 1975. *Studies in Tai Linguistics in Honor of William J. Gedney*. Bangkok: Central Institute of English Language, Office of State Universities.

Harris, Jimmy G., and Richard B. Noss (eds.). 1972. *Tai Phonetics and Phonology*. Bangkok: Central Institute of English Language.

Hartmann, John F. 1976. The Linguistic and Memory Structure of Tai-Lue Oral Narrative. Ph.D. dissertation, University of Michigan.

————. 1980. A Model for the Alignment of Dialects in Southwestern Tai. *Journal of the Siam Society* 68:72-86.

————. 1985. Dating White Thai and Black Thai Scripts. Paper read to the 18th International Conference on Sino-Tibetan Languages and Linguistics, Bangkok.

Hatton, Howard. 1978. First Person Pronominal Realization in Thai Autobiographical Narrative: A Sociolinguistic Description. Ph.D. dissertation, University of Pennsylvania.

Haudricourt, André-G. 1962. Comments. In Lafont 1962.

Haugen, Einar. 1971. The Ecology of Language. *The Linguistic Reporter* 13, supplement 25:19-25. Reprinted in Dil (ed.) 1972:325-39.

————. 1987. *Blessings of Babel: Bilingualism and Language Planning, Problems and Pleasures*. Berlin: Mouton de Gruyer.

Heimbach, Ernest E. 1969. *White Hmong-English Dictionary*. Ithaca: Southeast Asia Program, Cornell University.

Helm, June (ed.). 1967. *Essays on the Problem of Tribe*. Seattle: American Ethnological Society.

Henderson, E. J. A. 1951. The Phonology of Loan Words in Some South East Asian Languages. *Transactions of the Philological Society* 1951: 131-58.

Hendricks, Glenn, Bruce T. Downing, and Amos Deinard (eds.). 1986. *The Hmong in Transition*. Papers of the 1983 Hmong Research Conference, University of Minnesota. New York: Center for Migration Studies.

Henne, H. 1976. On Chinese Dialects in Lampang. *Lampang Reports* 5: 217-22.

Hermann, Albert, et al. 1966. *An Historical Atlas of China*. Chicago: Aldine Publishing Co.

Hiebert, Paul G. 1978. Conversion, Culture and Cognitive Categories. *Gospel in Context* 1:24-29.

Hinton, Peter. 1975. Karen Subsistence: The Limits of a Swidden Economy in North Thailand. Ph.D. dissertation, University of Sydney.

———. 1983. Do the Karen Really Exist? In McKinnon and Wanat (eds.) 1983:155-68.

Hildebrandt, Nancy, and Howard Giles. 1983. The Japanese and Subordinate Group: Ethnolinguistic Identity Theory in a Foreign Language Context. *Anthropological Linguistics* 25:436-66.

Hjejle, Benedicte. 1972. The Lampang Field Station in Thailand. *Newsletter of the Scandinavian Institute of Asian Studies* 5:3-8.

Hockett, Charles F. 1958. *A Course in Modern Linguistics*. New York: Macmillan Co.

Hogan, David W. 1967. Some Forgotten Tribes. *Echoes Quarterly Review* 19 (Oct.-Dec.).

———. 1972. Men of the Sea: Coastal Tribes of South Thailand's West Coast. *Journal of the Siam Sciety* 60:205-35.

———. 1976. Urak Lawoi' (Orang Laut). In Smalley (ed.) 1976:283-302.

———. 1985. Basic Structures of the Urak Lawoi' Language and Their Functions. Master's thesis, William Carey International University.

Horowitz, Donald L. 1985. *Ethnic Groups in Conflict*. Berkeley: University of California Press.

Hovemyr, Anders P. 1989. *In Search of the Karen King*. Uppsala: Studia Missionalia Upsaliensia.

Hudak, Thomas John. 1987. Thai. In Comrie (ed.) 1987:757-75.

Huffines, Marion Lois. 1986. Strategies of Language Maintenance and Ethnic Marking among Pennsylvania Germans. *Language Sciences* 8:1-16.

Huffman, Franklin E. 1970. *Modern Spoken Cambodian*. New Haven: Yale University Press.

———. 1976. The Relevance of Lexicostatistics to Mon-Khmer Languages. In Jenner, Thompson, and Starosta (eds.) 1976.

———. 1979. Descriptive and Comparative Study of Austroasiatic Languages in Thailand. Manuscript.

———. 1986. *Bibliography and Index of Mainland Southeast Asian Languages and Linguistics*. New Haven: Yale University Press.

Hussain, Zakir. 1982. *The Silent Minority: Indians in Thailand*. Bangkok: Chulalongkorn University.

Hutchinson, E. W. 1935. The Lawa in Northern Siam. *Journal of the Siam Society* 27:153-82.

Hymes, Dell (ed.). 1964. *Language in Culture and Society: A Reader in Linguistics and Anthropology*. New York: Harper and Row.

Ingersoll, Jasper C. 1963. The Priest and the Path: An Analysis of the Priest Role in a Central Thai Village. Ph.D. dissertation. Ann Arbor: University Microfilms.

Institute. 1986. *Four-Language Dictionary: Thai-Kuy-Northern Khmer-English*. Bangkok: Summer Institute of Linguistics and Institute of Language and Culture for Rural Development, Mahidol University.

Institute of Population Studies. 1981. *A Preliminary Report of the National Survey of Fertility, Mortality and Family Planning in Thailand, 1979*. Bangkok: Institute of Population Studies, Chulalongkorn University.

Isara Charanyananda. n.d. A Study of Children's Ability to Hear the Tones of the Thai Language. Master's thesis, College of Education, Bangkok.

Jadit Insawang. 1975 [BE 2518]. Chinese Pressure Groups and Interest Groups and Democratic Development in Thailand. In Thai. Master's thesis, Thammasat University.

Jenner, Philip N. 1974. Observations on the Surin Dialect of Khmer. In Nguyen Dang Liem (ed.) 1974:61-73.

Jenner, Philip N., Laurence C. Thompson, and Stanley Starosta (eds.). 1976. *Austroasiatic Studies*. *Oceanic Linguistics* Special Publication No. 13. Honolulu: University of Hawaii Press.

Jennings, Wanda. 1986. Lecture at Mahidol University.

Jessel, Levic. 1977. *The Ethnic Process: An Evolutionary Concept of Language and Peoples*. The Hague: Mouton.

Jiranan Komonkitiskun. 1985. Some General Characteristics of Lawa Grammar (La-Up Dialect). Master's thesis, Mahidol University.

Jirawat Wongswadiwat. 1973. The Psychological Assimilation of Chinese University Students in Thailand. Ph.D. dissertation. Ann Arbor: University Microfilms.

————. 1976. Assimilation through Marriage in Thailand. *Topics in Culture Learning* 4:23-24.

Johnston, Beulah M. 1976. Kuy. In Smalley (ed.) 1976:259-72.

Jones, Robert B. 1961. *Karen Linguistic Studies: Description, Comparison, and Texts*. Berkeley and Los Angeles: University of California Press.

————. 1966. Comparative Thai Studies: A Critique. In Ba Shin, Boisselier, and Griswald (eds.) 1966:160-63.

————. 1971. *Thai Titles and Ranks: Including a Translation of Traditions of Royal Lineage in Siam by King Chulalongkorn*. Ithaca: Southeast Asia Program, Cornell University.

Jones, Robert B., Ruchira C. Mendiones, and Craig J. Reynolds. 1976. *Thai Cultural Reader*, Book 1. Ithaca: Southeast Asia Program, Cornell University.

Joos, Martin. 1962. *The Five Clocks*. Bloomington: Indiana University Research Center in Anthropology, Folklore, and Linguistics.

Judd, Laurence C. 1964. *Dry Rice Agriculture in Northern Thailand*. Ithaca: Southeast Asia Program, Cornell University.

Kachru, Braj B. (ed.). 1982. *The Other Tongue: English Across Cultures*. Urbana: University of Illinois Press.

Kaeota Khanawan and Banchong Khanawan. 1980. *Language Qualification of Teachers in the Northeast Elementary Schools*. In Thai. Khon Kaen: Faculty of Education, University of Khon Kaen.

Kalaya Chuchote. 1984 [BE 2527]. The Satun Malay Syntactic Structures. In Thai. Master's thesis, Mahidol University.

Kalaya Tingsabadh. 1980. A Phonological Study of the Thai Language of Suphanburi Province. Ph.D. dissertation, University of London.

————. 1985a [BE 2528]. Thai Dialectology up to the Year 1984. *Science of Language*. Department of Linguistics, Faculty of Arts, Chulalongkorn University 5:75-102.

————. 1985b. Some Accents of Central Thai, a Tonal Study. Paper read at the 18th International Conference on Sino-Tibetan Languages and Linguistics.

————. 1986. Lecture at Chulalongkorn University.

Kalaya Tingsabadh and Amara Prasithrathsint. 1986 [BE 2529]. *The Use of Address Terms in Thai During the Bangkok Period*. Bangkok: Thai Studies Program.

Kanala Sukhabanij Eksaengsri. 1977. Political Change and Modernization: Northeast Thailand's Quest for Identity and its Potential Threat to National Security. Ph.D. dissertation, State University of New York.

Kanita Kanasut Roenpitya. 1973. A Semantic Study of Royal and Sacerdotal Usages in Thai. Ph.D. dissertation, University of California.

Kannika Nitayapakda. 1985. The Phonology of Urak Lawoi' Language on Lanta Island in Krabi Province. Master's thesis, Mahidol University.

Karnchana Nacaskul. 1979. A Note on English Loanwords in Thai. In Theraphan et al. (eds.) 1979:151-62.

Keen, F. G. B. 1978a. Ecological Relationships in a Hmong Economy. In Kunstadter, Chapman, and Sanga (eds.) 1978:210-21.

———. 1978b. The Fermented Tea (Miang) Economy of Northern Thailand. In Kunstadter, Chapman, and Sanga (eds.) 1978:255-70.

———. 1983. Land Use. In McKinnon and Wanat (eds.) 1983:293-306.

Keller, Barbara L. 1983. An Annotated Bibliography on the Relationship Between Language and Identity. *Notes on Translation* 28.

Kerr, A. F. G. 1927. Two 'Lawa' Vocabularies. *Journal of the Siam Society* 21.

Kershaw, Roger. 1979. Menace and Reassurance in Malay Circumcision: A Note on Some Attitudes of Kelantan Thais. *Journal of the Siam Society* 67:116-22.

———. 1981. Towards a Theory of Paranakan Chinese Identity in an Outpost of Thai Buddhism. *Journal of the Siam Society* 69:74-106.

Kesmanee Debavalya. 1983 [BE 2526]. A Linguistic Borderline between Central Thai and Southern Thai: A Tonal Study. In Thai. Master's thesis, Chulalongkorn University.

Keyes, Charles F. 1966. Peasant and Nation: The Integration of a Thai-Lao Village into the Thai National System. Ph.D. dissertation, Cornell University.

———. 1967. *Isan: Regionalism in Northeast Thailand*. Ithaca: Southeast Asia Program, Cornell University.

———. 1968. Tai-tribal Relations in a Frontier District of Thailand. Duplicated. Seattle: University of Washington.

———. 1971. Buddhism and National Integration in Thailand. *Journal of Asian Studies* 30:551-68. Also in *Visakha Puja* BE 2514:22-34.

———. 1976. Towards a New Formulation of the Concept of Ethnic Group. *Ethnicity* 3:203-13.

———. 1978. Ethnography and Anthropological Interpretation in the Study of Thailand. In Ayal (ed.) 1978.

———. 1979a. Introduction. In Keyes (ed.) 1979: 1-23.

———. 1979b. The Karen in Thai History and the History of the Karen in Thailand. In Keyes (ed.) 1979:25-61.

———. 1981. The Dialectics of Ethnic Change. In Keyes (ed.) 1981:4-30.

———. 1987. *Buddhist Kingdom as Modern Nation State*. Boulder, Colorado: Westview Press.

Keyes, Charles F. (ed.). 1979. *Ethnic Adaptation and Identity: The Karen on the Thai Frontier with Burma*. Philadelphia: Institute for the Study of Human Issues.

―――. 1981. *Ethnic Change*. Seattle: University of Washington.

Khachatphai Burutphat. 1983 [BE 2526]. *Minority Groups in Thailand and National Security*. In Thai. Bangkok: Phrae Phitthaya Press.

Kheuan Singkhampha. 1987 [BE 2530] *Northern Khmer Folktales*. In Northern Khmer. Surin: Non-formal Education.

Kheuan Singhanipa, Suwilai Premsrirat, and David Thomas. 1984. *Surin Khmer Conversation Lessons*. Bangkok: Institute of Language and Culture for Rural Development, Mahidol University.

Khubchandani, Lachman M. 1983. *Plural Languages, Plural Cultures: Communication, Identity, and Sociopolitical Change in Contemporary India*. Honolulu: University of Hawaii Press.

Kingshill, Konrad. 1960. *Ku Daeng―The Red Tomb: A Village Study in Northern Thailand*. Chiang Mai, Thailand: The Prince Royal's College.

Kirsch, A. Thomas. 1966. Development and Mobility among the Phu Thai of Northeast Thailand. *Asian Survey* 6:370-78.

―――. 1967. Phu Thai Religious Syncretism: A Case Study of Thai Religion and Society. Ph.D. dissertation, Harvard University.

―――. 1975. Economy, Polity and Religion in Thailand. In Skinner and Kirsch (eds.) 1975:172-96.

Kloss, Heinz. 1967. 'Abstand Languages' and 'Ausbau Languages.' *Anthropological Linguistics* 9:29-41.

Kloss, Heinz, and Grant D. McConnell (eds.). 1978-1989. *The Written Languages of the World*. Quebec: Les Presses de l'Université Laval.

Kobkua Suwannathat-Pian. 1988. *Thai-Malay Relations: . . .Seventeenth to Twentieth Centuries*. Singapore: Oxford University Press.

Kraisri Nimmanahaeminda. 1963. The Mrabri Language. *Journal of the Siam Society* 51:179-84.

―――. 1965a. An Inscribed Silver-Plate Grant to the Lawa of Boh Luang. In Siam Society 1965, vol. 2:233-28.

―――. 1965b. Put Vegetables into Baskets and People into Towns. In Hanks, Hanks, and Sharp (eds.) 1965.

Kraisri Nimmanahaeminda and Julian Hartland-Swann. 1962. Expedition to the 'Khon Pa' (or Phi Tong Luang?). *Journal of the Siam Society* 50: 165-86.

Kraus, Michael. 1992. The World's Languages in Crisis. *Language* 68:4-10.

Kukrit Pramoj. 1955. The Court Language. In Vilas and Van Beek (eds.) 1983:81-87.

Kunstadter, Peter. 1964. Research on the Lua' and S'Kaw Karen Hill Peoples of Northern Thailand. Duplicated.

———. 1965. *The Lua' (Lawa) of Northern Thailand: Aspects of Social Structure, Agriculture, and Religion.* Princeton: Center for International Studies, Princeton University.

———. 1967. The Lua' (Lawa) and Skaw Karen of Maehongson Province, Northwestern Thailand. In Kunstadter (ed.) 1967:639-76.

———. 1969. Report to the National Research Council of Thailand: An Outline of Anthropological Research, 1966-1969. Duplicated.

———. 1978a. Alternatives for Development of Upland Areas. In Kunstadter, Chapman, and Sanga (eds.) 1978:290-308.

———. 1978b. Subsistence Agricultural Economies of Lua' and Karen Hill Farmers, Mae Sariang District, Northwestern Thailand. In Kunstadter, Chapman, and Sanga (eds.) 1978:74-133.

———. 1979. Ethnic Group, Category and Identity: Karen in Northern Thailand. In Keyes (ed.) 1979:119-63.

———. 1983a. Highland Populations in Northern Thailand. In McKinnon and Wanat (eds.) 1983:15-45.

———. 1983b. Animism, Buddhism, and Christianity: Religion in the Life of Lua People of Pa Pae, North-Western Thailand. In McKinnon and Wanat (eds.) 1983:135-54.

Kunstadter, Peter (ed.). 1967. *Southeast Asian Tribes, Minorities and Nations.* Princeton: Princeton University Press.

Kunstadter, Peter, and Carl Helm. 1966. Computer Simulation of Competition between Human Populations. Paper read to Wenner-Gren Foundation Seminar No. 33 on the Inter-Relation of Biological and Cultural Adaptation.

Kunstadter, Peter, E. C. Chapman, and Sanga Sabhasri (eds.). 1978. *Farmers in the Forest: Economic Development and Marginal Agriculture in Northern Thailand.* Honolulu: East-West Center.

Kuo, Eddie C. Y. 1980. Language Planning in Singapore. *Language Planning Newsletter* 6.

Ladd, Thomas M. 1970. Local Authority and Development Programs in the Four Muslim Provinces in Thailand. In Van der Mehden and Wilson (eds.) 1970.

———. 1975. *Political Violence in the Muslim Provinces of Southern Thailand.* Singapore: Institute of Southeast Asian Studies.

Lafont, Pierre-Bernard. 1962. Les Écritures 'Tai du Laos. *Bulletin de l'École Française de l'Extrême-Orient* 50:367-94.

Lakhana Doomkum. 1984. A Syntactical Study of the Malay Dialect in Taba Village. Master's thesis, Mahidol University.

Landon, Kenneth P. 1941. *The Chinese in Thailand*. New York: Institute of Public Relations.

Larson, Donald N. 1984. Talk-Work Audit, East Asia Missions. Duplicated.

Larson, Donald N., and William A. Smalley. 1972. Reprint 1984. *Becoming Bilingual: A Guide for Language Learners*. Lanham, Maryland: University Press of America.

Larson, Mildred L., and Patricia M. Davis (eds.). 1981. *Bilingual Education: An Experience in Peruvian Amazonia*. Washington: Center for Applied Linguistics.

Leach, E. R. 1954. *Political Systems of Highland Burma*. Cambridge: Harvard University Press.

Lebar, Frank M., Gerald C. Hickey, and John K. Musgrave. 1964. *Ethnic Groups of Mainland Southeast Asia*. New Haven: Human Relations Area Files.

Lee, Gar Yia. 1981. The Effects of Development Measures on the Socio-Economy of the White Hmong. Ph.D. dissertation, University of Sydney.

————. 1986. Culture and Adaptation: Hmong Refugees in Australia. In Hendricks, Downing, and Deinard (eds.) 1986:55-71.

Lehman, F. K. 1963. *The Structure of Chin Society: A Tribal People of Burma Adapted to a Non-Western Civilization*. Urbana: University of Illinois Press.

————. 1967. Ethnic Categories in Burma and the Theory of Social Systems. In Kunstadter (ed.) 1967:93-124.

Lemoine, Jacques. 1972a. *Un Village Hmong Vert du haut Laos*. Paris: Éditions Centre Nationale de la Recherche Scientifique.

————. 1972b. Les écritures du Hmong. *Bulletin des Amis du Royaume Lao* 7-8:123-65.

Lewis, Paul W. 1985a. Three Lands—Three Words. Manuscript.

————. 1985b. Effects of Opium on Tribal People in Thailand. Duplicated.

Lewis, Paul, and Elaine Lewis. 1984. *Peoples of the Golden Triangle*. London: Thames and Hudson.

Li, Fang-Kuei. 1959. Classification by Vocabulary: Tai Dialects. *Anthropological Linguistics* 1:15-21.

————. 1960. A Tentative Classification of Tai Dialects. In Diamond (ed.) 1960.

————. 1977. *A Handbook of Comparative Tai*. Honolulu: University of Hawaii Press.

————. 1992. Tai Languages. In *Encyclopaedia Britannica* 22:731-732.

Liberman, Stanley. 1981. Language and Ethnic Relations: A Neglected Problem. In Dil (ed.) 1981:1-18.

Lightfoot, Paul, Theodore Fuller, and Peerasit Kamnuansilpa. 1983. *Circulation and Interpersonal Networks Linking Rural and Urban Areas: The Case of Roi-Et, Northeastern Thailand.* Honolulu: East-West Center.

Lim, Linda Y. C., and L. A. Peter Gosling (eds.). 1983. *The Chinese in Southeast Asia* 1: *Ethnicity and Economic Activity.* Singapore: Maruzen Asia.

Linton, Ralph. 1943. Nativistic Movements. *American Anthropologist* 45: 230-40.

Lyman, Thomas A. 1974. *Dictionary of the Hmong Njua.* The Hague: Mouton.

———. 1979. *Grammar of Mong Njua (Green Miao): A Descriptive Linguistic Study.* Published by the author.

McKinnon, John, and Bernard Vienne (eds.). 1989. *Hill Tribes Today: Problems in Change.* Bangkok: White Lotus Co.

McKinnon, John, and Wanat Bhruksasri (eds.). 1983. *Highlanders of Thailand.* Kuala Lumpur: Oxford University Press.

Maeda, Seiji. 1979. *Les Lawa, la plus ancienne population de la Thaïlande: étude monographique et socio-juridique.* Doctoral dissertation, École des Hautes Études en Science Sociales.

Maneerat Chitikakamthorn. 1981. A Comparative Study of Phonology in Satun Malay and Pattani Malay. Master's thesis, Mahidol University.

Maniratana Bunnag. 1966. *Sri Dhananchaya.* Bangkok: Khurusaphaa Lâatphráaw.

Manit Manitcaren. 1965. *Thai Dictionary.* Bangkok: Phrae Phithaya Wangburapha.

Marin, G. 1943. An Old Pwo-Karen Alphabet. *Man* 43.5.

Marlowe, David H. 1967. Upland-Lowland Relationships: The Case of the S'Kaw Karen of Central Upland Western Chiang Mai. Chiang Mai: Tribal Research Centre.

———. 1979. In the Mosaic: The Cognitive and Structural Aspects of Karen-Other Relationships. In Keyes (ed.) 1979:165-214.

Marshall, Harry I. 1922. *The Karen People of Burma: A Study in Anthropology and Ethnology.* Columbus: Ohio State University.

Matisoff, James A. 1983. Linguistic Diversity and Language Contact. In McKinnon and Wanat (eds.) 1983:56-86.

Mauzy, Dianna K. 1985. Language and Language Policy in Malaysia. In Beer and Jacob (eds.) 1985:151-77.

Mead, Margaret. 1966. *New Lives for Old: Cultural Transformation—Manus, 1928-1953.* New York: William Morrow and Co.

Met Ratanaprasit. 1965. *Thai Yuan-Thai-English Dictionary.* In Thai. Bangkok.

Mitani, Yasuyuki. 1978. Phonological Studies of Lawa: Description and Comparison. Ph.D. dissertation, Cornell University.

Moerman, Michael. 1964a. Farming in Ban Phaed: Technical Decisions and Their Consequences for the External Relations of a Thai-Lue Village. Ph.D. dissertation, Yale University.

———. 1964b. Western Culture and the Thai Way of Life. *Asia* 1:31-50.

———. 1965a. Ethnic Identification in a Complex Civilization: Who Are the Lue? *American Anthropologist* 67:1215-30.

———. 1965b. Ban Ping's Temple: The Center of a "Loosely Structured" Society. In *Anthropological Studies in Theravada Buddhism.* Cultural Report Series 13:137-74. New Haven: Southeast Asia Studies, Yale University.

———. 1966. Kinship and Commerce in a Thai-Lue Village. *Ethnology* 5: 360-64.

———. 1967a. A Minority and Its Government: The Thai-Lue of Northern Thailand. In Kunstadter (ed.) 1967:401-24.

———. 1967b. Reply to Naroll. *American Anthropologist* 69:512-13.

———. 1967c. Being Lue: Uses and Abuses of Ethnic Identification. In Helm (ed.) 1967:153-69.

———. 1974. Accomplishing Ethnicity. In Turner (ed.) 1974:54-68.

———. 1988. *Talking Culture: Ethnography and Conversational Analysis.* Philadelphia: University of Pennsylvania Press.

Molly Changbencharoen-Yong. 1986. Chinese Newspapers in Thailand: Chinese with Thai Mentality. *Bangkok Post* April 24:34.

Mottin, Jean. 1978. *Éléments de grammaire Hmong Blanc.* Bangkok: Don Bosco Press.

———. 1980a. *History of the Hmong.* Bangkok: Odeon Store.

———. 1980b. *Contes et légendes Hmong Blanc.* Bangkok: Don Bosco Press.

Mühlhäusler, Peter. 1989. On the Causes of Accelerated Linguistic Change in the Pacific Area. In Breivik and Sahr (eds.) 1989:137-72.

Mundhenk, Norman A. 1966. Unsigned introduction to Purnell, Hope, and Yuang 1966.

———. 1967. Kammyang Sound Features. Manuscript.

———. 1968a. *Auxiliary Verbs in Myang of Northern Thailand.* Hartford: Hartford Seminary Foundation.

Murashima, Eiji. 1988. The Origin of Modern State Ideology in Thailand. *Journal of Southeast Asian Studies* 19:80-96.

Narong Kongchatree. 1979. Thai-Malay Bilingualism. MA thesis. Bangkok: Institute of Language and Culture for Rural Development, Mahidol University.

Nash, Manning. 1989. *The Cauldron of Ethnicity in the Modern World.* Chicago: University of Chicago Press.

National Statistics Office. 1980. *Population and Housing Census: Whole Kingdom.* Bangkok: National Statistics Office, Office of the Prime Minister.

Newmeyer, Fredrick (ed.). 1988. *Language: The Socio-Cultural Context.* Cambridge: Cambridge University Press.

Nguyen Dang Liem (ed.). 1974. *South-East Asian Linguistic Studies.* Canberra: Department of Linguistics, Australian National University.

———. 1979. *South-East Asian Linguistic Studies.* Canberra: Department of Linguistics, Australian National University.

Nida, Eugene A., and William L. Wonderly. 1971. Communication Roles of Languages in Multilingual Societies. *The Bible Translator* 22:19-37.

Noss, Richard B. 1964. *Thai Reference Grammar.* Washington: Foreign Service Institute.

———. 1966. The Treatment of */r/ in Two Modern Khmer Dialects. In Zide (ed.) 1966:89-95.

———. 1967. *Language Policy.* Paris: UNESCO and the International Association of Universities.

———. 1983. *Varieties of English in Southeast Asia.* Singapore: Singapore University Press.

Noss, Richard B. (ed.). 1982. *Language Teaching Issues in Multilingual Environments in Southeast Asia.* Singapore: RELC.

Noss, Richard B., Andrew Gonzalez, Amran Halim, and Angkap Palakornkul. 1984. *An Overview of Language Issues in Southeast Asia, 1950-1980.* Singapore: Oxford University Press.

Nusit Chindarsi. 1976. *The Religion of the Hmong Njua.* Bangkok: The Siam Society.

O'Connor, Richard Allen. 1978. Urbanism and Religion: Community, Hierarchy, and Sanctity in Urban Thai Buddhist Temples. Ph.D. dissertation. Ann Arbor: University Microfilms.

Olney, Douglas P. 1983. *A Bibliography of the Hmong (Miao) of Southeast Asia and the Hmong Refugees in the United States.* Minneapolis: CURA, University of Minnesota.

Oranuch Sa-ard. 1984. Phrases to Sentences in Kuay (Surin). Master's thesis, Mahidol University.

Osgood, Charles E., and Thomas A. Sebeok (eds.). 1954. *Psycholinguistics: Survey of Theory and Research Problems.* Memoir 10, *International Journal of American Linguistics.*

Pailin Yantreesingh. 1980. The Phonology of the Kuay Language of Suphanburi, with Comparisons to the Kui Language of Surin. Master's thesis, Mahidol University.

Paitoon Mikusol. 1984. Social and Cultural History of Northeastern Thailand from 1868-1910: A Case Study of the Huamuang Khamen Padong (Surin, Sangkha and Phukhan). Ph.D. dissertation, University of Washington.

Patya Saihoo. 1971. Cultural Diversity and National Identity in Thailand. In Southeast Asia Social Science Association 1971:175-83.

———. 1974. Social Organization of an Inland Malay Village Community in Southern Thailand. Ph.D. dissertation, Oxford University.

Paulsen, Debbie. 1922. A Phonological Reconstruction of Proto-Plang. *Mon-Khmer Studies* 18-19:160-222.

Paulson, C. B., and R. G. Paulson. 1980. Language and Ethnic Boundaries. *Language Sciences* 2:69-101.

Payau Memanas. 1979. A Description of Chaobon (Ñahkur): An Austroasiatic Language in Thailand. Master's thesis, Mahidol University.

Payom Dhamabutra. 1985. Sound Symbolism. Paper read to the 18th International Conference on Sino-Tibetan Languages and Linguistics.

Paz, Octavio. 1979. Mexico and the United States. *New Yorker* Sep. 17: 136-53.

Phillips, Herbert P. 1987. *Modern Thai Literature: With an Ethnographic Interpretation*. Honolulu: University of Hawaii Press.

Photchanat Samoemit. 1983. The Phonology of Phlow Spoken in Si Sawat District, Kanchanaburi Province. Master's thesis, Chulalongkorn University.

Phunsrikasem Kasemsri. 1957. *The History of King Mongkut*. In Thai. Bangkok.

Pichai Ratanaphol. 1969. Development of Controls on the Chinese Schools in Thailand. In Thai. Master's thesis, National Institute of Development Administration.

Pike, Kenneth L. 1967. *Language in Relation to a Unified Theory of the Structure of Human Behavior*. 2nd ed. The Hague: Mouton.

Pira Sudham. 1983a. *Siamese Drama and Other Stories from Thailand*. Bangkok: Siam Media International Books.

———. 1983b. Monsoon Country. In Pira 1983a:77-135.

Platt, John, and Heidi Weber. 1980. *English in Singapore and Malaysia: Status, Features, Functions*. Kuala Lumpur: Oxford University Press.

Pojanee Sritararat. 1985. A Tonal Comparison of Phuthai Dialects Spoken in Nakhon Phanom, Kalasin and Sakon Nakhon Provinces. Paper read at the 18th International Conference on Sino-Tibetan Languages and Linguistics.

Pongsri Lekawatana. 1979. The So-called Passive in Thai. In Gething and Nguyen (eds.) 1979:1-9.

Poole, Peter A. 1970. *The Vietnamese in Thailand: A Historical Perspective*. Ithaca: Cornell University Press.

Post. 1985. Poaching Persists. *Bangkok Post Economic Review* Jan. 14:48.

——. 1986. Killing the Curse of the Poppies. *Bangkok Post* Jan. 19, Sect. 2.

Pranee Gyarunsut. 1983 [BE 2526]. Chinese Loanwords in Modern Thai. In Thai. Master's thesis, Chulalongkorn University.

Pranee Kullavanijaya and Peansiri Vongvipanondha. 1984 [BE 2527]. *Bibliography of Thai Grammar and Phonology*. Bangkok: Linguistics Department, Chulalongkorn University.

Prapart Brudhiprabha. 1980. *Study of the Dialect of Na Pho Village (Loei Province)*. Bangkok: Department of Linguistics, Srinakarinwiwot University.

Prasert Sriwises. 1978. *Kui (Suai)-Thai-English Dictionary*. Theraphan L. Thongkum and Jerry W. Gainey (eds.). Bangkok: Indigenous Languages of Thailand Research Project, Chulalongkorn University.

Preecha Kuwinpant. 1979. *Marketing in North-Central Thailand: A Study of Socio-Economic Organization in a Thai Market Town*. Bangkok: Social Research Institute, Chulalongkorn University.

Preecha Phintong. 1989. *Isan-Thai-English Dictionary*. Ubon: Siridharma Publishers.

Premasri, P. D. 1988. Minorities in Buddhist Doctrine. In de Silva et al. (eds.) 1988:42-58.

Premchit Chanavong. 1983. Nakorn Sri Thammarat Dialects. *Wicha* 7:204-35.

Puey Ungphakorn. 1974. Societies of Siam. *Journal of the Siam Society* 62: 1-6.

PULO. 1981. Appeal to the Islamic Summit: Patani Plea for Muslim Help. *The Journal of the Muslim World League* 8.

Purcell, Victor. 1965. *The Chinese in Southeast Asia*. London: Oxford University Press.

Purnell, Herbert C., Jr. 1965. Two Grammatical Features of Northern Thai. In Hanks, Hanks, and Sharp 1965:15-20.

——. 1970. Toward a Reconstruction of Proto Miao-Yao. Ph.D. dissertation, Cornell University.

Purnell, Herbert C., Jr., E. R. Hope, and Yuang Kao Sukantha. 1966. [Erroneously dated 1962]. *A Colorful Colloquial: An Introduction to the Study of Spoken Northern Thai*. 2nd ed. Chiang Mai, Thailand: Overseas Missionary Fellowship.

Queljoe, David H. de. 1971. *A Preliminary Study of Some Phonetic Features of Petani, with Glossaries*. DeKalb, Illinois: Center for Southeast Asian Studies.

Rachamanop. 1965 [BE 2508]. *Royal Language: Complete Edition.* In Thai. Bangkok: Bannakhaan.

Rajah, Ananda. 1990. Ethnicity, Nationalism and Nation-State: The Karen in Burma and Thailand. In Wijeyewardene (ed.) 1990:101-33.

Rambo, A. Terry, Kathleen Gillogly, and Karl Hutterer (eds.). 1988. *Ethnic Diversity and the Control of Natural Resources in Southeast Asia.* Ann Arbor: Center for South and Southeast Asian Studies, University of Michigan.

Regional Workshop. 1985. *Minorities in Buddhist Polities: Sri Lanka, Burma and Thailand.* Colombo, Sri Lanka: International Center for Ethnic Studies.

Renard, Ronald. 1988. Minorities in Burmese History. In de Silva et al. (eds.) 1988:77-91.

———. 1990. Correspondence from Northern Thailand. *Khosana* 24:5.

Rhum, Michael R. 1987. "Grapholatry" in Northern Thailand: The Magical Qualities of Written Words. Paper read to the Association for Asian Studies.

Riggs, Fred W. 1966. *Thailand: The Modernization of a Bureaucratic Polity.* Honolulu: East-West Center.

Rischel, Jørgen. 1982. Fieldwork on the Mlabri Language: A Preliminary Sketch of its Phonetics. *Annual Report of the Institute of Phonetics, University of Copenhagen* 16:247-55.

Rischel, Jørgen, and Søren Egerod. 1987. Yumbri (Phi Tong Luang) and Mlabri. *Acta Orientalia* 48:19-33.

Royal Institute. 1968. *Romanization Guide for Thai Script.* Bangkok: Royal Institute.

Royal Pages' School. 1932. *Royal Language.* Bangkok.

Royce, Anya Peterson. 1982. *Ethnic Identity: Strategies of Diversity.* Bloomington: Indiana University Press.

Rubin, Herbert J. 1973. Will and Awe: Illustrations of Thai Villager Dependency on Officials. *Journal of Asian Studies* 32:425-44.

Ruengdet Pankhuenkhat. 1980. *Thai Dialectology.* In Thai. Bangkok: Institute of Language and Culture for Rural Development, Mahidol University.

Ruhlen, Merritt. 1987, 1991. *A Guide to the World's Languages.* 1: *Classification.* Stanford: Stanford University Press.

Rustow, Dankwart A. 1968. Language, Modernization and Nationhood: An Attempt at Typology. In Fishman, Ferguson, and Gupta (eds.) 1968:87-105.

Ryan, Ellen Bouchard, Howard Giles, and Richard J. Sebastian. 1982. An Integrating Perspective for the Study of Attitudes toward Language Variation. In Ryan and Giles (eds.) 1982:1-19.

Ryan, Ellen Bouchard, and Howard Giles (eds.). 1982. *Attitudes towards Language Variation: Social and Applied Contexts*. London: Edward Arnold.

Sanneh, Lamin. 1989. *Translating the Message: The Missionary Impact on Culture*. Maryknoll, New York: Orbis Books.

Scherer, K. R., and Howard Giles (eds.). 1979. *Social Markers in Speech*. Cambridge: Cambridge University Press.

Schlatter, Donald. 1976. Lavüa' (Lawa, Lua'). In Smalley (ed.) 1976:273-81.

Schrock, Joanne L., et al. 1970. *Minority Groups in Thailand*. Washington: Department of the Army.

Scupin, Raymond. 1980. Islamic Reformism in Thailand. *Journal of the Siam Society* 68:1-10.

———. 1988. Language, Hierarchy, and Hegemony: Thai Muslim Discourse Strategies. In Smalley and Amara (eds.) 1988:331-51.

Sebeok, Thomas A. (ed.). 1960. *Style in Language*. New York: John Wiley.

Sebeok, Thomas A., Yuen Ren Chao, Richard B. Noss, and Joseph K. Yamigawa (eds.) 1967. *Current Trends in Linguistics 2: Linguistics in East Asia and South East Asia*. The Hague: Mouton.

Seidenfaden, Erik. 1918. Some Notes about the Chaobun, a Disappearing Tribe in the Korat Province. *Journal of the Siam Society* 12:1-11.

———. 1919. Further Notes about the Chaubun, etc. *Journal of the Siam Society* 13:49-51.

———. 1925. Supplementary Note and Lü Vocabulary. *Journal of the Siam Society* 19:185-209.

———. 1952. The Kui People of Cambodia and Siam. *Journal of the Siam Society* 39:144-80.

———. 1958. *The Thai Peoples: The Origins and Habitats of the Thai Peoples with a Sketch of Their Material and Spiritual Culture*. Bangkok: The Siam Society.

Shorto, H. L. 1979. The Linguistic Prehistory of Mainland South East Asia. In Smith and Watson (eds.) 1979:273-78.

Siam Society. 1965 [BE 2508]. *Felicitation Volumes of Southeast-Asian Studies Presented to His Highness Prince Dhaninivat Kromamun Bidyalabh Bidhyakorn*. Bangkok: The Siam Society.

Silverstein, Josef. 1990. Civil War and Rebellion in Burma. *Journal of Southeast Asian Studies* 21:114-33.

Skinner, G. William. 1957a. *Chinese Society in Thailand: An Analytical History*. Ithaca: Cornell University Press.

———. 1957b. Chinese Assimilation and Thai Politics. *Journal of Asian Studies*. 16:237-50.

————. 1958. *Leadership and Power in the Chinese Community of Thailand.* Ithaca: Cornell University Press.

Skinner, G. William, and A. Thomas Kirsch (eds.). 1975. *Change and Persistence in Thai Society: Essays in Honor of Lauriston Sharp.* Ithaca: Cornell University Press.

Smalley, William A. 1956. The Gospel and the Cultures of Laos. *Practical Anthropology* 3:47-57. Reprinted in Smalley (ed.) 1978.

————. 1961. *Outline of Khmu' Structure.* New Haven: American Oriental Society.

————. 1963a. Notes on Kraisri's and Bernatzik's Word Lists. *Journal of the Siam Society* 51:189-201.

————. 1963b. Dialect and Orthography in Gipende. In Smalley (ed.) 1963:138-47. Reprinted from *The Bible Translator* 9:63-69.

————. 1964a. Khmu. In Lebar, Hickey, and Musgrave 1964:112-17.

————. 1964b. Ethnolinguistic Survey of Northern Khmer and Kuy Speaking People in Northeast Thailand. Duplicated.

————. 1965. Ciaŋ: Khmu' Culture Hero. In Siam Society 1965 1:41-54.

————. 1972. Problems in Writing Thailand Minority Languages in Thai Script. In Harris and Noss (eds.) 1972:131-36.

————. 1976a. Writing Systems in Thailand's Marginal Languages: History and Policy. In Smalley (ed.) 1976:1-24.

————. 1976b. Bases for Popular Writing Systems. In Smalley (ed.) 1976: 25-42.

————. 1976c. The Problem of Vowels: Northern Khmer. In Smalley (ed.) 1976:43-83.

————. 1976d. The Problem of Consonants and Tone: Hmong (Meo, Miao). In Smalley (ed.) 1976:85-123.

————. 1976e. Outline of the Thai Writing System. In Smalley (ed.) 1976: 319-31.

————. 1985. Adaptive Language Strategies of the Hmong: From Asian Mountains to American Ghettos. *Language Sciences* 7:241-69.

————. 1986. Stages of Hmong Cultural Adaptation. In Hendricks, Downing, and Deinard (eds.) 1986:7-22.

————. 1988a. Thailand's Hierarchy of Multilingualism. In Smalley and Amara (eds.) 1988:245-61.

————. 1988b. Multilingualism in the Northern Khmer Population of Thailand. In Smalley and Amara (eds.) 1988:395-408.

————. 1991. *Translation as Mission: Bible Translation in the Modern Missionary Movement.* Macon, Georgia: Mercer University Press.

Smalley, William A. (ed.). 1963. *Orthography Studies: Articles on New Writing Systems.* London: United Bible Societies.

―――. 1976. *Phonemes and Orthography: Language Planning in Ten Minority Languages of Thailand.* Canberra: Department of Linguistics, The Australian National University.

―――. 1978. *Readings in Missionary Anthropology II.* Pasadena: William Carey Library.

Smalley, William A., Chia Koua Vang, and Gnia Yee Yang. 1990. *Mother of Writing: The Origin and Development of a Hmong Messianic Script.* Chicago: University of Chicago Press.

Smalley, William A., and Nina Wimuttikosol. Forthcoming. Another Hmong Messianic Script and Its Texts. *Journal of the Siam Society.*

Smalley, William A., and Amara Prasithrathsint (eds.). 1988. *Language Use in Thailand.* Special issue of *Language Sciences* 10.2.

Smith, J. Christina. 1987. *The Hmong: An Annotated Bibliography, 1983-1987.* Minneapolis: CURA, University of Minnesota.

Smith, Larry E. 1981. *English for Cross-Cultural Communication.* London: The Macmillan Press.

Smith, M. Estelle (ed.). 1972. *Studies in Linguistics in Honor of George L. Trager.* The Hague: Mouton.

Smith, R. B., and W. Watson (eds.). 1979. *Early South East Asia: Essays in Archeology, History and Historical Geography.* New York: Oxford University Press.

Smithies, Michael. 1972. Village Mons of Bangkok. *Journal of the Siam Society* 60:307-32.

Snit Smuckarn and Kennon Breazeale. 1988. *A Culture in Search of Survival: The Phuan of Thailand and Laos.* New Haven: Southeast Asia Program, Yale University.

Songsak Prangwattanakul. 1986 [BE 2529]. *Agreement on the Transliteration of Lan Na into Standard Thai Characters.* Chiang Mai: Center for the Promotion of Art and Culture, Chiang Mai University.

Sopher, David E. 1977 [1965]. *The Sea Nomads: A Study of the Maritime Boat People of Southeast Asia.* Singapore: The National Museum.

Sophon Ratanakhon. 1978. Legal Aspects of Land Occupation and Development. In Kunstadter et al. (eds.) 1978:45-60.

Sorat Makboon. 1981. A Survey of Sea Peoples Dialects along the West Coast of Thailand. Master's thesis, Mahidol University.

Spickard, Paul R. 1989. *Mixed Blood: Intermarriage and Ethnic Identity in Twentieth-Century America.* Madison: University of Wisconsin Press.

Stern, Theodore. 1965. Research upon Karen in Village and Town, Upper Khwae Noi, Western Thailand. Duplicated.

―――. 1968a. Three Pwo Karen Scripts: A Study of Alphabet Formation. *Anthropological Linguistics* 10:1-39.

————. 1968b. *Ariya* and the Golden Book: A Millenarian Sect among the Karen. *Journal of Asian Studies* 27:297-328.

————. 1979. A People Between: The Pwo Karen of Western Thailand. In Keyes (ed.) 1979:63-80.

Stewart, William A. 1968. Sociolinguistic Typology of Multilingualism. In Fishman (ed.) 1968:531-45.

Story, Joan H., and John H. Story. 1969a. Meo Villages Researched to Date. Duplicated.

————. 1969b. "Hill Tribes," the Target Audience. Duplicated.

Strecker, David. 1979. A Preliminary Typology of the Tone Shapes and Tonal Sound Changes in Tai: The Lan Na A-Tones. In Theraphan et al. (eds.) 1979:171-240.

————. 1987. Tai Languages. In Comrie (ed.) 1987:749-56.

Suchit Bunbongkarn. 1987. *The Military in Thai Politics, 1981-1986.* Singapore: Institute of Southeast Asian Studies.

Sudarat Leerabhandh. 1984. A Phonological Reconstruction of Proto-Orang Laut in Thailand. Master's thesis, Mahidol University.

Sujaritlak Dipadung et al. 1983 [BE 2526]. *Social, Cultural, and Political Roles of the Mon People.* Bangkok: Chulalongkorn University.

Sujit Wongthes. 1986 [BE 2529]. *The Thais Were Always Here: A Social and Cultural History of the Siamese People in Thailand.* In Thai, with English summary. Special issue of *Arts and Culture.*

Sukhuma-Vadee Khamhiran. 1980. Aspects of Bilingualism in Two Malay-speaking Communities in Southern Thailand: A Pilot Study. Duplicated.

————. 1981. When do Thai-Muslims Speak Thai? Paper read to the Third International Conference on Austronesian Linguistics. Denpasar, Bali, Indonesia 1981.

Sulak Sivaraksa. 1986. *A Buddhist Vision for Renewing Society: Collected Articles by a Concerned Thai Intellectual.* Bangkok: Tienwan Publishing House.

Sumon Yuesin. 1984 [BE 2527]. *Communication Behavior and Thai Cultural Assimilation: A Study of Chinese in the Chiang Mai Municipal Area.* In Thai. Master's thesis, Department of Public Relations, Chulalongkorn University.

Surai Phongthongcharoen. 1978. English Loanwords in Thai. *Pasaa* 8:65-88.

Sureeporn Yaysa-nga. 1985 [BE 2528]. A Comparative Study of the Phonetics and Phonology of Lavüa' Spoken in Ban Pa Pae, Ban Chang Maw, Ban Umphai and Ban Dong, Mae Hong Son Province. In Thai. Master's thesis, Chulalongkorn University.

Surin Pitsuwan. 1982. Issues Affecting Border Security between Malaysia and Thailand. Bangkok: Faculty of Political Science, Thammasat University.

———. 1985. *Islam and Malay Nationalism: a Case Study of the Malay-Muslims of Southern Thailand*. Bangkok: Thai-Khadi Research Institute, Thammasat University.

Suriya Ratanakul. 1985. The Phonology of Lawa. In Suriya, Thomas, and Suwilai (eds.) 1985:264-309.

———. 1972 [BE 2515]. *Thai-Hmong Dictionary*. Bangkok: Kesom Samphan Printers.

———. *English-White Meo Dictionary*. Bangkok: Institute of Language and Culture for Rural Development, Mahidol University.

Suriya Ratanakul and Lakkhana Daoratanahong. 1986 [BE 2529]. *Lawa-Thai Dictionary*. Bangkok: Institute of Language and Culture for Rural Development, Mahidol University.

Suriya Ratanakul, David Thomas, and Suwilai Premsrirat (eds.). 1985. *Southeast Asian Linguistics Presented to André-G. Haudricourt*. Bangkok: Institute of Lnguage and Culture for Rural Development, Mahidol University.

Suwilai Premsrirat. 1986. Müang Ling, a Multilingual Community. In Thai. *Language and Culture* 6.2.

Suwilai Premsrirat and Sophana Srichampa. 1990. *Formulating a Thai-based Northern Khmer Orthography*. In Thai. Bangkok: Institute of Language and Culture for Rural Development, Mahidol University.

Suwilai Premsrirat et al. 1987 [BE 2530]. *The Northern Khmer Writing System*. In Thai. Bangkok: Institute of Language and Culture for Rural Development, Mahidol University.

Suwilai Premsrirat et. al. 1988 [BE 2531]. *Health Manual*. In Northern Khmer. Bangkok: Institute of Language and Culture for Rural Development, Mahidol University.

Szanton, Cristina Blanc. 1983. Thai and Sino-Thai in Small Town Thailand: Changing Patterns in Interethnic Relations. In Gosling and Lim (eds.) 1983:99-125.

Tambiah, S. J. 1968. Literacy in a Buddhist Village in Northeast Thailand. In Goody (ed.) 1968:85-131.

———. 1970. *Buddhism and the Spirit Cults in North-East Thailand*. Cambridge: Cambridge University Press.

———. 1976. *World Conqueror and World Renouncer: A Study of Buddhism and Polity in Thailand against a Historical Background*. Cambridge: Cambridge University Press.

Tapp, Nicholas. 1982a. The Relevance of Telephone Directories to a Lineage-based Society: A Consideration of Some Messianic Myths among the Hmong. *Journal of the Siam Society* 70:114-27.

———. 1982b. How to Stop Opium Farming? *Royal Anthropological Institute News* 48.

———. 1986. *The Hmong of Thailand: Opium People of the Golden Triangle.* London: Anti-Slavery Society.

———. 1989a. *Sovereignty and Rebellion: The White Hmong of Northern Thailand.* New York: Oxford University Press.

———. 1989b. The Impact of Missionary Christianity upon Marginalized Ethnic Minorities: The Case of the Hmong. *Journal of Southeast Asian Studies* 20:70-95.

———. 1990. Squatters or Refugees: Development and the Hmong. In Wijeyewardene (ed.) 1990:149-72.

Tarone, Elaine. 1980. Communication Strategies, Foreigner Talk, and Repair in Interlanguage. *Language Learning* 30:417-31.

Taweeporn Suwannaraj. 1980. The Phonology of the Nyeu Language. Master's thesis, Mahidol University.

Teel, Stephen. 1988. Northern Khmer-Thai-English Dictionary. Duplicated.

Terwiel, B. J. 1989. *Through Traveller's Eyes: An Approach to Early Nineteenth Century Thai History.* Bangkok: Editions Duang Kamol.

Textor, Robert B. 1961. *From Peasant to Pedicab Driver.* New Haven: Yale University Southeast Asia Studies.

Thai/UN. 1984. Terminal Report of the Thai/UN Highland Agricultural Marketing and Production Project. Duplicated.

Theraphan L. Thongkum. 1984a. *Bibliography of Minority Languages in Thailand.* Bangkok: Research Division, Faculty of Arts, Chulalongkorn University.

———. 1984b. *Nyah Kur (Chao Bon)-Thai-English Dictionary.* Bangkok: Chulalongkorn University.

———. 1985a [BE 2528]. Minority Languages in Thailand. *Science of Language Papers* 4: *Languages and Dialects*: 29-74. Bangkok: Department of Linguistics, Chulalongkorn University.

———. 1985b. An Acoustic Study of the Register Complex in Kui (Suai). Paper read to the 18th International Conference on Sino-Tibetan Languages and Linguistics.

Theraphan L. Thongkum (ed.). 1985. *Aksornsart Niphon* 4: *Studies in Linguistics.* In Thai with English abstracts. Bangkok: Faculty of Arts, Chulalongkorn University.

Theraphan L. Thongkum, Pranee Kullavanijaya, Vichin Panupong, and Kalaya Tingsabadh (eds.). 1979. *Studies in Tai and Mon-Khmer Phonetics and Phonology: In Honour of Eugénie J. A. Henderson.* Bangkok: Chulalongkorn University Press.

Thomas, David. 1990 [BE 2533]. On the "Language Status" of Northern Khmer. *Journal of Language and Culture* 9:98-106.

Thomas, Dorothy. 1987. Changing the Northern Khmer Orthography: Thailand. Manuscript.

Thomas, David, and Dorothy Thomas. 1982. Word Play in Surin Khmer. *Language and Culture* 2:87-95.

Thomas, David, and Robert K. Headley, Jr. 1970. More on Mon-Khmer Subgroupings. *Lingua* 25:398-418.

Thurgood, Graham. 1985. Benedict's Work—Past and Present. In Thurgood, Matisoff, and Bradley (eds.) 1985:1-15.

Thurgood, Graham, James P. Matisoff, and David Bradley (eds.). 1985. *Linguistics of the Sino-Tibetan Area: The State of the Art.* Canberra: Department of Linguistics, Australian National University.

Tifveman, Lawrence H. 1972. Thai Political Integration: The Meo Hill Tribes of Northern Thailand. Master's thesis, University of North Carolina.

Tribal Research Centre. 1978. *Tribal Population Summary in Thailand.* Chiang Mai: Tribal Research Center.

Tribal Research Institute. 1986a. *The Hill Tribes of Thailand.* Chiang Mai: Tribal Research Institute.

———. 1986b. Tribal Population Summary in Thailand. Chiang Mai: Tribal Research Institute.

Trier, Jesper. 1981. The Khon Pa of Northern Thailand, an Enigma. *Current Anthropology* 22:291-93.

———. 1986. The Mlabri People of Northern Thailand: Social Organization and Supernatural Beliefs. *Contributions to Southeast Asian Ethnography* 5:3-41.

Truxton, Addison Strong. 1958. The Integration of the Karen Peoples of Burma and Thailand into Their Respective National Cultures: A Study of the Dynamics of Culture Contact. Master's thesis, Cornell University.

Tugby, Elise, and Donald Tugby. 1971. Inter-cultural Mediation in South Thailand. Paper read to the Seminar on Contemporary Thailand, Canberra.

Turner, J. C., and Howard Giles (eds.). 1981. *Intergroup Behavior.* Oxford: Blackwell.

Turner, Roy (ed.). 1974. *Ethnomethodology.* Harmondsworth: Penguin Education.

Uthai Dulyakasem. 1986. The Emergence and Escalation of Ethnic Nationalism: The Case of the Muslim Malays in Southern Siam. In Abdullah and Siddique (eds.) 1986:208-49.

Van der Haak, Feikje, and Brigitte Wykos. 1987. Dialect Survey of the Suay in Surin, Thailand. Manuscript.

Van der Mehden, Fred R., and David A. Wilson (eds.). 1970. *Local Authority and Administration in Thailand*. Los Angeles: Academic Advisory Council for Thailand.

Vang, Chia Koua, Gnia Yee Yang, and William A. Smalley. 1990. *The Life of Shong Lue Yang: Hmong "Mother of Writing."* Minneapolis: CURA, University of Minnesota.

Veena Chantanakomes. 1980. A Description of Moken: A Malayo-Polynesian Language. Master's thesis, Mahidol University.

Velder, Christian. 1963. A Description of the Mrabri Camp. *Journal of the Siam Society* 51:185-88.

Vella, Walter. 1978. *Chaiyo! King Vajiravudh and the Development of Thai Nationalism*. Honolulu: University of Hawaii Press.

Vichin Panupong. 1985. Word Geography in Nakhon Ratchasima: A Follow-up Study. Paper read to the 18th International Conference on Sino-Tibetan Languages and Linguistics.

Vilas Manivat and Steve Van Beek (eds.). 1983. *Kukrit Pramoj, His Wit and Wisdom*. Bangkok: Editions Duang Kamol.

Visit Prachuabmoh. 1972. *The Rural and Urban Population of Thailand: Comparative Profiles*. Bangkok: Institute of Population Studies, Chulalongkorn University.

Wales, H. G. Quaritch. 1969. *Dvāravatī: The Earliest Kingdom of Siam*. London: Bernard Quaritch.

Wallace, Anthony F. C. 1956. Revitalization Movements. *American Anthropologist* 58:264-81.

Wannaporn Thongmark. 1985. The Linguistic Borderline between Central Thai and Southern Thai: A Lexical Study. In Thai. In Theraphan (ed.) 1985:169-88.

Wantanee Pakornnodom and Dee Yu Palikup. 1978. *A Comparative Study of Sounds, Words and Sentence Patterns in Central Thai and Northeastern Thai (Khon Kaen Dialect)*. Khon Kaen: Department of Foreign Languages, Khon Kaen University.

Weaver, Robert W. 1956. Through Unknown Thailand. *Natural History* 65: 289-95, 336.

Weinreich, Uriel. 1953 [1963]. *Languages in Contact*. The Hague: Mouton.

———. 1957. Research Frontiers in Bilingualism Studies. In *Proceedings of the Eighth International Congress of Linguists*: 786-97.

———. 1968. Is a Structural Dialectology Possible? In Fishman (ed.) 1968:305-19.

Weinstein, Brian. 1990. *Language Policy and Political Development*. Norwood, New Jersey: Ablex Publishing Company.

Wijeyewardene, Gehan. 1990. Thailand and the Tai: Versions of Ethnic Identity. In Wijeyewardene (ed.) 1990: 48-73.

Wijeyewardene, Gehan (ed.). 1990. *Ethnic Groups across National Boundaries in Mainland Southeast Asia*. Singapore: Institute of Southeast Asian Studies.

Wilaiwan Kanittanan. 1975. The Phu Thai Language of Nakhon Phanom. In Thai. In Harris and Chamberlain (eds.) 1975:377-86.

———. 1976 [BE 2519]. *The Saek Language*. In Thai. Bangkok: Thammasat University Printing House.

———. 1977 [BE 2520]. *Phu Thai Language*. in Thai. Bangkok: Thammasat University Printing House.

———. 1979. How Much Is English Influencing the Language of the Educated Bangkok Thais? In Nguyen (ed.) 1979:55-59.

Wilson, David A. 1962. *Politics in Thailand*. Ithaca: Cornell University Press.

Wirawong. 1972. *Northeastern Thai-Central Thai Dictionary*. In Thai. Bangkok: Thai Watana Phanit.

Wonderly, William L. 1968. *Bible Translation for Popular Use*. New York: United Bible Societies.

Wright, Michael A. 1968. Some Observations on Thai Animism. *Practical Anthropology* 15:1-7.

Wu, David Y. H. 1982. Ethnic Relations and Ethnicity in a City-State: Singapore. In Wu (ed.) 1982:13-36.

Wu, David Y. H. (ed.). 1982. *Ethnicity and Interpersonal Interaction: A Cross-Cultural Study*. Singapore: Maruzen Asia.

Wu, David Y. H., and Brian L. Foster. 1982. Introduction. In Wu (ed.) 1982:1-12.

Wurm, S. A., and Shiro Hattori. 1981. *Language Atlas of the Pacific Area*. Canberra: Australian Academy of the Humanities.

Wyatt, David K. 1966. Northeast Thailand: An Historical Perspective. *Asian Survey* 6:353-54.

———. 1984. *Thailand: A Short History*. New Haven: Yale University Press.

Xiong, Lang, Joua Xiong, and Nao Leng Xiong. 1984. *English-Mong-English Dictionary*. Privately published.

Yanyong Cariyaphat. 1986 [BE 2528]. *The Atlas of Thailand*. In Thai. Bangkok.

Yang, Dao. 1975. *Les Hmong du Laos face au dévelopement*. Laos: Editions Siaosavath.

———. 1980. *Dictionnaire Français-Hmong Blanc*. Paris: Comité National d'Entraide.

Yawalak Yim-on. 1984. Language Shift and Language Maintenance in a Sgaw Karen Community in Thailand. Master's thesis, Mahidol University.

Young, Gordon. 1962. *The Hill Tribes of Northern Thailand*. 2nd ed. Bangkok: The Siam Society.

Zarechnak, Michael (ed.). 1961. *Monograph Series on Languages and Linguistics* 14. Washington: Georgetown University Press.

Zehner, Edwin. 1990. Reform Symbolism of a Thai Middle-Class Sect: The Growth and Appeal of the Thammakai Movement. *Journal of Southeast Asian Studies* 21:402-26.

————. 1991. Merit, Man and Ministry: Traditional Thai Hierarchies in a Contemporary Church. *Social Compass* 38:155-75.

Zide, Norman H. (ed.). 1966. *Studies in Comparative Austroasiatic Linguistics*. The Hague: Mouton.

Zinke, Paul J., Sanga Sabhasri, and Peter Kunstadter. 1978. Soil Fertility Aspects of the Lua' Forest Fallow System of Shifting Cultivation. In Kunstadter et al. (eds.) 1987:134-59.

Index

Accommodation (acculturative relationship), 347–49

Acculturation. *See* Accommodation; Adaptation by minorities; Assimilation; Incorporation

Adaptation by minorities: Chinese, 174, 208–9, 211–12, 215–17, 217–19, 220; Hmong, 240–41, 246, 247–48, 248–49, 250–51, 253–54; Karen, 124; Kuy, 149, 150–51, 151–53; Lavüa', 258–60, 261–63; Lue, 202; Mon, 225–26, 227–29; Northern Khmer, 141–45, 148, 151–53; Nyah Kur, 264–65; Pattani Malay, 159–61, 165, 166–68, 168–69, 171; Phlong, 129, 130–33; Phlow, 128; Phu Thai, 200; Pray, Mal, 231, 234–37; Saek, 197–99; Satun Malay, 157–58; Sgaw, 125–26, 130–33, 134–35; Ugong, 269–71; Urak Lawoi', 267–68

Agriculture, origins of, 294, 295. *See also* Swidden agriculture

Akha, 224, 283, 302, 365

Anglicization of non-English words, 203, 372–73, 375–77

Arabic script, 172–73, 283

Assimilation: channels of, 324, 327–30, 347–48, 352–53; Chinese, 208–10, 217–19; degrees of, 329–30; forced, 162; forces against, 352–54; Karen, 133–35; Lavüa', 261–62; Mon, 225–26; stages of, 311–12, 353–54;

Ugong, 269–71. *See also* Accommodation; Adaptation by minorities; Incorporation

Austronesian (language family), 299, 371

Austro-Thai (language family), 299

Ayuthaya, 31–32, 56, 188–90, 195

Bangkok, 29–31, 32–33, 88, 98–99, 109

Bhumibol, King, 99, 134, 323–25

Bilingualism. *See* Multilingualism

Bisu, 256, 302, 365

Borders between languages, 111–12, 137–40, 148–49, 157–58

Buddhism: assimilative character of, 130, 248, 324, 347–48; centered vs. bounded categories, 349; diversity in, 323–24; interface with Islam, 166–68; in Lao identity, 97–98; among minorities, non-Tai, 130, 225, 229, 235, 262; support for hierarchy, 345; temple education, 95–96, 247–48; in Thai ethnicity, 235, 323–24

Bureaucracy, 145, 162–64, 355–57

Cantonese, 213, 302, 365

Categories, bounded vs. centered, 330–33, 346–47, 349, 352

Central Thai. *See* Thaiklang

Change: in culture, 249–51, 294–97, 183–94, 355; in dialect, language,

427